MASTERPIECES

OF THE SPANISH GOLDEN AGE

MASTERPIECES
of the Spanish Golden Age

THE ABENCERRAJE

LAZARILLO DE TORMES

THE LIFE AND ADVENTURES OF DON PABLOS THE SHARPER

FUENTE OVEJUNA

THE TRICKSTER OF SEVILLE

THE GREAT THEATER OF THE WORLD

Edited by Angel Flores

NEW YORK *Rinehart & Co., Inc.* TORONTO

FOR at least two centuries, the sixteenth and the seventeenth, Spain stood proudly as the mightiest power in Europe. When Ferdinand of Aragon and Isabella of Castile married in 1479, they launched their newly united nation upon a dynamic program of Christian homogeneity, and of centralization, nationalism, and expansionism. In the portentous year 1492, not only did Columbus set the flag and Cross of Spain upon the New World, but Spain expelled the Jews and the Moors from the Hispanic Peninsula. This latter action may have seemed at the time to mark a great Christian triumph over the "infidels" who, upon conquering Spain in 711, had spread over the land to finally settle in its most desirable sector, Andalusia. However, it deprived Spain of the most productive segment of its population, and resulted not only in a loss of irreplaceable manpower, but also in a drop in its agricultural output. Moreover, the male population which remained, feeling superior to all practical immediacy, began an idealistic flight from reality. On all the battlefields of Europe they perished gloriously for their God and King, or, hallucinated by improbable El Dorados, were swallowed up in American jungles and mountain fastnesses; or, in mystical exaltation, they entered monasteries or joined religious missions.

All of this bespoke disaster. The defeat of the Spanish Armada (1588) pointed warningly to the beginning of the end, though Spain had another century in which to commit more blunders, bleed more profusely, and die a slow, agonizing death. For empires do not die suddenly. And the dynamic forces unleashed

by national centralization and the consequent expansionism resulted in a cultural renascence which came to fruition not at the
political apogee, but rather during the receding tide. Góngora's
baroque poetry, Calderón's and most of Lope de Vega's plays,
Quevedo's satires, *Don Quixote*, the Mystics—in short, the
greatest literary works of Spanish genius—were created years
after the Invincible Armada had proved vincible, and after the
sun had begun to set over the vast Empire.

The present collection of literary masterpieces reflects this
maturation without overlooking the previous decades wherein
many genres and forms were gestated which later developed
and spread over Europe.

The earliest of these masterpieces, *The Abencerraje*, dates
back to the middle of the sixteenth century. Of unknown au-
thorship, it was inserted by Jorge de Montemayor in Book IV
of his *Diana* (1559), a pastoral novel which was very popular in
Spain and England; translated by Bartholomew Young, it influenced the Elizabethans including Shakespeare, and it was
culled by Antonio de Villegas in his *Inventario* (1565). To this
day most textbooks erroneously attribute it to Montemayor or
Villegas.

Fictional forms had appeared in Spain earlier than in any
other European country, because of the impact of Arabic sensi-
bility upon Spanish letters.* Even before the Middle Ages,
Persians and Arabs were producing fables and tales galore—the
riper and more sophisticated *Arabian Nights* belongs to a much
later period (the fifteenth century)—and in the very first important collection of cautionary tales written in Spain, *Count
Lucanor* (1335) by Prince don Juan Manuel, their inspiration
and main sources prove to be Arabic. However, *The Abencerraje* is predominantly a product of the Spanish genius—it is the
earliest European short story, dependent no longer on a didactic
framework such as the "exempla" in *Count Lucanor*, Boccac-
cio's *The Decameron* (c. 1350), or Chaucer's *Canterbury Tales*
(1387).

---

* Cf. my Introduction to *Great Spanish Stories*. New York: The Modern
Library, 1956, pp. ix–xiv.

At the appearance of *The Abencerraje*, Spain, like the rest of Europe, relied for its literary entertainment on either the chivalric or the pastoral novels. The novels of chivalry, which were for the most part prose versions of late epics, were inflated yarns recounting the exploits of dauntless knight-errants who, for the greater honor of their lady loves, rode into the world to rid it of giants, monsters, and unknightly knights. The earliest and perhaps the best of these thrillers was *Amadís de Gaula* (1508), though it may be argued that the *very best* was *Don Quixote*, in which its author, Cervantes, succeeded through parody and caricature in his intention of killing the genre once and for all. *Amadís*, with its many sequels and countless imitations, was the rage throughout the first half of the sixteenth century; among its ardent admirers were Francis I of France, St. Ignatius of Loyola, and St. Theresa of Jesus.

The strongest competitor of the novel of chivalry was another artificial form of fiction: the pastoral. The first appeared in a hybrid verse-and-prose form, in the *Arcadia* (1504) by the Italian Jacopo Sannazaro, and found Spanish cultivators in Montemayor, already mentioned, Cervantes (*Galatea* [1564]), Lope de Vega (*Arcadia* [1598]), etc.

The Abencerraje is, then, unmistakably Spanish: a short story based on an episode from real life, narrated in the fifteenth century *Crónica del Infante don Fernando de Antequera*. Couched in correct Spanish, it mirrors qualities which are forever associated with the Spanish spirit: love, honor, courage, politeness. The tale's emotional control as well as its penetration and lofty psychological climate constitute its most unforgettable elements and may explain its sustained and ubiquitous influence, for it inspired writers as different as Lope de Vega, whose play *El remedio en la desdicha* dramatized *The Abencerraje*, Chateaubriand, Hugo, Alarcón, Washington Irving.

Equally Spanish in its roots and genesis was *Lazarillo de Tormes*, also by an unknown author. This masterpiece, published in Burgos, Alcalá, and Antwerp in the same year (1554), may be said to mark the birth of a new type of prose fiction: the picaresque. Judged from a purely literary angle, the picaresque

may be considered a reaction to the overidealized and plati-
tudinous chivalric and pastoral novels. The *Lazarillo* is, above
all, antiromantic and sociological. It peers with irony and pity
into the economic and social crisis of Spain for, as Chaytor
aptly puts it, "rich in gold and silver, Spain sorely lacked
bread." * The effects of reduced manpower curtailed agricultural production and the small native industries. Court and
courtiers lived parasitically from the American mines. The im-
ported metal went on to Paris to buy luxuries, thus nurturing
the incipient French middle classes and converting their country into a first-rate power. The disproportion between the very
wealthy and the very poor became so staggering in the Peninsula that a price revolution was forced upon the nation.** When
the wheat-producing Spain had to import wheat, the under-
privileged classes could not afford to purchase a loaf of bread.
The Golden Age was consequently the Age of Beggary and
Roguery due, principally, to starvation. Hunger became a literary
theme, replacing those of idealized love and doughty feat of
arms. For the first time in literary history, one of the lowliest, a
puny little rogue like Lazarillo, bereft of all social prestige or
moral stature, became a dramatic personage. Lazarillo was the
begetter of the French Gil Blas, the English Becky Sharp, Pick-
wick, David Copperfield, and the Russian Chichikov.

Despite its brevity, for *Lazarillo* is but a short novelette, the
hero emerges as convincingly alive as the three principal masters for whom he works. The first two are a blind beggar and a
priest, both great hoarders of food who, because of their stinginess, compel the famished boy to surpass them in craftiness.
The third master, even more memorable, is an impoverished
squire who, though too proud to work like any commoner, lives
worse than the beggar and has no compunction about eating
the food pilfered in the streets by his servant boy. A parasite of
parasites living in a parasitic age, he keeps a bold façade of pre-

---

* H. J. Chaytor, Introduction to *La vida de Lazarillo de Tormes*. Man-
chester University Press, 1922, p. xv.
** Cf. Earl J. Hamilton, *American Treasure and the Price Revolution in
Spain*. Harvard University Press, 1934.

tense. Is this a satiric portrait of the aristocrat of the period or of the Spanish nation at large? It can be readily seen that the comic verges on the tragic, for the novel faithfully mirrors that impossible-to-dampen cheerfulness emanating from the little victories of the meek over the proud, as much as the grim determination on the part of the downtrodden to make the best of things against overwhelming odds—a projection, as it were, of that quixotic faith which egged on the Conquistadores to do the impossible. *Lazarillo*, like a sensitive seismograph, recorded the sound of breaking, the chaos fast approaching the mighty Spanish Empire. No wonder its anonymous author has been accused of being a pupil of Erasmus!

Though *Lazarillo* was extremely popular and ran into numerous editions, forty-five years elapsed before the appearance of another picaresque novel: Mateo Alemán's *Guzmán de Alfarache* (1599). Were the writers afraid to develop a socially-conscious genre during Philip II's strict censorship? Notice that *Guzmán* was published the year *after* the King's death! Were they afraid of being accused of subversive Erasmian ideas? Or was the delay because the sudden vogue of the pastoral novel, especially popular during the forty-five years 1554–1599, had attracted to it the most gifted prose writers? Perhaps the best reply lies in a combination of all these factors.

What is certain is that after the appearance of *Guzmán de Alfarache*, a long, gloomy book reflecting the many vexations and frustrations of its author and the more tenebrous reality of a defeated Spain*—the Invincible Armada had been destroyed —the picaresque was continuously cultivated during almost half a century (1599–1646) by distinguished scholars and men of letters: besides Mateo Alemán, Francisco de Úbeda: *La pícara Justina*, 1605; Alonso de Salas Barbadillo: *La hija de Celestina*, 1612; Cervantes: *Novelas ejemplares*, 1613; Juan Cortés de Tolosa: *El español Gerardo*, 1615; Vicente Espinel: *Marcos de*

---

* "Hatred and disgust for life well up so automatically that we end by being reminded of a modern book—Céline's *Journey to the End of the Night*." Gerald Brenan, *The Literature of the Spanish People*. Cambridge University Press, 1951, p. 172.

Obregón, 1618; Dr. Jerónimo de Alcalá: *Alonso, mozo de muchos amos*, 1624; Francisco de Quevedo: *Historia de la vida del Buscón*, 1626; Alonso de Castillo Solórzano: *Las harpías de Madrid*, 1631, and the trilogy: *La niña de los embustes*, 1632, *Aventuras del Bachiller Trapaza*, 1637, and *La Garduña de Sevilla*, 1642; Luis Vélez de Guevara: *El diablo cojuelo*, 1640; Antonio Enríquez Yáñez: *El siglo pitagórico*, 1644, and on and on to the anonymous *Estebanillo González*, 1646.

Of these tales of roguery that followed *Lazarillo* the most arresting one is the *Historia de la vida del Buscón, llamado Don Pablos; Exemplo de vagamundos y espejo de tacaños* (*The Life and Adventures of Don Pablo the Sharper* [1626]) by Francisco de Quevedo y Villegas (1580–1643), one of the major writers of the Golden Age. Because Quevedo belongs fully to the turbulence of the age—he rubbed shoulders with kings and viceroys and dukes, and suffered accordingly the ups and downs reserved for the critically inquisitive and outspoken—his works bear significance and, most important, contain a full measure of prophecy. Of all the writers of the period, it was this Spanish Swift, with his ear close to the ground, who knew most intimately the goings-on and also the sinister course ahead. A magnificent poet, Quevedo offers a strange mixture of a depressingly coarse, often obscene, realism, and an Alice-in-Wonderland fantasy, not unlike that of his countryman Goya of the *Caprichos* and *Disparates*. Witness Quevedo's uncanny *Sueños* (1635), those visits in Hell to his pet aversions: doctors and tailors, barbers and bankers. Realism and fancy are found in *Don Pablos* too, but the former is preponderant because of the nature of the picaresque. With sardonic pen Quevedo traces the "education" of his "hero." But this seventeenth-century Wilhelm Meister has no steady, wholesome world before him: what he has is a cruel society bereft of all altruism and beautiful sentiments. He has to open his way through a veritable hell peopled by double dealers, sycophants, and cold calculators—in short, through a macabre universe conceivable only in a time of utter corruption.

Quevedo's style exhibits Spanish prose at its ripest. The

virtuoso kneads together the vulgar jargon of the gutter with refined euphuisms and the exaggerated punning then in fashion. It must be remembered that this is the period of the Spanish baroque and that Quevedo and his contemporaries, most notably Góngora the poet and Calderón the playwright, were hard at work conceptualizing and deforming literary expression and sowing ambiguities wherever there was room left for them— theirs was the era of stylized diction, Latinized syntax, and metaphoric language.

In sharp contrast to the sordid reality projected in the picaresque novels stands the glamorous world of the Golden Age theater with its colorful costumes, its grandiloquent gesturing and posturing, its make-believe and tinsel. The Spanish people have always loved the theater, almost as much as their spectacular bullfights. It was therefore only natural that at the apogee of their Golden Age, when most Spaniards were keenly and exultantly aware of their nationality, there should emerge a *national* theater. Growing as it did, like the Elizabethan theater, in *"corrales,"* i.e., backyards of inns and taverns, close to the common people, it was the very opposite of the refined, sophisticated Racinian theater of the French courts. There were no restrictions, no rules, no unities—the Spanish "comedia" mixed up the tragic with the comic, the real with the imaginary; it emphasized action rather than psychological analysis, and rarely delivered disturbing political messages. It was, in short, sheer entertainment, extremely fluid, at times almost like the musical comedy of today, with its dancing and singing, and as full of improvisation as the *commedia dell' arte.*

The most dynamic figure of this theater was unquestionably Félix Lope de Vega Carpio (1562–1635). Lope created the Golden Age theater, gave it impetus and direction, nurtured it, and even composed a treatise on the art of writing comedies.* "For half a century his sensitive impressionable versatile genius was the ready channel through which the spirit of the triumphant Spanish nation could flow and the classical drama be-

---

* *The New Art of Writing Plays.* Translated by W. T. Brewster. New York: Columbia University Dramatic Museum, 1914.

come finally nationalized. He added play to play; no single play represents his genius, but in their entirety they fully represent the Spanish nation." * Lope's life reads like a novel: ** picaresque, mischievous, exuberant, but at times darkened by misfortune. He lived it so intensely that one wonders how it left him time for anything else. Albeit this man or superman (Cervantes called him "Monster of Nature") managed to cultivate all the literary genres: he wrote epic poems, novels, some of the tenderest lyrics in Spanish (he began dictating his verses at the age of 5, before he had learned to write), and over 2000(!) plays, of which 500 have come down to us. Among his masterpieces: *Fuente Ovejuna, Peribañez, El Caballero de Olmedo, El mejor Alcalde, el Rey, El perro del hortelano, El castigo sin venganza, La dama boba.* . . .

From this vast assortment I have chosen *Fuente Ovejuna* (1619) for inclusion in this anthology. Most critics consider it Lope's signal achievement, and I prefer it especially because I find in it a felicitous harmony between form and content: it is put together unusually well (considering Lope's usual haste!), and it has something to say. Rather than just amusing the public, Lope seems to be demonstrating the convergence of interests between the honest, hardworking tillers of the soil—the simple, faithful, beautiful souls of rural Spain—and the exalted Spanish Majesty whom Lope always endowed with a lofty sense of justice and magnanimity. To him monarchs were always ready to protect the peasants from the predacity and abuses of the tyrannical, lecherous feudal lords. The inspiration for *Fuente Ovejuna* came to Lope while reading Rades y Andrada's *Crónica de las Tres Ordenes Militares* (Chronicle of the Three Military Orders [1572]), wherein he came across the well-known event dramatized by him and which actually had taken place, April, 1476, in Fuente Abejuna, later called Fuente Ovejuna. In the

---

* A. F. G. Bell, *Castilian Literature*. Oxford University Press, 1938, pp. 187–188.

** Angel Flores, *Lope de Vega, Monster of Nature*. New York: Brentano's, 1930. Also available in the Spanish translation of Guillermo de Torre. Madrid: Editorial La Nave, 1939, and Buenos Aires: Editorial Losada, 1949.

province of Cordoba, bordering Extremadura, there existed a farming community, rich in pasturelands and produce: wheat, olives, wines, hogs, sheep, cows. The Romans called it Melaria because of its abundant flavorsome honey; the Spaniards translated the name to Fuente Abejuna, i.e., *fuente de las abejas*, well of bees, source of honey.* In 1400 Fuente Abejuna freed itself from the *Castle* of Calatrava, joining the free city of Cordoba. The feudal lords recaptured it in 1430, assigning it to don Pedro Téllez Girón, Gran Maestre of the Order of Calatrava. At his death, Fuente Abejuna fell into the hands of his son Rodrigo Téllez Girón, the young Maestre in Lope's play, who in turn gave it to be administered by the lecherous, cowardly Fernán Gómez de Guzmán, the *Comendador* (since Fuente Ovejuna was his *encomienda*). The historical background also emphasized the fraudulent plans of King Alfonso of Portugal who, after Enrique IV's death, coveted the whole of Spain. While the feudal lords, always involved in treacherous machinations, sided with the Portuguese pretender, the common folk defended the Catholic sovereigns Ferdinand and Isabella.

The struggle, therefore, was between a popular, unified state, comprising monarchy and common folk, and the rebellious separatists, the barons and counts of the "Castles," the legacy of feudalism. The peoples' insurrections, which proliferated throughout Europe under different names (revolts of the *pagesos de remensa* of Catalonia, of the *forenses* of Mallorca, of the *agermanados* of Valencia, as well as the *peasants' revolts* of Germany and the *jacqueries* of France) led to the emancipation of the serfs and, ultimately, to the formation of the bourgeoisie. Lope adroitly combined the various conflicts and tensions into an intensely moving play of love, revenge, community spirit, and justice triumphant thanks to the people's solidarity and the intelligence and benignity of the Monarchs. The play, variously interpreted, has been as successful in Catholic Spain and democratic France as in communist Russia.

Another *comedia* of tremendous appeal was *El Burlador de*

---

* By Lope's time Abejuna (pertaining to bees) had changed through popular usage to Ovejuna (pertaining to sheep).

Sevilla (*The Trickster of Seville* [1630]) by Tirso de Molina (1584–1648), which contributed the character of Don Juan to world literature. Tirso, whose real name was Gabriel Téllez (the illegitimate son of the Duke of Osuna, and scion of the Téllez Girón in *Fuente Ovejuna*), was born in Madrid, the theatrical capital of Spain, and spent most of his life in convents there and in Toledo, as interested in academies, theaters and literary pursuits, which embraced poetry, fiction, and drama, as in his multiple religious devotions and duties as friar and visitor for the Order of the Mercèd.

Tirso enriched the Golden Age theater with his theological plays [e.g., *El condenado por desconfiado*, which dramatized one of the subjects of polemics at the time: predestination) and with numerous profane plays (*La prudencia en la mujer, La villana de Vallecas, Don Gil de las calzas verdes, La gallega Mari-Hernández, Marta la piadosa*) which proved him to be a keen observer of human nature, especially of female psychology. He opposed frequently the conceited nobles, perhaps a compensatory attitude traceable to his bastardy. And because Tirso was not sold entirely on the many dead shibboleths and hollow knightly ideals and conventions of the Golden Age (*punto de honor*, i.e., honor at all costs, etc.), he delved with greater sincerity into the immediacy of Spain. His characters are therefore more real and in their relationships there is a freshness, a living quality, a resilience, a spark—one is tempted to say, a *joie de vivre*, even in tense moments—not to be found in the baroque, thunderous, death-dealing playwrights of the day.

However, Tirso's renown depends to a great extent on *The Trickster of Seville*, not so much because of its dramatic qualities as because with it he introduced the new myth of Don Juan to European literature. Many of the elements in the play were not original*; they existed before him in legend, folksong, folktale, and in the exploits of actual people famous for their—donjuanism. Tirso's main contribution consisted in choosing the right ingredients and mixing the theme of the libertine who

---

* Cf. Victor Said Armesto, *La leyenda de Don Juan*. Buenos Aires: Espasa-Calpe, 1946 (New edition, Colección Austral).

seduces women and then runs away from them, with the theme of the banquet with a dead man, who on taking his revenge administers divine punishment. Tirso elevated the superficial elements of folklore (lechery, inconstancy, sexual abnormality) to a more complicated psychological plane (the struggle of the sexes, the irresistible call to adventure, to danger, etc., which beckons every man). Furthermore, Tirso infuses a dramatic dichotomy into his character: on the one hand, Don Juan seizes avidly upon everything life offers him; yet within him there exists, on the other hand, deep repugnance toward the things desired or attained. Like a reckless gambler, Don Juan stakes everything he has on a card: even his mortal life, even his life after death. This recklessness and this constant communion with ever-increasing odds and hazards lends him tragic grandeur. And by introducing the Stone-Guest motif to this adventurous existence, Tirso elevated the action to a moral or rather to a theological plane. One of his favorite problems, predestination, once again is brought to the fore.

With a louder romantic accent the nineteenth-century poet-playwright José Zorrilla created *Don Juan Tenorio* (1844), which has become inextricably bound to the Spanish tradition: this play is produced in the theaters of all the Spanish-speaking nations on November 2, the *día de los muertos* (day of the dead), All Souls' Day. After visiting the cemeteries (realm of death), the crowds attend the performance of *Don Juan* (realm of life), a symbolic act which points to the ancestral roots of the Rites of Spring, the origins of Greek drama, the Orphic and Eleusinian mysteries, in fact all sorts of life-death-resurrection myths. This mystery or the motif of the seducer has recurred over and over again in many literatures; some of the world's outstanding writers and musicians have tried their hands at it: Molière, Goldoni, Gluck, Mozart, Byron, Pushkin, Mérimée, Dumas, Rostand, Richard Strauss, Bernard Shaw, Arnold Bennett . . . .*

---

* There exists abundant critical material on the Don Juan motif. Cf., for instance, G. G. Bevotte, *La Legende de Don Juan*. Paris: Hachette, 1929, 2 vols., and John Austen, *The Story of Don Juan*. London: Martin Secker,

Lope died in 1635; Tirso in 1648; and no writer was as notably endowed to take over the scepter of the Spanish theater as Don Pedro Calderón de la Barca (1600–1681). All these men belonged to the same Golden Age and therefore shared many things in common and reacted often very similarly—but how vastly different they were! While Lope's life was a veritable novel, Calderón's was totally devoid of glamor. In his youth, which seems to have been rather short, he campaigned in Flanders and Italy; in his old age, he became a priest: soldier and priest, nothing more common in the Spain of the times! Quiet, taciturn, thoughtful, he devoted all his effort to his art, inextricably bound to his Catholicism. His philosophical temperament, on the one hand, and his stylistic formalism, on the other, led him to create an art so allegorical and contorted that our highbrow contemporaries are calling him "highbrow." Calderón never attained the *popular* successes of Lope, nor was his name associated with any of the literary quarrels of the day. His prestige derived from the Court; Philip IV granted him titles of nobility and the Cross of Santiago.

Calderón's playwriting alternates between a reworking, as it were, of the plots and themes of Lope and his contemporaries (compare, for instance, Lope's *El Alcalde de Zalamea* with Calderón's *El Alcalde de Zalamea*) and a meditative theater somewhat distant from human contingencies, a theater focused on philosophical and religious allegorizations (*La vida es sueño*, *El mágico prodigioso*). Because the heroic drama is well represented in this volume with Lope's *Fuente Ovejuna* and Tirso's *The Trickster of Seville*, I have chosen the devout *El gran teatro del mundo* (*The Great Theater of the World*) to exemplify the work of the least known, but perhaps greatest, genius of the Golden Age theater. The reader should remind himself, however, that the same Calderón also wrote such plays as *Amar después de la muerte* (*Love after Death*), in which the audience is transported to the atmosphere of *The Abencerraje* and the relations of love, war, and chivalry between Moriscoes and

---

1939. For savory Shavian comments, see the Introduction to *Man and Superman*.

Christians. Love, war, death, noble Moors, and repentant Christians: the melodramatic threads are all there in this old tale of the civil wars of Granada, and in the hands of Calderón they become a rich tapestry of pathetic beauty and intense dramatism.

How different the romantic *Love after Death* (yes, Romanticism in the mid-seventeenth century!), with its flair and piquancy, with its emotional tensions, its exotic background, its exquisite poetry, its fateful love and its death and revenge—from the quiet *autos sacramentales!* It is as if there were two Calderóns! *The Great Theater of the World* is a kind of theological *Everyman*. It is a play within a play, in which the Author has for his disputants a motley crew: a Poor Man, a Rich Man, a Farmer, the King, a Child, Beauty, Discretion; and through them, at times humorously, at others tragically, the message comes out, vividly, unequivocally: that life is but a temporary station, a preparatory step for life after death. The message, a Roman Catholic message, seems to echo Matthew 6:19–21: "Lay not up for yourselves treasures upon earth where moth and rust doth corrupt, and where thieves break through and steal. But lay up for yourselves treasures in heaven, where neither moth nor rust doth corrupt, and where thieves do not break through nor steal: For where your treasure is, there will your heart be also."

Queens College,   ANGEL FLORES
Flushing, New York.

1479–1504 *Ferdinand the Catholic of Aragon and Isabella of Castile*

1481   Founding of the Holy Office of the Inquisition at Seville; birth of Ignatius Loyola.

1483   Appointment of Torquemada as Inquisitor General for Castile and Aragon; birth of Luther.

1492   Discovery of America; conquest of Granada, ending Moorish dominion in Spain (711–1492)—Moors settled in the kingdom of Granada since 1238; expulsion of Jews.

1493   Papal bull granting New World to Spain.

1501–4   Victories of the Gran Capitan in Italy; conquest of Naples and Italy.

1504   Death of Queen Isabella.

1504–1516 *Ferdinand the Catholic*

1508   Cardinal Cisneros inaugurates University of Alcala; *Amadís de Gaula.*

1512   Conquest of Navarre.

1516–1556 *Charles I of Spain—Emperor Charles V of Holy Roman Empire*

1519–21   Conquest of Mexico by Hernán Cortés.

1520   Rebellion of the Holy Junta.

1521	Promulgation of the first edicts of Charles V against heresy in the Netherlands; excommunication of Luther by the Pope.
1521–22	War of the Comunidades.
1525	Bloody suppression of the Peasants' revolts in Germany.
1527	Assembly in Valladolid to examine doctrines of Erasmus.
1531–32	Conquest of Peru by Pizarro.
1535	Expedition of Charles V against Tunis.
1540	Society of Jesus founded by Ignatius Loyola.
1541	Disastrous expedition of Charles V against Algiers.
1545	Assembling of Council of Trent.
1551	THE ABENCERRAJE (licensed for printing).
1554	LAZARILLO DE TORMES; first *Index Expurgatorius*.
1556	Abdication of Charles V.

1556–1598 *Philip II*

1557	War against France and battle of San Quentin.
1559	Law forbidding Spaniards to study at foreign universities; Jorge de Montemayor: *Diana*, includes THE ABENCERRAJE.
1560	King Philip transfers court to Madrid.
1562	Birth of *LOPE DE VEGA*.
1563	Closing of the Council of Trent.
1565	Villegas: *Inventario*, includes *The Abencerraje*.
1566	Beginning of organized resistance to Philip II in the Netherlands, formation of the League of the Gueux or "Beggars": war of Liberation in the Netherlands lasts from 1568 to 1648.
1567	Founding of the library of the Escorial.
1568	Decree of the Inquisition condemning the people of the Netherlands to death, the Prince of Orange opens war against Spain.
1571	Naval battle of Lepanto, defeat of the Turks by Don John of Austria; Cervantes was wounded in this battle.

1572	Polyglot Bible of Antwerp edited by Arias Montano; expulsion of the Spaniards from Holland and Zeeland by Beggars.
1579	Union of Utrecht.
1580	Conquest of Portugal by Spain; birth of QUEVEDO.
1581	Formal declaration of Independence by the Dutch provinces of the Netherlands.
1584	Birth of TIRSO DE MOLINA.
1588	Destruction of the Invincible Armada.
1596	Capture of Cadiz by the Dutch and English.

1598–1621 Philip III

1599	Mateo Aleman: Guzman de Alfarache; birth of Velazquez.
1600	Birth of CALDERON DE LA BARCA.
1605	Cervantes: Don Quixote (Part I).
1609	Expulsion of the Moriscoes.
1615	Cervantes: Don Quixote (Part II).
1616	Death of Cervantes and Shakespeare.
1619	LOPE DE VEGA: Fuente Ovejuna.

1621–1665 Philip IV

1621	Renewed wars of the United Provinces with Spain.
1626	QUEVEDO: Life & Adventures of Don Pablos the Sharper.
1630	TIRSO DE MOLINA: The Trickster of Seville.
1635	Death of LOPE DE VEGA; Quevedo: Sueños.
1640	Recovery of national independence by Portugal, with the House of Braganza on the throne.
1642	CALDERÓN: The Great Theater of the World.
1643	Victory of the French over the Spaniards at Rocroi; death of QUEVEDO.
1646	Capture of Dunkirk from Spain by French and Dutch.
1648	Peace of Westphalia: acknowledgment of the in-

dependence of the United Provinces by Spain; death of *TIRSO DE MOLINA*.

1651   *Calderón: Love after Death.*

1655   Alliance of England and France against Spain; English conquest of Jamaica.

1659   Treaty of the Pyrenees between France and Spain and marriage of Louis XIV to Spanish Infanta; Spain looses Roussillon and Cerdagne.

1660   Death of Velazquez.

1665–1700   *Charles II*

1678   Peace of Nimwegen: Spain ceded Franche-Comte to France.

1681   Death of Calderón.

1700   Death of Charles II of Spain, bequeathing his crown to Philip, Duke of Anjou (Philip V of Spain, 1700–1746), thus beginning the Bourbon dynasty of Spanish kings.

BIBLIOGRAPHY

(References in English)

Aníbal, C. E. "The Historical Elements in Lope de Vega's *Fuenteovejuna*," PMLA, XLIX, No. 3 (1934), 657–718.

Austen, John. *The Story of Don Juan. A Study of the Legend and the Hero*. London: Martin Secker, 1939.

Bell, A. F. G. *Castilian Literature*. Oxford: Clarendon Press, 1938.

Bertrand, L. and Sir C. Petrie. *History of Spain*. New York: Appleton-Century Company, 1934.

Bourland, C. B. *The Short Story in Spain in the Seventeenth Century*. Northampton, Massachusetts: Smith College, 1927.

Brenan, Gerald: *The Literature of the Spanish People*. Cambridge, England: University Press, 1951.

Bushee, A. H. *Three Centuries of Tirso de Molina*. Philadelphia: University of Pennsylvania Press, 1954.

Castro, Américo. *The Structure of Spanish History*. Princeton University Press, 1954.

Chandler, F. W. *Romances of Roguery*. New York: Columbia University Press, 1899.

Chaytor, H. J. *Dramatic Theory in Spain*. Cambridge, England: University Press, 1925.

Davies, R. Trevor. *The Golden Century of Spain 1501–1621*. London: The Macmillan Company, 1937.

Deferrari, Harry Austin. *The Sentimental Moor in Spanish Literature before 1600*. Philadelphia: Pennsylvania University Publications, 1927.

Fitzmaurice-Kelly, J. *Chapters of Spanish Literature*. London:

A. Constable and Company, 1908; *Lope de Vega and Spanish Drama*. Glasgow: Gowans & Gray, 1902.

Flores, Angel. *Lope de Vega, Monster of Nature*. New York: Brentano's, 1930.

Ford, J. D. M. *Main Currents of Spanish Literature*. New York: H. Holt and Company, 1919.

Gouldson, Kathleen. "The Spanish Peasant in the Drama of Lope de Vega," in E. Allison Peers, ed., *Spanish Golden Age Poetry and Drama*. Liverpool: Institute of Hispanic Studies, 1946, pp. 63–89.

Haan, F. de. *An Outline History of the Novela Picaresca in Spain*. The Hague: Martinus Nijhoff, 1903.

Hamilton, Earl J. *American Treasure and the Price Revolution in Spain*. Cambridge, Massachusetts: Harvard University Press, 1934.

Haring, C. J. *Trade and Navigation between Spain and the Indies in the Time of the Hapsburgs*. Cambridge, Massachusetts: Harvard University Press, 1918.

Howells, W. D. "Lazarillo de Tormes," in *My Literary Passions*. New York: Harper & Brothers, 1895.

Hume, Martin A. S. *Spain: Its Greatness and Decay, 1479–1788*. Cambridge, England: University Press, 1913; *Spanish Influence on English Literature*. London: E. Nash, 1905.

Keller, Daniel S. "Lazarillo de Tormes, 1554–1954: An Analytical Bibliography of Twelve Recent Studies," *Hispania*, XXXVII (1954), pp. 453–456.

Klein, Julius. *The Mesta, a Study in Spanish Economic History*. Cambridge, Massachusetts: Harvard University Press, 1920.

Lea, H. C. *A History of the Inquisition of Spain*. 4 vols. New York: The Macmillan Company, 1922.

Lewes, G. H. *The Spanish Drama. Lope de Vega and Calderón*. London: Knight, 1846.

Madariaga, S. de. *Shelley and Calderón*. London: A. Constable and Company, 1920.

Marañón, Gregorio. *Antonio Perez*. New York: Roy Publishers, 1955.

Mariejol, J. H. *Philip II.* New York: Harper & Brothers, 1933.

Marni, Archimede. "Did Tirso Employ Counterpassion in His Burlador de Sevilla?" *Hispanic Review,* XX (1952), pp. 123–133.

McClelland, I. L. *Tirso de Molina. Studies in Dramatic Realism.* Liverpool: Institute of Hispanic Studies, 1948.

Menéndez Pidal, Ramon. *The Spaniards in Their History.* New York: W. W. Norton and Company, 1950.

Merimée, E. and S. Griswold Morley. *A History of Spanish Literature.* New York: H. Holt and Company, 1930.

Merriman, R. B. *The Rise of the Spanish Empire in the Old World and the New.* 4 vols. New York: The Macmillan Company, 1918–1934.

Nichols, Madaline A. "A Study in the Golden Age," in *Estudios Hispanicos. Homenaje a Archer M. Huntington.* Northampton, Massachusetts: Wellesley College, 1952, pp. 457–476.

Oliveira Martins, J. P. *A History of Iberian Civilization.* Oxford, England: University Press, 1930.

Oppenheimer, Max. "The Baroque Impasse in the Calderonian Drama," *PMLA,* 65 (1950), pp. 1146–1165.

Parker, A. A. *The Allegorical Dramas of Calderón.* London: Dolphin Book Company, 1943.

Pound, Ezra. "The Quality of Lope de Vega," in *The Spirit of Romance.* Rev. ed. New York: New Directions, 1952, pp. 179–213.

Prescott, W. H. *History of the Reign of Emperor Charles.* 3 vols. Philadelphia: J. B. Lippincott Company, 1875; *History of the Reign of Philip the Second.* 3 vols. Philadelphia: J. B. Lippincott Company, 1883.

Ranke, Leopold von. *Ottoman and Spanish Empires in the Sixteenth and Seventeenth Centuries.* New York: The Macmillan Company, 1912.

Rennert, H. A. *The Spanish Stage in the Time of Lope de Vega.* New York: Hispanic Society, 1909; *The Life of Lope de Vega.* Reprint. New York: G. E. Stechert & Company, 1937.

Roaten, Darnell. "Wölfflin's Principles Applied to Lope's *Fuenteovejuna,*" *Bulletin of the Comediantes* (University of Wisconsin), IV (1952), #1, no pagination.

Roaten, Darnell and F. Sánchez Escribano. *Wölfflin's Principles Applied to the Spanish Drama, 1500–1700.* New York: Hispanic Institute, 1952.

Roth, Cecil. *The Spanish Inquisition.* London: R. Hale, Ltd., 1937.

Schevill, R. *Dramatic Art of Lope de Vega.* Berkeley: University of California, 1918.

Seaver, H. L. *The Great Revolt in Castille.* New York: Houghton Mifflin Company, 1928.

Selig, Karl L. "Concerning Gogol's *Dead Souls* and *Lazarillo de Tormes,*" *Symposium,* VIII (1954), pp. 138–140.

Seymour, Willard C. *Popular Elements and the Idea of Justice in the Comedies of Lope de Vega.* Stanford University dissertation, 1953.

Silva, R. "The Religious Dramas of Calderón," in E. Allison Peers, ed., *Spanish Golden Age Poetry and Drama.* Liverpool: Institute of Hispanic Studies, 1946, pp. 119–205.

Spitzer, Leo. "A Central Theme and Its Structural Equivalent in Lope's Fuenteovejuna," *Hispanic Review,* XXIII (1955), pp. 274–292.

Ticknor, George. *History of Spanish Literature.* 3 vols. Boston: Houghton Mifflin Company, 1891.

Trench, R. C. *Calderón: His Life and Genius.* New York: Redfield, 1856.

Trend, J. B. *The Civilization of Spain.* New York: Oxford University Press, 1944; "Calderón and the Spanish Religious Theatre of the Seventeenth Century," in *Seventeenth Century Studies Presented to Sir Herbert Grierson.* Oxford: Clarendon Press, 1938, pp. 161–183.

Weir, L. E. *The Ideas Embodied in the Religious Drama of Calderón.* University of Nebraska Studies, 1940.

Wilson, E. M. "The Four Elements in the Imagery of Calderón," *Modern Language Review,* XXXI (January, 1936).

(*References in Other Languages*)

Alonso Cortés, Narciso. "Sobre *El Buscón*," *Revue Hispanique*, 43 (1918), pp. 26–37.

Asensio, Manuel J. *El "Lazarillo de Tormes": Problemas, crítica y valoración*. University of Pennsylvania dissertation, 1955.

Astrana, Marín, L. *La vida turbulenta de Quevedo*. 2nd ed. Madrid: El Gran Capitán, 1945.

Barja, César. *Libros y autores clásicos*. 3rd ed. Brattleboro: Vermont Printing Company, 1923.

Bataillon, Marcel. *Erasme et l'Espagne*. Paris: E. Droz, 1937; in Spanish as *Erasmo y España*. 2 vols. Mexico: Fondo de Cultura Económica, 1950.

Bouvier, Rene. *L'Espagne de Quevedo*. Paris: E. Droz, 1936; *Quevedo, homme du diable, homme de Dieu*. Paris: H. Champion, 1929.

Castro, Américo. *Semblanzas y estudios españoles*. Princeton, New Jersey: privately printed, 1956.

Cotarelo, E. *Ensayo sobre la vida y obras de don Pedro Calderón de la Barca*. Madrid: Revista de Archivos, Bibliotecas y Museos, 1924.

Díaz Plaja, Guillermo. *Historia General de las Literaturas Hispánicas*. Barcelona: Editorial Barna, 1953, Vol. III, "Renacimiento y Barroco."

Durán, Manuel E. *Motivación y valor de la expresión literaria de Quevedo*. Princeton University dissertation, 1954.

Entrambasaguas, J. de. *Vida de Lope de Vega*. Barcelona: Labor, 1936; *Estudios sobre Lope de Vega*. 2 vols. Madrid: Consejo Superior de Investigaciones Científicas, 1946.

Freden, Gustaf. *La cena del amor (estudios sobre Calderón)*. Madrid: "Insula," 1954.

Friedrich, Hugo. *Der fremde Calderón*. Freiburg: Schultz Verlag, 1955.

Frutos Cortés, Eugenio. *Calderón de la Barca*. Barcelona: Labor, 1949.

Igual Ubeda, A. and J. Subias Galter. *El Siglo de Oro*. Barcelona: Seix & Barral, 1951.

Papell, A. *Quevedo, su tiempo, su vida, su obra*. Barcelona: Barna, 1947.

Pfandl, Ludwig. *Spanische Kultur und Sitte des 16, und 17. Jahrwunderts*. Kempten: Kösel & Pustet, 1924; in Spanish as *Cultura y costumbres del pueblo español de los siglos XVI y XVII*. Barcelona: Araluce, 1929; *Geschichte der spanische National-literatur in ihrer Blütezeit*. Freiburg. i. B.: Herder, 1929; in Spanish as *Historia de la literatura nacional española en la edad de oro*. Barcelona: Gili, 1933.

Ramírez de Arellano, R. "Rebelión de Fuenteovejuna," *Real Academia de la Historia*, XXXIX, pp. 446 ff.

Revue Hispanique (symposium devoted to Quevedo's *El Buscón*), XLIII (1918), pp. 1–78.

Río, Angel del. *Historia de la literatura española*. New York: The Dryden Press, 1948, Vol. I.

Ríos, Blanca de los. *Del Siglo de Oro*. Madrid: B. Rodriguez, 1910; "El *Don Juan* de Tirso de Molina," *Archivo de Investigaciones Históricas* (Madrid), Año I (1911), pp. 7–30.

Sánchez y Escribano, F. *Cosas y casos de los albores del siglo XVII español*. New York: Hispanic Institute, 1951.

Serrano Plaja, A. *España en la Edad de Oro*. Buenos Aires: Atlántida, 1944.

Shaeffer, Adolf. *Geschichte des spanisches Nationaldramas*. 2 vols. Leipzig: F. A. Brockhaus, 1890.

Spitzer, Leo. "Zur Kunst Quevedo in seinem *Buscón*." *Archivum Romanicum*, XI (October-December, 1927), pp. 511–580.

Valbuena Prat, Angel. "Los autos sacramentales de Calderón," *Revue Hispanique*, LXI (1924), pp. 1–302; *Literatura dramática española*. Barcelona: Labor, 1930; *Calderón*. Barcelona: Juventud, 1941; *La vida española en la Edad de Oro*. Barcelona: A. Martin, 1943; *Historia de la literatura española*. Barcelona: Gili, 1953, Vols. I and II.

Vossler, Karl. *Realismus in der spanischen Dichtung der Blütezeit*. Munich: Bayerische Akademie der Wissenschaften, 1926; in Spanish as *Algunos caracteres de la cultura española*. Buenos Aires: Espasa-Calpe, 1942; *Lope de Vega und sein*

Zeitalter. Munich: Beck, 1932; in Spanish as *Lope de Vega y su tiempo*. Madrid: Revista de Occidente, 1933; *Einführung in die spanische Dichtung des goldenen Zeitalters*. Hamburg: C. Behre, 1939; in Spanish as *Introducción a la literatura española del Siglo de Oro*. Reprint. Buenos Aires: Espasa-Calpe, 1945 (Colección Austral); "Tirso de Molina," *Escorial* (Madrid), II (1941), pp. 167–186.

Wardropper, Bruce W. *Introducción al teatro religioso del Siglo de Oro. La evolución del auto sacramental, 1500–1648*. Madrid: Revista de Occidente, 1954.

CONTENTS

MASTERPIECES

OF THE SPANISH GOLDEN AGE

THE ABENCERRAJE

ANONYMOUS

Translated by Angel Flores

THE STORY goes that in the time of the brave Prince Don Fernando, who conquered the city of Antequera, there lived a knight named Rodrigo de Narvaez, renowned for his courage and feats of arms. In the struggle against the Moors, he wrought many valiant deeds, especially in the campaign and battle of Antequera wherein he proved himself worthy of perpetual fame. But this Spain of ours values courage so little (since here it is so natural and ordinary a quality) that it seems no matter how bravely one may act, she underrates one's courage. Spaniards are unlike those Romans and Greeks who, when a man risked death but once in his whole life, immortalized him in their writings and extolled him to the skies.

Now this knight did so much in the service of his army and his King that, after the city had been conquered, he was appointed Governor of it, so that he might play as important a part in its defense, as he had previously played in its capture. He was also made Governor of Alora; thus he found himself in command of two garrisons, and by dividing his time between them, he always managed to help the one in direst need. He lived the greater part of the time at Alora. Within this fortress he kept fifty knights, paid by the King to defend it; and like the Immortals of King David, their number never diminished, for when one died another was put in his place. They all had so much faith and reliance in the courage of their leader that no undertaking ever intimidated them. Consequently they were not in the least hesitant about provoking their enemies or protecting themselves from them. In each of their skirmishes they won honor and spoils; and for this reason they were always rich.

One very calm night, after supper, the Governor spake unto them, saying: "Nobles, lords and brethren, it seems to me that naught enlivens a man's spirits so much as the continuous exercise of arms, because in this occupation one gains confidence in oneself and ceases to fear others. This assertion needs no proof as you yourselves will readily attest. I say this because much time has elapsed since we have done aught to increase our fame. I should be discrediting myself and my rank if, as leader of such valiant folk and such a brave regiment, I should make light of time without any worthy accomplishments. Since night protects us, I venture (if you deem it wise) that it will be worth our while to advise our enemies that the defenders of Alora never sleep. I have spoken; do as you think best."

They told him that he should command and that they would obey him. Then, choosing only nine of his men, so that the fortress might remain well guarded, he ordered them to take arms. When fully equipped, they went out through a secret door of the fortress so that no one might see them. As they advanced on their way, they came to a crossroad. "Now, if we all follow this road," quoth the Governor, "perhaps the enemy will go off by the other. Therefore, you five take this road and I, and the remaining four, will take the other. So, if perchance some of us should meet the enemy, and be outnumbered, let one of you sound his horn, and at the given signal the rest of us will hasten to your aid."

The five knights traveled onward talking of diverse matters, when one of them said:

"Stop, comrades, for if I am not mistaken, someone is coming."

They hid in a small wood bordering on the road, until presently they espied a handsome Moor mounted on a roan stallion coming toward them. So gallant and comely a gentleman was he and of such goodly grace and countenance that his personage alone attested to his noble blood and extraordinary valor. He wore a long cloak of crimson damask, and over it a burnoose embellished with gold and silver thread. On his right sleeve was embroidered the image of a beautiful lady. In his hand he held a two-headed lance. He carried a shield and scimitar, and wound thickly about his head he wore a Tunisian turban, which served both for the ornament and defense of his person. Fair was he, and pleasant to look upon; tall and shapely of body; and as he traveled, he sang a ditty in praise of the sweet memory of his love, as follows:

> In Granada was I born
> In Cartama was I bred;
> But in Coin by Alora
> Lives the maiden I would wed.

Albeit the melody was not artistic, the Moor appeared happy and, as he was in love, he lent a charm to all he sang.

The knights, overjoyed at seeing him, stepped aside a bit to let him come forward until they could fall upon him. They caught him off guard, but he defended himself with utmost courage. Then four of his attackers withdrew, leaving one alone to fight him; but as the Moor knew more about jousting, he cast both horse and rider to the ground with a single thrust of the lance. When the remaining four saw this, three of them attacked him, for he seemed very powerful. Thus there were three Christians against the Moor, each ordinarily powerful enough to overcome ten Moors; but in this case all of them were powerless against the one. Then, suddenly, the Moor's lance broke and the knights pressed in upon him closely. Pretending to flee, he spurred his horse and rushed upon the unhorsed knight. Then, swooping down from his saddle like a bird, he grasped his victim's lance and again faced his enemies. They still followed him, thinking he was abandoning the fight; but so skillfully did the Moor wield his lance that in no time at all he had two out of three on the ground. The one who remained, seeing his companions in such narrow straits, blew his horn and rushed in to help them. Now the skirmish waxed

fiercer, for they were piqued to see their adversary hold out so
well against them. As for the Moor, he had more at stake than
his own life.

At this moment one of the two knights jabbed him in the
thigh with his lance; and if the blow had not glanced off, his
fate would have been sealed on the spot. Furious at seeing
himself wounded, the Moor put up his defense and jousted with
his opponent until, with one thrust of his lance, he cast him
and his horse to the ground.

Rodrigo de Narvaez, sensing the need of his companions,
spurred his horse and, crossing the road, hastened to help them.
As he had a better horse, he soon was in the lead. Seeing the
five wounded knights, and how valiantly the Moor had fought,
he realized that this was no ordinary man. Then he spake unto
him, saying:

"Such is your noble valor and rare strength, brave Knight,
that by overcoming you one may win but glory and great
honor."

A heated combat began between these valiant men-at-arms,
but since the Governor was fresh, and the Moor and his horse
badly wounded, he pressed in so relentlessly that the latter could
hardly defend himself. The Moor knew that on this one battle
both his life and happiness depended, and thus he dealt Rodrigo
a blow which, if not for his shield, would have vanquished him
forever. Rodrigo answered swiftly with a thrust at the Moor's
right arm. Then he rode in close to him and struck him with
such force that, casting him out of his saddle, he also fell with
him to the ground, crying:

"Yield, Sir Knight, if you hold your life dear, for it is now
in my hands."

"It is in your hands," said the Moor, "to kill me, as you
say; but Fortune shall never turn on me in this way, for I have
long since succumbed to the one who shall be my conqueror."

The Governor did not then reflect upon the mysterious meaning of these words but, acting in his usual merciful way, he
helped the Moor to rise, for the latter was overcome with
fatigue, and with loss of blood from his wounds, neither of

which was very serious. Then Don Rodrigo bound up his wounds with some bandages given him by the knights and helped the Moor mount one of his men's horses—since his own had been wounded—and they started back toward Alora. As the Governor rode on, commenting on the Moor's great prowess and good nature, the latter heaved a long, deep sigh, and muttered a few words in Arabic which no one understood.

Rodrigo de Narvaez considered the Moor a man of parts, and gracious of visage, and remembering how valiantly he had defended himself, judged such melancholy too great for so brave a heart. Desirous of knowing more about the matter, Rodrigo said:

"Be advised, Sir Knight, that the prisoner who loses heart and courage for fear of imprisonment, hazards the right of freedom. Remember that in war men must win or lose, for chance is unpredictable, and it seems a shame that one so courageous as yourself should now be in such a sad plight. If you are sighing because of the pain of your wounds, rest assured you will have the best of care, and if you are grieved at the prospect of prison, remember that Chance is the sister of War, and that all who pursue the one must be prepared to accept the other. And if you are troubled by some other secret grief, tell me, and on my honor I swear I will do all I can to help you."

The Moor raised his sorrowful eyes and asked:

"Who are you, Sir Knight, who thus comfort me in my sadness and show such concern for my misfortune?"

"My name is Rodrigo de Narvaez," replied the knight, "and I am Governor of Antequera and Alora."

Almost joyfully the Moor turned to face him and said:

"Now certainly have I lost many reasons for complaint. Your merits have long been known to me and, albeit I have never seen you before, I venture to deem you worthy of my trust. Thus, I pray you, gentle Knight, command your company to withdraw, that I may speak with you freely."

The Governor did so, whereupon the Moor began thus to speak:

"Rodrigo de Narvaez, most valiant Governor, now hear

my story and judge if my misfortunes do not warrant a heavy heart. Know that my name is Abindarraez the Younger, distinct from an uncle, my father's brother, who is also called so. Descended I am from the noble house of the Abencerrajes in Granada, whom you must have heard mentioned many times, and though of late my luck has been the worst, yet I would tell you of myself:

"Know that in Granada dwelt a noble lineage of lords and knights, called Abencerrajes, who were the flower of all that kingdom in gentility, refinement and humanity. They surpassed all the rest in valiant deeds. By kings and noblemen they were highly esteemed, and the common folk adored them. From all skirmishes they emerged victorious, and in all tournaments they won renown. They innovated court dress and etiquette, so that it might well be said that in both peace and war they were the example and the mirror of the entire kingdom. It is said that there never lived an Abencerraje who was cowardly, niggardly, or ill-disposed. He who did not pay court to a lady was not considered an Abencerraje, nor was she who did not have an Abencerraje to pay court to her considered a lady. But Fate, hostile to their exceptional good fortune, willed that they should lose this superiority in the manner that you will hear:

"The King of Granada, influenced by false rumors circulated about them, did a notorious and unjust injury to two of these knights, who were the best of their family; and it was said, although I do not believe it, that these two, assisted by ten others, conspired to kill the King and divide the kingdom among them, to avenge their injury. This conspiracy, whether true or false, was discovered before it could be put into effect. The King, fearful of scandalizing the people of the realm, who loved the accused dearly, had them all beheaded on the same night; because had he delayed this unjust act, he would have been powerless to commit it.

"Large ransoms were offered in exchange for their lives but the King rejected them all—such was his severity! When the people saw that there was no hope of saving their lives, they wept and lamented with all their hearts: the fathers who begot them; the mothers who gave them birth; the ladies whom they served; and the knights who fought beside them in battle, all wept for them. And all the common folk raised such a hue and cry that it seemed as if the city were being invaded by the enemy. So it is evident that if their lives could have been purchased with tears the Abencerrajes would not have perished so miserably.

"Here you see how such an illustrious line of noble knights came to its end! Consider how long it takes for Fortune to raise a man to the pinnacle of success and how quickly she hurls him down from it! How slow is a tree in growing, and how readily it goes up in flames! With what great difficulty a house is built, and how easily it burns down! How many people could take warning from the fate of those unfortunates who, albeit illustrious, famous, and favored by the King himself, innocently suffered public disgrace! Their homes were demolished, their property confiscated, and themselves proclaimed traitors to the King.

"The result of this miserable affair was that no Abencerraje could live in Granada, except my father and an uncle of mine who were found innocent of the crime. This concession was granted on condition that the sons born to them should be reared in some other city and should never return to their own, and that the daughters should marry men who lived outside the realm."

Rodrigo de Narvaez, who kept noticing how grieved the Moor was in relating his misfortunes, said:

"Your story, Sir, is certainly strange. You have cause, Abindarraez, to lament the fall of your noble house and kinsmen, whose heads could never hatch so great a treason."

"This gentle opinion which you have of the goodness of my ancestors I know not, worthy Governor, how to requite except with unfeigned and humble thanks. You will see how all the Abencerrajes learned to be unhappy from then on. Soon I was born and my father, not to disobey the King's edict, sent me to be nursed and brought up in a certain fort called Cartama, committing me to the charge and care of the Governor thereof, with whom my father had a long-standing familiarity and acquaintance. This man had a daughter, almost my age, whom he loved more than himself; because, besides being his only child, she was very beautiful, and moreover, had cost him his wife, who had died in giving her birth.

"I was brought up with her from childhood, and, as we were generally thought to be brother and sister, we came so to regard ourselves. I do not remember ever having spent an hour in which we were not together: together they brought us up, together we walked, ate, and drank. From this close companionship there sprang up in us a natural love which increased as we grew older. One warm afternoon as I entered the garden of jasmines, I found her seated near the fountain combing her beautiful hair. Dazzled by her beauty, I fixed my look upon her, and she looked to me like Salmacis. I thought to myself, 'Oh, if I were only Hermaphroditus to appear before this beautiful Goddess!'

"I can not express how much it pained me to call her sister. I could wait no longer; I went to her, who, as soon as she saw me, came to receive me with open arms. When I sat down beside her she asked me, 'Why have you, good brother, left me so long alone?'

" 'Sweet lady,' I replied, 'I have long been seeking you in every place. At last my heart conjectured where you were. But tell me now, I pray you, what certainty have you that we are brother and sister?'

" 'No other,' said she, 'than the great love I bear you, and the fact that everyone calls us so.'

" 'And if we were not brother and sister,' said I, 'would you then love me as much as you do?'

" 'Can you not see,' she continued, 'that if we were not brother and sister, my father would not permit us to go so continually together and all alone?'

" 'Even so,' said I, 'I should be far happier than in my present misfortune.'

"Thus she spoke, and as she did so, her fair face kindled

with vermilion blush, and she said to me, 'And what do you lose by it if we were brother and sister?'

" 'I lose myself and you,' I said.

" 'I do not understand you,' said she, 'but it seems to me that the mere fact that we are brother and sister is enough to compel us to love each other quite naturally.'

" 'It is only your beauty that compels me to love you. Rather it seems that our relationship chills me.'

"At these words I lowered my eyes and saw her image in the crystalline waters of the nearby fountain. I seemed to find her image wherever I turned, and in my heart I found the truest one of all. I said to myself, and I should have been sorry if anyone had heard:

" 'Oh, were I now to drown in this fountain where I proudly behold my sweet lady, how much more fortunate should I die than Narcissus! If she should love me as I do her, how happy should I be! If fortune would let us live ever together, what a happy life should I then lead!'

"As I was saying this, I rose up, and gathering some jasmine and myrtle from around the fountain, I wove a fair and redolent wreath, and, after placing it on my head, I returned to her crowned and conquered. Her eyes rested on me more sweetly, I thought, than ever before, and removing the garland from my head, she put it on her own. She seemed to me, at that moment, more beautiful than Venus when she appeared at the award of the golden apple. And looking upon me, she said,

" 'How do you like me now, Abindarraez?'

" 'You look,' I answered, 'as if you had just conquered the world, and were being crowned queen and mistress of it.'

"At which words, rising from her place, she took me by the hand, and said to me, 'If it were so, indeed, my brother, you should lose nothing by it.'

"I made no reply but to follow her out of the garden.

"We continued this deceitful life for a long time until cruel Love, wishing to wreak vengeance on us, discovered our deceit; for as we grew older I cannot say how she felt when she first became aware of this, but never in my life was I happier than at this time, although afterwards I paid for it dearly. The moment we were sure of our love, that pure and healthy love we felt for one another, it began to torment us, and turned into a rabid affliction that will last until we die. In our case there were no premonitory symptoms to dissimulate; because the start of our love affair was a pleasure and delight, founded on all that was good; and later on the disease developed not gradually, but suddenly and all at once.

"By this time she had become my one and only happiness in life and my whole being was wrapped up in hers. Beauties which were not hers seemed ugly to me, useless and without any value in the world. My every thought was of her. By this time our diversions were different; sometimes I looked at her fearing she would notice I was even envious of the sun that touched her. Her presence made my existence pitiable and her absence weakened my heart. But in spite of this I believed that nothing was owed me for she paid me in the same coin. Fortune, jealous of our sweet love, wished to deprive us of our joy, and how she did so I shall tell you directly.

"The King of Granada, in order to promote the Governor of Cartama, sent an order that he should leave the fortress immediately and go to Coin, the territory which borders yours, and that I should be left at Cartama under the authority of the Governor who was to come there.

"When my lady and I heard this unlucky news, you may imagine, noble gentleman, if at any time you have been a lover, what a world of grief we conceived. We both went into a secret place to weep and lament our misfortunes, and the departure and loss of each other's company. There did I call her my sovereign mistress, my only joy, my hope, and other sweet names that Love did put into my mouth. Weeping I said to her:

" 'When the view of your rare beauty shall be taken from my eyes, will you then sometimes remember me?'

"At this point, my tears and sighs cut off my words. Forcing myself to speak more, I uttered I know not what foolish words, which I can not remember, for my dear mistress carried away my wits, senses, and memory with her.

"But can I ever tell you what sorrowful things she said, although to me they seemed but few! She whispered many sweet words that still ring in my ears; but finally not to prolong our suffering, we bade each other farewell with many tears and sobs. In token of our love, each left the other a fond embrace accompanied by a sigh, wrested from the very depths of our hearts.

"Then, because she saw my dire distress and my deathly countenance, she said to me:

"'Abindarraez, since I cannot bear to leave you, and know that you feel the same, I will be yours until death; my heart belongs to you; my life, my honor, my possessions are yours to keep; and in witness thereof I shall send for you the very first chance I have. Then you will come wherever I may chance to be, and there, as your wife, I will give you that which I alone possess for you. Neither your loyalty nor my soul would consent to have it otherwise, and all the rest of me will be yours eternally.'

"With this promise my heart was somewhat lightened and for this infinite favor which she promised me when time and occasion should serve, I kissed her dainty hands.

"The next day, after their departure, I felt like one who had wandered over wild, craggy mountains, who suddenly finds himself in an eclipse of the sun. I began to feel her absence keenly and sought in vain for remedies against it. Sometimes I looked upon the windows where she used to stand, sometimes at the fountain where she bathed, or at the bed wherein she slept and the garden where daily she used to disport herself. I visited in turn her accustomed haunts, and in every one of them I found a reflection of my sorrow. In truth, her plan to send for me eased my pains a little, and with it I dissembled some part of my woes, though at times my despair was such that I almost preferred losing all hope.

"But by some great stroke of luck my lady had sent for me

that very morning, for her father had been summoned to Granada by the King. Awaked from my heavy slumber and melancholic cares by this inopinate and happy news, I regained my composure and waited for nightfall, so that I might depart in secret. I donned my present garb to show my lady the rejoicing of my heart. Truly, I thought myself invincible in battle, for I carried my mistress in my heart. Wherefore, Rodrigo, if you conquered me, it was not your strength alone that did so but an evil omen written in the stars. Consider now, at the end of my true tale, the happiness which I lost, and all the misfortune which I possess! The journey from Cartama to Coin seemed unending, for in my eagerness I could not bear to wait another moment: my lady had sent for me and soon we would marry and partake of our mutual joy! But now I am a wounded, conquered captive, and that which grieves me most is that the last opportunity for the realization of my happiness ends tonight. Oh suffer me then, Christian, to comfort myself with sighs, and do not consider them a sign of weakness, though it were a great deal better for me to have the courage to endure this hard and sinister turn of fortune."

Rodrigo de Narvaez was deeply moved by this discourse, and amazed by the Moor's strange story; and, being as he was, so sympathetic, he decided not to hinder him with any delay. The valiant Governor said to him:

"Abindarraez, I want you to know that my virtue surmounts your ill fortune, for if you will promise me on your honor as a knight to return to my prison within three days, I will set you free so that you may continue your amorous enterprise, for it would grieve me to cut short so fine and honest an undertaking."

When the Moor heard this, he was so happy that he threw himself at the Christian's feet in token of thanks, and said to him:

"If you do me this unexpected favor, noble Governor of Alora, you will show the greatest gentility of any man, and you shall restore me again to life. Take whatever security you desire; I will not fail to do whatsoever you command."

Rodrigo de Narvaez called his squires and said to them:

"Gentlemen, entrust this prisoner to me, for whose ransom I, myself, will be a pledge."

After they had agreed that he might dispose of him at his pleasure, Rodrigo, taking the Abencerraje by his right hand, said, "Do you promise me on your honor to come back to my castle at Alora and there to yield yourself as my prisoner within three days?"

"I do," replied the Moor.

"Then go," said Rodrigo, "and good fortune be with you. If you have need of my person to accompany you or of anything else to help you in your enterprise, speak, and you shall have it."

The Moor thanked him greatly but took only a horse, and he rode as fast as he could towards Coin. Rodrigo de Narvaez and his squires returned to Alora, talking along the way of the valor and goodly behavior of the Abencerraje. The Moor was not long, due to the great speed at which he rode, in coming to the fort at Coin. He went straight to the castle as he had been bade and did not stop until he found a postern gate; there he stayed a little to look about him on all sides to see if anyone was on guard. But when he perceived that all was quiet, he knocked on the door with the butt end of his lance, for that was the password his mistress had given him through the gentlewoman. Presently this same gentlewoman let him in and said:

"What has detained you, my lord? Your long tarrying put my lady in a great fear. Alight, and I will take you to where she attends your presence in great perplexity."

He then dismounted and hid his steed in a secret place nearby, wherein he also left his lance with his shield and scimitar. The gentlewoman took him by the hand and very softly led him up a pair of stairs, for fear of being heard by the people in the castle; and brought him into the room of the fair Xarifa (for thus was that lady called). She ran to receive him with open arms; and they both fell into such a passionate embrace that neither could utter a word to express the overwhelming joy they had at each other's sight. Then the lady said to him:

"What may be the cause of your delay I know not, my loving lord, but the sorrow and anxiety I have experienced at your slow coming, my eager love may attest."

"I hope you know, fair lady," quoth he, "that it is through no fault and negligence of mine; but men's designs do not always fit their desires. Rest assured that it was not in my power to come sooner than I have."

She led him by the hand to a secret chamber. There she seated herself on a bed, and said to him:

"I was desirous, my thrice beloved, to have you see how captives of love can fulfill their promises, for from the very day when I gave you my word as the pledge of my heart, I have sought the means to discharge myself of it. So I ordered you to come to my castle to be my prisoner, as I am yours. I mean to make you lord of myself and of my father's treasure, under the honorable name of a lawful husband; although this, I understand, will be much against his will. Since he is ignorant of your valor, and does not know your deserts as well as I, he will perhaps bestow some richer husband on me, but I esteem your noble personage and your virtuous and valiant mind more than the greatest riches in the world."

As she uttered these words she lowered her head, blushing not a little at having so greatly revealed herself and in so plain and open terms declared her affection unto him. The noble Moor took her in his arms and kissed her white hands many times for such loving and courteous words, and thus spake unto her:

"In return for all the great good you have wrought in my behalf, sweet lady of my soul, I have naught to offer you that is not yours already, except this pledge of love, in proof whereof I take you as my lady and my wife."

They called the gentlewoman and they became husband and wife. Being married, they went to bed where they rekindled the flames of their enamored hearts. In which amorous enterprise there passed on either side many loving words and deeds, which are rather to be contemplated than described in writing. After this the Moor lay so sad and pensive and heaved so profound and painful a sigh that the fair Xarifa, perceiving it, was much amazed and troubled to see so sudden an alteration, whereupon, unable to suffer so great an insult to her beauty and willingness, she rose up a little in the bed, and though somewhat troubled, said in a sweet and merry voice:

"What means this, Abindarraez? It seems that you are offended at my mirth. I hear you sigh as you toss and tumble from side to side. If I am your only joy and delight, why do you not tell me for whom you sigh; and if I am not, why do you deceive me? If you have found any flaw in my beauty, consider my zealous and loving heart which is sufficient to supply many wants. If you serve another, let me know her, that I may serve her too. But, if you have any other secret grief I shall not be offended if you tell it to me and I will either die or rid you of it."

The Abencerraje, ashamed of what he had done, and thinking that his silence would fill her head with jealousy and suspicion, heaved a passionate sigh.

"My sweetest life," said he, "if I did not love you more than my own soul, I would never have shown such signs of inward grief, because the trouble I had when I was alone I bore with better courage, but now that I am constrained to leave you, I have no strength to endure it. Thus you know my sighs are caused rather by too much faithfulness than by lack of it; and so that you may not be left in suspense and in ignorance of the cause of my sorrow, I will tell you what has lately come to pass."

Then he told her the whole matter, finishing his narrative with these words:

"So that your captive, fair lady, is also the prisoner of the Governor of Alora. I do not dread the pain of that imprisonment, since you have taught my heart to suffer; but to live without you will be worse than any death."

With a merry countenance, she said to him:

"Trouble not your mind, Abindarraez, for I will take the care and remedy of this grief upon me, as a thing that touches me most of all; and the more, since it is not denied any prisoner that has given his word to return to prison to satisfy his captors by sending the ransom that shall be demanded of him. Wherefore do you yourself set down whatever sum you deem suitable, for I have the keys to all my father's treasure, which I will put in your hands and leave at your disposal. Rodrigo de Narvaez is a courteous gentleman and a good knight; he once gave you your liberty, and as you have acquainted him with the trust of these affairs, he is now the more bound to employ greater virtue and gentleness towards you. I am sure he will be contented with this arrangement, for, having you in his power and prison, he must perforce set you at liberty when he has received the value of your ransom."

The Abencerraje answered her:

"I see well, fair lady, that the strength of your love for me does not permit you to give me the best counsel; I will never commit so foul a fault as this. For if I was bound to keep my word, and was responsible only for myself, now that I am yours, the bond is greater. I will therefore return to Alora, and surrender to the Governor, and when I have done my duty, let Fortune deal with me as she will."

"Heaven never willed that you should be a prisoner and I should go free!" said Xarifa; "for being your captive, I am duty-bound to accompany you in this journey, for neither the extreme love I bear you nor the fear of my father's frowns, which I have purchased by offending him, allow me to do anything else."

The Moor, weeping with joy, embraced her, saying:

"You never cease, my dearest soul, to heap your favours upon me. Now do as you will, for this is my resolution."

With this decision, they rose before daybreak and after providing some necessary things for their journey, they departed in utmost secrecy for Alora. Xarifa wore a veil for fear of being recognized. As they pursued their way, conversing on various matters, they came upon an old man, and Xarifa asked him whither he was bound.

"I am going to Alora," he replied, "to confer with the Governor, who is the most honorable and virtuous gentleman I have ever seen."

Xarifa was overjoyed to hear this, for it seemed to her that since all found this gentleman so virtuous, he would treat them likewise, for they were in great need of it. Turning to the traveller, she said to him:

"Tell us, brother, know you of any remarkable deed that this man has performed?"

"I know of many, but when I have told you of one you will understand all the rest. This gentleman was first Governor of Antequera, and there he spent much time, enamored of a very fair lady in whose service he performed deeds of chivalry that are too numerous to mention; and albeit she recognized his bravery, she loved her husband so much that she practically ignored him. Thus it happened that one summer day, after dinner, she and her husband were strolling in their garden, inside the castle walls. He carried a sparrow hawk on his wrist. This pet he launched among some birds, who became frightened and flew away to seek refuge in the bramble bushes. The sparrow hawk, stretching his body, put out his claws, seized, and killed many of them. The gentleman fed him and turning to his lady said to her:

"'What do you think of the cleverness with which the sparrow hawk surrounded the birds and killed them? This, you may know, is the procedure of the Governor of Alora in a skirmish with the Moors. Thus does he follow them and kill them.'

"She, pretending not to know the Governor, asked her husband who he was.

"'He is the most valiant and virtuous knight that I have ever seen,' he answered, and then began to praise the knight very highly; to such a degree, indeed, that a certain compunction came over the lady, and she exclaimed:

"'How all men are enamored of this knight! Why should

I not be, if he be enamored of me? Surely I will be excused
for what I might do for him, since my husband has informed
me of his worth.'

"Later on, when her husband had gone out of the city, the
lady, unable to restrain her eagerness, sent her servant to call
the Governor. Rodrigo de Narvaez was in a frenzy to please
her albeit he did not believe that she was sincere, for she had
always repulsed him coldly. Nonetheless, at the appointed
hour, very cautiously, he went to see the lady, who was waiting
for him in a secret place. Thereupon she realized the mistake
she had made in shamefully desiring to have the one by whom
she had for so long been desired. She was also thinking of
rumor, which discovers everything, and fearing the fickleness
of men, and she bethought herself of the injustice she would
be doing her husband. All these obstacles, as is customary,
conspired to attract her the more, so that disregarding them
all, she received him sweetly and put him in her bedroom.
There they exchanged loving words, until at last she said to
him:

" 'Sir Rodrigo de Narvaez, from now on, I am yours except
that there remains something which is still not yours. Do not
thank me for this, because all your passion and assiduity,
whether false or true, raised you but little in my esteem; but
thank my husband for it, for he told me things about you
which have put me into my present state.'

"Then she told him what her husband had said, ending her
speech thus:

" 'Certainly, Sir, you owe my husband more than he owes
you.'

"These words impressed Rodrigo de Narvaez so deeply that
they confused him and made him repentant of the evil which
he was doing to the one who had spoken so well of him; and
withdrawing from her, he said:

" 'Lady, it is certain that I love you a great deal, and I shall
love you more from now on; but God never willed that I
should do such cruel hurt to the man who has spoken of me so
affectionately. From this day on I must treat your husband's

honor as my very own. In no better way can I repay him for the good things he has said of me.'

"And without waiting longer he returned whence he had come.

"The lady had to remain the butt of a joke and certainly, in my opinion, good lord and lady, the knight displayed great virtue and courage, for he conquered his passion."

The Abencerraje and his lady were surprised at the story. They praised him a great deal, and the Moor said that he had never seen greater virtue in any man.

She answered, "Before God, Sir, I would not want so virtuous a man. He must have been little in love thus to have departed; the honor of the husband carried more weight with him than the loveliness of the woman."

And after his reply she said other very charming words. Soon they arrived at the fortress and knocked at the gate. It was opened by the sentinels, who already knew of their coming. One man ran to call the Governor and said to him:

"Sir, in the castle is the Moor whom you conquered, and he brings with him a noble lady."

The Governor's heart told him who it might be, and he went down below and received them courteously. Abindarraez, taking his wife by the hand, brought her unto him and said:

"See, Rodrigo de Narvaez, if I am not true to my promise to return your prisoner. One was enough to overcome many; instead of one, I bring you two. Behold here my lady, and judge if I have not justly suffered for her sake. Accept us now as yours, for in your virtuous and noble mind rests my whole trust and confidence, and into your hands I commit her dear and most precious honor."

Rodrigo de Narvaez was very glad to see them both, and said to Xarifa:

"I know not, fair lady, which of you excels the other in love and courtesy, but truly I consider myself greatly bound to you both. Therefore enter and rest yourselves and henceforth consider this house and its master as yours indeed."

After this friendly conversation they went with him into his dining room, where they partook of refreshment, for the journey had somewhat tired them. Then the Governor asked the Moor:

"Sir, how are your wounds?"

"I think, Sir, that, with the journey, they are somewhat rankled."

Fair Xarifa, appalled, and altered in countenance, said:

"Alas, how comes this to pass, my lord? Have you any wounds about you and I know them not?"

"My lady, he whose heart endures the wound of your love need care little for any others. Truth it is that in the skirmish the other night I received two slight wounds which my troublesome journey and my negligence in curing have made somewhat worse."

"It is best," the Governor said, "that you lie down and I will send for a surgeon, who is here in the castle, to cure them."

Following which counsel the fair Xarifa, much altered and troubled in her mind, began to undress him. Then the surgeon came to see him, and, examining his wounds, said that they were not dangerous; and with a certain ointment which he made himself, the pain was assuaged; and in three days he was as sound and whole as he had been ever before.

One day, just at the end of dinner, the Abencerraje spoke thus to the Governor:

"As you are wise, Rodrigo de Narvaez, and as you have shown us such consideration, I have hopes that by your advice and help you will bring this painful affair to some good end. This is the fair Xarifa of whom I told you; this is my lady and my dearly beloved wife. She would not stay at Coin for fear of her father. For though he knows not what has passed between us, yet she fears lest this accidentally be discovered at some time. I know well that the King loves you and, though you be a Christian, bears you special good will for your valor and your virtuous disposition. Wherefore I beseech you, gentle Knight, to help us secure her father's pardon."

The noble Governor said to them, "Comfort yourselves, Abindarraez and fair Xarifa, I promise I will do whatever I can." Whereupon he called for ink and paper to write a letter to the

King of Granada, which in few words and true, went as follows:

"Most mighty King of Granada, Rodrigo de Narvaez, Governor of Alora, your servant, by these presents kisses your royal
hands and gives Your Majesty to understand that the Abencerraje Abindarraez, born in Granada, grown to manhood in
Cartama, and being under the charge and government of the
Captain of that fort, became enamored of Xarifa, the latter's
fair daughter. Then did it please Your Majesty to invest in the
said Captain the government of Coin. The two lovers, to bind
themselves in a mutual and permanent bond, betrothed their
faith before her departure. Now, in her father's absence she
sent to Cartama for the Abencerraje. As he was going to Coin,
I met him on the way; and there took place a certain skirmish
between us, wherein he showed himself a valiant and courageous man-at-arms. I made him my prisoner. Then he told me
his pitiable story, and my heart was moved with compassion at
his grief. I set him free for two days. He went on his way to see
his lady, and in that journey he won his wife and lost his
liberty. But seeing the Abencerraje had to return to my prison,
she came with him also, and here they are both in my power.

"I beseech Your Majesty, let not the word *Abencerraje*
offend you, for this gentleman and his father were blameless
in the conspiracy which was made against Your Royal Person,
in testimony whereof they are yet both living. Wherefore, I
humbly beseech Your Majesty to devise between Your Grace
and me a remedy for these hapless lovers, whose ransom I will
frankly waive, and willingly set them free. May it only please
Your Majesty to procure the lady's pardon from her father
and to entreat him to receive the gentleman into his affinity
and good likings. By doing which, besides the singular favor
that Your Highness shall do me, Your Majesty shall do no less
than is expected of the wonted virtues and bounty of your royal
and magnificent mind."

With this letter he dispatched one of his gentlemen, who,
coming before the King, delivered it into his own hands.

When he knew from whom it came, the King was very much pleased, for he loved this Christian especially for his valor and goodly personage. And reading it, he turned to the Governor of Coin, who was standing there, and, calling him aside, said to him:

"Do you read this letter which I have received from the Governor of Alora."

Upon reading it, his countenance manifested how much he was grieved in mind, which thing the King perceived and said to him:

"Be not offended nor sorry, although you have good cause, for there is no reasonable thing that the noble Governor of Alora requests at my hands which I will not do for him. Therefore, I command you to go immediately to Alora and to pardon your daughter and son-in-law, and carry them to your castle; in recompense whereof I will not forget to bestow on you continual favors."

It grieved the old Moor to the very heart; but, seeing he must not disobey the King's command, by counterfeiting a merry countenance and borrowing a little courage from his daunted spirits, he said that he would do so. Then he left for Alora, where it was already known, from the account of the messenger, all that had occurred at the palace. The Governor of Coin was courteously received.

The Abencerraje and his wife, tainted and appalled with shame and fear, came and kissed his hands. He received them joyfully and said:

"I come not hither of my own accord to repeat nor entreat of things past, but by commandment of the King, who wills that I pardon your misdeeds and your sudden marriage without my consent. And as for the rest, daughter, you have chosen a better husband for yourself than I could have given you."

Rodrigo de Narvaez was very glad to hear this gentle greeting of the old Moor, for whose entertainment he made many feasts and banquets. One evening, after they had dined in the garden, he said to them, "I value the privilege I have had of helping bring this affair to such a successful end; for nothing else could have made me more content. Therefore, I say that in itself the honor of having held you my prisoners is sufficient ransom. Wherefore, Abindarraez, you are free, in testimony whereof, I give you leave to go whither it please you, and whensoever you will."

Then they kissed his hands for the kindness he had shown them and the good he had done them. And the next morning they left the fortress, with Rodrigo de Narvaez bearing them company part of the way. When they arrived at Coin, great triumphs, banquets, and feasts were made in public celebration of the marriage. Xarifa's father, taking them both aside one day, said to them, "My beloved son and daughter, now that you are in peace, and possessors of my riches, it is only right that you show the gratitude due to Rodrigo de Narvaez for the good he has done you; also because of the great kindness with which he has treated you, he should not lose the right of your ransom; rather on this account is he the more deserving of it. I will give you six thousand double ducats. Send them to him, and from now on value him as a friend; indeed, even though your creeds differ."

The Abencerraje thanked him very humbly, and, taking the money and four fair Barbary horses, four lances, and four targets with bars and heads of pure gold, he sent them to the Governor of Alora with the following letter:

"If you think, noble Rodrigo de Narvaez, that by giving me my liberty in your castle, to return to mine, you gave me permanent freedom, you have deceived yourself; for when you liberated my body you imprisoned my heart. Kind deeds are the eternal prisoners of noble hearts. If you, in order to win accustomed honor and fame, are wont to do good to those whom you could destroy, I, in order to resemble my ancestors, and not to degenerate from the noble blood of the Abencerrajes, but rather to encompass in my veins all of their good traits, am obliged to thank you and serve you. This small gift is but a token of the sender's good will, which is very great, and also that of his wife, the fair Xarifa."

The valiant Governor valued highly the magnificence of the gifts; and, accepting the horses, lances, and targets, he thanked the Moor profusely and wrote to fair Xarifa the following letter:

"Abindarraez has not wished, fair Xarifa, to allow me to enjoy the real triumph of his captivity, which consists in forgiving and doing good. Since I have never on this earth had the opportunity of doing such a generous deed, nor one so worthy of a Spanish Captain, I should like to erect a monument in its honor and thus spread its fame unto future generations. The horses and arms I accept to aid him against his enemies; and if by sending me the ducats he has proved himself a generous knight, by accepting them I would seem a despicable lover of money. I am indebted to you both for the favor that you have granted me in making use of me and my castle; also, fair lady, know that I am not accustomed to rob ladies, but to serve and respect them."

With the letter he also returned the ducats. Xarifa, upon receiving them, said, "Whoever thinks he can surpass the valiant Rodrigo de Narvaez in martial deeds or in gallantry and liberality, is greatly mistaken."

In this manner they all remained satisfied and content with one another, bound together by a noble friendship which lasted forever.

LAZARILLO DE TORMES

ANONYMOUS

Translated by Mack Hendricks Singleton

PROLOGUE

I CONSIDER it right well that matters which are of moment should come to the attention of many persons and not be buried, unseen and unheard, in the tomb of oblivion, for it is quite possible that some readers who might chance to stumble onto such material would therein find information of great interest, and others, reading less deeply, could at least find entertainment.

In this regard Pliny tells us that there is no book, no matter how bad it may be, that has not something good about it. It is obvious that not all tastes are alike, for what one person will not eat, another dies for. Certain things which are disprized by some are greatly esteemed by others. This situation fortunately allows nothing to be thrown aside or destroyed (unless it be very greatly detestable), and permits many things to be widely disseminated, especially things which are harmless and impart useful knowledge.

Few would write for a single reader, for writing is a hard job; and writers who have done their work wish to be rewarded, not with money, but with the knowledge that their works are widely known and read, and—if they merit it—praised. In this regard Cicero tells us: "The desire to be held in esteem creates all the arts."

Does the first soldier who scales a wall hold his life to be less dear than any of the others do? Not at all. What impels a soldier to act dangerously is the desire to be admired. The same thing holds true for those who practice the Arts and Letters. The friar preaches very well, for he wishes to save souls; but ask him whether he is displeased when he is told: "How marvellously Your Reverence preached today!" A certain gentleman jousted very poorly—and then gave his armor to a trickster who praised him for having borne himself so well in the field. What would he have done if the compliment had been true?

It was ever thus. And I will confess I am no more saintly than my neighbors. Therefore, I shall not be disappointed if this little trifle of mine, though written in so prosaic a style, is received and enjoyed by all those readers who find pleasure in perusing the true account of a man who has had so many adventures and experienced so many dangers and adversities.

I beg Your Worship to receive this poor offering of one who would have made it richer had his gifts and his desires been of equal magnitude.

Since Your Worship writes me to relate these matters very fully, I have thought it best to start not in the middle but at the beginning. In this way Your Worship and others may receive a complete account of my life.

It will be clearly seen from this narrative that those who have inherited noble houses ought not be presumptuous, since they have been favored by Fortune.

And it will likewise be seen that those to whom she has not been partial have often done much more than those who have inherited their wealth, for many times, through their own energy and pluck, the less favored have, despite ill fortune, eventually reached port.

CHAPTER I

Lazarus tells of his life and whose son he was

I must first, sir, tell you that my name is Lazarus of Tormes, and that I am the son of Thomas González and Antonia Pérez, natives of Tejares, a village near Salamanca. I was born in the Tormes River, and so took Tormes as my surname. It happened in this manner:

My father (God forgive him!) was in charge of a watermill on the banks of that river for more than fifteen years. One night, my mother being great with child, gave birth to me there; so that in all honesty I may say I really was born in that river.

Now, when I was eight years old my father was accused of having performed various surgical operations on the bags belonging to the people who came to the mill to have their grain ground. He was arrested, confessed and denied not, and so was prosecuted.*

At that time an expedition was being sent against the Moors, and my father joined it, for he was in exile because of the scandal previously mentioned. He went as muleteer with a gentleman who had decided to go on the expedition; and like a faithful servant, my father ended his life at the same time as his master.

I pray to God that he is now in Paradise.

My widowed mother, being then without husband and protection, decided to take up her abode among worthy people, since she was herself so, and came to live in the city. She rented a little cottage and began to prepare meals for students and to wash clothes for the horseboys of the Comendador of the parish of La Magdalena, so that it was necessary for her to frequent the stables. And thus she became acquainted with a dark man who helped take care of the horses. He sometimes

---

* There is in here, it seems to me, an untranslatable pun.

came to our house in the evening and would leave on the following morning. On other occasions, he would come to the door on the pretext that he wished to buy eggs, and then he would enter the house.

When he first began to visit us, I did not take to him at all. I was really afraid of his black color and unprepossessing appearance. But when I saw that the quality of our food greatly improved with his visits, I began to grow fond of him, for he always brought bread and pieces of meat with him, and when winter came he would bring firewood, which kept us warm.

So it came about that as he continued to stay with us, and as he and my mother became thicker, she eventually presented me with a pretty little colored brother, whom I played with and helped keep warm.

I recall now that once when my stepfather, the negro man, was playing with the little fellow, the latter chanced to observe that my mother and I were white but that his father was not. He ran to my mother and pointing back with his little finger, said: "Mother! *Bogey-man!*" And my stepfather replied, laughing: "*You* little rascal, you! *You* little whoreson!" And, although still very young, I took note of the expression my baby brother had used, and I said to myself: "How many there must be in the world who flee from others—simply because they cannot see themselves!"

As our luck would have it, the activities of Zaide—so my stepfather was called—reached the ears of his supervisor, and when an investigation was made, it was discovered that he had stolen half of the provender bought for the horses, and, furthermore, he had pretended that many articles were lost, including bran, firewood, currycombs, aprons, and the blankets and coverings for the horses. When my stepfather could find nothing else to pilfer, he would unshoe the horses and take the horseshoes to my mother. They were later sold to a blacksmith, and the money he gave us for them helped feed and clothe my little brother.

Let us not marvel that a cleric or a friar should steal from the poor or from their own houses in order to give gifts to the ladies who are their devotees, or help someone of their own sort, when we have seen how a poor slave was impelled for love's sake to do the same thing.

Zaide was convicted of all that I have mentioned, for when they asked me threateningly what I knew, I—in my boy's way and out of fear—revealed everything, even to the fate of those horseshoes he had had me sell to the blacksmith. My poor stepfather was whipped till the blood came, and my mother was ordered on pain of a hundred lashes not to enter the Comendador's house again or to receive the unfortunate Zaide into her own.

My poor mother exerted herself to obey the sentence, and, to avoid danger and flee from slanderous tongues, she went to work for some persons who at that time lived at the Inn of La Solana. There, undergoing a thousand hardships, she brought my little brother up to an age when he could walk, while I, at the same time grew to be a good-sized lad who could fetch wine or candles or anything else the guests required.

At this time a blind man chanced to stop at the inn. Considering that I would be a good guide, he asked my mother whether he might not take me along with him. She commended me to him, saying that I was the son of a good man, who to exalt our Holy Faith, had given his life on the expedition to Gelves. She said she trusted in God that I would turn out to be no worse a man than my father had been, and she besought the blind man to treat me well and care for me as properly as a fatherless child deserved. He replied that he would do so and said he accepted me not as a servant but as his son. And so I began to serve and guide my new old master.

After we had been in Salamanca for a few days, it appeared to the blind man that he could not earn there as much as he desired, so he decided to leave the place. When the time for our departure drew near, I went to see my mother, and, the two of us weeping, she gave me her blessing, saying:

"Son, well do I know I shall not see you ever again. Try

hard to be good, and may the Lord direct you. I have brought you up to your present age, and I have now given you a good master. From now on, you must take care of yourself."

And so I left her and went back to my master, who was waiting for me.

We left Salamanca, and when we reached the bridge we observed there a stone animal which had almost the form of a bull, and the blind man requested me to approach the animal. When I had come near, he said to me:

"Lazarus, place your ear up close to the beast and you will perceive a great sound within him."

I, in my simplicity thinking it to be so, obeyed. When my master felt that I had my head alongside the stone, he knocked it with a terrific blow of his hand against the beast, so that I had a headache for three days afterwards from my butting of the bull.

And he said to me:

"Idiot! Be now aware that a blind man's boy has to know somewhat more than even the devil himself."

And he laughed heartily at his little trick.

I seemed at that instant to awaken from the naïveté in which like a little boy I had slept, and I said to myself:

"He is very right, and I must indeed have an alert eye and I must be ever watchful, since I am on my own, and I must learn to take care of myself."

We began our journey, and in a few days the blind man taught me some thieves' slang; and when he saw I was an intelligent lad, he was quite pleased and said to me:

"Gold and silver, I can give you none, but wise counsels for living, I can give you many."

And so it was indeed; for, after the Lord God, my old master took best care of me, and, although he was blind, he illuminated me, and in his own way gave me the only education I ever had.

I am happy, sir, to recount to you these childhood memories to demonstrate how virtuous it is for men to rise from low es-

tate, and, contrariwise, how vile it is to fall low from high position.

Now, to return to my excellent blind man and to proceed
in the narration of matters concerning him, I would, sir, inform
you that since the Creation, God has not produced a blind man
who was as he so very wise and so very sagacious. In his profession he was a very eagle. He knew a hundred-odd prayers by
heart. He had a deep and resonant voice which echoed
throughout the church when he said his prayers. When he had
finished, he would apparel his face with pious mien—but he
made no faces or grimaces with eyes or mouth, as others are so
often wont to do.

He had a thousand ways of getting money. He said he
knew prayers for many different situations—for women who
could not bear children and for those who were in travail; and
for those who had made unhappy marriages he had prayers
that would cause their husbands to love them dearly. To pregnant women he could predict whether the baby would be a
boy or a girl. And in medical matters he said that Galen knew
not half so much as he when it came to teeth, faints, and female ailments. In a word, no one could report any sickness to
him without receiving advice of this sort: "Do this, you must
do that, eat such an herb, take such a root. . . ."

And so, he was universally looked up to—especially by
women, who believed everything he told them; and, because
of those skills of his which I have mentioned, women greatly
contributed to his income. Indeed, he could earn more in a
month than a hundred other blind men could have earned
in a whole year.

But, sir, you must also know that although he had acquired a
great deal and kept it, there never was, I think, in all the world
so miserly and niggardly a man as he—so very much so, indeed,
that he almost starved me, for he never gave me the half of
what my necessities required. I shall tell you in all frankness
that if with my wit and tricks I had not managed to supply my
wants, I should certainly have died of hunger. For despite all

his craft and wisdom I so outwitted him that always—at least, *almost* always—I emerged the winner. To accomplish this I was in the habit of playing upon him the most devilish tricks, some of which I shall now relate to you—although I did not always come out unscathed.

He kept his bread and other things in a canvas bag which could be fastened with an iron hoop locked with a padlock, and when he put things in it or took them out he did so with such vigilance and nice calculation that it was utterly impossible for anyone to filch anything from him, even a crumb. (I may assure you that I took every crumb I could get from him, although I could easily do away with all I got in just two mouthfuls.)

After he had closed the padlock he would relax his vigilance, thinking me occupied with other matters; and then I would often bleed the stingy bag by means of a rip which I had made in it and was careful to sew up again every time; and I took out of it good-sized hunks of bread, pieces of bacon, and some sausages. . . .*

What I could filch and steal I converted into half-farthings; and when the blind man had been ordered to pray and was given whole farthings for that purpose, I conveniently had one of my half-farthings ready and would pop the whole one into my mouth the second it was presented, no matter how hard the blind man tried to get it first, and would then give him my own half-farthing in exchange. The wicked old fellow complained to me about it because he could *feel* the coin and tell it was not a whole farthing; and he would say:

"How in hell can this be? Ever since you have been with me I have been getting only half-farthings, though formerly I was given full farthings and very often a whole maravedí. My ill luck must somehow be due to you."

He had the habit of cutting prayers short—he would, indeed, say only half a prayer if the person who had commis-

---

* The sentence that follows in the text is based on the terms of a Spanish game and is untranslatable.

sioned it went away—on which occasions I was instructed to give his cloak a tug. This I would do, and then he would again start calling out: "Who wishes to have a prayer said?"—which is the way the question is often put.

At our meals he usually set a little jug of wine beside him. I would then swiftly grab it and give it a couple of furtive kisses and then return it to its place. But this went on only a short while, for he knew by the number of draughts left in the bottle how much was missing, and so to protect his wine he thereafter never let go of the jug but always held it tightly by the handle. But no magnet ever more successfully attracted iron to itself than I attracted that wine—this time by means of a rye-straw which I had prepared for that very occasion. I would put it in the mouth of the jug and then proceed to suck my fill of the wine within. But since the old villain was so sagacious, I am sure he caught on, for after that he changed his habit and began to place the jug between his legs, where he could cover it over with his hand; and so drank fully protected against me.

Now, being accustomed, as I was, to the drinking of wine, I was dying for it. And seeing that my little scheme of using a straw no longer produced results, I decided to make a little hole in the bottom of the jug so that the liquid would subtly drain out, and I used a little dab of wax to fill up the hole. When mealtime came I pretended to be cold and sat down between the blind man's legs to keep warm before the miserable little fire we had. When the bit of wax I had used was sufficiently warm with heat from the fire, the little hole in the jug began to let the wine drip into my mouth—and I maneuvered myself into so favorable a position that not the least drop got away. When the poor old devil started to drink he found the jug completely empty. He was amazed, he cursed himself, and, not knowing how that could be, sent the jug and the wine to the devil.

"At any rate, Uncle," I said, "you cannot accuse *me* of drinking it, for you never let it out of your hand."

He turned the jug so much about and about that he finally found the little drain and caught on to my trick; but for the time being he said nothing but pretended he still did not understand what had occurred. The next day when my jug was beginning to ooze in its usual way, I sat down according to custom, not suspecting the damage in store for me or that the blind man knew what I was doing. I sat imbibing those sweet draughts with my face upward and my eyes somewhat closed, the better to savor that delicious liqueur. The savage old blind man realized that now was the time for him to take revenge on me; so with his full strength he lifted up that—for me—bittersweet jug and with full force let it fall upon my mouth, so that your poor Lazarus, who was expecting nothing of the sort—but was, rather, carefree and joyful—really felt that the heavens and everything therein residing had fallen on top of him. The blow was such that it addled my pate and left me senseless, and the blow from the jug was so great that the pieces of it stuck in my face and tore it in several places, and it also knocked out my teeth, so that until this present day I have been toothless.

From that time on I had an aversion to that bad blind man, for although he was nice to me and treated me well and helped me recover, I knew perfectly well he was delighted with the chastisement he had given me. He bathed with wine the wounds the jug had caused me, and would often smiling say:

"How odd it is, little Lazarus! You are being healed by the very thing that hurt you." And he made further remarks in the same vein, which I did not like a bit.

When I was half recovered from my dreary punishment and my bruises, I began to consider that the cruel old man could easily put an end to me with a few more blows of the same kind, and so I decided to get away from him. But I did not leave him immediately, because I wished to put some plans into effect, carefully and to my best advantage. Although I should have liked to forget my grudge against him and forgive him for breaking the jug over my head, I was not encouraged to do so by the rough treatment he gave me from that time on, for he would strike me without cause or reason, knocking my head about and pulling my hair. And if anyone asked him why he treated me so roughly he would straightway relate the jug incident, saying:

"Do you perchance think this lad of mine is some young innocent? The devil himself could hardly think up better tricks than this lad here."

And those who heard him would cross themselves, saying:

"Who would ever have thought that such a little fellow could have done such a wicked thing?"

And they would laugh over the trick, saying:

"Chastise him, Uncle, chastise him well, and heaven will reward you for it."

Which, with such encouragement, is precisely what he did.

Whereupon I began to lead him down the worst roads possible—and on purpose, in order to hurt him and endanger him. If there were stones ahead, we went that way; if there was mud we went through the deepest part of it; and although I did not emerge from it as dry-shod as I might have liked, I would have been perfectly happy to lose one of my own eyes if I could have caused him to lose both of his—if he had had any to lose.

During all this time he kept poking me in the back of my head, which was now always covered with bruises, and seemed almost bald because he had pulled so much of my hair out. And although I swore I was not doing what I did out of malice, he never believed me at all—such was the discernment and great understanding the old villain had.

Now, that you may, sir, observe how very acute the old fellow was, I shall relate to you one of the incidents that happened to me while I was with him—an incident that fully convinced me how great his astuteness really was. When we left Salamanca, his intention was to move on to Toledo, because he said the people there were better off, even though less prone to give. He gave great importance to the following proverb: "More giveth the niggard than the naked." And so we took this road, passing through the best towns. We would stop along the way wherever we found welcome and profit; and when we found neither, we made our departure the third day after our arrival.

It chanced that we came to a town by the name of Almoroz, where a man who was harvesting grapes (for it was that time of year) charitably gave my blind man a bunch of grapes. Since grape baskets get rough treatment, and, too, because the grapes are very ripe at that particular season, the bunch he had received began to fall apart in his hand. If he had placed it in his pack it would certainly have turned into grape juice—it and everything with which it came in contact. So he decided to have a feast, not only because he could not take the grapes with him but also to give me some entertainment, for he had that particular day administered me a great many blows and proddings with his knees. We sat down on a fence and he said:

"Now I wish to show you how generous I am. Let us both eat this bunch of grapes, dividing it equally between us. We shall share it this way: you take one and I'll take one, but you must promise me not to take more than one at a time. I will do the very same until we have finished, and in that way no tricks will be played."

The agreement having thus been made, we began to eat. But at the very second round the old traitor changed his tactics and began to eat two grapes at a time, assuming, I suppose, that I must be doing the same. When I saw that he was breaking the contract, I determined not to be satisfied with just going along with him. I outdid him; I ate two at a time or three at a time, however I could. When we had finished the bunch, the blind man sat there for a while with the stem in his hand. Finally, shaking his head, he said:

"Lazarus, you were trying to deceive me. I would swear to God that you were eating three grapes at a time."

"I really wasn't," I replied. "But why do you suspect that?"

The supremely sagacious blind man answered me:

"Do you know why I was aware that you were eating them three grapes at a time? Well, when I was eating them two grapes at a time you didn't say a thing."

I laughed to myself, and although but a boy I perceived the blind man's great and discerning discretion.

To avoid prolixity, I shall not tell you all of the many amusing and profitable things which happened to me while I was with this my first master. And so I will tell you only of my leave-taking, and then bring this part of the narrative to an end.

While we were at an inn in Escalona, which is the residence of the Duke of that name, the blind man gave me a sausage to be roasted. After the juice had dripped out and had been lapped up, the blind man took a coin from his purse and told me to go and buy a maravedí's worth of wine at the tavern. The devil—the old thief-maker, they call him—placed in my imagination the trick I was to perform.

There was beside the fire a spindly little turnip which was so wretched looking it had no doubt been thrown there because it was no good for the cooking pot. At the moment nobody was present but the blind man and me. Since I had such a ravenous appetite because of the invasion into my very being of the savory smell of that sausage—which I knew I was destined to eat—I lost all my inhibitions and putting aside all fear in the hope of achieving my desire, I grabbed the sausage while the blind man was taking the money out of his purse, and swiftly put the spindly old turnip on the spit. Then when my master had given me the money, he took up the spit and began to turn it before the fire and thus tried to roast something which because of its very shortcomings had previously escaped being cooked.

I went for the wine and on the way devoured the sausage. When I got back I found that the blind old sinner had lodged the turnip between two slices of bread without having caught on—since he had not touched it—that it was not his sausage. When he took up his sandwich and bit into it thinking to get a good bite of sausage, his hopes were dampened by the drab old turnip, and he became angry and said:

"What is the meaning of this, Lazarus?"

"Poor me!" I said. "And must you blame me for this too? Haven't I just returned with the wine you sent me for? Someone else was here and did this to play a trick on you."

"No, no, that cannot be," he said. "I did not let the spit out of my hands. What you say is impossible."

I began again to swear and perjure myself, saying that I was guiltless of the substitution of the turnip for the sausage; but it little availed me against the shrewdness of the accursed blind man, from whom nothing could be hidden. He got up and seized me by the head and, like a good hound, began to smell my breath to assure himself of the truth of the matter. In his great excitement he opened my mouth a little more than was bearable, and without being careful about what he was doing, stuck his nose in. Now, that part of his person was long and pointed, and, with his vexation on this particular occasion, it had expanded to a length of around nine inches. The tip of it then reached down into my throat. Because of my great fear and the recentness of my eating the sausage, that object had not yet settled in my stomach. The groping around of his very generous nose in my throat half choked me, and encouraged my unsettled stomach to reveal my guilt and greediness by returning the blind man's sausage to him. So it was that before he could get his beak out of my mouth, my stomach was so greatly moved that the nose and the poorly chewed sausage left my person at the very same instant.

O Lord! I only wished at that moment to be buried, for dead I was already. The fury of the wicked old blind man was so terrible that if people had not come to my rescue I really do think he would have killed me. They got me out of his hands, which held on to what had been the little hair remaining on my head. My face was scratched, and my neck and throat all torn. Well, the latter certainly deserved the treatment, for its sins had brought so much punishment my way. The blind man told everyone who came there of my misdeeds, and related all over again the jug incident and the grape story and also what had just happened.

The laughter of all those people was so great that everyone who came along the street approached to see the fun. And I, though weeping and so greatly maltreated, felt I did an injustice to the blind man by not laughing at his account of my wiles, for he told his tale with such skill and relish.

Meantime I was reminded of a weak and pusillanimous action I had committed, and I cursed myself for my negligence. I *should* have bitten his nose off, for, since he had himself set the stage for it, I only needed to close my teeth upon that beak of his; and since it belonged to that old scoundrel, my stomach might better have retained it than it had the sausage—and so, no evidence would have been forthcoming, and I should have been able to deny any accusation. I wished to God I had done that. It would have been wonderful.

The innkeeper's wife and others who were there patched up matters between us, and they washed my face and throat with the wine I had brought back to be drunk. The blind man's commentary on this occasion was very humorous.

"Really, this fellow makes me spend more yearly on wine to wash him with than I spend on wine to drink in two whole years. It may even be said, Lazarus, that you should be more grateful to wine than to your own father, for if he begot you once, wine has given you life a thousand times."

And then he would tell how many times he had beaten me about my head and bruised my face and then healed my wounds with wine. And he said:

"I do really believe that if any man is ever going to be blessed with wine it will be you."

And those who were washing me laughed greatly when they heard this, though I was cursing.

But the blind man's prediction came true; and since that time I have had many occasions to remember that man (who doubtless had the gift of prophecy), and I feel sorry because of the vexations I caused him, although I made restitution, as you shall see, sir, as my story proceeds.

Considering all this and the low tricks the blind man had played upon me, I decided to leave him for good. Since this determination was constantly on my mind, I felt that after

the last trick he played on me I had better leave him now as
soon as I could. And so it came about, and in the following
manner.

The next day we went about the town begging alms. It had
rained heavily the night before, and now because it was still
pouring the blind man stood praying on an open kind of porch
which there chanced to be in that town. As night came on and
the downpour did not cease, the blind man said to me:

"Lazarus, this shower is interminable, and it gets worse the
darker it gets. Let us seize this opportunity to reach an inn."

To get to this place we had to cross a perfect rivulet that had
formed in the street.

I said to him:

"Uncle, the stream that has formed here is very wide. But,
if you wish, I can find a place where we may cross quickly without getting wet. I see one spot which is quite narrow. There we
shall be able to cross dry-shod."

He accepted my suggestion.

"You have a lot of good sense," he said. "That is why I am
so fond of you. Take me to that place where the water is narrow. It is dangerous to get wet in winter; it is especially dangerous to get wet feet."

I, who saw that everything was set for my trick, led him from
the protection of the porch straight into the square before one
of several pillars that constituted the support of the projecting
upper stories of several houses there, and then said to him:

"Uncle, this is the narrowest place in the stream."

It was raining hard and the poor devil was getting wet; so, because of our haste and more especially because God blinded
his understanding at that moment to give me my revenge, he
let himself believe me and said:

"Set me properly ready for the jump, and then you jump over
the water yourself first."

I set him immediately in front of the pillar and then jumped
over the water and got behind the pillar—like one awaiting the
charge of a bull, and I said:

"Ready! Jump as hard as you can and you will make it!"

I had scarcely got the words out of my mouth when like a he-goat the blind man plunged forward with all his might, even taking a previous step backward to jump all the harder. He struck the pillar head-on with such force that the sound of the collision made was very much as if a big pumpkin had struck the stone; and with his head split open he fell back half dead.

"So!" I cried. "So you could smell the sausage but not scent the post? Goody, goody!"

And I ran off, leaving him in the care of many people who were coming to his aid.

I reached the gates of the town in one long trot; and before nightfall I was in Torrijos.

I never learned what happened to the blind man after that; nor did I ever bother to find out.

CHAPTER II

How Lazarus entered the service of a priest,

and then what happened

On the following day, not feeling completely safe there all alone, I went to a place called Maqueda, where my sins led me into the company of a priest, who asked me, when I went to beg alms, whether I could act as altar boy. I said I could—which was quite true; for the blind man, although he treated me very roughly, taught me among many good things to act in such a capacity. The priest decided to receive me into his service. But, as the saying goes, I only escaped the thunder to be struck by the lightning. The blind man had been stinginess itself, but compared to my new master he was a very Alexander in magnanimity. I will only say that the priset presented a living portrait of the utmost niggardliness. I do not know whether he was so by nature or whether he had acquired the habit with his clerical garb.

He had an old chest with a lock on it, the key to which he

carried with him attached to a leather thong around his cassock. When the holy bread came from church he popped it into this receptacle, which he immediately locked. Throughout the whole house there was nothing to eat except what was in that box. In other houses you may often see bacon hanging by the chimney, a cheese on a shelf or in the cupboard, or some little basket containing pieces of bread left over from the table. But not in *this* house. I really believe that even though I had not been allowed to eat the things I have mentioned, the sight of them would have still provided me with some consolation.

The only other food in the house was a string of onions locked away upstairs. I was rationed one of them every four days. And when I asked the priest for the key to go and get one he would thrust his hand into his breastpocket and, if anybody was present, would say with great solemnity:

"Well, take it, but return it to me immediately, and do really try to keep from stuffing yourself all the time." As if that key would open a pantry filled with all the jams of Valencia! But there was nothing at all in that room, as I have said, but a string of onions hanging from a nail. The priest had counted them so exactly that if (for my sins!) I had taken more than my allotment I should have paid dearly for my daring.

I really came near starving to death. But, though the priest had little charity for me, he treated *himself* rather well, for he allotted himself five farthings a day for food and drink. I *will* say that he divided his broth with me. But of the meat all I got was the sight of it; and of the bread only a little—not, alas! even half of my requirement. It happens that in that region they have sheepshead on Saturdays, and the priest used to send me to get one that cost three maravedís (or six farthings). He would cook it and eat its eyes and tongue and neck and brains and the flesh of the jaws, and then he would give me the gnawed bones remaining on the plate, saying:

"There you are! Take them and celebrate—the world is yours! You live more royally than the Pope himself!"

"May God reward you in this same fashion!" I would say to myself.

At the end of the three weeks I was with him I became so weak that from pure hunger I could hardly stand. I saw myself headed for the grave unless God and my astuteness came to my aid. I had no way of using my tricks, for there was no opportunity to filch; but even though there had been, I could not have blinded the priest as I had blinded my first master. (May God forgive him if he died from that crash against the pillar!) Because of *his* condition he could never see what I was doing; but the priest was possessed of the finest eyesight in the world. When we were at offertory, not a farthing fell into the bowl without his immediately spotting it. He kept one eye on the people and one on my hands. His eyes danced in his head as if they had been made of quicksilver. He was aware of every single farthing given him. And when offertory was over he would take the bowl from me and put it on the altar.

I was unable to sneak a farthing from him during the whole time I lived—or, rather, died—with him. I never brought him a farthing's worth of wine from the tavern, either; for the little bit of it he received at offerings was popped into the chest immediately and then measured out so frugally that it lasted him for a whole week. And to conceal his great miserliness he would say to me:

"See, lad, priests must be very temperate in eating and drinking, and for that reason I do not pamper myself as others do."

But the wretched man lied a great lie, for at funerals and meetings of brotherhoods, where we were paid to pray, he ate like a wolf and drank more than a quack doctor.

And now that I have mentioned funerals—God forgive me!— I never was an enemy of our human lineage except on those occasions, and that was because we ate well. I wished, and even prayed, that God would call one of His own unto Himself. When the sacraments, especially Extreme Unction, are given to the sick, the priest calls upon all those present to pray. You may be sure that on those occasions I was certainly not the last to fall to prayers. With all my heart and soul I besought the Lord *not* to treat the patient according to His will (as people say) but very positively to carry the sick man away from this world. When anyone escaped my prayers, I hoped he might go to the devil; but if anyone died, I, with equal enthusiasm, gave him all my blessings. During my sojourn of around six months there no less than twenty people died, and I think I killed them—or perhaps I should say they died at my behest. It must have been because the Lord, seeing my prolonged and raging death, was pleased to take those people unto Himself in order to give life to me. But my suffering at the moment found no cure. For if on the day of a funeral I found some alleviation, when there was no burial, I, accustomed to my surfeit, returned to my hunger with all the greater misery. So in nothing could I find relief except in death, which as for others I likewise desired for myself; but, though I felt it continually within me, I never experienced it.

I often thought of leaving my wretched master; but I gave up the idea for two reasons. First, I did not trust my legs because of the great weakness that came to me from sheer hunger. The other reason was, as I told myself: "I have had two masters. The first starved me, and the second has brought me down to the doors of my tomb. So, if I leave this one and find another one worse, what will that be but death itself?" I was therefore unable to budge, for I was certain that I would find my new masters progressively worse. And one step lower would be the end of poor old Lazarus.

May the Lord deliver every faithful Christian from the affliction I was in! Well, one day my wretched, miserable, bad master went out of town. When I was left alone I began to think over my difficulties in order to find some sort of solution for them. The only thing I could see was that I was going from bad to worse. At any rate, while I was so occupied in thought, a tinker chanced to come to the door. I do believe he was a very angel sent to me in that guise by the hand of God. He inquired whether I had anything to repair. To myself I said: "There is a plenty to repair about me, and if you succeeded in *that* job you would have performed wonders." But, as it was no time to jest, I said to him, illuminated as I was by the Holy Spirit:

"Uncle, I have lost the key to this chest, and I am afraid my master will beat me. Do please see whether among those keys you have with you there might not be one that could replace my loss, and I will pay you well."

My angel-tinker tried several of the keys he carried with him on a long string, and I helped him with my feeble prayers. When I let my imagination wander I could see the loaves inside take on the likeness of the face of God. When the chest was open, I said to the tinker:

"I have no money to give you for the key, so please take one of the loaves here instead."

He took one of the loaves of holy bread—the one he thought the best—and went away quite pleased, leaving me even more so. But for the nonce I touched nothing so that nothing would be missed, and, too, I saw myself the master of so much wealth I thought that hunger never would dare attack me again. My wretched master came home, and it was God's will that he did not miss the funeral offerings I had given the tinker.

The next day, as soon as the priest had got out of the house, I opened my bread-filled paradise and took up in my hands and teeth a loaf of holy bread and in the time you could say two credos I had made it invisible and then locked the chest again. I began sweeping the house with great joy, for it seemed to me I had finally found the cure for my troubles. And so I continued to be merry for the rest of that day and the following too. But it was not my lot to find very long-lived happiness, and on the third day I really had a shock.

It happened that quite unexpectedly I saw my murderer bending over our chest and moving the bread about and about, counting and recounting the loaves. I pretended not to notice what he was doing, and in my secret prayers and devotions I kept saying: "O Blessed Saint John, Patron of Servants, blind him!" After the priest had calculated a while, by days and fingers, he said:

"If this box were not so well guarded, I would really say that someone had taken some loaves of bread from me; but from this moment on, I intend to keep a good count of my bread. There are nine loaves and a piece left."

"May God send you ill tidings," I said to myself, for it seemed to me that his words were like a huntsman's arrow piercing my heart. My stomach began to groan with hunger, seeing itself put back on its former fare. The priest now left the house. I, to console myself, opened the chest, and, seeing the bread, began to worship it, but did not dare kiss it, even. I counted the loaves just in case the wretched priest had made a mistake in his calculation, but I found his accounting far more exact than I could have desired. All I could do was to give the bread a thousand kisses as gently as I could, and then break off a little bit around the edge of the extra piece. With that I spent the rest of the day—but not quite so merrily as the day before.

But as my hunger was growing—especially since I had habituated my stomach to receive more bread than usual on those two or three days I have mentioned—I was dying a miserable death, and, when alone, could do nothing but open and close the chest in order to contemplate there the blessed face of God (as children are wont to call bread). And God Himself, Who cometh to the aid of the suffering, when He saw me in that predicament, brought to my mind a little remedy, for, after considering the matter, I said:

"This big old chest is worn in some spots, though the holes are small. It would be perfectly plausible to think that mice had got inside and attacked the bread. I must not take the bread out all at once, for he who is my ruination would perceive the raid on his box. This must be done bit to bit."

And I began to crumble the bread onto some not very precious cloths that were there, taking crumbs from three or four of the loaves. Then, as one savoring very delicate candy, I ate my crumbs and was somewhat comforted. But when the priest came home to supper and opened the box, he saw the depredation and doubtless thought the damage had been done by mice, for my artifice had so carefully imitated the workings of those animals. He looked the chest up and down and saw certain holes which he suspected to have been the entrance of the little fellows. He called me and said:

"Lazarus, look! Just see what a raid there has been on our chest this past night!"

I pretended to be quite amazed and asked what had happened.

"It's obvious," he said. "It's the mice. They destroy everything."

We began our supper, and God caused me to be fortunate once more, for I received more bread than was my usual pittance, because the priest cut away all that part of the bread he thought the mice had nibbled, and gave it to me, saying:

"This is for you. Eat it: mice are clean things."

And so, that day, with the bread which my hands—or, rather fingernails—had got me and the pieces the priest had cut off for me, I finished my meal—though I had hardly begun.

But, all of a sudden, I was thunderstruck again, for the priest went about taking nails out of the walls and looking for little boards with which he nailed up all the holes in the old chest.

"Ah, dear Lord!" I said to myself. "To what misery and ill luck and disaster are we poor mortals not subjected! How fleeting are the pleasures of this burdened life! Alas for me, who thought with this wretched little scheme to alleviate my misery! I was, a while, joyful and fortunate, but my ill luck would not let me so remain. My ill fortune has awakened my miserable master, and his subtlety is now more acutely sharpened than it has ever been (for such as he are at all times provided with piercing sagacity), and he has gone and stopped up the holes in the chest and by so doing has closed the gates against my comfort and opened up the dams of my suffering."

Thus did I lament, while my diligent carpenter, with many nails and boards, made an end to his labor.

"Now," said he, "Messrs. Mice, you traitors, you must perforce change your plans, for you shall find no profit in this house."

As soon as he had gone out, I went to see what he had accomplished, and I found that he had not left a single hole big enough for a gnat to get through! Well, I opened the chest with my now useless key, but without hope of profit. I saw the two or three loaves I had started on—the ones my master thought the mice had gnawed—and I derived some wee satisfaction from touching them very fleetingly—in the manner of a deft fencer.

Since necessity is a wondrous sharpener of wits, I, since my need was so very great, spent my days and nights trying to think up some way of keeping body and soul together. And I really do think that in finding the wretched solutions I *did* find, I was actually illuminated by hunger; for it is rightly said that the wit is mightily sharpened by a lack of food and that a surfeit, on the contrary, produces dullness. And I may honestly say that I am a living witness to the veracity of that maxim.

It so happened that being one night wide-awake and thinking hard how I might again get control of that chest, I was aware, from my master's customary snorts and snores, that he was sound asleep. I got up very gently and went for an old knife I had found and left in a special place, and brought it back. (This all happened according to a plan I had made during the day.) I went to the dreary old chest and, using my knife as a gimlet, attacked it at the spot where it was least well defended. Since the aged chest made no great resistance—it was, rather, soft and worm-eaten—I was rewarded with victory when it allowed me to make a nice big hole in one of its sides. When this was done, I opened the wounded receptacle and gropingly performed on the pieces of bread in the manner previously described.

Feeling somewhat comforted, I locked the old thing up and went back to my straw, upon which I reposed and slept a bit. But not much—because, I thought, of my hunger. And so it must have been, for at that time not all the cares of the King of France should really have kept me awake. On the following day my master saw the damage that had been inflicted on his bread, and also the hole in the chest. He began to send the mice to the devil, saying:

"Now, what *is* the meaning of this! This is the first time there have *ever* been mice in this house!"

He most indubitably must have spoken the truth; for if there was in the whole kingdom a house that deserved to be favored by the absence of mice it certainly must have been his, because "foodless" and "mouseless" are synonymous.

My master started a new search through the house and along the walls to find nails and boards to patch up my destruction. When night came, and his repose, I was with my equipment directly alert; and what he did by day did I undo by night.

Thus matters stood in this race we were running. The old saying must have been invented for this very situation: "Where one door closes, another one opens." In brief, we seemed to be repeating that old story about Penelope—what my master wove by day I unravelled by night. In a few days and nights the poor old chest really looked more like a dilapidated breastplate than like its own self, so much nailing and patching had it been subjected to.

As soon as my master saw that all his precautions availed him nothing, he said:

"This old chest is so rickety and the wood is now so old and flimsy that it provides me no protection at all against mice. If we keep it, the way matters are now we shall soon have nothing at all left. And the worst part about it all is that, although it is no longer really serviceable, if I get rid of it I will be put to the expense of buying another one at an outlay of three or four reals. The best thing I can see to do, since our previous thinking has produced no results, is to set up something *inside* the chest to catch the little beasts."

He then went and borrowed a mousetrap, and with some cheese parings, which he also borrowed from the neighbors, he immediately proceeded to set up that mock cat of his on the inside of the chest. And an extraordinarily fine help it was to me! For, although I required few sauces for my diet, still I was regaled with those bits of cheese I got from the trap, and at the same time I did not give up nibbling away at the holy bread.

When the priest found that his bread was being nibbled at and his cheese eaten but that the mouse went uncaught, he sent himself to the devil and inquired of the neighbors what it could be that was extracting the cheese from the trap and eating it, and *how* it could happen that the mouse got out of the box even though the trap was sprung. The neighbors assured him that no mouse had done this damage because, if it had been one, it most certainly would have been caught.

One neighbor said to him:

"I now recall that once upon a time there was a snake loose in your house. That must be the cause of your trouble. It makes sense too, for since that beast is long, it is able to seize the bait and, even though the trap falls upon it, enough of its body remains outside the chest for it to be able to pull itself free."

What this fellow said seemed sensible to all who were present. It gave my master quite a turn, and he thenceforth did not sleep as soundly as before. He even went so far as to think that any worm eating away in the middle of the night must be the snake gnawing away at the chest. He would then get up, and, with a club which he had placed at the head of his bed when he had heard about the snake, he would give the sinful old chest a heavy beating in the hope of frightening the serpent away. He even kept the neighbors awake with his noises, and I could get no sleep either. He would come over to my straw and muss it all up—and me too—thinking the snake had found refuge with me in my straw or shirt. He had been told, you see, that those animals at night very often seek warmth in cradles with babies, at times even biting them or harming them in some way or other. Most of the time I pretended to be asleep, and on the following morning he would say to me:

"And heard you nothing last night, lad? I was hot in pursuit of the snake and I got so far as to think that it was in your bed, for snakes are chilly beasts and always seek warmth."

"Oh, how afraid of him I am!" I would say. "God forbid he should bite me."

Well, my master kept so wide-awake and so alert that, upon my word, the snake (little-boy snake that it was) no longer dared gnaw by night or even approach the chest. But by day when the priest was at church or uptown, I performed my assaults. And my master, seeing the damage I had created, and his little success in combating it, walked the nights, as I have observed—a very ghost.

Now, I greatly feared that with all his precautionary measures he would come across the key I kept under the straw, and it occurred to me that it would be safer for me to put it in my mouth at night.

It so happened that during my stay with the blind man I had transformed my mouth into a purse, and I could often keep the equivalent of twelve or fifteen maravedís—in little coins—in my mouth without being inconvenienced while I ate. Otherwise, I should never have possessed a farthing of my own without the blind man's spotting it, since from time to time he inspected every seam and patch I had on me. So then, as I have observed, I nightly placed the key in my mouth and slept with it there without fear the old fiend my master would detect its presence. But, I must go on to say, when misfortune is slated to come, it *will* come, no matter what diligence you post against it.

My fate so willed it—my sins, I should rather say—that one night while I was asleep the key so maneuvered itself in my mouth, which was open, that the passing of air caused by my breathing made a sound as it proceeded through the hole in the hollow top part of the key, and so—as my ill luck would have it—produced a definite and prolonged whistle. My ill fortune used this stratagem to catch my master's attention. Frightened by the sound, he doubtless thought it must be the hissing of the serpent—and indeed it must have sounded very much like that.

He got up very deftly with his club in his hand, and, gropingly and guided by the sound of the serpent's hiss, approached where I lay sleeping—very cautiously in order not to be perceived by the beast. When he was quite close, he concluded that the creature, lured by the heat from my body, must be lying in the straw. He lifted his cudgel aloft directly over where he considered the hisser to be, and, having prepared to give the fellow a blow that would terminate its existence, he discharged upon my head a blow of such magnitude that it left me senseless and with my head crushed.

I made such an immediate lamentation because of that dreadful blow that the priest realized what he had done, and he later recounted how he came to me, and, making a great outcry, tried to recall me to consciousness. When he touched me with his hand he felt the blood flowing freely out of me, and so became fully aware of what he had done. He then hastily went for a light. Holding it over me, he found me suffering greatly but with the key still in my mouth. Half of it was sticking out just the way it was when I was whistling through it.

My serpent-killer was amazed and puzzled at the sight of the key. He took it completely out of my mouth and saw what it was, for it was fashioned exactly like his own. He went and tried it out, and so proved my duplicity. The savage old snake-hunter must have said to himself something like this: "That mouse-and-serpent that was devouring my estate is in my power now."

What happened during the following three days I shall not relate, for that period was for me like those days Jonah spent in the belly of the whale, and I have here limited myself to an account of the brief things which I heard the priest tell his visitors when I had recovered my senses.

After three days I was fully conscious, and, as I lay on my straw, my head covered with plasters and oils and balms, I said, in my amazement:

"What has occurred?"

The cruel priest answered me:

"Nothing indeed but this: I have at last trapped the mice and snakes that were devouring me."

I looked myself over, and seeing my dilapidated condition suspected what the cause of my misfortune had been.

At that time an old woman healer and the neighbors came in. They began to take the bandages off my head and to treat the wound caused by the cudgel. And when they found I had recovered my senses they were very pleased and said:

"He has finally come to. God grant it be of no importance."

Then they began once again to tell of my plight and to laugh at me, which caused me—sinner that I was—to lament my ill-fortune. But they *did* give me something to eat—though I was so hollow with hunger that they could supply hardly half my wants. So, recovering bit by bit, I was able after two weeks to get up and go about and feel fairly sure I was out of danger—but I was still desperately hungry and only half healed.

The day after I got out of bed my master the priest took me by the hand and led me outside the door; and when once we were in the street, he said to me:

"Lazarus, from now on you belong to yourself—no more to me. Seek yourself a new master, and good-by, for my household cannot afford such a diligent servant as you. I do really believe the only explanation for your actions is that you must once have been a blind man's boy."

And, crossing himself to ward me off as if I had been full of devils, he turned his back upon me and, closing the door after him, went back into the house.

CHAPTER III

How Lazarus found work with a country

gentleman and what happened to him

So, out of the great weakness in which I found myself I was forced to squeeze enough strength to carry on. With the aid of good people, I managed to reach this famous city of Toledo, where after two weeks and with God's mercy my wounds were healed.

While I was ill, I was invariably given alms, but after I recovered my health everyone said to me:

"*You* suspicious character, *you* tramp! Why don't you look for a master?"

"And where might I find one?" I asked. "Where, unless God, as He created the world, creates me one *to* find?"

Carrying on such conversations from door to door with little profit to myself (for charity had there taken flight to heaven), I was finally rewarded by the Lord's leading me into the presence of a country gentleman whom I chanced to meet on the street. He was dressed with some distinction, he was well-kempt, and his gait and progress were perfectly correct. He looked at me, and I looked at him, and he said to me:

"Lad, seek you perchance a master?"

"Yes, sir," said I.

"Then come along with me," he replied. "And thank the Lord for having allowed you to come my way. You have, I daresay, prayed a good prayer today."

I followed him, thanking God for the words I had just heard and for the appearance of a master whose dress and bearing indicated that he was precisely the kind of superior I was looking for.

It was still morning when I met this my third master. He led me over much of the city. We passed through several squares where bread and other provisions were being sold. I thought (it was wishful thinking) that he intended to have me carry home some of the food that was being sold there, it being the proper time of day for him to have purchased his necessary provisions; but briskly and with full stride he hastened through those utilitarian parts of the town. And I said: "It may be he is not satisfied with what he sees here. He doubtless wishes to make his purchases in some other locality."

In this manner we moved along until the clock struck eleven. Then he entered the cathedral, I following him; and he very devoutly heard mass and participated in the other parts of divine service, up to the very end, when all the people finally left. Then we too left the cathedral.

Briskly and with full stride we started down the street. I was now the happiest person in the world to see that we had *not* bothered to buy food, for I imagined that my new master must be a man who made purchases in large quantities, and I suppose that dinner would soon be ready for us—a meal of the sort I so fondly hoped for and so urgently needed.

At this time the clock struck one, and we reached a house before which my master and I stopped. Throwing one side of his cloak over his left shoulder, he took a key from his sleeve and opened the door, and we entered the house. It had a dark, lugubrious, and frightening entrance, although there were decent-looking rooms and a little courtyard within.

As soon as we were comfortably inside, he took off his cloak, and, asking whether I had clean hands, he allowed me to help him shake it out and fold it; then, after blowing lightly on a little stone bench, he laid the cloak upon it. He then sat down by the garment and inquired extensively of me where I was from and how I had happened to come to this city.

I replied with a somewhat longer account than I really cared to indulge in, for it seemed to me to be much more properly the time of day for him to have had the table laid and a stew dished up than it was for me to have to tell him a lengthy tale. However, I satisfied his curiosity about my person as best I could lie, stressing my good qualities and covering up the rest, for it seemed to me the latter truths were not exactly for genteel ears. When I had finished, I waited a little; and then I perceived an ominous sign, for it was almost two o'clock, and still I saw no more of a desire in him to dine than if he had been a corpse.

And then I thought over his locking the door, and I recalled having heard neither up nor downstairs the steps of a living soul. I had seen walls but no chairs, no meat block, no bench or table—not even a chest like that of bitter memory. To put it succinctly, the house appeared to be enchanted. While I was thus engaged in thought, he said to me:

"Have you, lad, *dined* perchance?"

"I have not, sir," I replied, "for it was only eight o'clock when I met Your Worship, and I have not eaten since."

"Oddly enough," he said, "although it was very early when we met this morning, I had already had a good big breakfast, and I must inform you that when I thus eat so heartily at an early hour, I have nothing else to eat all day long. Therefore, get along the best you can for the moment, and we shall sup a little later."

You may, sir, very well believe that when I heard those words I almost fell down dead, not so much from hunger as from suddenly acquiring the knowledge that once more Fortune was against me. I pictured in my mind's eye the hardships I had undergone, and I was saddened by the memory of my woes. I also recalled the idea I had had when I left the priest—that, although he was wretched and mean, I still might find a master who could be even worse. In a word, hot were the tears I could have shed on that occasion, and my sorrow for my burdened life and fast-approaching death were very great indeed.

However, I concealed my feelings the best I could and said to him:

"Sir, I am a mere boy, and I am not greatly concerned with food—for which God be praised. I am very proud of my record on that score, for among the young fellows of my age I have always had the reputation of best being able to abstain from overindulgence. Because of this characteristic of mine I have been repeatedly praised by the masters I have had."

"A splendid virtue," he said. "Because of it I shall hold you in greater esteem. For pigs surfeit themselves, but to eat moderately is a virtue possessed by men of character."

"I know what you mean," I said to myself. "Damned be the curative and healing powers that all my masters have found in hunger!"

I went over to one side of the vestibule and stood there. I took some pieces of bread out from under my shirt—bits that I still had left from my begging. When my master saw them he said:

"Come over here, lad. Let me see what you are eating."

I approached him and showed him the bread. He took one of the three pieces I had—the biggest and the best.

"That looks like excellent bread, I do declare," he said.

"Do you really think so?" I said.

"I do indeed," said he. "Where did you get it? Was it kneaded by clean hands?"

"That, sir, I do not know. I can, however, say that the smell of it is very enticing."

"May it please God," says he. And lifting it to his mouth he began to devour it as voraciously as I was devouring the other pieces.

"Delicious bread," he said. "Delicious."

When I realized what his trouble was, I intensified the zeal of my own operations, for I gathered from the gusto of his attack that if he finished before I did he would insist on showing me the courtesy of accompanying me further. And so we finished at almost the same instant. Then he began to crumb the front of his shirt (very tiny crumbs they were, too) and when he was through, he went into a small adjacent chamber and came back with a neckless old jug. When he had drunk, he offered the jug to me. In order to keep up my pretense of abstemiousness I said:

"Sir, I drink no wine."

"Oh it's water," he said. "You may drink as much as you like."

I took the jug from him and drank—not very much, for my ailment was not thirst.

Things went on that way until night came. We talked about my background, and I gave him the best account I could of it. Finally, he took me into the room where he had got the jug, and said to me:

"Now, young fellow, stand over there and you shall see how this bed is to be made, so that henceforth you will be able to do it all by yourself."

I got on one side of the bed and he got on the other, and we made the wretched thing. There was really little to do because it was nothing but a wicker framework resting on some benches. On top of this was a filthy mattress and over that were spread the bedclothes. The former, because it had been so infrequently washed, hardly looked like what it was supposed to be, although it had to pretend. It had even less than the minimum requirement of cotton wadding. Well, we stretched this object out, making a show of softening it up—which was impossible, because it was positively adamant—and you cannot soften a stone. Besides, there was so little stuffing in it that it was hardly worth while making the effort. When the poor thing was laid on the wicker framework all the reeds below stood forth clearly: they had the exact appearance of the back of a scrawny pig. On top of the starving mattress lay a quilt of the same family, the color of which I was unable to ascertain. When the bed had been made and night had fallen, my master said to me:

"Lazarus, it is growing late and it is a considerable distance from here to the square. Furthermore, there are in this city many snatch-cloaks who prowl by night. Let us therefore manage the best we can tonight and tomorrow early . . . God will provide. You can see that because I am alone I am not properly set up for housekeeping, so I have preferred to dine out during the past few days. But from now on we shall proceed in a different manner."

"Sir," I said, "do not be concerned about me, for I can spend a night without eating—and much longer, if necessary."

"Good. You will live longer and enjoy better health for so doing," said he. "As we were saying during the day, there is no better guarantee of a long life than a small intake of food."

"If that is the way to survive," said I to myself, "then I shall be immortal, for I have always had to live by that prescription, and it looks to me as if I would continue to live by it forever and ever."

My master then went to bed, using his trousers and doublet as a pillow. He told me to lie at his feet, and I did so. But what a sleep I slept! With my miseries and hardships and my hunger there was not a pound of flesh on my body, and the reeds of the wicker framework and my protruding bones did not the whole night long cease their contentions and duelling. Besides, since I had that day eaten almost nothing, I was ravenous with hunger, which is ever the enemy of sleep. God forgive me, but I cursed myself and my dreadful luck a thousand times during most of the night, and, worst of all, I did not dare move about much for fear of waking my master; and so I many times prayed to God that I might die.

The next morning we got up. My master began to clean and brush his trousers and doublet, and his shirt and cloak, while I merely looked on without doing anything. And then he got dressed in the most leisurely fashion you can imagine. I poured out water for him to wash with, and he combed his hair and put his sword in its belt, saying as he did so:

"Ah, if you only knew, lad, what a blade this is! I would not trade it for the best gold mark in the whole world. No indeed! Anthony the Armorer of Toledo never among all the swords he made tempered a blade like that."

And he took it from its sheath and ran his fingers along the blade, saying:

"Just look at that! I would wager I could cut through fleece with that."

And I said to myself:

"And *I* would wager that with my teeth, though they are not of steel, I could cut through a four-pound loaf of bread."

He put the blade back and girded his sword on his belt,

to which he attached a string of beads. And with genteel and reposed step, and refined little movements and swayings of head and body—he would at times throw one side of his cloak over his shoulder and at times would put it under his arm—he placed his right hand on his side and with stately carriage went out the door saying:

"Lazarus, take good care of the house while I am at mass, make the bed, and go to the river—it is just down the way— and get a pitcher of water, and be sure to lock the door so that no one can get in and steal anything, and leave the key here at the threshold, so that if I should return in the meantime I shall be able to get in."

And he went down the street with such refined bearing and exquisite gait that people who did not know him must have considered him a near relative of Count Claros or, at the least, that valet of his who handed him his clothes while he dressed.

"Lord be praised," said I when left alone. "Thou sendest the ailment and the cure at one and the same time. Could anyone meeting my master have the slightest suspicion (such is his manifest self-satisfaction) that he had not last night supped and then couched himself in a fine bed? Is there anyone who would ever guess that, despite this early morning hour, he had not well breakfasted? Great are Thy secrets, O Lord, unsuspected by Thy people! Is there anyone who would not be impressed by his genteel manner and stylish shirt and cloak? Who would ever divine that such a dignified gentleman had the whole day yesterday dined only off that crust of bread his servant Lazarus had for a day and a night carried around in his bosom—where certainly it could not have been contaminated by overcleanliness? Who would imagine that today after he had washed his hands and face, he had, for lack of a towel to dry himself with, used his shirttails? *That*, no one would ever suspect. Ah Lord, how many there must be of the likes of him in this Thy world! They suffer from the dark disease of honor more than they would ever suffer in service of Thee!"

I stood there by the door mulling and meditating until my

master had got all the way down the long and narrow street. I went back into the house, and before you could have said "credo" I had gone through it from top to bottom without making a stop—there was nothing to stop for. I made the hard black bed and took the jug and went to the river, where, in a nearby park, I saw my master in very intimate tête-à-tête with two veiled ladies—of the kind that apparently is never absent from that territory. Many of them, indeed, make a particular point of going out early on summer mornings to refresh themselves along the riverbank and try to get a free meal—for the gentlemen of the town have accustomed them to expect an invitation to breakfast.

My master, I was saying, was with two of them, acting like that poet and lover Macías of the olden days and uttering more dulcet things than Ovid ever wrote. When the ladies observed that he was becoming affectionate, they had no embarrassment in asking him to take them to breakfast—offering the customary payment their sort can always make.

But he, feeling his purse to be as cold as his stomach was hot, fell into such a chill that the color fled from his countenance, and he began to show some confusion in his remarks and to offer some rather unlikely excuses. They, who knew their business well, caught on and left him for the cheat he was.

I, who was eating some cabbage stalks—my only breakfast—returned home with due diligence (as was befitting a new servant) without my master's seeing me. Once there I decided it would be well to sweep part of the place—but there was nothing to sweep with. I stopped to think what I would do next, and I thought best to wait for my master until midday, when he might possibly return with something to eat; but vain was my expectation.

When I saw that it was two o'clock and he still had not returned, I, with the torment of my hunger upon me, locked the door and left the key where he had told me to, and then went back to my old trade. With low and feeble voice and with my hands clasped before me, with the image of God before my eyes and His name upon my lips, I began to beg for bread before those doors and houses which, because of their size, seemed to me most promising. And since this business came to me so naturally (as if I had imbibed it with my mother's milk —indeed, who ever had a greater teacher than my blind man?), I proved myself so adept that, although the town was not given to charities, nor had the year been a good one, I had, before the clock struck four, stowed away in my body an equal number of pounds of bread plus two more which I carried in my sleeves and shirt.

I started back to our house, and as I was passing a meat market I begged from one of the women there a piece of cow's heel and a little cooked tripe, and she gave them to me.

When I got home my worthy master was already there. He had folded up his cloak and placed it on the bench, and he was at the moment walking about the courtyard. When I came in, he approached me—I at first thought to scold me for my tardiness, although the matter turned out quite otherwise. He asked me where I had been, and I replied:

"I was here until two o'clock, sir, and when I saw that Your Worship did not return, I wandered about over the city commending myself to the good people I met, and they gave me what you here see."

I took out the bread and tripe from a fold in my shirttail and showed them to him. His countenance brightened up considerably, and he said:

"Well, I waited for you to come home so that we could dine together, but since you did not appear I ate all alone. However, I must commend you for what you have done. It is far better to beg honestly in God's name than ever to steal. You have indeed done well, so God help me. But, in order that my honor will not be diminished, I must request you to allow no one to know that you stay with me. I daresay no one has got wind of it, for I am practically unknown in this city. I wish I had never come here, either!"

"Do not be concerned, sir," I replied. "I cannot imagine anyone asking me, and I certainly would not tell even if I were asked."

"Now then," said my master, "fall to, you young sinner. God willing, we shall soon be out of want, though I may tell you that since I came to this house I have not had a minute's good fortune. It must have been built on an unlucky spot. For there *are* unlucky houses with spells upon them, and they bring their inhabitants only ill luck. This one is indubitably of that sort. But I promise you that I shall get out of here by the end of the month. I would not stay on here if they gave me the place."

I sat down on one side of the bench without mentioning the lunch I had had, lest he should consider me a glutton. I began to gnaw away at my bread and pieces of tripe and on the sly kept an eye on my wretched master, whose gaze never wandered away from my shirttails, which on that occasion I was using as a plate. May the Lord ever feel as merciful towards me as I felt towards my master, for I knew how he felt, having myself gone through the same tribulation so many a time previously—and still. I wondered how he would take it—as a courtesy on my part or not—if I invited him to share my meal with me. After all, he had informed me that he had already had dinner. Still, I hoped the poor sinner might relieve his misery by sharing in what had relieved mine. I wanted him to eat with me as he had done on the previous day, especially now that I was supplied with more and better food and less of a hunger of my own.

It was God's will that my wish should have fulfillment—and I think it was my master's will too. Because when I began to eat, he stopped his promenading about and came over to me and said:

"Lazarus, I do believe that in all my life I never saw a man enjoy his food with such zest as you manifest. Really, just to see you eat so heartily would make anyone watching you hungry—even though he had just dined."

I said to myself:

"It is your own hunger that makes me seem to eat so zestfully." However, to give him some encouragement (for he was working hard and had certainly given me a lead), I said:

"Sir, the better the tools, the better the workman. This

bread is very delicious and this cow's heel is so well cooked and seasoned that few could resist its savor."

"Cow's heel, did you say?"

"Yes, sir."

"Cow's heel," he said, "is really the finest dish in all the world. I consider pheasant not better flesh."

"Why don't you have a bit of it, sir? Tell me what you think of the taste of it."

I delivered over the cow's hoof into my master's claws and added two or three helpings of the whitest bread. He sat down beside me and began to eat, as one who very much needed to, gnawing away at every one of the little bones more efficiently than a greyhound could have done.

"This is excellent when served with garlic sauce," he said.

"The sauce *you* are eating with now is the finest sauce in the world," I said in a low voice.

"Honestly, young Lazarus, from the way I am enjoying this you might think I hadn't had a bite to eat all day long."

"God grant," I said to myself, "*I* never speak more falsely."

He asked me to get the jug, and I brought him the water I had got that morning from the river. It was clear that since he required water he had actually not had too much to eat. We drank and went to bed as on the previous night.

To avoid prolixity, I shall only say that we continued to exist in this way for a matter of a week or ten days. My master would go forth in the morning with that look of satisfaction and that reposed gait of his, to kill a bit of time, knowing that he could return and live off his poor old Lazarus.

I often contemplated my ill luck at having escaped the other wretched masters I had had, only, in my search for improvement, to end up with one who not only could not feed me but had to rely on me to feed him. However, because he had absolutely nothing and no choice, I had a fond fellow-feeling for him. I felt pity for him but held no grudge against him, and many times, to lighten his wants, I deprived myself of the fruits of my own begging.

One morning after the poor fellow had got up and gone to the roof of the house to satisfy a certain pressing need, I felt I could clear up a specific wonderment of mine, and so I unfolded his doublet and trousers, which were at the head of the bed, and I found a smooth velvet purse which had a hundred folds in it but not a single farthing, nor did I see any indication there *had* been any in it for quite some time.

"He is poverty-stricken," I said. "No one can give what he does not have. But the stingy blind man and the wretched close-fisted priest both had the wherewithal to help me. They both made good livings, one with his glib tongue and the other in his professional capacity. They deserved no loyalty, but this one is greatly to be pitied."

God is my witness that to this day when I run across one of his sort with that gait and pomp, I feel deep pity for him when I think that he may be suffering the same way my master was suffering. When all is said and done, I was happier serving him than any of the others, for the reason I have previously given. I had but one cause of dissatisfaction: I only wished he had not put on the airs he did. He should have humbled his fancy as his needs increased. But I have reason to think that his kind, though they have never a penny to their name, consider it to be supremely important to have their hats set jauntily on their heads when they appear in public. Only the Lord can cope with this situation (which may He do); otherwise they must die of their ailment.

Well, sir, being in the circumstances I have just described and leading the type of life I was leading, my ill fortune (which never tired of pursuing me) so arranged matters that I was forced to discontinue the particular—and I may say, difficult —way of life I have just told you about. It happened that there had been a crop failure in this region, and so the City Council decided that all poor people from out of town would have to leave the city. It was therefore publicly proclaimed that any such persons henceforth discovered would be lashed. And so it was that four days after the proclamation was made and the law was put in force, I saw a procession of poor people being lashed in Cuatro Calles Square. The sight so frightened me that I never again had the temerity to beg publicly.

Our house was the bleakest sight imaginable. Dark was the gloom and deep the despondency of its inhabitants, whose fortunes had fallen so low that they very often went two or three days without eating or even talking. My only help came from some women who lived next door, and spun cotton and made caps to earn their livelihood. I became friendly with them and felt somewhat at home at their house. They would give me a little share of the pittance they earned, and with that I just managed to survive.

I really felt not so sorry for myself as for my poor master, who had nothing to eat for a week. At least I can say that he had nothing to eat at our house, for there was absolutely nothing there *to* eat. I don't know where he went or what he did or what he ate—*if* he ate. Yet you should have seen him striding down the street at noon, straight and stately as a greyhound of most distinguished pedigree. You should have seen him—to speak now of matters pertaining to his honor—take one of the straws from our house (and there were not even too many of them) and go to the door and pick his teeth—where nothing had lodged—ever complaining of that ill-favored house and saying:

"A sad sight! This unfortunate dwelling, I tell you, is the cause of all our ill luck. It is, as you can see, dark, gloomy, and lugubrious. We shall continue to suffer as long as we stay here. I long for the end of the month when I can leave for good."

Now, while we were undergoing this dreadful and tormenting starvation, it happened, I know not because of what stroke of luck, that my poor master came into the possession of a real. He came home with it as proudly as if he had got hold of all the treasures of Venice, and with merry and smiling countenance he handed it to me, saying:

"There, Lazarus! The Lord is at last beginning to show his generosity. Go to market and buy bread, wine, and meat. Let

us defy the very devil! And furthermore, that your young heart
may jump for joy, I must tell you that I have rented a new
house and we shall move from this ill-starred place as soon as
the month is up. Cursed may it be, and cursed be the man
who laid its first tile! It was in an evil hour that I entered the
place! I swear to you that never since I came here have I enjoyed a drop of wine or a bite of food, nor have I had any
peace of mind—the place is so bleak and lugubrious! Go and
return quickly, and we shall this day dine in the manner of
counts."

I took the real and my pitcher and, quickening my pace,
started up the street, directing my way towards the square. I
was filled with a very great joy. But what availed that happiness, since it was so written in the constitution of my dreary
fortune that no enjoyment should ever come to me unaccom-
panied by misery? So did it happen on this occasion.

For as I was going up the street, figuring out how I ought
best to spend the money and praising the Lord for His bounty,
I quite by chance ran into a funeral procession made up of
churchmen and others who came down the street bearing a
body on a litter.

I snuggled close to the wall to give them plenty of room to
get by, and as soon as the body had passed, a woman I assumed to be the wife of the deceased came alongside the litter.
She was dressed in mourning and was accompanied by other
women, and she was wailing high and loud:

"O my dear husband and my lord! Where do they bear you
now? Alas, to that sad and cheerless dwelling where there is
never eating or drinking!"

When I heard that my heaven collapsed and I said:

"O woe is me! They are taking the dead man to our very
house!"

I left the course I had taken and, plowing my way through
the people, I went running back as fast as I could to our house.
When I got there, I swiftly fastened the door and invoked the
protection of my master. I threw my arms around him and

begged him to keep anyone from coming through the door.
He, somewhat taken back, and imagining I must be referring
to something else, said to me:

"What has got into you, lad? What is the meaning of your
outcry? Tell me what your trouble is. Why have you closed
the door so frantically?"

"O sir," I cried; "Come quickly. They're bringing a dead
man here."

"What do you mean?" he asked.

"I ran into them up the street and the widow kept saying: 'O
my dear husband and my lord! Where do they bear you now?
Alas, to that sad and cheerless dwelling where there is never
eating or drinking.' They are bringing him here, sir!"

When my master heard this he burst out laughing and kept
it up for a long time without being able to speak—though he
really had little occasion for mirth at any time. Meantime, I had
bolted the door and placed my shoulder against it for added
defense. The people passed me by with their dead man, but I
continued to fear that they intended to deposit him in our
house. When my master had laughed his fill (and his laughter,
I may add, was the only filling thing in the house), he said:

"It is true that as the widow put it you had some reason to
make the interpretation you did; but now that God has taken
care of the matter, and they have passed us by, open the door
and go get us something to eat."

"Let me wait, sir, till they have gone the whole length of the
street," I begged.

My master finally came to the street door and opened it
much against my will—I was still so frightened and upset—
and then I went my way.

Although we ate well that day I took no joy in my food, nor,
indeed, did I recover my color for the following three days. But
my master was amused, and smiled whenever he was reminded
of that old consternation of mine.

In this manner I stayed on with my third and poorest master
—this country gentleman—and all the while I was curious
about the purpose of his coming to this town and the reason

for his stay here. I had, from the very first day I began to work for him, known him to be an out-of-towner because he had no acquaintances among the inhabitants here.

My curiosity was finally satisfied, and I was told what I desired to know. One day after we had had a fairly substantial meal, and my master was feeling in rather good spirits, he told me about his background. He said he was a native of Old Castile and that he had left his region to keep from having to take his hat off to a gentleman who was his neighbor.

"But, sir," I protested, "if he was all you say he was and if he outranked you, were you not in error *not* to take your hat off first? You say that he would take his hat off to *you*."

"Yes, he is all I say he is, and he did indeed take off his hat to me. But when you consider how many times I took mine off first, it certainly would not have been unbecoming in him to have beaten me to it and taken *his* off first once in a while."

"I do not, sir, think that I myself would be very much concerned with that sort of thing, especially with my superiors in rank and those who are better off."

"You are but a boy," he replied, "and you cannot deeply comprehend these matters of honor—a concept which today includes the most precious treasures a respectable man possesses. Now you must bear in mind that I am, as you see, a gentleman; and I swear to God that if I should meet the Count in the street and he did not deign to remove his headpiece with a very affirmative gesture, I would, the next time I saw him, go into some nearby house, pretending to have business there, or, before he reached me, I would take another street if there were one at hand—simply not to have to take my hat off to him first. A gentleman, Lazarus, owes nothing to anyone except God and King, nor is it right that he should for a moment fail to give the proper consideration to the rights and privileges appertaining to his person. I recall that one day I reprimanded a tradesman in my country. I really wished to lay hands on him because every time he met me, he would say: 'God preserve you.' 'Watch your manners, you scoundrel,' I said to him. 'Do you think you can say "God preserve you" to *me* as if I were just any old body?' Well, from that day on he always took off his hat to me and addressed me in the proper manner."

"But, sir," said I, "isn't it a nice way to greet a man to say to him that you hope God will preserve him?"

"O no," he said, "that's very bad. That's what you say to people of no great sorts; but to people of station (like me) you must at least say: 'I kiss Your Grace's hands.' Or, perhaps: 'Sir, I kiss your hands'—especially, if your interlocutor is a gentleman. So, you see why I could not abide that fellow back home who crammed his 'God preserve you' down my throat; nor would I—and I never will—suffer any man of less station than the King himself to address me with a 'God preserve you.'"

"Now," said I, "I know why He does not preserve you any better than He does. You won't allow anyone to ask Him to."

"I am rather particular about these things," he went on, "for in my region I own a little cluster of houses (they are sixteen leagues from the spot where I was born—on the Valladolid slope), which, if they were in good repair and had not fallen down, would fetch me more than two hundred thousand maravedís—they have such possibilities of being enlarged and improved. And too, I own a pigeon house, which, if it were not in such a dilapidated condition, would net me over two hundred birds yearly. There are other interesting items, too, which I will not go into; but I gave up everything because my honor was at stake. I then came to this city hoping to find an opening for my talents, but I have had no luck. I have contacted many priests and gentlemen of the cloth, but they are such close-fisted people that nobody in all the world can do anything with them. Gentlemen of moderate importance have asked me to associate myself with them, but if I did, I am afraid I would find that sort of thing very difficult. I would be little more than a yes-man—not a real associate at all; and if I objected they would soon find occasion to show me the door. Payments are few and far between; most of the time you do well to get your meals in return for your labors. And when they wish to ease their conscience and repay your sweat, they take you to the wardrobe and present you with a sweat-stained doublet or a threadbare cloak or shirt. Yet if you take a place with a man of title, you have to put up with a lot more misery. Now, do I not have the ability to serve and give satisfaction to such as these? I tell you, Lazarus, that if I ever met the right one of them, I think I could become his favorite, and I should perform a thousand services for him, because I could lie to him as well as anyone else and please him most marvellously. I would die laughing at his witticisms and sallies, even though they were not the best in the world. I would never say anything to him that might upset him—even though it would be to his advantage if I did so. I would be very solicitous about his person in word and deed, but I certainly would not go out of my way to do anything for him unless I was sure it would come to his notice. I would make it a point to pick quarrels with the serving-people in his presence, in order that he might think I took very seriously all that concerned his affairs. If he quarrelled with one of his servants, I should pretend to try and patch up the trouble by making a few sly observations that might *seem* to be in favor of the servant but which would really only irk the master more. I should tell him all manner of nice things about himself, but, on the contrary, I should be malicious and mocking when it came to the people of his household and elsewhere; and I would make investigations and pry into other people's lives in order to tell him tales; and I should do other charming things of the sort that today are so frequent in high places and are so much favored by the lords of palaces. The great do not wish to have virtuous men about them. They detest men of character, rather, and depreciate them, and hold them to be of little worth. They call them fools and say they are not men of affairs in whom they can put their confidence. And when shrewd fellows get hold of them, they treat them as I have previously described—and I should do the same if I could only find one to get hold of."

In this manner did my master lament *his* adverse fortune as he gave me an account of his worthy person.

At this time a man and an old woman entered the house.

The man asked my master for the rent on the house and the old woman asked for the rental of the bed. They figured how much it all came to, and, for a two months' period, the amount was more than my master could have got together in a year. The sum, if I recall, was twelve or thirteen reals. Well, he gave those people a very nice reply, saying he had to go to the square and change a two-real coin and promised them he would return in the afternoon. But he never did.

The two came back that afternoon; but it was too late, as I told them. When night had come and my master had not, I was afraid to stay alone in the house, so I went over to my neighbors, the spinners, and told them what had happened, and stayed there with them.

When morning came, the creditors returned and asked about my master; but the bird had flown. My friends the spinners answered:

"This is his serving-boy, and this the key to the door."

I was questioned about my master, and I told them I did not know where he was. He had not, I said, returned home after he went out to change the coin. He had, I suspected, taken to his heels.

When they heard that, they went for the bailiff and a notary. They all came back and took the key; and calling me and other witnesses, they opened the door and went in to attach my master's property until he had paid them what he owed them. They went all through the house, and finding it completely bare, they inquired of me:

"What has become of your master's property—his chests and tapestries and jewels?"

"That I do not know," I replied.

"Doubtless," they said, "those things have been taken away during the night and deposited somewhere else. Mr. Bailiff, arrest this boy. He must know where everything is."

At this moment the bailiff came up and grabbed me by the collar of my doublet, saying:

"Boy, you are under arrest unless you discover to us where your master's properties are."

I had often been grabbed by the collar by the blind man, who had held on to it gently while I led him down the way he could not see; but I had never been in quite this sort of situation before, and I was terribly afraid and promised to tell them everything they had asked me.

"Very good," said they. "Just tell us what you know and do not be frightened."

The notary sat down on the bench to write the inventory. He asked me what my master possessed.

"Sirs," said I, "my master has told me that he owns a cluster of houses and also a pigeon house, though the latter is a shambles."

"Splendid," said they. "However little they are worth, they will still recompense us for what he owes us. Now, what part of town are those properties in?"

"They are not here but in his part of the country," I replied.

"Well, really! A fine thing!" they said. "And where might his part of the country be?"

"He said he was from Old Castile," I said.

The bailiff and the notary laughed heartily at this, and said to the others:

"You see he has more than enough to pay his debt."

My spinning friends, who were present, said:

"Gentlemen, this boy is innocent. He has only been with the country gentleman for a few days and knows no more about him than Your Worships do. Besides, he has been coming over to our house, and, out of the goodness of our hearts, we have been feeding him the best we could. At night he has been going back and staying with his master."

My innocence was apparent and they let me go free. The bailiff and the notary then requested their fees of the man and the old woman. About this they all had quite an argument and made a great deal of noise. The man and the old lady contended that they were not obliged to pay anything. There was no reason to, they said, for nothing had been attached. The officials said they had given up another bit of business to take on this affair.

Finally, after a lot of shouting, the old lady loaded her bedding on the back of the bailiff—and I may say he was not overly encumbered by his burden. All five of them took off yelling. I don't know how it all turned out. I guess the poor old wad of bedding finally paid all their bills. I think it deserved it too, for instead of staying quietly at home and reposing from its past labors it *would* go out and get rented.

So, as I have related, my third poor master left me; which brought home to me how very low my fortunes had fallen. For when all these adverse circumstances were added up, it became apparent to me that my affairs were so very much upside down that, although masters are usually left by their servants, in my case the contrary occurred, and I was left by my master.

CHAPTER IV

How Lazarus found work with a friar of the
Order of Grace, and what happened to him

I looked for a fourth master and found one in the person of a friar of the Order of Grace. My friends the spinning women helped me make the arrangements. They said he was a relative of theirs. He had no love for choirs or meals at the monastery. His principal passion was to gad about, and he greatly enjoyed secular affairs and seeing people on all sorts of business— so much so, indeed, that he wore out more shoes than anyone else at the monastery. He gave me the first pair of shoes I ever wore out in all my life. They lasted me exactly one week. But I could not have stood trotting about after him for a longer period. For this reason and because of some other little things I leave in the inkpot, I went my way.

CHAPTER V

How Lazarus found work with a seller of
indulgences and what happened to him

My fifth master happened to be a seller of indulgences—the
most barefaced and shameless one I have ever seen, and, I may
say too, the most successful promoter in the business. He had
many ways of selling his wares, and he was ever on the alert to
invent new and tricky devices.

When he entered towns where indulgences were to be offered,
he first presented some little tokens of esteem to the local
clergy—things of no great value, like a head of Murcian lettuce when it was in season, a couple of limes or oranges, a
peach, or a green-skinned pear. In this way he won the churchmen's good will in the hope that they would support his undertaking by calling on the faithful to take his indulgences.

When these reverend gentlemen expressed their gratitude, he
would determine how much learning they had. If he found
that some were well educated, he would never utter a word in
Latin, in order not to give himself away. On such occasions he
would resort to the use of a glib and well-turned patter in
Spanish. But if he found out that other gentlemen of the cloth
had reached their eminence through the influence of money
rather than as the result of merit and learning, he would act
like a very St. Thomas Aquinas and talk in Latin for two hours
on end. At least it *sounded* like Latin.

When the people did not willingly take his indulgences he
sought ways of forcing them to, willy-nilly. At times he could
be a perfect nuisance; on other occasions he resorted to sheer
trickery. Now, since it would be prolix to recount all the tricks
I saw him play I shall relate only one of them—and a very
clever and funny one it was, too. I shall thereby be able to
show you his great sufficiency.

There is in the district called Sagra de Toledo a town where

he had preached for two or three days, making all of his customary exhortations; yet, despite his efforts, no one would take
any indulgences, nor, it seemed to me, did anyone have the
slightest intention of doing so. He cursed himself repeatedly because of his failure; but trying hard to think up some sort of
scheme to help increase sales, he decided to convoke the whole
town in order to issue indulgences the following day.

That night, after supper, he and the bailiff began to gamble
to see who would pay for the refreshments. A quarrel eventually
ensued, and hot words passed between the two of them. My
master called the bailiff a thief, and the bailiff called my master
a crook. At this, my master grabbed a short thick lance that
was standing by the door near where they were playing.
Whereupon, the bailiff drew his sword. There was a great deal
of noise, and at our shouts the guests in the inn and some of
the neighbors came running in and mixed in the fray. The two
battlers, with murder in their eyes, tried furiously to disengage
themselves from those who were restraining them; but since
the house was now overflowing with people who had been attracted by all the noise and confusion, the two could no longer
do each other any bodily harm, and had to rely only on insults
to win the fight. Among these little compliments the bailiff
called my master a crook, and said that the indulgences offered
were false.

The people of the town, finally seeing that it was impossible
for them to make peace between the two contenders, decided
to take the bailiff away from the inn to another part of town.
That infuriated my master; but after the guests had besought
him to be calm, he went to bed. And so then did we all.

The next morning my master went to the church and had
the bells rung for mass and for the sermon he was going to
preach when he dispensed the indulgences. The people came
in. They were very critical of the indulgences, saying they were
false and that the bailiff himself during the fight had said so.
Whereas they previously had shown no enthusiasm about buying the indulgences, they now absolutely abhorred the idea of
doing so.

My master the Pardoner climbed into the pulpit and began his sermon to encourage the people not to forego the great advantages and blessings the indulgences would bring.

When he had reached the high point of his sermon, lo! the bailiff came in, and when he had said a prayer, he rose up, and in a resonant and deliberate voice began with great dignity to say:

"My dear friends, hear now a word from me, then later you may hear whomsoever you desire. I came here with this crook who is preaching to you. He told me that if I would give him my support in his trickery, he would divide the spoils with me. But now, seeing the hurt it would do my conscience and the damage it would do to your pocketbooks, I, repenting of what I have done, make this clear declaration: 'His indulgences are phony.' Do not, therefore, believe a word he says, and do not take any of the indulgences. I myself will not either directly or indirectly be a party to this hoax. And as of now I surrender my staff, which is the symbol of my authority. And if this fellow eventually should be punished for his fraud, be you my witnesses that I publicly state that I have no dealings with him, nor will I ever consent to lend him any aid whatsoever. Rather do I prefer to open your eyes to his swindle and make public his wickedness."

And in this way he concluded his address.

Some honest fellows who were there made a move to rise and throw the bailiff out of the church to avoid a scandal. But my master, who had maintained silence during the address, restrained them and ordered them on pain of excommunication not to interfere with the bailiff, but, rather, to allow him to say whatever he chose.

As soon as the discourse was over, my master asked the bailiff whether he wished to say anything further, and requested him, if he did, to say it.

The bailiff replied:

"I do indeed have a considerable amount more to tell these good people about you and your frauds, but for the moment I will say no more."

At this my master knelt down in the pulpit and, with hands together in prayer and eyes turned aloft to heaven, said:

"Lord God, from Whom nothing is ever hidden, but contrariwise, to Whom all things are manifest and patent—to Whom nothing is impossible, but, contrariwise, to Whom all things are possibility—*Thou* knowest the Truth, and *Thou* knowest how unjustly I have here been affronted. As for myself, I forgive him, in order, Lord, that Thou mayest forgive me. Pay Thou no heed to one who knows not what he does or says. But do not, Lord, turn a deaf ear to the injury done *Thee* here, lest some of these good people should, through hearing the false words uttered by this evil man, desist from taking the indulgences they had originally planned to take. Since such a refusal would, O Lord, be so very grave an error on the part of my fellow men, I pray Thee, let this accusation not pass without Thy notice. Show us, we pray, a miracle and in this wise: If what he says is true, and I am really the incarnation of evil and falsehood, let this pulpit sink with me down into the earth full seven fathoms deep where neither it nor I will ever by mortal eyes be seen again. But if what *I* say is true, and if *he,* pawn of the devil, has spoken falsely in order to deprive the congregation of the great blessing the indulgences are, then let him be singularly punished, and let his wickedness be rendered apparent to all the world."

Scarcely had my pious master concluded his prayer when the wretched bailiff fell plumb to the floor with such impact that the whole church vibrated with resonant reverberation. He forthwith began to bellow, and to foam at the mouth. His lips were twisted and he made grotesque grimaces. His hands and feet twitched, and he tossed about all over the floor.

The confusion of the people and their cries were so very great that no one could hear his neighbor in the tumult. Some were amazed and fearful, and some prayed: "God help and protect us!" But others said: "He deserved it for giving false testimony."

At last some of the congregation approached the ailing bailiff (not, I thought, without fear) and tried to hold his arms tight—although he gave some hardy fisticuffs to those who were nearby. Others grabbed him by the legs and held on tightly too, because no treacherous mule in all the world has ever kicked as hard as that bailiff could kick when his legs were free. They held on to him for quite a while. There were a good fifteen men on top of him, and he continually dealt out his blows to them—and when they were not alert, they were sure to get one right in the snout.

Meanwhile, my master was still kneeling in the pulpit, his hands and eyes directed towards heaven. He was so deeply transported into the divine essence that the confusion and noise in the church were not sufficient to call him back from his holy contemplation.

Those good men approached him, and crying out to him aroused him from his ecstasy. They besought him to come to the aid of the poor dying man; they begged him to let bygones be bygones and to forget all the evil things that had been said, for now the wretched bailiff had received his just reward. They pleaded with him in God's name to do whatever he could to free the sick man from the suffering he was undergoing. They said they now saw who the culprit really was. They perceived my master's goodness and truthfulness, since the Lord had so graciously acceded to his plea by immediately punishing the bailiff.

My master, as one awakened from a sweet sleep, looked at them, and then at the delinquent, and thereafter at all those who were present, and slowly and deliberately said to them:

"Good people, you should not intercede on behalf of a man in whom God has so clearly manifested His will and might; but since He orders us not to return evil for evil but to forgive those injuries which are done to us, we may confidently beg His Majesty to fulfil what He ever commands *us* to do—namely, to forgive this man who has sought to impede the work of His Holy Faith. Let us, then, pray for him."

My master then descended from the pulpit and earnestly requested the congregation to pray devoutly that Our Lord would in His infinite goodness forgive the miserable sinner and restore him to health, and heal his mind; and, further, that He would cast out the devil from him, if it had come about that His Divine Majesty, because of the man's great sin, had permitted the Tempter to enter his heart.

All knelt down and, with the clergy, began to chant a litany in a low voice before the altar. And then my master came forward with a cross and holy water, and after having chanted over the body of the bailiff, he lifted his hands toward heaven, and with only a little of the whites of his eyes showing, began a prayer that was as long as it was pious, and so caused all the people there to weep (as happens at sermons on the Passion when both preacher and congregation are really devout.) Since Our Lord, he said, could not wish the death of this poor sinner but his life and repentance instead, he prayed that His Majesty would forgive him and revive him and restore him to health, for the unfortunate man had been tricked by the devil and overwhelmed by sin and death; and, my master continued, he was confident that if the Lord would resuscitate the wretched man, he would then repent and confess his sin.

My master then had an indulgence brought and placed on the bailiff's head; whereupon the sinful fellow began little by little to recover physically and mentally. When he was fully restored, he threw himself at the feet of my seller of indulgences and begged his forgiveness. He confessed to have spoken through the mouth of the devil and with his connivance—first, to do harm to my master and so be avenged for the insults of the preceding evening; and second, and even more important, he had acted as he did because the devil was terribly troubled to think of the good work that would be performed there when the indulgences were issued.

My master forgave him freely, and they immediately became close friends again. There was then such haste in taking the indulgences that hardly a person in the whole town could stand to be without one—husbands and wives, sons and daughters, or maids and boys.

What had happened soon became common knowledge in neighboring towns, so that when we reached them, it was not necessary for us to give a sermon or attend church, for the people came to our inn for their indulgences as if they had been coming for free pears. So that in the ten or twelve towns in that region my master sold several thousand indulgences without preaching a single sermon.

When the scene I have described was first enacted, I was, I will confess, amazed. I thought, as so many others thought, that it was authentic. But when later I saw the fun my master and the bailiff were having over it, and heard their laughter, I realized I too had been hoodwinked by my sly and scheming master.

And despite my being so young, I was amused, and I said to myself:

"How many such tricks these jokers must have played on poor innocent people!"

To bring this matter to a close I will only add that I was with my fifth master nearly four months, and I cannot truthfully say that my life with him was exactly a bed of roses.

CHAPTER VI

How Lazarus found work with a chaplain and

what then happened

After all this, I found work with an artist who painted tambourines. I was required to grind colors for him. And I underwent a thousand hardships.

Being now a pretty good-sized fellow, I one day entered the cathedral, and a chaplain there engaged my services. He put me in charge of a good donkey, four big jars, and a whip; and I then began to peddle water around town. This was my first real progress on the way to a better life. Now for the first time I had enough to eat. Every day I would give my master thirty maravedis and keep what I took in over that amount, and on Saturdays I kept everything I took in.

I was so successful at this work that at the end of four years, by having taken good care of what I made, I had saved enough to be able to provide myself decently with some old clothes. I bought myself a doublet of old fustian with braided sleeves and open collar, and a cloak that had once been fuzzy, and an old-fashioned sword made by the swordmaker Cuéllar. As soon as I saw that I was apparelled like a respectable man, I told my master to take back his donkey, for I no longer cared to continue at that sort of work.

CHAPTER VII

How Lazarus found employment with a bailiff

and what then happened

After I left the Chaplain I became an agent of the law with a bailiff. But I stayed not long with him, for the work seemed dangerous. Especially after my master and I had one night been pelted with stones and beaten with sticks by some fugitives. My master, who stayed behind, was manhandled, but they never caught *me*. After that I handed in my resignation.

Then considering in what manner I ought to live in order to settle down and earn something for my old age, I found that God had illuminated me and directed me into a profitable course of action. With the favor of gentlemen and friends, all the miseries and trials I had previously suffered were rewarded when I achieved what I had long sought: one of those official positions so greatly esteemed in our time, since without one nobody can really get ahead.

In this work I live today—in the service of God and Your Worship. I am in charge of making public proclamations about the wines that are sold in this city and at auctions. I make announcements when things have been lost, and I accompany persons who are being prosecuted by the law and I cry out the crimes they have committed. I am, in a word and in good old-fashioned Spanish, a *pregonero,* or town crier.

Things have gone so well with me, and I have occupied my-self so diligently, that all the matters I have mentioned above now pass through my hands. I am now so influential that if in all the city any man wishes to sell his wine or anything else, Lazarus of Tormes had better be informed of it, or the business will not go well.

At this time my lord the Archpriest of San Salvador, Your Worship's friend and humble servant, observing my abilities and my model way of life, arranged a marriage between me and a servant of his. Considering that from such a worthy person nothing could come but good and profit, I accepted the arrangement.

And so I married her, and I do not at all regret having done so, because, in addition to her being a good and diligent help-mate, I have received full favor and aid from my lord the Archpriest. During the year he gives her, off and on, a supply of wine, some meat on holidays, an occasional loaf or two of holy bread, and the old trousers he discards. He has got us to rent a little cottage next door to his house, and we dine with him almost every Sunday and on most holidays.

But evil tongues—they were never lacking and they never will be—leave us no peace, saying all sorts of things about us—specifically that my wife goes to make his bed and cook for him. I only hope that such people's reward in heaven is better than the brand of truth they tell. My wife is certainly not the woman to feel happy when she hears these jibes, and my lord has promised to do something I know he will carry out.

"Lazarus of Tormes," he said to me, "if you are sensitive to slanderous tongues, you will never get ahead. I say this to you because I would not be surprised if people wonder at seeing your wife come here to my house and then leave. Well, I can assure you she comes in all honor to herself and to you. There-fore, pay no heed to what people say, but fix your attention, rather, on what is of most importance to you—your own profit, I mean."

"Sir," I said, "I have determined to associate with people of excellence. It is true that certain friends of mine *have* mentioned something of the sort to me, and they have further assured me that she had had three babies before I married her—speaking with proper reverence before Your Worship, especially since she is here present."

Then my wife swore so great an oath that I thought the house would fall in. She burst out crying and cursing the man who had arranged our marriage. It was so dreadful that I wished I had died rather than to have uttered the remark I had made. But the Archpriest and I worked hard to placate her, and she finally ceased her weeping when I swore never again to mention anything of the sort as long as I lived. I further said that I heartily approved of her coming and going by day or night to his house, for I was convinced of her honorable intentions. And thus we three came to terms.

Since that time no mention has ever been made of the matter. Rather, when I feel that someone is on the point of referring to this ticklish situation, I cut him short by saying:

"Now look: if you are my friend say nothing that will trouble me, for I consider no one a friend of mine who does so. Especially, if what is said might embroil me with my wife. For in all the world she it is whom I must love and cherish—I value her even more than I value myself. Since she became my wife God has been very good to me—much better than I deserve. And I do solemnly swear by the Sacred Host that she is as virtuous as any woman living within the walls of Toledo. And if any man say to the contrary, then he is my mortal enemy."

And so my friends say nothing at all to me on this score.

This all occurred the same year our victorious Emperor Charles V entered this great city of Toledo and here held court, when so many wonderful celebrations and fiestas took place, as Your Worship has undoubtedly heard.

And I sir, at this time was living in all prosperity and at the height of my good fortune.

THE LIFE AND ADVENTURES
OF DON PABLOS THE SHARPER

FRANCISCO DE QUEVEDO

Translated by divers hands and
revised and edited by Mack Hendricks Singleton*

CHAPTER I

He tells who he is and where from

I AM, sir, a native of Segovia. My father's name (may he rest in peace!) was Clemente Pablo. His life and deeds are well known. He was a barber by trade. However, he had such lofty ideas that he took it as an affront to be called *barber* and insisted that he was rather a "masseur of cheeks" and a "tailor of beards." It is said that he came from a good family. That might very well be true, for he was given to drinking.

He married Aldonza de San Pedro, who was the daughter of Diego de San Juan, and the granddaughter of Andrés de San Cristóbal. The townspeople held her Christianity to be suspect and considered her to be of Moorish or Jewish descent—although she left no stone unturned in her attempt to trace her lineage

---

* Clarity, verisimilitude, and interest have been the criteria used in choosing from among variant readings. Even so, a few very difficult phrases in the original versions have not been translated. These omissions are generally indicated by suspension points. Literal renderings of word-plays in the original have been replaced by similar word-plays in English. These substitutions, if lengthy, have usually been placed within brackets. Brackets are also used when something has been added for clarity.

right back to very Litany itself. She was attractive, and she was so celebrated in her lifetime that nearly all the popular song writers in Spain spent some time on her. Shortly after her marriage she underwent great hardships (and for a long time after that, too) because evil tongues maligned my father, saying that he had itchy fingers. It was very convincingly shown that every time he shaved his customers he would, while he rinsed their faces, maneuver them into such a position that my little seven-year-old brother could rifle their pockets. That dear angel died of a whipping in jail. My father took it very hard, for the little fellow was so good that he could even steal your heart away.

Because of these tricks of my father's—and there were others, too—he served some time in jail—though I have been told that he left the place in great honor. He was, you see, so red from the beatings he had received that people took him for a cardinal. It is said that the ladies crowded around the windows to get a glimpse of him, for my father made quite an impression both on foot and on horseback.

I relate these things not out of vanity, for everyone knows that vanity is not a part of my nature.

My mother had her problems, too. Once an old woman who had been my nursemaid praised my mother and said that she was so charming she bewitched everyone who had any dealings with her. Mention was also made of the Evil One and flying—which made it seem likely that my mother might be provided with feathers so that she could fly in public. She was known to be an expert in restoring virginity, dying gray hair, and curing baldness. Some called her a "weaver of mundane pleasures," others called her a "healer of dislocated longings," and still others thought she was nothing but a common bawd. For some, she was a go-between, if, indeed, she was not (when opportunity offered) a go-getter on her own. It was known that she had innumerable ways of wheedling money out of people. You should have seen how proud she was and how heartily she laughed when she heard others speak of her accomplishments! I shall say nothing about her acts of penance. She had one room accessible to herself alone—though I, because I was so little and harmless, was allowed to go there. It was all lined with skulls, which, she said, were to remind her of death or perhaps, too, of the longings we have in this life. The bedsprings were made of hangman's rope. "What do you think?" she would say. "I keep these relics because I know that most of those who were hanged are saved."

My parents showed some difference of opinion as to which of their professions they thought I should follow. But I, who since my childhood had always aspired to be a gentleman, would follow neither of their trades. My father often chided me, saying: "Son, a thief does not follow a mechanical but a liberal art." And after a while he would, with folded hands, sigh and add: "He who does not steal in this world cannot survive. Why do you think the police and the magistrates hate us so much? At times they exile us; and on other occasions they give us the noose for no particular reason other than to let us get the hang of it. I cannot help weeping when I think of it." And the good old man would indeed cry, and like a child, when he remembered how often they had dusted his back, simply "because they did not want any thieves but themselves and their stooges around. However, astuteness is a handy weapon. That is why, when I was young, I was always hanging around churches—and not just because I was a Christian, either. Oftentimes I would have been flogged if I had admitted my guilt; but I never confessed, except, of course, in matters specifically designated by Holy Mother Church. And so, I have been able to make a living for your mother as honestly as I could." "What do you mean— you have made a living for me?" my mother asked angrily, fuming because I had not chosen to follow the profession of witch. "I have both supported you and bailed you out of jail with my wit," she went on, "and I even provided you with spending money when you were in prison. If you did not always confess, was it because of your courage, or was it because of the potions I provided for you? Be grateful to my witchcraft.

Were it not that passers-by in the street might overhear me, I would remind you of the time I let myself down the chimney and brought you out through the roof."

She was so angry she might have said much more, but it happened that a rosary she had made of dead men's teeth became unstrung with her gesticulations. I pacified my parents by affirming that I wished to learn virtue and pursue my own good intentions. I begged them to put me in school, since I could accomplish little by remaining illiterate. They seemed to find my suggestion acceptable, although they grumbled and growled a bit about it. My mother went back to stringing teeth, and my father went out to trim someone—whether purse or hair, I do not know. I was left alone, thanking God for giving me such sharp parents, who were ever unrelentingly zealous in watching out for my best interests.

CHAPTER II

How I went to school and what happened

to me there

The next day, after my parents had spoken to the teacher and bought me a reader, I went to school.

The teacher was happy to see me, and told me I had the look of a sharp and understanding fellow. That morning, in order not to undeceive him, I recited my lesson well. He had me sit close to his desk, and, because I was almost always the first to arrive, he put me in charge of discipline. I was also the last to leave because I would often run errands for the "Missus"—the name we gave the teacher's wife. I had them both much in my debt for such little services. But the other children very quickly became jealous of me because I was such a favorite. I was careful to make up to the sons of aristocrats, especially Diego, who was the son of Don Alonso Coronel Zúñiga. I became such a good friend of his that I would help myself to anything he brought along for lunch, and he reciprocated. On holidays I used to go to his house and play, and I was at his side every day. But the other children, either because I would not talk to them or because they thought me presumptuous, began to call me names that had to do with my father's business. Some called me Mr. Razor, and others, Mr. Cupping-glass Swindler; and one of them, out of sheer jealousy, said that my mother had by night sucked the blood from two of his younger sisters; and still another taunted me, saying that my father had been called to his house to exterminate the mice because (he said) my father had had some connection with a cat house. The others then began to call out "scat," and others would say, "Kitty, kitty." One said: "I threw two eggplants at your mother during her coronation"—referring, of course, to the time when the Inquisition had made her wear the cap of infamy in public. But in spite of their jibes, they kept their distance—thanks be to God. And though I was embarrassed to death, I pretended to ignore what they said.

I bore everything bravely until one day a boy called me the son of a witch-bitch at the top of his voice. If he had said it softly I would have ignored it. But things being as they were, I picked up a stone and clouted him over the head with it. I ran home to my mother and hid. I told her everything, and she replied briefly: "You behaved properly. You have given a good account of yourself. You erred, however, in not asking him who told him such things." After she had spoken, I said to her (for I always had the finest thoughts in my head): "Oh, Mother, I am only sorry for one thing. Some of those who were present at that scene said I had no real cause to feel offended —and I forgot to see whether it was just because my opponent was so young." Then I begged her to tell me outright whether I was in a position to have given them the lie. I asked her to tell me whether I was the result of the general collaboration of many men or the son of one father alone. She laughed and said: "Devil take you! You understand all about such things, don't you? You are no fool; you really aren't. You are a very clever lad. And you were quite right in clouting him over the head, for even if such things are true, they had better be left unsaid." What I heard left me as if dead; and a determination to pack what I could and quickly leave my parents seized me —so great was my embarrassment. But for the moment I said nothing. My father took care of the boy and healed him, and then smoothed things out and sent me back to school. The teacher was angry with me until he heard the cause of the quarrel, but afterwards, when he realized I was right, he took me again to his bosom.

Meanwhile, Don Diego came to see me frequently, for he had taken quite a liking to me. You see, I would trade my tops with him when mine were better than his, and I would give him part of my lunch without asking for anything in return. And besides, I bought him prints, taught him how to wrestle, played at bullfighting with him, and entertained him all the time. So that when his parents saw how much Diego enjoyed my company, they begged my father and mother to allow me to dine and sup with him and even to stay all night with him almost every night.

It happened that on one of the first school days after Christmas a man called Pontius Aguirre, who was known to be a converted Jew, was coming down the street, and my friend Diego urged me to call out the name Pontius Pilate—and then run. In order to please Diego I called out "Pontius Pilate." The man blushed, and then started after me with a bare knife, obviously with the intention of killing me. I was obliged to break into my teacher's house, shouting for help. The man followed me in, but the teacher kept him from doing me any harm by assuring him that he would punish me. The "Missus" pleaded with her husband on my behalf, but he nevertheless ordered me to lower my pants and he proceeded to flog me, saying after each lash: "Are you ever going to say 'Pontius Pilate' again?" And I would answer every time: "Never, sir!" I had to repeat that twenty times, for such was the number of lashes he gave me. I received on that occasion such instruction never to say "Pontius Pilate," and I had such a fear of pronouncing that name, that when on the following day the teacher told me to say prayers as usual in the presence of the other boys, I, when I reached the Credo and it was time to say, "He suffered under Pontius Pilate," remembered that I must never again say "Pilate" and (observe, sir, my simplicity), instead, I said: "He suffered under Pontius Aguirre." The teacher was so greatly amused at my stupidity and the fear I had of him that he laughed and put his arm around me. Then he gave me a signed statement saying that he would not give me a beating on the first two occasions when I had them coming. I was not exactly unhappy to hear that.

Well, to make a long story short, Shrovetide came, and the teacher, wishing his boys to have a good time, arranged to have them play a game known as "King of the Roosters." Twelve of us who had been previously chosen by the teacher cast lots, and as a result I was chosen king. I then asked my parents to get me some appropriate finery. On the appointed day I made my appearance on a tuberculosis-ridden and rickety nag, which seemed all the time to be bowing courteously—but that was not out of politeness but from sheer lameness. Its rear end was hairless, like a monkey's, and its neck was longer than a camel's. It was blind in one eye and disabled in the other. As for its age: all it needed was to have someone close its eyes. In short, it looked more like a wooden horse than a real one. And if it had only had a scythe it would have looked like what the horse-world considers its symbol of death to be. Its entire appearance bespoke of fasting, and it was perfectly clear that the poor thing had been much given to abstinence and penances. It had indubitably never made the acquaintance of barley or hay. But what provoked most laughter in onlookers was the abundance of bald spots it displayed. Indeed, if it had had a lock on it, it would have looked very much like a living old moth-eaten horsehair trunk.

Well then, swaying from side to side on this contraption, like a pompous Pharisee, I led the parade, and all the boys in their fine array followed after me. In the very greatest majesty I rode along on the aforementioned specter, and we all finally came to the square (it frightens me still to think of it),

and drew near the market stalls of the female vegetable dealers
(from whom, Oh Lord, deliver us!). My horse, if such it could
be called, snapped up a cabbage, which disappeared immediately
into the long tunnel that led to its stomach—though it had
to spend considerable time before it reached its destination.
The vegetable seller, impudent as her kind always is—began to
shout. Instantly her companions hastened to her side, followed
by a lot of riff raff. They picked up some enormous carrots,
some massive turnips, eggplants, [and some bad eggs], and
began to pelt the poor thing with them. Since I was not
expecting that kind of ovation, I started to dismount; but
they gave my poor steed such a wallop in the face that he
started to rear up and then promptly tumbled into—I hope
you will excuse my language—into an open latrine, and took
me along with him. I was a sight frightful to behold! But
by this time my companions, now well armed with stones,
were chasing the women away, and they managed to crack
open the heads of a couple of them. As for myself, after
that fall into the latrine, I became much more privy to what
was going on than anybody else. But shortly thereafter the
police appeared and began to make inquiries; they arrested
the vegetable sellers and the boys; they examined them for
weapons and took away from some of the boys the daggers
and swords they had at first worn solely as decorations but had
later drawn in the fray. Finally, the officers came to me and
frisked me for weapons, and when they saw I had none (for I
had hidden them in a house), they asked me where they were.
I said I had no offensive weapons except for my smell. In passing, I must confess, sir, that when they began to pelt us with
the eggplant and the turnips, I, since I was wearing feathers
in my hat, concluded that they had taken me for my mother,
and that they were throwing the things at her as they had done
so many times before; and so in my little-boy simplicity I said:
"Sisters, although I am wearing feathers, I am really not Aldonza
de San Pedro, my mother"—as if they could not see it from my
face and dress! I may plead fear as an excuse for my show of
stupidity, and then, too, the suddenness with which things hap-

pened had something to do with the way in which I expressed myself.

But to return to what I was saying. The policeman wanted to take me into custody, but he did not do so simply because he could find no place to get hold of me—I had become so filthy. Finally the people dispersed, and I went home, inflicting martyrdom on all the nostrils I met along the way. I entered the house and told my parents what had happened. They were so angry to see me in such a wretched state that their first intention was to give me a drubbing. I tried to excuse myself by throwing the blame on that elongated, shrivelled old nag. I tried to appease them, but when I saw that their anger did not subside, I went out to find my friend Don Diego and finally located him at his own house with his skull cracked and his parents vowing never again to allow him to go to school. There I was informed how my nag, finding itself in so great a predicament, had summoned sufficient strength to kick up its heels, and had thereby, out of sheer debility, dislocated its haunches and fallen down in the mud, where it lay at death's very door.

Seeing, therefore, that the holiday was spoiled and that everyone in town was scandalized—my parents, embarrassed—my friend, hurt—and the horse, dead—I decided to return neither to school nor to my parents, but instead stayed on as a servant —or, rather, companion—to Don Diego. His parents were quite pleased with this decision because they felt my friendship for the lad was a fine thing for him. I wrote home and told my people that I had no further need of going to school, because, although I had not learned to write very well, I was quite aware that if the plan I had of becoming a gentleman ever materialized, the most important requisite for such a way of life would be to write very badly. So I decided to forego further schooling in order not to burden my parents with additional expenses, and I also wished to stop living at their house in order not to cause them greater annoyance. I told them where I was staying and explained the arrangements I had made; and I told them also that I should not see them until they asked me to.

CHAPTER III

How I went to a boarding school as the servant of Don Diego Coronel

As a result of what had happened, Don Alonso decided to send his son to a private school, in order, first, to get the boy used to being away from his father's solicitous care, and, secondly, to place him in surroundings that would not cause his father to worry about him. He heard that in Segovia a gentleman by the name of Cabra, a graduate of the university, had set up a school for the education of young gentlemen; and so Don Diego was dispatched to that place and took me along as his servant and companion. On the first Sunday after Lent, therefore, we were delivered over into the dreadful clutches of Living Hunger, for to state the matter any less bluntly would be an out-and-out prevarication. Cabra (the Old Goat, we called him) was a very peashooter of a clergyman, generous only in height. He had a small head, red hair (need anything more be said?), and a pair of eyes set so far back in his head that he seemed all the time to be peering out of caves. They looked so sunken and shadowed that they might have been thought to be in the sort of place storekeepers delight in, so that they can deceive customers when the latter are examining defective goods. His nose was flat and had been partially destroyed by some sort of ailment that was probably not venereal—for to contract that sort of thing costs money. His beard had turned white purely from the fear it had of the mouth adjacent to it—a mouth which threatened to eat it up at any moment out of sheer hunger. He was missing several teeth, which he had lost through lack of exercise. His windpipe was long like an ostrich's; and his Adam's apple stood forth prominently in search of something to eat. His arms were dried up and his hands each had the exact appearance of a bundle of twigs. The bottom part of him looked like a two-tined fork, or a pair of compasses. He had long, skinny legs, and he walked very slowly. When he was annoyed, his bones rattled like the wooden clappers lepers use when they beg alms. One of our boys used to cut his hair, but Cabra never shaved—he refused to spend money on such a luxury. Besides, he said, the very thought of a barber's hands on his face made him sick. He often said he would rather be killed than shaved.

On sunny days the Goat wore a threadbare bonnet that looked as if mice had been nibbling at it—it had so many holes in it, and it was thickly embellished with grease. It had originally been made of cloth, but with time it had acquired the consistency of dandruff, more than anything else. His cassock was a very wonder, because no one could tell what color it was. Because it was completely hairless, some thought it must have originally been made of frogskin. Others called it a mere optical illusion. When you were close to it, it looked black, but from a distance it looked blue. Cabra did not wear a cord or collar or cuffs. With his long hair and wretched cassock he looked like Death's very lackey. Each of his shoes looked like Goliath's tomb. And his room? Why, there were not even spiders there. He exorcized the mice for fear they might gnaw on some bits of bread he kept by him. His bed was the floor—and he slept on one side to keep the sheets from wearing out. In a word, he was arch-poor and proto-impoverished.

Well, this was the sort of person into whose clutches Don Diego and I fell. The night we arrived the Old Goat showed us to our room, and in order not to spend much time about it (he was so stingy he disliked to spend time, even), he gave us a very short talk and told us what our duties were. We kept busy with these chores until dinner, and then we went to the table. We served our masters, who, of course, ate first. The refectory was about as large as a half-peck measure, and the astounding number of five young gentlemen managed to squeeze in around the board. The first thing I did was to look around for cats; and when I saw none, I asked one of the older servants (whose thinness branded him as belonging to our boarding-house) for an explanation of their absence. He replied with a dejected note in his voice: "*Cats*? Do you think that cats have any interest in fasting and penance? I can see from your plumpness that you are new around here." Hearing this, I was deeply distressed, and I became even more so when I noticed that all those who had lived for some time at the boarding-house were like awls, and their faces looked as if they had been washed in an astringent.

The Goat sat down and said grace. The dinner before the company was very much like Eternity—it had neither begin-ning nor end. Some broth was brought in in wooden bowls, and such was its crystal clarity that it could have provided Narcissus with a better mirror to look into (at his peril) than the fountain he actually did look into. I noticed the anxiety with which the young gentlemen's emaciated fingers swam after the solitary orphan of a chick-pea lying at the bottom of the bowl. After each swallow Cabra would say: "No matter what others may tell you, there is nothing in all the world com-parable to stew. All else is vice and gluttony." And saying this, he downed his broth, saying: "This is really healthful food, and besides it sharpens the mind in a wonderful way." "I wish it were a sharpened knife right in the middle of *you*," I said to myself. And then I observed a skinny half-ghost of a lad with a plate of meat in his hand. It looked as if it had come off his own body. An adventurous turnip was lying on the plate be-side the meat. When the master saw it, he said: "Turnips to-day? As far as I am concerned, partridge itself cannot compare with turnip. Well, fall to, lads, and let me rejoice to see you regale yourselves." And taking a knife he pricked the turnip with it, and conveying it to his nose, popped it into his mouth, and said, shaking his head as he did so: "They are really very good for you—have quite a tonic effect, you know." It was plain to see that he was a great admirer of vegetables. He gave us so little lamb that between what stuck to our fingernails and what lodged in our teeth not very much was left for our stomachs. The Goat looked at the boys and said: "Eat, eat! After all, you are young. How I do rejoice to see your healthy appetites! Oh what a banquet, this! And only a moment ago you were yawning with hunger!" They finished, leaving some little bits of bread on the table and two pieces of skin and a couple of bones on the plate. Then the master remarked: "We must leave this for the serving-boys. They too shall eat. Let *us* not eat everything." "May God forsake you!" I said to myself. "And may what you have eaten do you no good, for your threats against my stomach." The dominie then again said grace, and after that observed: "The serving-boys may now take over. As for the rest of you, you need some exercise until two o'clock. That will keep you from getting sick from all you have eaten." I opened my mouth very wide at this: I simply could not restrain my laughter. Cabra became very much annoyed with me and told me to mind my manners. Then he added some old saws to what he had just said, and left the room.

We sat down. I could see that things were not too promising. My insides were now demanding justice; so I, being stronger and in better condition than the others, attacked the plate, and so did the rest of them. I greedily downed two of the three pieces of bread and one of the skins that had been left on the table. When the others started to make a great outcry, the Goat entered the room, saying:"Eat like brethren, for God has given you the wherewithal to do so. Do not contend, for there is an ample sufficiency for all." Then he left us and went back to enjoy the sun.

I swear on my honor, sir, that I really saw what I am about to relate. One of the diners was so hungry and so out of practice in the exercise of his eating-equipment that he twice pushed a bite of food into his eyes and then had to try three times more before he was able to guide his hand safely to his mouth. I asked for some water to drink (an activity which they in their fasting did not engage in). No sooner had I lifted the glass to my mouth than the ghost-boy snatched it away from me just as it if had been a communion lavatory. I got up sorely distressed, for I realized that I was in a house where I had made the gesture of drinking to the health of my insides, but they had not received my kindness cordially, and still, unplacated, growled. I next felt an urge to relieve myself—of what I do not know, for I had eaten nothing—; and so I asked one of the old-timers if there was a privy there where I could take care of my needs. He answered: "In this house we have no such needs, and therefore there is no privy. If you ever have such a need again, any place around here is as good as any place else. I have been here for two months and have had no occasion to use those facilities except the first day I came here, and that, mind you, was from the dinner I had had at home the night before." How shall I ever be able to express fittingly my sadness and dejection on that occasion? For they were so very deep that, considering how little food was to enter my body during my stay there, I concluded that even though I might be in a mood to lighten myself, I did not dare expel from my person anything that had already lodged there.

We kept busy until evening. Don Diego asked me several times what he could do to persuade his insides that they had eaten, for they obstinately refused to believe that he had. People often have a bloated feeling after a heavy meal. We had a bloated feeling too, but it came from the oversized vacuum in our middles. Dinnertime came round (there was not the slightest hint about our having the afternoon snack people usually have) and we were given even less than we had had at the previous meal. There was no lamb and just a little roast goat —a not too tender linguistic reminder of our dear master. Only the devil himself could have invented that meal. "It is very healthful," said Old Goat, "to dine lightly, in order to keep the stomach clean." And he proceeded to quote a string of hellish doctors. He praised dieting and said that it prevented nightmares—although he knew that everybody in his house had the same recurrent dream of food. They dined, we dined; and nobody dined.

We went to bed, but neither Don Diego nor I could sleep the whole night long. He lay there making plans to ask his father to extricate him from this place, and I kept encouraging him to act. And yet, after thinking the matter over a bit, I finally asked: 'Do you know for sure, however, that we are still alive? I really think we were killed in that battle with the vegetable sellers and are now only souls in purgatory. Unless someone includes us in his prayers, or helps us out of our misery by having some very special masses said for us, it is, I think, useless for you to ask your father to get us out of here." And so in this sort of colloquy, and with an occasional cat nap, we spent the rest of the night, and finally got up.

At six o'clock the Goat called for morning lessons, and we all went to class. I sat there with bared teeth—they were yellow with despair. I was told to read the introductory matter, but my hunger was such that I swallowed half the words for lack of better intake. I know you will believe what I have written when I tell you that Cabra's servant assured me that when he first came there Cabra brought home with him two Friesian horses, which after two days were so light and svelte that they positively flew through the air. He said, too, that he had seen Old Goat bring heavy mastiffs there, which in three hours turned into the lankest greyhounds imaginable. One Lent, he said, many men came to the door of the house and some stuck their feet in and others their hands, and others even came all the way in. This went on for quite some time, and people actually came from out of town to do this. He said he had asked one of them what this meant, for Cabra showed some annoyance when anyone asked him about it. One man said that some of those people were being eaten up by the itch and others were being devoured by chilbains, but that when they entered the Goat's house all eating and devouring promptly ceased, and they were immediately cured. The boy assured me that what he said was really true, and I, having made the acquaintance of that house, certainly believed everything he said. I am telling you all this so that you will not think I have been guilty of exaggeration in my report.

Well, Old Goat held his class, and we recited our lesson in unison. Things went on very much as I have been describing them. The only observable change was the addition to the stew of a bit of pork, which Cabra apparently felt he should have around—just to show he was an old Christian. He had a perforated little iron box that normally contained sand used to blot ink with. He opened this contraption and put inside of it as much pork as it would hold. Then, dangling it from a string, he dipped it into the stew and let a little of the fat ooze out. Then he took the box and pork out and put them aside to be used again on the following day. He must, however, have later come to the conclusion that he was being extravagant, for he gave up the custom of putting the box and pork *in* the stew and only wafted them back and forth over the pot.

We bore all these tribulations as you can well imagine. Don Diego and I were in such a sad plight that, being unable to get any food, we tried to find some relief for our misery by staying in bed. And so we said we could not get up because we were ill. We dared not say we had a fever, for anyone could easily see that we had none. Toothache and headache were not satisfactory excuses either, so we said that we had a severe stomach ache and had not been to stool for three whole days. We felt sure that Cabra would never spend a penny on medicine for us, and so would let us alone. But the devil ordered otherwise. It happened that our master had an old enema he had inherited from his father, who had been a druggist. He got it out, prepared an infusion, and called in his seventy-year-old aunt, who also acted as his nurse, and asked her to give each of us an enema.

They started on Don Diego; but when he bent down, the old woman, instead of putting it in, shot it up into the space between his shirt and his back and hit him on the back of the head with it—so that what was supposed to act as a lining within became an embellishment without. Don Diego began to yell. Cabra then came in, and when he saw what had happened, said they had better try me out next and then come back later to Don Diego. I fought wildly, but little good did it do me, because, while the Goat and others held me, the old lady succeeded in giving me the works—and I succeeded in giving the works right back to her—and in the face, too. At that, Cabra lost his temper and swore he would throw me out of the house. Anyone, he said, could see that it was all just a scurvy trick. I prayed to God that the Goat *would* send me away, but my luck would not have it so.

We complained to Don Alonso, but Old Goat convinced him that we had acted the way we did just to keep from studying. And so, our supplication produced no result.

Cabra now brought the old woman in to keep house for him and do the cooking and wait on the boarders. He did this because he found some bread crumbs on his servant's doublet one morning. What we experienced from the old woman—only heaven knows. She was so deaf that we had to scream to make her understand us, and she was almost completely blind. She was a great one for prayers, too; and so one day her rosary broke and fell in the stew, and she served us the most pious broth I have ever seen. Some of the boarders tried to analyze the contents of the broth and said: "What? *Black* chick-peas? The Ethiopian variety, doubtless." Others said: "Chick-peas in mourning? Did some of their loved ones pass on?" My master was the first to close in on one of the beads, and when he bit down on it, broke one of his teeth. On Fridays the old lady used to give us eggs that looked so venerable and bearded with white hairs from her head that you might have thought them hoary judges or reverend magistrates. It was also usual for her to stir the soup with a fire shovel instead of a ladle, and she frequently sent us in a bowl of pebbly broth. And many a time I found in the stew—insects, sticks and the tow she used to spin with. She put practically everything in the food, in order, apparently, to provide us with plenty of roughage.

We continued to undergo these hardships until the following Lent, when, at the beginning of that season, one of our friends fell sick. Old Goat had no desire to spend any money on a doctor, and he therefore did not call one in until the sick man began to ask for a priest. Old Goat then called in an apprentice doctor, who took the boy's pulse and said that starvation had finally won. The Sacraments were then administered, and the poor lad, when he saw them, (he had not said a thing for a day), uttered these words: "My Lord Christ, it has been necessary for me to see Thee in this house to persuade myself that I was not in hell." These words touched me deeply. The unfortunate boy died, and we buried him very poorly, because he was from another part of the country.

The story of the whole horrible business soon spread all over town, and it eventually came to the ears of Don Alonso Coronel. Since Don Diego was his only son he began to have his doubts about Cabra's statements, and from then on paid more attention to the two shadows we had by now become.

He came to get us out of the boarding school, and although he looked straight at us, asked where we were to be found. When he realized what had happened, he gave Licentiate Fasting a good verbal drubbing and then sent us home in sedan chairs. We said farewell to our friends, who followed us with their best wishes; and with their eyes manifested the same gloomy sorrow that the Algerian captive shows when he sees the Trinitarian brothers come and ransom his companions, and forsaking him, they leave for home.

CHAPTER IV

Of my convalescence and my studies at the University of Alcalá

When we entered Don Alonso's house we were put to bed very gently lest our hunger-gnawed bones should fall apart. They brought explorers to hunt for our eyes; and since my work at Cabra's had been harder and my hunger greater than Don Diego's, it took the investigators some little more time to find my two faded orbs than it did his. They brought in doctors and had them dust out our mouths just as you might dust off an altarpiece. They gave us some broths and juices. No one will ever be able to describe properly the celebration our insides put on when we drank our first almond juice and ate our first bowl of broth—which delicacies must have been considered by our inner regions to be absolutely exotic. The doctors prescribed that no one might speak out loud in our room for nine whole days, for our insides were so hollow that a loud word would certainly echo and re-echo indefinitely down there. With these and other provisions for the future we began to regain some of our lost energy, but our cheeks and jaws were so wasted away and unworkable that they had developed pleats; and so it was decided that they should be put back in shape with the use of a pestle—just as shoes are reshaped with a last. After forty days we got up, though we still looked like other men's shadows, for we were as thin and jaundiced as the seed of the fathers of the desert.

We now spent the whole day thanking God for having delivered us out of the hands of that dread Goat, and we begged the Lord never to allow another Christian soul to fall prey to his fearful talons. It sometimes happened, while we were at table, that we were reminded of the wicked old principal of that boarding school, and our hunger on those occasions would become so great that the household expenses increased considerably on that day. We told Don Alonso how at meals Cabra would hold forth on the thousands of ailments that come from gluttony—although he had himself never known any such illnesses in all his life. Don Alonso laughed when we told him that in the commandment *Thou shalt not kill*, Cabra included partridges, capons, hens and all the things he did not wish to give us—and in the commandment he also included hunger itself, for he seemed to think it was a sin not only to kill hunger but even to injure it in the slightest, if we are to judge from the kind of food he served us.

Three months went by in this fashion, and then Don Alonso took it into his head to send his son to Alcalá to complete his studies in grammar. He asked me whether I would like to go along; and since what I wanted most was to get as far away as I could from the name of that damned persecutor of stomachs, I offered to serve his son in whatever capacity he might indicate. After this matter had been settled, he gave his son a steward by the name of Tomás de Baranda to take care of his lodgings and handle his current expenses, for the payment of which he gave Don Diego money orders to present to a certain Julián Merluza.

We piled our baggage on a wagon operated by a man by the name of Diego Monje. It consisted of a cot and a small bed made of cord to roll under mine and the steward's, five mattresses, eight sheets, eight pillows, four carpets, a trunk filled with linen, and other household equipment.

We took a coach and left about an hour before nightfall, and shortly after midnight we reached a forever-accursed inn of Viveros.

If Moriscos are said to be dogs and thieves are said to be cats, then I never in all my life saw dog and cat keep such peaceful company as they did in the person of the innkeeper that night. He made a great fuss over us, and since he and the carter's men were hand in glove (the latter had already arrived with the baggage half an hour earlier, for we had travelled slowly), he rushed up to the coach, gave me his hand and helped me down from the footboard, and asked me whether I was planning to become a student. I answer affirmatively; whereupon he took me inside where there were two rough characters, some women of rather doubtful repute, a priest in prayer, a greedy old merchant who was trying to forget to eat supper, and two scurvy-looking students on the lookout for some way to fill their stomachs.

Because of his youth and because, too, he was the last to arrive, my master then said to the host: "Sir, please give me just anything you have—but enough, if you please, for me and my two servants."

The rough characters immediately spoke up and said: "Your Grace, we are *all* your servants here. We can assure you, host, that this gentleman will appreciate anything you do for him. So empty the larder."

One of them helped Don Diego take his cloak off, and added: "Do rest yourself, my lord," and then put the coat on a bench.

This made me feel as proud as if I had been the owner of the inn. One of the nymphs then chimed in: "What a fine-looking young man! Does he intend to become a student? Are you his servant?"

I replied that they had surmised correctly—that the other fellow and I were indeed his servants.

They asked me his name, and it had scarcely left my mouth when one of the students approached him almost in tears, and embracing him with great emotion, said: "Oh my lord Don Diego! Who would have ever thought that after ten years I should see you again, sir, and in such a way as this! Ah me! And have I changed so much that Your Grace no longer really recognizes me?"

My master and I were astonished, for we both could have sworn that neither of us had ever laid eyes on him before.

The other scholar continued to look at Don Diego's face, and finally said to his friend: "Is this the gentleman about whose father you have told me so many fine things? If so, then great is our fortune to have found him and to have been able to recognize him, now that he is grown up so. God protect him!" And he began to cross himself.

You would most certainly have believed that we had all actually been brought up together. Don Diego answered them graciously; and while he was asking the student what his name was, the innkeeper came in to set the table, and catching on to the trick that was coming up, said: "Enough, enough! You can talk after supper. The food is getting cold."

One of the ruffians immediately brought up seats for the company, and a chair for Don Diego, and the other ruffian brought in a dish that was ready. The students said: "Now, fall to, your Lordship, and while they are scraping up some more for us, we will wait on you at table."

"Oh really!" said Don Diego. "You must sit down too. You must, by all means."

To which the ruffians replied, although Don Diego had not spoken to them: "Later, good sir, for not everything is ready yet."

When I observed that some were being invited and that others had taken it upon themselves to issue their own invitations,

I was disturbed and feared that what in fact really happened *would* happen, because the students took the salad, which was a rather nice dish, and looking at my master, said: "It is not right that in the presence of such a noble gentleman these ladies here should go unprovided for. Wouldn't Your Grace care to ask them to have a bite too?"

My master, hoping to appear gallant, invited the ladies to join him. They sat down posthaste; and with but four mouthfuls they and the two students left only a little leaf on the plate. The wretched student handed it to Don Diego, saying as he did so: "Your Grace had a grandfather—my father's uncle—who could not stand the sight of lettuce. It is very bad for the memory—lettuce is—especially in the evening. Besides, the salad they served us tonight was very bad."

Don Diego ate the last of the lettuce.

The student now interred a roll, and his companion did away with a second. The two bawds were engrossed in annihilating the bread; but the one there who ate most was the priest—though he ate only with his eyes.

The two rough-looking characters now sat down to half a roast kid, two slabs of pork, and a pair of roasted doves. They had the brazenness to say: "Well, Father, what are you doing over there? Pull yourself up a chair and join us, for milord Don Diego has invited us all to supper." The priest was seated at the table even before the echo of their words had died away.

Now, my master, seeing that they were taking advantage of him, began to feel quite distressed. They divided it all up and gave Don Diego a few bones and wings, remarking that according to an ancient proverb those were the most succulent parts. It follows that we ate the proverbs and they ate the doves. The priest and the others gulped down the rest.

The rough-looking monsters now slyly suggested: "Don't eat too much, sir, or you will be ill."

And one of those revolting students added: "And besides, you have to get used to eating lightly if you are going to Alcalá."

The other servant and I were imploring God to put it in their hearts to leave something for us. When they had eaten every-thing, and the priest was re-examining the bones the others had left, one of the ruffians returned to the table and said: "Oh, how can I forgive myself! We have left nothing for the servants. You two come here. Host, give them anything you can stir up."

My master's imaginary relative—the knavish scholar, I mean —jumped forward instantly and said to the bully: "Pardon me for saying it, sir, but you seem to know very little about cour-tesy. Do you perchance not know my dear cousin? He will him-self provide for his servants, and he would do the same for ours—if we had any, just as he has done for us." And turning to Don Diego, who was very much taken back, he pleaded: "Do not be angry with him, sir. He didn't realize you are the way you are."

When I saw such duplicity, I cursed him roundly.

The tables were then cleared, and everyone suggested that it was high time for Don Diego to go to bed. He wanted to pay for the supper at that moment, but they told him there would be plenty of time on the following morning for that. They all talked a while, and the student, on being asked his name, said that it was Pedro Coronel. May the trickster burn in the hottest of everlasting flames for that! He looked at that greedy merchant and saw that he was asleep. "Would you like to have a good laugh?" he asked. "Then let's pull a trick on this nasty old fellow who hasn't eaten anything but words dur-ing the whole trip, even though he has enough money to burn."

The ruffians agreed. "The scholar is right," they said. "Let's do it. It's a capital idea."

With this, the student crept up, took from under the sleeping old man's feet a knapsack, and unfolding it, found a box, which could not have attracted more people even if it had been a drum. They all crowded up close while it was being opened. It was soon discovered to be filled with sweetmeats. The trickster took them all out and replaced them with stones, sticks, and whatever else he could find. Then he relieved himself on all this, and on top of the filth placed about a dozen pieces of old plaster. Having closed the box again, he said: "But this won't do, for he has a bottle too." He removed all but a little of the wine from the bottle, and taking apart a cushion from our coach, he filled the bottle with wool and tow and capped it up again. With this, everyone lay down to sleep for the hour remaining, while the student put everything back in the knapsack, and placed a big rock on the hood of the old fellow's greatcoat. Then he too lay down to sleep.

As the time drew near for our departure, everyone woke up except the old man, who slept right on. They called him, but when he tried to get up he could not lift the hood of his coat. Seeing what the trouble was, the innkeeper, who was fully aware of what had happened, scolded him, saying: "Look here now! Couldn't you find anything else but that stone to make off with, Uncle? What do you gentlemen make of this? Why, if I hadn't seen it in time! . . . Gentlemen, I value this stone more than a hundred ducats, because it is a charm to be used to get rid of the stomach ache." The merchant raved and swore that he had not put that silly stone in his hood.

The ruffians added up the bill, which amounted to sixty reals, but even the greatest mathematician would not have been able to understand how they arrived at such a figure. The students then spoke up: "We shall be happy to be of service to you in Alcalá to repay you for your hospitality." And we stood there, astonished at the expense.

Later, as we proceeded to eat a bite, the old man reached for his knapsack. And so that we should not see what he took out, and to keep from having to share it with us, he untied it underneath his coat. Grabbing a sticky piece of plaster he popped it into his mouth and bit down on it with the tooth and a half he still had, and in the process almost lost those. He began to spit and make gestures that expressed his nausea and misery. We all ran up to him, with the priest in the lead, and asked him what the matter was. He commended himself to the devil, and dropped the knapsack as the student approached him, saying: "Get thee behind me, Satan. The cross is before you." Another one opened a prayer book, and they made the poor man believe that he was bewitched until he explained what the trouble was and asked them to let him rinse out his mouth with a little wine he had in his bottle. They gave him permission to do so; and taking it out, he opened it and poured out into a small glass some of the wine, which came out all mixed with wool and tow—a disgusting, bearded and hairy mess that could neither be drunk nor strained. With this, the old man lost his patience; but seeing that laughter in the others had become uncontrollable, he thought it best to keep his peace and so got into the wagon with the ruffians and the women.

The students and the priest piled up on two donkeys, and we got into the coach. We had hardly begun to move when first some, and then others, began to laugh at what they now openly acknowledged to have been the trick they had played on my master. The innkeeper said: "The young gentleman, with a few initiations like this, will certainly mature right quickly."

To which the priest added: "I am a priest, and I will repay him by saying some masses for him." And the hated student taunted Don Diego with—"The next time, dear cousin, scratch when you itch and not afterwards." . . .

We decided to pay no attention to it all, but God knows how abashed we were.

With these and other things we finally reached Alcalá at nine o'clock, and then spent the rest of the day trying to figure out just what we had spent so much money on; but we were never able to make heads or tails out of the whole mess.

CHAPTER V

Concerning our arrival at Alcalá, the initiation fee,

and the tricks played on Pablos as a newcomer

Before nightfall we left the inn and set out for the house that had been rented for us outside the Santiago Gate. It was a sort of students' dormitory, although we shared this one with only three other lodgers. The landlord was one of those hypocrites who believe in God not because they have good reason to but just for appearance's sake. In short, he was a Morisco, of which tribe, Lord knows, there is a great abundance (like their generous noses—which can smell out anything but pork). I say this, but I must hasten to add that there is very great nobility indeed in the upper class.

So, the landlord received me with less grace than if I had been the Holy Sacrament. I do not know whether he did it to inculcate respect in me at the very outset, or whether it was just natural for such people to be like that—for it certainly seems natural for a bad disposition to go hand in hand with a false belief. We took our things in, prepared our beds and made other like arrangements, and slept there that night.

At dawn, lo and behold!—all the students in the house came in to ask my master for his initiation fee. He did not know what all this was about, and had to ask them what they meant. I, meanwhile, had made ready for anything that might happen, and was ensconced cosily between two mattresses with only half my head sticking out, so that I presented something of the appearance of a turtle. They wanted two dozen reals. On receipt of that sum they set up a dreadful hubbub, yelling: "Long live our companion! He shall be admitted to our fraternity! He shall enjoy all our rights and privileges! He may have the itch, go about dirty, and starve like all the rest of us!" And having granted my master those rights, they scurried downstairs;

and Don Diego and I dressed immediately and set off for school.

My master was taken care of by some members of the school who were friends of his father's, and he went directly to his classroom; but I, who had to go to another, began to tremble. I started into the patio; but I had hardly put one foot in, when some people met me and started to yell: "A new one!" I thought I had better laugh and pretend that what they had said had not made me apprehensive. But that did not work, because eight or nine of them approached me and began to laugh. I turned red. I wish God had never allowed it to occur, but one of them who was near me immediately put his hand on his nose, and then moving away, said: "Judging by the way he smells, this Lazarus is ripe for resurrection."

At this, they all moved away, holding their noses. Hoping I might escape, I too put my hand to my nose and said: "You are right; something *does* smell bad here."

This occasioned another burst of hilarity, and the students —there must have been almost a hundred of them—drew apart. They began to sound the alarm and make odd rasping noises; and from the opening and closing of mouths I could see that they were coughing up phlegm. Then a dirty fellow with a horrible cold boastfully approached me, and suiting his actions to his words, said: "Take that!"

Seeing my dreadful predicament, I cried: "I swear to God I'll mur. . . ." I was going to say "murder," but the bombardment and rainfall that overwhelmed me were such that I could not finish my sentence. Some seemed to be throwing their intestines at me—such was the length of their missiles; others, when they had exhausted their saliva, resorted to the contents of their noses, and showered upon me such hard little nasal pellets that my cloak was all battered and dented from them. I had covered my face with this garment, but it was such a good target that not a one of them missed his mark. I was by this time snowy white from head to foot; but one of the villains, seeing me covered up and with no filth on my face, pushed for-

ward, saying angrily: "That's enough. Don't kill the poor fellow."

Considering the way they were treating me, it seemed a distinct possibility that they might do exactly what he had said.
So I removed my cloak from my face to see what was happening, and just as I did so, my protector (I *thought*) who had
hoarded up a supply of black-green mucus, suddenly let it go
and planted a great gob of it right between my eyes. Lord,
how miserable I was! The hellish mob raised such an outcry
that it stupefied me, and I, seeing how they had emptied their
stomachs on me, thought that to save themselves the money
usually spent on doctors and medicines, these fellows apparently were in the habit of lying in wait for new students to
purge themselves on. After all this they would have liked to
give me a beating, but there was no place for them to hit me
without carrying away on their hands a goodly portion of the
slime that plastered my cloak, which, alas!, was no longer black
but utterly white.

They left me, and I went home.

I could hardly find the place. Fortunately, it was still morning, and I met only three or four boys, who must have been
good fellows, because they threw only four or five filthy rags at
me and went their way.

I went in, and the Morisco, when he saw me began to laugh
and to act as though he too had the intention of spitting on me.
Afraid that he indeed might, I hastened to say: "This is no occasion for an *Ecce Homo*."

I should never have said that, for he gave me a pretty sound
drubbing. Having received that little gratuity, I went upstairs—though I was hardly able to get there—and spent quite
some time looking for a place to get hold of my clothes and
take them off. Having finally achieved this, I hung them out
on the roof and got into bed.

My master soon came home, and finding me asleep and
knowing nothing of my nauseating adventure, he became
angry, and started pulling my hair with such vigor that if he
had given it just two yanks more, I should have awakened

bald. I got up yelling and complaining, and he, angrier than ever, said: "Is this the way a servant should act, Pablos? This is quite a new life you've taken to."

I, hearing something about another life, decided that I must be dead, and said: "You offer me fine consolation in my tribulation. Look at that cloak—it has been used as a handkerchief for bigger noses than you ever saw in a Holy Week parade. Look at these ribs." And with that I began to blubber.

When he saw my tears, he believed me; and looking for the cloak and finally seeing it, he gave me his sympathy, saying: "Pablos, keep your eyes open, or they'll take advantage of you. You must look out for yourself, for here you have no father or mother other than your own self."

I told him everything that had happened; whereupon he told me to undress and go to my room, where four other lodgers' servants slept.

I went to bed and slept so soundly that after I had supped well, I felt almost as strong as if nothing had happened to me. But when misfortunes begin, there is no end to them, for they are linked each to each, and the one that comes first inevitably drags the others after it.

The other servants came in to go to bed. They greeted me and asked me whether I was ill and why I had gone to bed.

I told them what had happened; and with an air of assumed purity they at once began to cross themselves, affirming that such a thing would never have happened even among Lutherans. "Is it possible that such iniquities are really being perpetrated?" one of them asked. Another said that in his private opinion the president of the University was to blame, because he should have made arrangements to forestall such shameful goings-on. "Do you suppose he knows the identity of the culprits?" inquired a third. I replied that he probably did not, and thanked them for their friendly interest in me. By this time they had finished undressing and had got in bed, and then they put out the light. I soon fell asleep, for now I felt quite at home—just as if I had been there with my father and my brothers.

It was around midnight, I think, when I was awakened by one of my roommates, who was shouting at the top of his voice: "Help! Murder! They are killing me!" And I heard something in his direction that sounded like the lashings of a whip. I raised my head and said: "What's going on here?" And no sooner had I done so than a whip began to dance across *my* back in furious tempo. I began to yell and tried to get up. The other victim was moaning, but with little cause, for the attackers were devoting their attention strictly and exclusively to me. I managed to say: "God's mercy!" but the blows were now falling upon me with such frequency that my instinct of self-preservation impelled me to seek refuge under the bed. They had already stripped off the cover from over me, and so I was able to make my transfer with little loss of time. As soon as I was safely under the bed, the three who had been asleep also began to shout; and from the reverberations coming from the whip I concluded that someone from the outside had set upon the whole lot of us. Meanwhile, that scoundrel who had been next to me moved over into my bed and left a carefully concealed calling card there; and while he was returning to his own bed, the blows ceased, and all four boys got up, loudly demanding that the perpetrators of this piece of knavery should most certainly be punished. I was still under the bed, all doubled up very much like a greyhound with the cramps, and complaining like a dog with his tail caught in a door. The others now pretended to close the door, and I then came out of my hiding place and asked them if by chance anyone had got hurt, for they were all bitterly complaining. Then I climbed into my bed.

I lay down and pulled the covers up over me and then turned over and went back to sleep; but since I tossed and turned so much in my sleep, I woke up to find myself filthy all the way up to my chest. Everyone except me then got up. I pretended to be indisposed because of the beating I had received. I can assure you that no manner of devils could have ever budged me. In my confusion I thought that because of my fright, perhaps, and the excitement of the preceding evening I might have involuntarily ejected that vileness from my person, and I even went so far as to imagine that I might have committed it in my sleep. In short, I felt that I was incriminated, though innocent, and yet I did not know how to exonerate myself. My companions came in complaining, and, to keep the show going, asked how I was. I told them I was pretty wretched because of the many lashes I had received. I asked them just what had happened there during the night. One of them replied: "The fellow who did this is not going to escape even if we have to get an astrologer to tell us who did it. But the important thing is to see whether you are injured or not, for you have been complaining a great deal." And so saying, he started to pull back the sheets to expose my delinquency. At this point my master came in and said: "Pablos, can't I really depend on you any more? What do you mean by staying in bed until eight o'clock? Get right up—although I must say this is no time of day for anyone to be getting up." The others intervened in my behalf and told Don Diego the whole story, and asked him to let me sleep. One of them said: "If Don Diego doesn't believe it, just let Pablos get up and show him." And with that he took hold of the sheets, which I had clenched between my teeth in order to hide the filth that covered me. When the others saw that they could achieve no results with the technique they were using, they said: "God's body! How it stinks in here!" Don Diego said the same thing (which was quite true). Then following his lead, they all began to search the room to see whether there was a chamberpot there. Someone said it was impossible to stay in the room, and another said that all this was not very conducive to studying. They searched all the beds and then moved them about and looked under them. Then one said: "There must be something in Pablos' bed. Let us transfer him to one of the other beds and look in his." When I saw there was no way out for me, and that they were going to move me over, willy-nilly, I pretended to be having a heart attack. I clutched the bedstead and made the most horrible faces. They knew what my real trouble was, however, and closed in on me, saying as they did so: "What a shame!" Don Diego tried to help out by pulling my middle finger. And finally, the five of them managed to get me up; and when they lifted the covers and saw the complex designs on the sheets, they almost brought the house down with their laughter. "Poor thing!" the rascals said. I pretended to faint, and one of them said: "Please pull his middle finger, Don Diego, and pull it hard." So my master, trying to be helpful, pulled so hard on my digit that he dislocated it. The others were trying to garrote my thighs, and one of them remarked: "The poor thing must have done this while he was experiencing his attack." I can never properly express what I experienced then with my embarrassment, my dislocated finger, and the fear I had of being garroted. Finally, because of the fright they had given me (they had already put the cords about my thighs), I pretended to come to; and I did so just in time, for the rascals had gone so far in their practical joke as to leave a couple of marks on each of my legs. Then they left me, saying: "Heavens! You really ought to learn to control your natural functions better." I cried out in anger, and when they heard me, they said: "But you should be thankful you have regained your health. You should not mind in the least having soiled yourself. So don't complain." And they washed me, and put me back to bed, and went their way.

When I was alone, I could not help observing that more, almost, had happened to me that one day in Alcalá than had happened to me the whole time I stayed at the Goat's. At noon, I dressed, and cleaned my cassock the best I could— washing it like a saddlecloth—and waited for my master, who, when he came home, asked how I was. Then they all had dinner, and I ate with them—although I had little appetite and did not care for much to eat. After dinner the other servants all gathered in the hall for a session of small talk. After teasing me for a while, they finally confessed to having played that trick on me. They all laughed; which only made my embarrassment twice as great. And I said to myself: "Well, Pablos, you really must keep your eyes open from now on." And so, I resolved to turn over a new leaf. After this we all became close friends —brothers really; and from that time on nobody ever bothered me again as long as I was in school.

CHAPTER VI

Concerning the housekeeper and the pranks I played

"In Rome, do as the Romans do," says a wise proverb. Heeding its lesson, I resolved to be a knave among knaves, and even to outdo the rest of them if I could. I do not know whether I succeeded or not, but I can assure you that I exerted every possible effort to do so. First, I sentenced to death any pigs that chanced to come inside the house, and I passed the same sentence on the housekeeper's chickens when they came from the yard into my room. It so happened that one day two of the finest pigs I ever saw in my life strayed into the house. I was playing around with the other servants when I heard them grunting. I told one of the boys to go and see who was grunting in our house. He came back and said that there were two pigs in the house. When I heard this, I became so angry that I went in, saying that it was the height of impudence for them to come and grunt in somebody else's house. I stabbed one of them in the breast, and we finished them off by striking them on the back of their necks. So that the noise they made would not be heard, we all shouted at the top of our voices as though we were singing. Thus did those swine meet death at our hands. We took their entrails out and gathered up the blood. Then we took them to the back yard and singed them with burning straw. It was not a very good job; but when our masters returned, it was all over—except for the entrails. The stuffed tripe on this occasion was not well done, and that was not because of a lack of time on our part. To make matters easy, you see, we had left half the contents of the entrails still inside them, and so, to save trouble, we ate the tripe sausage just the way the pig itself had stuffed it while it was still in his body.

Don Diego and the steward found out about the whole thing and became so angry with me that the other guests . . . could not refrain from smiling, and felt obliged to come to my rescue. Don Diego asked me what I would say if they accused me and set the law upon me. I told him that I would say I had been driven to it by hunger—an excuse that is always a valid sanctuary for students. I told him, too, that I would say the pigs had entered our house without knocking, just as if they had been at home, and so I had assumed they belonged to us. All the students laughed at that sally, and Don Diego said: "By my faith, Pablos, it doesn't take you very long to pick up new tricks, does it?" The difference between my master and me was remarkable, for he was so quiet and religious, and I was so mischievous, that the contrast between us brought out very clearly the basic characteristics each of us had.

The housekeeper got along royally with me because the two of us had made an alliance to raid the larder. I was a very Judas of a steward, for I was henceforth possessed of a great longing to betray the larder—a feeling that seems inherent in the nature of stewards. Meat in the housekeeper's hands did not follow the rules of rhetoric, for it ever diminished and never increased. When she could use goat's meat or mutton she never used lamb; and if there were bones, there was no pork. So the stew was always teary, from sheer debility; and if her broths had been congealed, it could have been used to make glass beads out of. On feast days and as a special treat she would throw some old tallow candle ends into the stew to enrich it. She had the habit of saying to my master, when I was present: "There certainly isn't a better servant than Pablos to be found anywhere—if he just weren't so mischievous. Don't ever let him go, for his loyalty far outweighs his waywardness. He brings home the very best the market has to offer." I would, in my turn, compliment her in like fashion, and so we fooled everybody there.

We sometimes bought things in large quantities, and then we would hide half the charcoal and the pork, and at an opportune time, she would say: "Please, gentlemen, try to be a little more economical, for if you do not use things with a little more moderation, the King himself will not be able to pay our bills. We are out of oil and charcoal again. I just don't know how you could have used it up so fast. Well, you must buy some more—and I *do* hope you will put it to better use. Do give Pablos the money to get it with."

This they would do, and she and I would pilfer half of the new supply. And we did this on not just one or two occasions but all the time. And sometimes when I bought things at the market place, she and I would deliberately quarrel about the amount I had spent. "Do you really mean to tell me, Pablos, that you paid two whole pennies for these greens?" I would pretend to cry and blubber and would go and complain to my master and press him to send his steward to find out the truth, and so silence the housekeeper, who, as part of the game, kept insisting on her point. The steward then went and found out that what I had said was substantially correct; and in this way the housekeeper and I were assured of the good will of both my master and his steward. The former thus valued me for my loyalty and esteemed the housekeeper because of her concern for our welfare. Don Diego, to show his satisfaction with me, often said to her: "I only wish Pablos were as virtuous as he is loyal."

We continued to suck them dry in this manner—the way leeches do. I'll bet you would be surprised to learn how much money we had accumulated by the end of the year. And we felt no obligation to return any of it, either, for the housekeeper confessed and took communion every week and I never once heard her profess the slightest intention of returning anything—and she was such a very saintly creature, too. Around her neck she always displayed so big a rosary that she must have felt she was wearing a bundle of faggots. It made quite a clatter when she moved around. She was in the habit of blessing her stews; and when she skimmed the foam off, she would make signs of the cross with her ladle. I think she did that to conjure up their ghosts; for flesh and bone, they had none. From this rosary hung many images, crosses and large pardoner's beads. She said she prayed every night for her benefactors with every bit of that woodpile. She would appeal to her "Blessed Intercessors," and in very truth she had need of every single intercessor among them to redeem her from all her sins. She slept in a room directly over my master's, and he could hear her praying more prayers than a blind man ever prays. She would start out with one to the *Just Judge* and end with the prayer *Quick-come-to-a-halt* (as she pronounced the prayer beginning "Quicumque vult . . . ," followed by a *Salve, Regina*. She said her prayers in Latin to impress us and make us think she was very innocent. And indeed, we were so very much impressed that we nearly split our sides laughing at her.

She had other talents, too. She was a soother of longings and a minister of delights—I mean a "madam," and the excuse she gave me was that it ran in her family, just as the king of France is said to inherit the ability to cure scrofula.

Do you think we were always on good terms? Well, everyone knows that two friends, if they are greedy and are together a lot, will inevitably try to deceive each other.

Now, it happened that the housekeeper kept chickens in the back yard. She had twelve or thirteen friers, [and one day while she was picking one she had just killed, she inadvertently mentioned that part of a bird's anatomy which is known as the *pope's nose*]; so I began to cry out: "Merciful heavens, woman! Why couldn't you have killed a man or stolen money from the King's own treasury—anything, for that matter, that I could have kept quiet about, instead of doing the one thing I cannot possibly keep to myself! Oh, woe is me . . . and you too!" When she saw me so distraught, she became quite disturbed and said: "Why, Pablos, what have I done that is so bad? If you are up to another one of your pranks, you may just as well spare yourself the trouble." "Another one of my pranks! Good Lord, woman! Don't you see that now I have no choice but to inform the Inquisition of what you have said. If I don't,

I shall be excommunicated." "Inquisition?" she said weakly; and began to tremble. "Why, what have I done that is against the Faith?" "You have just done something very terrible, so you had better not take the Holy Inquisitors lightly. Now, confess that you have been a very foolish woman, and retract what you have said, and don't deny your blasphemy and irreverence." In the greatest fright she said: "Pablos, if I retract what I have said, will they then punish me?" "No," I replied; "they will absolve you." "Well then, I retract it," she said. "But won't you tell me what I am retracting?—for as my dead ancestors are my witnesses, I really don't know." "Is it really possible that you don't know what you just said? The very thought of repeating it frightens me terribly. Don't you really remember calling [a certain part of that chicken *the pope's nose*]? Popes are the Vicars of God on earth and the Head of Mother Church. Now you can see what a terrible thing you did." She was horrified, but was finally able to say: "Pablos, I did say that, but may God deny me forgiveness if I said it with any bad intent. I take it back. Now reconsider, and see if you can't find it in your heart not to accuse me, for I think it would really kill me if I had to go before the Inquisition." "If you will swear upon the altar in church that you did not say that with any bad intent, then I will be sure you are innocent, and I will not accuse you. But you will have to give me those two chickens that were eating here just now while you were saying that bad expression. They have become impure by association. I will take them to a friendly familiar of the Inquisition, who will purge them with fire. And after that you will have to swear never to repeat the offense." The housekeeper was overjoyed and said: "Take them, Pablos; take them at once. Tomorrow I will swear that I was innocent of any bad intent." In order to make my position a little more secure, I hesitated, but finally said: "The worst part of it all, Capriana" —such was her name—"is that I am taking all the risk, because the familiar will probably think I am the guilty one, and he may give *me* a little trouble. On second thought, you had better take them yourself, because I am simply afraid to." "Pablos," she said when she heard this; "for the love of God, go and take them with you. Don't make me suffer any longer. Nothing is going to happen to you." I let myself be convinced and finally agreed to take them, since it was what we both wanted. I hid them in my room and pretended to have gone out. After a while I returned, saying: "It went better than I had thought possible. The familiar wanted to come back with me and see the guilty woman, but I managed to get him involved in a conversation and he completely forgot all about it." She gave me a thousand hugs and another chicken for my services. I took the latter and put it with its companions. Later, I had a pastry cook made a chicken pie out of them, and I shared it with the other servants. The housekeeper and Don Diego eventually found out about the trick, and the whole house was soon celebrating it. The prank distressed the housekeeper so much that I thought she was going to die from sheer embarrassment. She came pretty close to reporting my thefts to my master, and if she had not herself been involved, I think she would most certainly have done just that.

Since I was now in the bad graces of the housekeeper and could not put anything over on her, I had to look elsewhere for means of amusing myself, and so I finally took up the game which students there used to call "snatch-and-run." While I was engaged in this pastime, many amusing things happened to me. I went out one night about nine o'clock when the streets were practically deserted, and while I was walking along the one called Calle Mayor, I saw a confectionery shop with a basket of raisins sitting up front. I approached it unobtrusively and snatched it up and started to run. The proprietor and his servants and neighbors all set out after me. I had the disadvantage of carrying a basket, and I saw that even though I had a good head start, they were going to catch up with me eventually. So, turning a street corner, I put the basket down and sat on it. I wrapped my cloak about my leg, and pretending to be a beggar, put both hands around my leg and began to say: "God forgive him, but he ran right over my foot!" They heard me and started to come over to where I was. I began the usual "In Our Lady's name" and the customary laments—"In an evil hour it happened to me" and "Alas, the poisonous air," and the like. They came up yelling like mad and said to me: "Did a man come running by here, brother?" "Yes," I said. "There he goes! He ran right over my foot—God be praised." And they set off down the road again. When I was sure they were out of sight, I took the basket home, and told them there about the trick. They refused to believe it had happened just the way I told it, although they did speak highly of the idea itself. For that reason I felt I ought to invite them to watch me purloin a box of sweetmeats some other evening.

They came with me that time; and when they saw that the boxes were so far back in the shop that I could not possibly get to them with my hands, they concluded that it would be impossible for me to make my boasting good. Besides, the confectioner was on the lookout for trouble, for he had, you see, heard about what had happened to the other shop-keeper and his raisins. I was determined, however, to carry out my plan, and so I went right on. I moved some dozen steps away from the shop and then ran forward with my hardy rapier in my hand. When I reached the store I made a lunge at the confectioner, who fell down crying for confession. I thrust the rapier into one of the boxes, ran the blade in, and lifted the box and ran off with it. My friends were amazed to see what I had been able to do; and later they almost died laughing when the confectioner asked them to examine him, for he was convinced he had been gravely wounded. He swore, too, that he even knew who his assailant was—someone, he said, with whom he had recently had words. But when he looked around and saw that the boxes were in considerable disarray—because I had extracted one of them from the very midst of the pile—he caught on and crossed himself over and over and over.

I must confess that I never ate anything that tasted so good. My companions said that all by myself I could keep the house stocked with the food I "snitched" (which means the same thing as steal, but sounds somewhat nicer).

I, being still pretty young, and hearing myself praised for

the skill with which I had accomplished those bold feats, was encouraged by what I heard to try a few more of them. Every day I came home with a lot of little pitchers I had stolen from some nuns whom I had asked to give me a drink. It was I, indeed, who caused the convents there to establish the custom of requesting security of some sort before they gave anything out.

One day I promised Don Diego and my companions that I would relieve the night watch of their swords some night. The hour for the adventure was chosen, and we all went out together—I first, of course, with one of the servants. When the watch appeared, I approached in a great distress and said: "Is this the watch?"

They replied that it was. And then I asked:

"Is the chief magistrate here?"

They answered that he was. Then I went and knelt down before him and said:

"In your hands, sir, lie both the solution of my problems and, at the same time, the means by which I may have revenge. At the same time you will have the opportunity of performing a great public service. If you wish to make an extraordinary arrest, lend me your ear for a few minutes in private."

The magistrate stepped aside. The constables already had their hands on their swords, and the bailiffs were tightly grasping their staffs.

I said to the magistrate: "Sir, I have come from Seville in pursuit of some of the most notorious men in the world. All of them are thieves and murderers. Among them there is one who wantonly murdered my mother and one of my brothers—without the slightest provocation, either. What I am saying has been proved. And they are now in the company of someone who is acting as a spy for the French, and I have every reason to suspect from what I overheard them saying, that he comes from none other than [that archtraitor], Antonio Pérez himself!"

When the magistrate heard this, he jumped right up in the air and began to shout:

"Where are they?"

"In that brothel there, sir," I said. "Do not lose a single minute! The souls of my mother and my brother will repay you with prayers for what you do, and the King will reward you too."

"Gad!" he said. "That's right. Let's not waste a second more. Men, follow me. Let me have that buckler there."

Whereupon I said to him, aside:

"Allow me to point out, sir, that if you go in armed you will quite likely lose out. The best thing would be for you gentlemen to go in one by one and without your swords, for those fellows are in the rooms and they all have pistols about them. If they see us come in armed with swords they will be sure to fire, because they know that only the police are permitted to carry swords. It would be much better for us to go in there with only our daggers, and seize them from behind. There are certainly enough of us here to do that."

The magistrate liked the idea very much, for he was exceedingly eager to capture my criminals. Meantime, we came nearer the inn; and the magistrate, whom I had instructed well, ordered his men to hide their swords in the grass growing in a field that lay almost directly in front of the house they planned to enter. The men did as they were ordered. Then all of them went inside.

I had previously told my companions to get the policemen's swords as soon as they had put them down in the grass, and then to take off with them at once for home. They followed my instructions carefully. When the magistrate and his men started into the house, I took care to be the last one to enter. Then, while they were mingling with the other people in the place, I gave them the slip and raced along a narrow lane which opens out near the Convent of La Victoria. I sped along so swiftly, indeed, that no greyhound in all the world could have ever overtaken me.

When the police had got in and saw that there was nobody present but students and rascals—which is to use two words to refer to the same thing—they started to look for me; and when they failed to find me anywhere, they began to suspect a trick.

They went to get their swords, but, of course, they could not find a single one of them. No one will ever be able to give a proper report of the discussions that took place that evening between the magistrate and the president of the University! They toured the whole campus, scrutinizing faces and looking for the weapons they had lost. By the time they came to our place, I had invented a plan to keep them from recognizing me. I was lying in my bed with a nightcap over my head, a candle in one hand and a crucifix in the other; and a friend of mine, a student of Divinity, was praying there with me, and my other companions were on their knees in prayer all around the bed.

When the president of the University and the police came in and saw that scene, they left immediately, being quite unable to imagine that a trick was being performed in such an atmosphere as that. They did not examine anything at all. Indeed, the president asked whether I was unconscious and even uttered a prayer for my soul when he heard that I was. With that, the president and the police left, deeply distressed at not having found the culprit they were after. The president swore up and down that he would deliver up the offender if he should ever run across him, and the magistrate vowed that he would hang the scoundrel, even though he might turn out to be the son of a grandee.

I got out of bed after they had left.

This story has been told countless times since then, and, indeed, it is still frequently heard.

To avoid being tedious, I shall say that I came to consider everything in the market place to be legitimate prey when I was on the hunt, and I no sooner spotted a cloth shearer's box, or a silversmith's, than I had them stowed safely away at my house. I did not spare the stalls of fruit sellers or vegetable women, either, for I had not at all forgotten about the incident that occurred when I was King of the Roosters. So with what I managed to steal I kept our house well provisioned the whole year round.

I shall say nothing at all about my raids on the vineyards and gardens in that vicinity.

Because of these and several other little frolicsome antics I became quite famous as a very sharp prankster. The young gentlemen there held me in such great esteem that I scarcely served Don Diego as I should have, though I always treated him with the utmost respect because of the deep affection he had for me.

CHAPTER VII

Concerning Don Diego's departure, the news of

my parents' death, and the resolve I made

concerning my future course of action

About this time Don Diego received a letter from his father, and it so happened that in the envelope it came in there was a letter for me too—one from my Uncle Alonso Ramplón—a man who was deeply devoted to the exercise of virtue. He was also very well known in Segovia for his strict execution of justice, for he had played an important part in every execution performed there in the course of forty years. If I am to tell the truth, then I must confess that my Uncle Alonso was the public hangman; but he had such a knack at his craft that the very sight of him in the performance of his duties gave onlookers a very itch to have him hang them too. As I was saying, this worthy person wrote me a letter from Segovia. It read as follows:

My dear Son Pablos [he loved me so much, you see, that he always addressed me as "son":

The numerous duties that I am required to perform in this position which His Majesty has given me have hitherto prevented me from writing you; for if there is any drawback to a man's serving the King, it is the work involved—although there is, to be sure, some compensation in knowing that people realize you are one of the King's own servants.

I am deeply grieved to have to inform you of something you will not be pleased to hear. Your father died a week ago—and with the greatest courage ever shown by any man in all this world. I tell you this, because I am the one who hanged him. He got right up on the donkey without using the stirrup. The frock we put over him looked as if it had been made to order. Indeed, with the crosses before him, he bore himself with such dignity that no one would ever have taken him for a man about to be hanged. He rode along completely at ease, looking up at the windows, and bowing to those who had left their work to watch him. He even went so far as to twirl his mustachios a couple of times. He told his confessors to be at ease, and applauded what they said. When he came to the gallows, he did not crawl up as a cat might have done, but firmly planting his foot on the step, he went right up, and nimbly too. When he saw that one board was cracked, he turned to the official in charge and suggested that the step should be repaired before the next victim came along, for not all men were possessed of the courage he had. I cannot possibly stress sufficiently how well your father looked to everyone there. When he reached the top, he sat down; and then pulling the folds of the frock back, he himself placed the rope around his neck. Then, seeing that the brother confessor wished to preach him a little sermon, he turned to him and said: "Father, I understand your remarks as if you had already made them. Say a little of the Credo, and let's get this business over with quickly. I have no desire to be boring." Well, no sooner said than done. He asked me to move his pointed hood a little to one side, and freshen up his beard and put it in order. This I gladly did, and then, down he dropped—without bending his legs or performing any of those other usual ugly actions people engage in at such times. He maintained such a grave countenance all the while that no one could have asked for a better performance. I afterwards cut him up and scattered his pieces along the highway. God knows how sad I feel when I think that he became the pièce de rèsistance at vultures' tables. But I feel sure that the pastry makers in this part of the country will use him for their meat pies, and thus bring some consolation to his relatives.

I have no good news to bring you of your mother, either. She is a prisoner of the Inquisition in Toledo, for, whereas scandal-mongers cause the dead to turn over in their graves, your mother, who never had a mean tongue, preferred to dig them up in person. It is further said that she had cultivated a habit of kissing the old he-goat of a devil every night—on the eye that has no pupil. At her house they found more legs, arms, and heads than there are in a chapel commemorating miracles. And besides, she was always producing counterfeit maidens and ren-ovated virgins. They tell me she is to appear in an auto-da-fe on Trinity Sunday. I am deeply affected by the dishonor she has brought upon us all—indeed, I have more of a right to feel that way than any of you, for, after all,—am I not the King's good servant? Relatives like your mother are not the sort of people who lend lustre to someone who has such a position as mine is.

My son, there are a few little things here that your parents left you—all told, I should imagine, around four hundred ducats' worth. I am your uncle, and what I have also belongs to you. This being the case, I would like to have you come here and stay with me, for with your knowledge of Latin and rhetoric you could be eminently and artistically successful as a hangman.

Write me as soon as you can, and in the meantime, God guard you well.

From Segovia, etc., etc. . . .

I cannot deny that I was deeply moved by these fresh calami-ties; but, at the same time, I did derive some pleasure from con-templating their significance. It came home to me very clearly that when the father leads a life of vice and evil the child may find some consolation in reflecting that when the man is done for, so is the vice.

I immediately ran over to Don Diego. He was still reading

that letter from his father, who therein had instructed him to leave Alcalá—and me, for he had been told about some of my recent doings. Don Diego said he would, of course, obey his father's instructions, although he was very sorry to have to leave me. He said he would find me a place with another gentleman —a friend of his.

I laughed and said to him:

"I am a new man now, and my ideas are different from what they were. From now on I should like to move up a little higher on the rungs of the social ladder and have a little more standing. If up to now I have had some little social prestige, from this time on I shall receive very positive backing."

I told Don Diego how my father had been carved up and piece-mealed. If in this life he amounted to nothing, after his death, at any rate, he may be said to have become a man of parts. I told my master everything my dear uncle had written me—all about my father and also about my mother's imprisonment—for, since my master knew everything about my background, I could tell him everything without embarrassment. He was very sorry to hear what I told him, and asked me what I intended to do. I told what I had in mind.

The next day he very sadly left for Segovia, but I stayed on at our place, trying not to show how much my misfortune had afflicted me. I burned my uncle's letter lest someone by chance might see it; and I then began to make preparations for returning to Segovia to receive my bequest and meet my relatives —and promptly run away from them.

CHAPTER VIII

Concerning my journey from Alcalá to Segovia, and what
happened along the way to Rojas, where I slept
that first night

The day finally came when I had to give up the finest way of
life I ever knew. God alone knows how moved I was when
the time came for me to leave the many friends and comrades I
had known there. I sold what little I had, and with a few well-
turned lies I managed to realize around six hundred reals on my
properties. I rented a mule and left the inn, with nothing but
my shadow as my baggage. I can never suitably relate to you the
laments of the shoemaker for the shoes he had sold me on credit,
or the disappointment of the housekeeper about her pay, or the
shouts of the landlord demanding my rent. One said: "I just
knew it would be like this. . . ." And another said: "The people
who said he was a crook were absolutely right." I finally got
away, taking with me (I should like to think) the good will of
all, for I left one half of them weeping and the other half laughing at the tears the others shed.

I whiled away the time along the road thinking all these
things over, and eventually crossed a stream called the Torote.
Here I came up to a man riding along on a pack mule. He was
talking to himself very fast. He was so deeply engrossed in conversation with himself that, even when I came alongside him,
he did not see me. I greeted him; then he greeted me. I asked
him where he was going, and after we had exchanged a few
polite observations, our conversation turned to the subject of
the Turks; and we discussed the possibility of their descent
upon us, and wondered how large the King's forces were. My
companion expressed some opinions about how to recover the
Holy Land and how to overcome Algiers; and with this I very
quickly perceived that he was completely out of his head

when it came to matters of international politics and government. We continued our conversation in the manner of rascally schemers, and finally got to talking about Flanders. At this point my companion began to sigh and said:

"Sir, that country occupies my thoughts more than it does the King's even. I must tell you that for the past fourteen years I have been working on a project which would, if it were possible for me to put it into effect (which it is not), be able to settle all our problems there."

"I would like very much," I said, "to hear about such a project, which, though so rich in promise, you still find impossible to put in practice."

"Who ever told Your Grace that it couldn't be put in practice?" he inquired. "It *can* be done. Its being impracticable is quite another matter. And if I did not fear I might bore you, I would tell you exactly what it is. But in due time the whole world shall know, for my intention is to publish it with some other little essays I have written, and in my book I shall show the King two different ways of taking Ostend."

I begged him to tell me about this strategic possibility, and so he finally pulled a large piece of paper out of his pocket. It was a map of the enemy's fortifications and ours.

"Now, if you will observe carefully," he said, "you can see that the real difficulty about all this stems from the presence of this inlet here. Therefore, what I propose to do is sponge up all the water in it and so solve the problem."

I burst out laughing when I heard this wild scheme. But he looked me straight in the eye and, unflinching, said:

"Everyone I have told my scheme to has laughed just as you did. It appears to make people feel very happy."

"Yes," I said, "it really is comforting to hear about something so new and yet so well thought out. But I might point out that whenever you sponge any of the water out of the inlet, the sea will just come right back and fill it up again."

"Nothing of the sort," he countered. "I've got that all figured out too, and I can set your mind at rest upon that score. I have, you see, thought up an invention that will lower the sea twelve fathoms all around there."

I did not dare argue with him about that. I was afraid he might tell me he had cooked up some scheme to bring the heavens down upon us. I really never saw such a crackpot in all my life! He told me that Juanelo, the famous engineer who had raised the level of the Tagus at Toledo, had not done anything particularly important compared to what *he* had in mind —which was to do the same sort of thing much more simply, and that was by means of a spell. Now, did your Lordship ever hear anything as ridiculous as that?

My friend's concluding remarks were:

"I don't intend to do anything about all this for the time being. The King must first put me in charge of the project— a position for which I am, I need not say, very well equipped. I can also show that my pedigree is completely unspotted."

With this sort of conversation we finally reached Torrejón, where my friend stopped to see his cousin.

As for myself, I moved on, almost dead from laughing at the absurd projects he had cooked up.

After some time had elapsed, I happened to see in the distance what appeared to be a man standing beside a loose mule. He seemed to be looking at a book and drawing some lines on paper with the aid of a pair of compasses. From time to time he would turn around and jump about, and he would occasionally place one finger on top of another, and then make many unusual motions with the two of them. I confess that for a long time (and I was careful to keep my distance) I thought him to be a sorcerer. That was the reason why I hesitated to pass him. However, I finally did approach him. When he saw me, he closed his book; and as he was putting his foot in the stirrup, he slipped and fell. When he got up he said: "I didn't measure the proportion right in order to make the proper circumference in rising."

I didn't understand a thing he said; and I began to dread that he was going to be what he really did turn out to be: the most absurd man that was ever born of woman. He asked me whether I was going straight to Madrid or whether I was taking a "circumflex" road; and, although I did not understand him, I answered: "circumflex." He asked whose sword I was wearing. At the time I did not realize he was interested in knowing who had made it, so I foolishly answered that it was mine. Looking at it, he said:

"Those quillons should be longer to protect you, so that you can parry the cuts that are made in the center of the rapier thrusts."

And he began to talk in such a high-flown fashion that I became curious and asked him what his profession was. He told me that he was a skilled fencer, and that he could give a good demonstration of his ability anywhere and at any time. Overcome by laughter, I said to him:

"Well, really, from what I saw you doing in that field just now—weaving your circles, I mean—I would have taken you to be a conjurer more than anything else."

"That," he said, "was because a thrust in quart had occurred to me by means of which I could fetch a greater compass and engage my adversary's sword, in order to kill him before he could say 'boo'—and no one would ever know who did it, you see. And I was just trying to work it out mathematically."

"Is it possible," I asked, "that this sort of thing is a matter of mathematics?"

"Oh my, yes," he replied. "Not only mathematics, but theology, philosophy, music, and medicine as well."

"Of one thing I have no doubt," said I, "and that is that what you are doing has a great deal to do with medicine, for that is the science of killing men."

"Don't laugh," he said, "because I am now learning an excellent guard—the 'brush-off,' I call it—which will give greater cuts that at the same time will include within their own scope the spiral movements of the sword."

"I really don't understand a word of what you have said," I told him.

"Well," he replied, "this book, which is called *The Wonders of the Sword*, tells all about these things. It is a very good book, and it tells about the most *incredible* things. And so that you will be able to understand and believe what I have just been saying, I plan tonight to show you the most marvellous things imaginable when we reach Rojas. You shall see me do wonders with two spits. Do not for a moment ever forget that if you read this book you can kill anyone in the whole world. Some great scholar wrote it. I am even tempted to put it a little stronger than that."

We continued to discourse on these matters until we reached Rojas. We dismounted before an inn, and while we were about it, my companion very vociferously advised me to make an obtuse angle with my legs, convert them into parallel lines, and then lower myself perpendicularly to the ground.

The landlord saw me laughing, and he laughed heartily too. He asked me whether that gentleman might not be a red Indian, to judge from the way he was talking. When I heard this, I almost doubled up with laughter.

My companion then approached the landlord and said to him:

"Pray, could you not lend me a couple of spits, sir? I assure you that I will return them almost immediately. I would just like to show my friend here what an hypotenuse is like."

"Well, sir," replied the landlord, "if you want to give the creatures to me, I'll have my wife roast them for your pot o' noos right away—though I will confess that I never in all my life heard of a bird called a 'noo.' "

"They aren't birds at all," my companion said to him; and turning to me, he continued: "It is unfortunate that he knows so little about things. Just let me have the spits, my good man. I only want to use them to fence with. It may be that what I am about to show you will be the most valuable thing you have ever learned in all your life."

It happened that the two spits were being used at that moment, and so we had to resort to two long ladles instead. Such absurd goings-on had never been seen before in all the long history of the world. My friend jumped way up in the air and said:

"With this motion I gain more and at the same time gain the degrees of the profile. Now I take advantage of the remiss movement to kill the natural movement. This should be a slash and this a cut."

He let me be, and went jumping all over the place with his ladle. He was not tempted to use me as the mannequin fencers often use; and so it was the pot that stood in danger of being used as a target. Finally he said to me:

"Well, you can now see very clearly that this is the really correct way to fence and you will have no time for the silly nonsense those rascally fencing masters teach. All they know how to do is drink."

He had hardly got the words out of his mouth when, with his fangs bared, a big mulatto came out of the next room. He had on a hat that was as big as an umbrella, and a buff jacket beneath a short loose cloak that was all fluttering with ribbons. He was as knock-kneed as the Imperial Eagle, and he had a great scar right across his face, which was a mask of menacing mustachios and bristling whiskers. He wore a dagger that had as much complicated metalwork on it as a nun's window.

This personage looked at the floor and said:

"I have passed my examinations in fencing, and I have my certificate; and by the sun that ripens the wheat, I will slice up in little pieces anyone who says anything against fencing masters."

I saw that trouble was brewing, and so I stepped between the two of them and told the mulatto that my friend was not referring to him at all, and so there was no reason for him to lose his temper.

The mulatto replied:

"Take out your sword—if you have one—and we shall see what good swordsmanship really is. You are convincing no one with your ladlemanship."

My poor companion opened his book and cried out:

"This is what the book says, and it was printed with the King's permission; and I will maintain that what the book says is so—with a ladle or without a ladle, here or anywhere you choose. And if you don't believe me, let us measure it!" And he took out his pair of compasses and continued: "This angle is an obtuse angle." Whereupon the fencing master took out his dagger and said: "I don't know who this Obtusangle is, nor did I ever in all my life hear such a funny name as that; but with my dagger in my hand I intend to slice you up in little slivers."

And he threw himself upon the poor fellow and began to slash away at him. My poor companion ran all around the house, crying:

"You can't touch me! I won the degrees of the profile!"

The innkeeper and the other guests and I finally quieted them down. By this time I was sick from having laughed so much.

They gave my poor friend and me a room, and we then had supper. Finally all the people at the inn went to bed.

At two o'clock in the morning my friend got up and began jumping around the room in his nightshirt, and uttering a lot of mathematical gibberish. He awakened me; but not satisfied with that, he went down and woke the innkeeper too and asked him for a light, because, he said, he had come to a clear understanding of what he called the "sagitta" thrust. The innkeeper told him to go to the devil for having awakened him, and also called him addled for having caused so much disturbance. My friend came back to our room and told me that if I would get up, he would show me a feint he had devised for use against the Turks and their scimitars. He said he felt he should show it to the King immediately, because it would certainly prove to be a mighty bulwark for the Catholic religion.

It was dawn by this time; and so we all dressed and paid for our accommodations. We made peace between my companion and the fencing master, who went his way, saying that the sword book was all right. The only thing wrong with it, he said, was that it was so incomprehensible that it produced more madmen than it did fencers.

CHAPTER IX

Concerning a poet I met on my way to Madrid

I went on to Madrid. My addled companion, who was going in a different direction, said good-by to me—although, after he had gone on only a short distance, he came back in great haste, yelling all along the way. And even though we were right out in the open country, he whispered to me:

"I must beg you never to breathe a word about the deep secrets I have confided in you about the art of fencing. You have good judgment. Therefore keep everything to yourself."

I promised to do so. With which he again moved on and left me laughing merrily.

I travelled along for more than a league without meeting anyone. I busied myself with the thought that I had suffered many hardships in my attempt to pursue a course of honor and virtue. My first task was to draw a veil of oblivion over the activities of my parents; and after that had been done, I would have to conduct myself so honorably that no one would ever suspect the kind of background I really had. I was so pleased with these thoughts that I came to have a certain feeling of gratitude toward myself, for, as I said to myself:

"I deserve all thanks for this, for I never had anyone to learn virtue from, and I was never able to have anyone direct me properly. And so, what I have done is more important than what people do who simply inherit their patterns of conduct, for I have had to work out these problems all by myself."

I was proceeding along my way with these thoughts in my head when I came across a very old clergyman riding on a mule. He at once asked me where I was from. I told him Alcalá.

"God damn all the bad people there," he said, "for there is not a single person in that town who shows the slightest intelligence."

I asked him how that could be, for Alcalá boasted the pres-

ence of many great and erudite scholars. He rejoined very angrily:

"*Scholars?* Let me tell you something, young man. For fourteen years I have been a sacristan in the town of Majalahonda
and not one single time during that long period have those
people at Alcalá given me a prize for some fine songs I have
composed on various occasions. Now, you shall see how unfair
they have been to me, for I am going to read my poems to you.
I know you are going to enjoy listening to them."

And so saying and so doing, he unsheathed a roll of pestif-
erous verses. I shall repeat one of them for you. By it you may
judge how all the rest were.

> *Shepherds, feel you not quite frisky*
> *This feast of blest Saint Corpus Christi?*
> *This is the day of happy omen*
> *When the lowly lamb sans spot*
> *Tarries not a little lot*
> *And visits our abdomen,*
> *And in this merry, joyful moment*
> *Enters in our hungry guts.*
> *Sing ye out, ye tuneful sackbuts!*
> *Let's lift high the wine and whiskey!*
> *Shepherds, feel you not quite frisky,*
> *This feast of blest Saint Corpus Christi?*

"Now what," said he when he had finished his reading,
"—now what better could the very inventor of festivious verse
have done than what I have done? Observe that word *shepherds*. Oh, that word is simply pregnant with symbolical significance. I spent more than a month studying the problem before the word *shepherds* occurred to me."

I could not help laughing at this. The peals of merriment
gushed from my eyes and nose; but in the middle of my parox-
ysm I managed to say:

"Excellent, excellent! There is only one little criticism that
I should like to make, however, and that is this: You speak of

Saint Corpus Christi, but Corpus Christi is not a saint at all, but a festival in honor of the Eucharist."

"Oh, go on!" he said, assuming I was just making a little joke. "I can very easily show you on the calendar that he has really been canonized. I would wager my very head on that."

I did not care to pursue the argument. I could hardly have done so even if I had wished to—I was exhausted from having laughed so much. I told him I thought his verses most certainly merited a prize, for I had really never heard such ingenious poesy in all my life.

"Well then," he said at once, "just listen to part of a book I have written about the eleven thousand virgins, for each of whom I have composed fifty octaves. It is perfectly delightful."

To spare myself this new castigation I besought him not to read me anything of a sacred nature. So he began to recite a play that had more acts than the road to Jerusalem has stopping places. Finally he said:

"I wrote that in just two days. This is only the first draft, too."

It must have filled five whole quires of paper. The title was *Noah's Ark,* and the conversation in it took place among various animals—roosters, mice, donkeys, foxes, wolves, and wild boars—just as if it had been a collection of Aesop's fables. I praised the plan and artistry of the piece, and he replied:

"It is all my own idea, too, for nothing quite like it has ever been done before. The most appealing thing about it is its freshness. If anyone doubts *that* I should like to see his reaction when it is performed. No. My play is surely destined to become quite famous."

"But how could such a play as yours ever be performed?" I asked. "The characters in it are all animals, and animals can't talk."

"I acknowledge," he said, "that what you say may be true, and it does indeed present a grave difficulty. But if that problem could be solved, I think the play would be perfectly marvellous. And it did occur to me once to put the words in the mouths of parrots, thrushes and magpies, and also to use monkeys in the interludes between acts."

"This is indeed a remarkable piece of work," I said.

"Oh, I've done better," he said. "I have written something for a lady I love and it is far better than this. I've done nine hundred and one sonnets and twelve quatrains." He seemed to be counting his pounds penny by penny. "And all to my lady's legs!"

I asked him whether he had ever seen his lady's legs; and he replied that he had not, because of the orders he had taken. But he added that he hoped the sonnets would turn out to have been prophetic.

Now to tell you the truth, I was really enjoying the conversation very much, but I was dreadfully afraid I would have to listen to more of his terrible verses, and so I tried to turn the conversation to other matters. I remarked that I noticed some hares along the way, and when I did, he jumped and said:

"Well, I will begin a new poem in which I compare my lady to a hare."

He was going right to work on it, so I tried to divert his attention by remarking:

"Did you notice those stars shining brightly right in the broad daylight?"

And he replied: "When I finish what I am doing, I will recite to you my Sonnet XXXIII, in which I refer to my lady as a star, for she seems to know just what is on their minds."

I was beginning to be quite put out, because I could not mention anything without the sacristan's referring to some foolishness he had written about it. I was pleased no end, therefore, when I realized that by this time we were quite close to Madrid. I expected that my friend would now be quiet to keep from being embarrassed; but it turned out quite otherwise, because he wished to have everyone know he was a poet, and so the minute we hit the city he started talking louder than ever. I begged him to stop, and reminded him that if the children of the town smelled out a poet, every vegetable stalk within the city limits would be thrown at us. I explained to him that a decree denouncing poets as madmen had just been made public. It was one that had been prepared by a former poet after he had given up his disorderly way of life. My companion became very much distressed when he heard this, and asked me to read him the document if I happened to have it with me. I promised him that I would read it to him as soon as we reached an inn.

We stopped at a place where my companion was in the habit of staying. There were more than a dozen blind men at the door. Some of them recognized my friend by his voice; others, by his smell. They welcomed him with great uproar. He embraced them all, and they asked him for a prayer in grave and sonorous verses to the Just Judge—one that would stimulate hearers to give. Others asked him to write prayers for poor souls in purgatory. Business arrangements were then discussed, and each of the blind men gave the sacristan eight reals as down payment on the poems they were to receive. He then let them go, and said to me:

"I'll make no less than three hundred reals off these blind men. So, if it is all right with you, I would like to retire a little while and compose some of the poems for them, and then after supper we shall hear that decree."

Oh wretched, miserable life! Yet none is more wretched or miserable than the life of a man who lives off the unfortunate and needy!

CHAPTER X

What I did in Madrid and what happened to me

in Cercedilla, where I stayed that night

My companion withdrew for a while to mull over the heresies and follies he intended to perpetrate on the poor blind men. Dinnertime came meanwhile, and then my friend asked me to read him the decree. For lack of anything better to do, I took it out and read it to him. I feel I should quote it here, because it seems to me that its criticisms are very apt.

Here it is:

DECREE

A CONDEMNATION OF ADDLED, INSIPID, AND EMPTY-HEADED POETS

The sacristan laughed heartily when he heard this and said: "You should have told me ahead of time what it was about! Heavens! I thought you had me in mind when you first mentioned it, but now it turns out to be directed at empty-headed poetasters!"

I was very much amused to hear him say that, for he seemed to think he was Poetry Incarnate. I omitted the prologue and started right in with the first section, which read:

"*With full cognizance on our part that the species of vermin commonly designated as poets is, notwithstanding, composed of our fellow men and Christians (although bad ones), and whereas during the course of the whole year they express their adoration of eyebrows, teeth, ribbons, hair, and slippers, and furthermore, commit other and even greater crimes,* WE COMMAND, *during that season of the year known as Holy Week, that all public poets and idlers on the corners of the thoroughfares in this commonwealth be gathered together as if they were indistinguishable from women of ill repute, and* WE *furthermore* ORDER *that they be subjected to the hearing of preachments, the contents of which shall be aimed at and directed toward the achievement of their ultimate conversion, for which purpose* WE *do hereby* DECREE *that houses of penitence be set aside; and, furthermore,*

"WHEREAS *it has come to our attention that the heavy and sultry heat which is experienced in the canicular, dogday, and unremittingly discrepuscular and denocturnalized verses of the Poets of the Sun (as dried out and desiccated as raisins, from the light and heat of their own suns and orbs),* WE IMPOSE *upon the aforementioned poets an unrelentingly perpetual and sempiternal* SILENCE *in all matters that deal with or appertain to the heavens and* WE APPOINT *certain months of the year to be called* CLOSED SEASONS *for cultivation of and communing with* MUSES, *which ladies shall, for these purposes, be considered as belonging and appertaining to the category of game and fish, in order that the number of said* MUSES *may not be decimated, diminished, or consumed to the point of vanishment. And, furthermore,*

"WHEREAS *it has come to our attention that the aforesaid infernal sect of men, which has been sentenced to perpetual conceptizing and the uninterrupted dissecting of words and the confounding of the ordinary processes of thought and reason, has gravely infected the females of our time with the fearsome plague of poetry,* WE DECLARE, *because of this evil which the aforesaid poets have perpetrated on the aforesaid females, that we have been avenged for the evil and pernicious crime which the* FIRST FEMALE *committed with the* APPLE; *and, furthermore,* WE COMMAND, *since the age in which we live is indigent and penurious, that the verses of the aforesaid poets should be* BURNED *like old rags, in order to extract therefrom the quantities of gold, silver, and pearls therein contained, for the reason that the aforesaid poets in the greater number of their compositions construct the females with whom their writings deal from different and various metals, as was the case with the statues of Nebuchadnezzar."*

Here the sacristan could not contain himself. Rising up, he said:

"No, no! That is equivalent to depriving us of our property. Go no further, sir, because I intend to appeal this case—I will go to the Pope himself and spend every penny I have, if necessary. A fine thing! That I, a churchman, should have to suffer this affront! I shall prove that the verses of a clergyman-poet are not subject to the mandates of that decree, and after that I intend to take the matter to court."

I very much wanted to laugh, but in order not to delay (for it was getting late) I said to him:

"Sir, this decree was written just for fun. It is not binding, nor can it be put in force, simply because there is no authority back of it."

"Well, sinner that I am!" he exclaimed. "You should have told me that at first! You could have spared me the greatest shock I ever had. Do you by any chance know what it is like to be a man who has composed eight hundred thousand verses and hear *that?* Well, continue, and God forgive you for the turn you have just given me."

I went on reading:

"*. . . and* WHEREAS, *having observed that after they discontinued the pernicious habit of composing Moorish ballads (although some vestiges of this art are still to be found in their works), they proceeded to try their hand at composing pastorals (because of which act flocks have wasted away and become languid from having imbibed so many tears, and they have been scorched by such ardent emotions and so dazed by the music they have heard that they no longer care to graze),* WE DO ORDAIN, *therefore, that these same persons renounce and abandon the said profession, and do hereby* ASSIGN HERMITAGES *to those of their number who might prefer seclusion and solitude, and* WE FURTHER ORDAIN *that the rest of them shall devote themselves to the occupation of muleteer.*"

"Some fairy, bugger, cuckold, harlot or Jew must have ordered such a nasty thing as that is," my companion cried. "And if I only knew who that was, I should dedicate to him a satire composed of such stanzas as would completely devastate him— or, for that matter, anyone else who chanced to read them. Now, just imagine how befitting a place a hermitage would be for me—why, I don't even have a long beard! And just feature how jolly being a muleteer would be for a buretticized and sacristanicized old fellow like me. This, sir, is very, very hard to bear."

"I have already observed, Your Grace," said I, "that these are nothing but jokes and jests. I think you ought to take them in that spirit."

I thereupon continued:

"FURTHERMORE, *and as a precautionary measure for curbing the practice of stealing and passing off the works of other authors as one's own,* WE FURTHER COMMAND *that no stanzas shall henceforth and hereinafter be brought from Aragon to Castile or from Italy to Spain, and the poet who resorts to such practices shall be condemned to walk about the streets properly dressed; and if he should by any chance relapse into the vice aforementioned,* WE ORDER *that he shall be forced to* TAKE A BATH."

My old friend enjoyed this last part immensely. (He was wearing a very soiled old cassock which was sufficiently encrusted with enough dirt and grime to bury him in; and the cloak he was wearing was so filthy you could have used it to fertilize two large farms.)

And so, chuckling to myself, I went on to inform him that the order further prescribed that:

"WOMEN *who shall fall in love with such poets shall be included among the numbers of those who are so afflicted that they hang themselves or fling themselves headlong from precipices and who, because they have taken their own lives, are not given Christian burial.*

"FURTHERMORE, *having noted the abounding number of quatrains, songs, and sonnets that have been circulating in these poetically fertile years,* WE ORDER *that those which have escaped the spice shops should be tossed without the slightest hope of appeal into privies by the bundle.*"

I finally came to the last article, which read as follows:

"*But being mercifully aware that in this republic there are three kinds of persons who are so especially wretched that they cannot live without the services of the poets aforementioned—to wit, actors, blind men, and sacristans,* IT IS THEREFORE PERMITTED *that some public journeymen may exercise this craft,* PROVIDED THAT *they secure a license therefor from the poets' guild in their vicinity—with, however, these three restrictions:*

"1. *That would-be poets shall not conclude their interludes by introducing cudgelings or devils, or end their plays with marriages; and they shall omit the usual fanfare from the action.*

"2. Blind men shall not have everything happen in Tetuán or say pleasant peas for 'present piece'; and they shall furthermore put aside these terms: 'beloved Christian,' 'brotherly' and 'points of honor.'

"3. And, furthermore, sacristans shall no longer compose carols with names in them like Gil or Pascual, or insert plays on words, or contrive pieces that may be used again and again with only a change of names.

"And, IN CONCLUSION, WE ORDER that all poets, specifically and in general, shall cease to use the names of Jupiter, Venus, Apollo, and other like gods, on penalty that if they do not so do, they shall be forced to receive those heathen deities as their mediators at the hour of their death."

All those who had heard the decree thought it very well done and asked me for copies of it. Only the sacristan was displeased with it. He began to swear by the solemn vespers, the *introitos* and the *Kyries* that the piece, because of what it said about blind men, was a satire really directed at him. But, he said, he knew his own business better than anyone else. And last of all he said:

"I am a man who has lodged in the same inn with Liñán, and I have also dined more than twice with Espinel." He went on to say that in Madrid he had been as close to Lope de Vega as he was to me and that he had likewise visited Don Alonso de Ercilla a thousand times. Furthermore, he had in his house a portrait of the "divine" Figueroa and, besides all this, he had purchased the pantaloons that Padilla discarded when he became a friar—and he still wore them, for that matter, he said, though they were in pretty poor condition. He showed them to us, and this so tickled the audience that no one would leave the inn.

It was now two o'clock and time for us to be on our way, and so we finally left Madrid. I was indeed sorry to have to take leave of my old friend.

I took the Fuenfría Pass, and the Good Lord, to keep me from entertaining evil thoughts, so willed it that I overtook a soldier, with whom I struck up a conversation. He asked me whether I had just been in Madrid, and I replied that—yes, I had been there recently but for only a short time.

"That's as much time as the place deserves," he said. "I swear to Christ that I would much rather be anywhere else—even with snow up to my middle, and weighed down by as much iron as they put in a belfry-clock, and eating wood—I'd rather be *anywhere* else just to keep from having to put up with all the tricks they play on honest men back there in Madrid."

I remarked that there were all sorts of people in Madrid, and that decent men and men of quality were highly esteemed there.

"I don't know how you can say that," he replied angrily. "I was there six months trying to get a commission, and I had no success at all, even though I have been in the Army for twenty long years and have shed my blood in the King's service—as these wounds here testify."

He showed me a span-long scar on his groin—at least, he called it a scar, though I am positive it was nothing but a swollen lymphatic gland. Then he showed me two others marks on his heels, which he said were bullet wounds. But I suspect that they were nothing but chilblains—if I may judge from the two that I have myself. He took off his hat and showed me his face. There were sixteen stitches on it and these (he said) were from a deep gash he had received along the nose. His physiognomy boasted three more scars; and all these put together caused his features to bear a striking resemblance to a map.

"I received these in my defense of Paris—in the service of my God and my King; and because of them I must ever present these disfigurements to the world. And, do you know? —I have never received anything at all in return for what I have done, except nice words—which they are very liberal with, in order to keep from making even a poor gesture of tangible return. Now, by your life!—read these documents here, and you shall see that—I swear to Christ! God's Blood!—there was never in all the world a soldier who was of such marked competence as I am."

Marked he was, but only facially. He then brought out a couple of tin boxes, which must have belonged to the person whose name he had doubtless assumed. I read them and then praised him to high heaven, and said that he really did have a better military record than either the Cid or Bernardo del Carpio.

He caught me up sharply:

"What do you mean—the Cid or Bernardo del Carpio! Why, my record is better than the record of García de Paredes and Julián Romero and I don't know who else! Why, damn it," he went on. "It was easy for them in those days—there wasn't no artillery then. Bernardo couldn't last a single hour now. I swear to God, he couldn't. You just go up Flanders-way and ask them there about the deeds of Big Snaggletooth, and you'll see what they say."

"Is that you, by any chance?" I asked.

"Is that *me*?" he asked. "Who else do you suppose it is! Don't you see how snaggle-toothed I am? But—enough, enough! It is not proper for a man to utter his own praises so much."

While we were engaged in this dialogue, we overtook an emaciated old hermit, who was riding peacefully along on his donkey. He was clad in brown clothes, and his beard was so long that it actually swept the dust.

He greeted us with the customary "Deo gratias," and began to praise the crops and the bountifulness of the Lord of which they were a manifestation.

The soldier burst out:

"Ah, yes, Father; but many a time I've seen pikes thicker about me than the wheat spikes over there. But I swear to Christ I did my little bit at the siege of Antwerp. I did indeed, God's blood!"

The hermit reproved him for swearing so much, and he replied to this admonition:

"It is sure as clear as day *you're* no soldier, Padre. If I ever stopped swearing, I would certainly not be living up to the requirements of my profession."

I was greatly amused to see him playing soldier—or what he thought was soldier. It was by that time perfectly clear to me that he was nothing but a cowardly scoundrel, for among authentic soldiers of any prominence—if, indeed, not among all—there is no more detestable vice than the custom of swearing.

By this time we had reached the foothills of the pass. The hermit began to tell his beads on a very woodpile of a rosary. Every time he said an Ave Maria he produced a thud like the sound made by croquet balls hitting against each other. The soldier, meanwhile, rode along comparing the mountain crags to castles he had seen, and pointing out the best location for strongholds and the most suitable positions for artillery.

I, for my part, said nothing, but kept looking at them, quite as suspicious of the hermit's gigantic rosary as I was of the soldier's fabrications.

The latter once said:

"I would give anything to be able to blow up a lot of this pass and perform a really good service for travellers."

In this manner we finally reached Cercedilla at nightfall. The three of us went into the inn and ordered some supper (it happened to be Friday). Then the hermit said:

"We must find something to do while we wait, for idleness is the parent of vice." And he let fall from his sleeve—a deck of cards! When I saw that and thought of all his beads, I could not keep from laughing.

The soldier said: "Why don't we have a little friendly game with stakes up to a hundred reals—that's all I have with me."

In my greediness I said I could go as high as that myself; and the hermit said he would like to be a good sport and play too. He said he had about him a little "oil for the lamp"—as he called it—two hundred reals' worth of it. I confess that I hoped to be the owl that would suck up every drop of that oil. But my luck was so bad I would never wish it on anyone but a Turk. The first game we played was something like "monte." The hermit pretended he did not know that game and asked us to teach it to him. The saintly creature let us play two rounds, and then took us both in so royally that there was not a penny left on the table. By doing so, he appointed himself our heir and inherited everything we had while we were still alive. He did not bother to pick the coins up one at a time—he just swept them in with those haunches he had for hands—a sight that was very sad to behold. He was very sly and would make it a point to lose when the stakes were low and win when the stakes were high. After every round the soldier would let out a dozen resonant *I-swear-to-God*'s and a like number of *damn-it*'s, fortified by liberal doses of *by-the-life-of*'s. While I sat there biting my nails, the friar sharpened his own on my money. He invoked every saint in the calendar; and our luck was like the Messiah— it was ever expected but it never came. After the hermit had completely fleeced us we asked him to lend us something so that we could go on playing and try to win back some of our losses; but, after having won every one of my six hundred reals and the soldier's hundred too, the hermit said that he had had enough fun, we were all brothers, and there was no need to pursue the matter further.

"Don't swear at me," he said. "I commended myself to God and He caused things to go my way—that's all."

We did not at the time realize what a cardsharp he really was, and so believed what he said. The soldier then swore to swear no more, and I did the same.

"Damn it!" cried the poor second lieutenant (for he told me at that time that he was one). "I have been among Lutherans and Moriscoes, even, and yet I was never taken in like this before."

The hermit laughed. He took out his rosary again and started to pray.

I asked our saintly companion to pay for my supper and lodging until we reached Segovia, because the two of us were absolutely broke, and he promised to do so.

When suppertime came the hermit managed to stow away [ten] eggs at one sitting. I never saw anything like it in all my life. Then he said he was going to bed. We all slept in one big

room with some other people who were there, because the
regular rooms were all taken. I went to bed in the greatest dejection. The soldier called the landlord and entrusted to his
keeping those tin boxes with his papers in them and also a
bundle of shirts that had seen better days. When we were all
in bed the friar made the sign of the cross, and the rest of us
crossed ourselves. He went right to sleep, but I could not close
my eyes, thinking over—as I was—all sorts of ways of getting
that money back again. The soldier kept talking in his sleep
about those hundred reals he had lost—as if they were not gone
for good!

Morning came, and time to get up. I asked for a light, and
they brought me one. The innkeeper then came in with the
soldier's bundle, but he had unfortunately forgotten his papers.
The poor second lieutenant then began to bring the house
down with his shouts. He said to the innkeeper:

["You're in all this to rob me too!"]

The innkeeper was so frightened that he only heard the first
part of the soldier's confused shout—"You're-in-all . . ."] The
rest of us were all shouting by this time to encourage the innkeeper to do something. So he dashed off and came right
back with three chamber pots, thinking [that he had heard the
lieutenant shout *urinal*], and that we must have all had an
attack of dysentery.

"Here," he cried, "is one for each of you. Anything else?"

The hubbub then really began. The soldier got up with his
sword in hand, and in his shirt took off after the innkeeper,
swearing he would kill him for playing a joke like that on him
and yelling that he had been at the Battles of Lepanto, the
Battle of Saint-Quentin, and others [and that he had all his
official papers with him]. We all ran after him and tried to subdue him. The innkeeper protested:

["Sir, I really thought I heard you ask for a urinal, and so I
brought you one."]

We finally managed to calm the lieutenant down, and then
we returned to our room. The hermit, through sheer fear, had
stayed in bed, saying that the commotion had indisposed him.

He paid our bills, and we left the town and proceeded towards the pass, angry that the hermit affair had turned out the way it had and that we had been unable to take his money away from him.

On our way we met a Genoese, one of those economic anti-Christs of our time here in Spain, who was going up the pass with a page behind him holding a parasol very ostentatiously over his head. We struck up a conversation with him. He could talk of nothing but money, for people like that are born with moneybags in their hands. He mentioned Besançon and said he wondered whether it was a good thing to lend money to Besançon. The soldier finally asked him who that gentleman was, and the Genoese replied:

"That is a town in Italy where businessmen ('pen-and-ink crooks' we call them here) meet to determine what the rates of exchange are going to be."

From all this we surmised that Bensançon was a center for bankers and usurers and such thieves. The Genoese went on to say that he was deeply distressed because he had lost 60,000 ducats in a recent transaction. This he swore on his conscience —although, it seems to me, conscience in a merchant is about as common as virginity in an easy woman—much advertised but nonexistent. Merchants seem to have heard that conscience needs but little provocation to sting, and so they discard it at birth and leave it behind with their umbilical cords.

We could now see the walls of Segovia ahead of us, and I will confess that I was happy to see them—although the memory of Cabra somehow watered the wine of my pleasure. I reached the town; and there at the entrance I saw my father scattered along the way and waiting to be taken in quarters and bags to the Valley of Jehosaphat [where the dead will come together on Judgment Day]. A bit affected, I went on, feeling that I was somewhat of a stranger now and that few would recognize me. I had now grown a beard, you see, and was well dressed. I took leave of my companions; and casting about in my mind to ascertain who in the town might know my uncle best, I could not think of a soul—except, perhaps, one of those persons whose heads had been exposed publicly on pillars after their execution. I approached several people and asked them if they knew Alonso Ramplón, but no one had even heard of him. I was feeling happy to see so many honest men in my town, when I happened to hear the town crier approaching very audibly, followed by uncle enthusiastically at work. Along came a procession of culprits followed by my uncle. They were bare and without hoods; and my uncle, wielding his cowhide, played a veritable passacaglia on the ribs of five living lutes—and in this musical performance no strings were used, but only ropes. I stood watching all this next to a man whom I had told I was a great gentleman (at the time I was inquiring of him whether he knew my uncle). When my esteemed relative's eyes fell on me, he rushed over to embrace me and cried: "Nephew!" I thought I would die from sheer embarrassment. I could not summon up enough courage even to wish my companion a good day as I hastily went away with my uncle.

"You can come along with us," he said, "while I take care of these people here. We'll be right back. You must come and have dinner with me today."

I was mounted and looked so beaten myself that I could certainly have been taken for one of the criminals, and so I told Uncle Alonso I would wait for him there; and then I drew aside, so frightfully embarrassed that if the recovery of my inheritance had not been at stake, I would never have spoken to him as long as I lived, or even appeared there in public again.

THE LIFE AND ADVENTURES OF DON PABLOS THE SHARPER • 155

CHAPTER XI

Concerning my uncle's hospitality and some of his

visitors. I receive my inheritance and

return to Madrid

My uncle's lodging was at a water-carrier's near the slaughter house.

We went in, and my uncle said:

"This place is not exactly palatial; but I assure you, Nephew, that it is very conveniently located to my work."

We went upstairs.

I was filled with the greatest anxiety about what might befall me at the top, for it had just occurred to me that what I was then doing was indeed very much like ascending the steps to the gallows.

We entered a room with such a low ceiling that we had to walk along with heads bowed, as though in the act of receiving a blessing. My uncle hung his whip on a nail among an assortment of ropes, lassos, knives, meat hooks, and other accouterments of his profession. He then invited me to take my cloak off and sit down. I replied that such was not my habit. God knows how greatly I was afflicted to see what a low creature my uncle really was.

He went on to say that I was very lucky to have run across him on that particular day, for I was going to be treated to a fine dinner as my reward. He had planned, he said, a special celebration and had invited some friends in for it.

At that moment one of those people who beg for souls in purgatory came in. He was dressed in a long purple robe that hung down to his very feet. He rattled his poor box and said to my uncle:

"I have made as much off my lost souls today as you have made off your lashees. Congratulate me."

They chucked each other affectionately under the chin, and then the impious beggar-for-souls-in-purgatory tucked up his robe and revealed to our gaze two knock knees and a pair of linen pantaloons. He began to dance around and ask whether Clemente had got there yet. My uncle said he had not. And then, lo and behold!—in comes a hornpipe player of the ácorny variety—a swineherd, I mean. I knew him to be such because he had in his hand a horn (and please forgive me [for reminding you of those imaginary projections that cuckolds wear on their brows]). All he really needed to do to be authentic was to take that musical object out of his hand and place it on his brow.

He greeted us, after a fashion; and then in came a left-handed, cross-eyed mulatto who was wearing a hat with a brim on it as broad as the slope of a mountain, and a crown that looked very much like the top of a walnut tree. He wore a buff jacket. The quillons of the cross guard on his sword were more numerous than sparrow hawks at a royal hunting party. His face was all slashed, stitched, and scarred. He came in and sat down; and greeting those who had already assembled, he said:

"By my faith, Romo and Gairoso certainly paid well, Alonso."

The beggar-for-souls-in-purgatory jumped up and said:

"I gave four ducats to Flechilla, the hangman at Ocaña, to goad the donkey on and not use the heavy whip when I was being thrashed."

"God lives!" said the constable, "I paid Lobuzno in Murcia handsomely; but the donkey moved along so slowly I thought it was trying to imitate a turtle; so the scoundrel kept plastering me—but it only raised welts."

And the swineherd said:

"My shoulders are still virgins." And shrugged them.

"Every dog has his day, and every pig his St. Martin's," said the beggar-for-prayers.

"I may say," said Uncle Alonso, "that among those who wield the whip I am one who will do whatever I can for those who commend themselves to me. I got sixty today, and I gave them only some little friendly caresses with the 'easy' whip."

I must confess that I blushed when I saw the sort of honest folk my uncle associated with. And I was so inept in covering up my embarrassment that the bailiff spotted me and said:

"Is this the father who had his backside dusted off the other day?"

I replied that I was not the sort of person who would ever experience the kind of punishment they were talking about.

My uncle got up and said:

"This is my nephew. He has a master's degree from the University of Alcalá, and he is a man of very elevated position."

The others begged my forgiveness and said they were my humble servants.

By this time I was dying for something to eat; and besides, I was terribly eager to get my bequest—and then flee from my uncle immediately.

They now set the table, and by tying a string to a hat they did what prisoners do to get alms from below, and so brought up a meal from a cheap restaurant located at the back of the house. The repast was delivered on remnants of plates and in portions of pitchers, and in earthen vessels. No one will ever be able to imagine how wretched and insulted I felt.

They all sat down at the table. The beggar-for-prayers appropriated the head of the table for himself, and the others took their places around it without order or ceremony.

Of the food we had I shall only say that it was all liquid. The bailiff drank my health three times—and he drank it straight; but I was careful to water my wine. The swineherd outdid us all. They seemed to have forgotten there was any such thing in the world as water—and they revealed no desire whatsoever to discover any.

There now appeared on the table five meat pies of the four-real variety. They removed the filling, and taking up an aspergillum they said a prayer for the dead, with a *requiem aeternam* for the soul of the victim who had furnished the meat for the pie. My uncle said:

"You no doubt recall, Nephew, what I wrote you about your father."

I no doubt did.

Well, they all ate, but I contented myself with the bottom part of the pie. I have since then always maintained that custom, and whenever I have meat pie I always say an Ave Maria for the salvation of the victim.

They killed off two more pitchers of wine—some half a gallon of it; and the bailiff and the beggar-for-prayers got into such a state that on the appearance of a plate of sausages looking very much like black fingers, one of them asked why they were bringing in baked joss sticks. My uncle was now in such a state that when he reached over to get one he said—and his voice was rather harsh and rough, and his eyes were swimming in new wine:

"Nephew, by-this-God's-bread, which He created in his likeness and image, I never ate anything better in all my life."

The bailiff now reached out and picked up the saltcellars and said, "This broth is hot." The swineherd took up a handful of salt and said, "This is the stuff to make you drink,"—and popped it all in his mouth. When I saw this I could not help laughing—even though I was boiling with rage below.

Then some soup came, and the prayer-fellow took up a bowl of it with both hands and said:

"God has blessed cleanliness."

Then he lifted it up towards what he thought was his mouth but what actually turned out to be his cheek, and spilled the broth all over his person. He was then a sight to behold. When he saw himself in this fix, he started to get up; but his head was pretty heavy, and so, when he tried to balance himself by holding onto the table (which was not too steady), he turned it over and gave the rest of the company a perfect shower. He said the swineherd had pushed him. The latter, when he saw the prayer-fellow practically on top of him, got up and clouted him with the (pardon me) horn. They gave each other a pretty good walloping and in the midst of the fray the prayer-fellow bit the other one on the cheek. With this and the tumblings-about and confusion, the swineherd vomited up everything he had eaten right in the face of the prayer-fellow. My uncle, who was still a little more himself than the others, asked who had brought so many gentlemen of the cloth into his house. I could see that he was beginning to see more than double. I finally separated the two and put an end to the brawl. I got the constable up off the floor, where he lay moaning and crying, and I finally got Uncle Alonso in bed, though he first insisted on bowing politely to a wooden candlestick he kept there, thinking it no doubt to be one of his guests. Then I took the horn away from the shepherd. Now that the others were asleep he wanted to play on it more than ever. He said that no one could make it produce prettier airs than he could. He said he wanted to make it compete with the organ.

At last, when they were all asleep, I went out. I spent the afternoon looking over my native region, and I even dropped by Cabra's house, where I was told that he had died of starvation. After four hours I returned home. I found one of the guests crawling about on all fours, looking for the door and saying that he could not find his house. I got him up off the floor. The others slept until eleven o'clock that night. My uncle started to stretch about then and inquired what o'clock it was. The swineherd replied that he still had a hangover and intended to sleep it off, because it was too hot and muggy to get up. The beggar-of-prayers asked where his little box was and said:

"The souls in purgatory are very happy to support me the way they do."

He started away, but instead of going to the door, he went to the window. When he saw the stars brightly shining above he started calling to the others and told them the stars were all out, even though it was only midday. He said there was a great eclipse of the sun. They all crossed themselves and kissed the floor.

When I realized what a scoundrel the beggar-for-souls really was, I was shocked no end, and decided never again to have anything to do with men of that ilk.

By this time I had had quite enough of this base, vile atmosphere, and I felt a growing urge to find my place among gentle-men and people of quality.

I took care of them one by one . . . , and then settled down the best I could on my clothes and the garments of some of those who by that time were in Glory. We spent the night in this manner, and the next morning I talked over the matter of my bequest with my uncle. He woke up and said that he felt absolutely beaten. The room itself was in a horrible condition. It looked like a pool—what with the liquids that had come from their mouths and those they had deposited there from other fountains.

My uncle finally did get up, and we talked at some length about my affairs. It was very hard for me to keep the conversa-tion going—because my uncle was such an alcoholic and so boorish. I finally managed to get him to tell me about part of my legacy, but not all; and he gave me around three hundred ducats my father had earned with his own hands and left in the keeping of a good woman [who was the ringleader of a bunch of thieves].

In order not to bore you, I will say that my uncle gave me what belonged to me except for what he had drunk up (which was no mean amount). He thought I could take the money and go ahead and get my degree, and then by applying myself I could become a cardinal and wear a red cassock. He had made so many people under his whip look like cardinals that he thought it was no great task to achieve that eminence. When I had my money safely stowed away, Uncle Alonso said:

"You should feel very guilty if you do not become somebody and make a name for yourself, because you have had [in me] a splendid model to follow. You have money, and I will always be ready to help you. Yes; all that I have, and all that I am, I place in your service."

I thanked him very much for his kind offer, and we spent the rest of the day in rather foolish conversation. When evening came my uncle and the swineherd began a game of cockal. . . . You should have seen how they played around with that cockal—catching it in mid-air and balancing it on their wrists.

. . . And, meanwhile, the pitcher was never absent from their sides.

Night came and the guests departed. My uncle went to his bed, and I went to mine—for I had provided myself with a mattress this time.

When morning came, and while Uncle Alonso was still asleep, I got up [with the intention of] going to an inn. I locked the door behind me and threw the key into a cathole and then went off to hide at an inn until I could find a way to get to Madrid. I had left in my uncle's room a sealed letter in which I announced my departure and gave my reasons for it. I told him not to try and find me, for no matter how much of eternity he might consume in seeking me out, he would never, never find me—ever.

CHAPTER XII

Concerning my departure and what happened to me

on my way to Madrid

A muleteer was leaving the inn that morning with a load of goods for Madrid. He had a donkey with him, and I rented it. I went to a gate outside the place and waited for him there. He finally came. I made myself comfortable, and then started off.

All along the road I kept saying to myself: "Stay where you are, you scoundrel, you scourge of men's honor, you hangman, you!"

When I got to thinking that I was going to Madrid (and I was very much comforted when I thought of that), I realized that I would have to rely there entirely on my own talents. I therefore decided to put away my old clothes, and get some of those new short garments that were then so much in style.

Let us for a moment return to my uncle and imagine how he reacted to my departure. He must have been terribly offended when he read my letter, which said:

Mr. Alonso Ramplón:

Since God has been so merciful as to have taken my good father unto himself and to have placed my mother safely in Toledo, where she has so much at stake (her own, I mean, when the Inquisition gets through with her), I need only one thing more to make my happiness complete; and that is to see you given the same treatment you so much enjoy giving others. It is my desire to have from this time on only one person in my family—myself, I mean. I refer to myself as "one" with some reservation, for Your Grace might after all get hold of me and make four out of me. Do not try to find me or even mention my name, for I am determined to disown any relationship to you.

Serve God and the King.

It would be quite impossible to enumerate the amount of curses and anathemas he must have poured forth upon me.

Let us now return to my trip.

I was riding along comfortably on my La Mancha donkey and in no mood at all to meet anyone, when I saw a gentleman coming along the road at a pretty good clip. He wore his cloak and his sword genteelly, and his trousers were nicely corded to his doublet. He wore boots and a big fashionable collar, and his hat sat jauntily on one side of his head. I suspected he was some gentleman who had come on ahead of his coach, and so when he came up to me I greeted him.

He looked at me and said:

"Sir Licentiate," he said, "you must be far more comfortable on that donkey than I am with all my equipment."

I thought he must be referring to the coach and servants following him. I replied:

"Actually, sir, I do find it much easier to ride this way than to have to be cooped up in a coach, and although Your Grace no doubt finds a coach more luxurious, I cannot myself quite stand the bouncings one has to put up with in coaches."

"What coach are you talking about?" he said in some concern.

And as he turned full round to look back, the cord that held his trousers up broke, and they came right off. When he saw me laughing, he asked me to lend him a string.

Then I saw that there was only a hint of shirt showing and that his tail was half exposed. I said:

"You had better wait for your servants, for I cannot help you at all. I have only enough string to keep my own self together."

"Look," he said, "if you are trying to make a joke out of this, then please stop. I just don't know what you mean when you refer to my servants."

And then he confessed to me how very poor he really was, and after a half league told me that if I did not let him get up on my donkey for a while he could not go on—he was so very weary of holding up his trousers with his hands. I was moved to compassion and got down and helped him up, for, of course, he could not let go of his trousers and get up all by himself. While I was about this I was quite surprised to discover that the back of his garment was pretty well fretted with openwork —over a background of unadulterated buttock. When he realized that I had seen what I *had* seen, he discreetly tried to explain the situation by saying:

"Sir Licentiate, not all is gold that glitters. You must surely have thought, when you saw my fancy collar and my bearing, that I was no less a personage than the Duke of Arcos or the Count of Benavante. Well, my exterior adornments serve to hide from the world what you are now palpably aware of."

I confessed to him that I had indeed formed a different idea about his social status.

"Well, you haven't seen anything yet," he said. "And there is certainly a very great deal to see in me—I have so little to cover myself with. You see before you a real authentic gentleman of an old La Montaña estate and family. And if my nobility had as much concern for me as I have for it, I would have nothing to complain about now. But no matter how good the blood is, it still has to be nourished with good bread and meat, for (God's clemency be praised!) the same red blood is the common property of us all. And an impoverished person may try his best to be a man of rank but the only thing *rank* about him will be his poverty. I realized one day how valueless my letters patent of nobility really were. On that occasion I had had nothing to eat, and yet no one at a restaurant I tried would give me a thing just because I had a pedigree. And they call those letters of gold! It would be better to use the gold to make pills with—that would at least produce *some* benefit— and, after all, there are not many letters of gold anyway. I have even had to sell the site of my grave—and so I shall have no place to fall down dead upon. You see, my father, Don Toribio Rodríguez Vallejo Gómez de Ampuero [y Albardín] (and he bore all those surnames)—my father, I was saying, once offered his estate as bail—and lost it. The only thing I now have left to sell is my right to be called Sir [but nobody particularly wants that title, for, after all, look at the commonplace things that are already called Sir: Sir Loin, Sir Mount, Sir Pass, Sir Round and Sir Render]."

I will confess that although there was something amusing about this gentleman's misfortunes, I was still rather touched when I heard about them. I asked him what his name was and where he was going and on what business. He repeated all those names his father bore—Don Toribio Rodríguez Vallejo Gómez de Ampuero [y Albardín]. It sounded like something rung by a bell, for at one end was a DIN(G) and at the other a DON(G)—[ding-dong, ding-dong, ding-dong . . .].

My companion then told me that he was going to Madrid because in a small town it was no pleasant matter to have been left as penniless as he had been. He had simply not been able to make a go of it. So he had decided to leave his province and come to the capital, where there was room for all and free meals for stomachs adventurous.

"The minute I get to Madrid," he said, "I have a hundred reals in my purse right away and a place to sleep, something to eat and a little off-color fun, for ingenuity there is like the philosopher's stone—it turns everything it touches into gold."

The future began to look very rosy to me. I begged my companion to brighten up our journey by telling me how his sort of penniless people managed to get along, and with whom—for what he had told me seemed to me to be a bit hard to believe. We are rarely content to mind only our own affairs but must concern ourselves with other peoples' too.

To which he replied:

"There are people of the one sort and people of the other. But I can tell you one thing. Flattery is the master key that wins everybody over in a town like Madrid. Now, I think you will find my statements a little more credible if you will let me tell you about my schemes and experiences there, and I think that then you will doubt no more."

CHAPTER XIII

In which the gentleman continues both his journey and the promised story of his life and habits

"The first thing you must know," he continued, "is that you will find there side by side the greatest folly and the greatest wisdom, the greatest wealth and the greatest poverty. Madrid is a place of extremes in everything. There, good men and bad men are on the surface almost indistinguishable. Furthermore, you will meet there a certain class of persons (like me) who are not known to have any past or property or family tree. We give ourselves different names. Some of us speak of ourselves as No-Account gentlemen; others call themselves Flops, Phonies, Dunghills, Long-Diets, and Hungrywolves. Our most skillful adjutant is astuteness. Our stomachs are usually empty, for it is no easy task to persuade other people to feed them. We haunt every banquet; we are the vermin in every eating house; and people entertain us only when there is no way out. We have little but air to thrive on, but we are really not unhappy. We are the kind of people who eat leeks and pretend they are capons. Whenever you come to see us you will find the floors of our rooms covered with chicken and mutton bones and fruit peelings. The doorways are all cluttered up with hen and capon feathers and rabbit fur. We go around town nights and collect all this rubbish in order to show it off by day. When a guest enters our place we act very much annoyed and say: 'I simply cannot get that maid to sweep the place up properly. I do hope you will forgive me for having such a mess; but some friends of mine were over here for dinner, and . . . well, you know how servants are these days . . .' or something of the sort. If our company does not know what we really are like, they believe what we tell them—that we honestly did have a feast there.

"Now shall I tell you about the way we manage to dine in other people's houses? It does not take us very long to find out where our acquaintances live, and then we call on one of them right at dinnertime—just at the moment he is about to sit down at the table. We pretend we have come to pay our respects to one of such incomparable wisdom and nobility. And if we are asked whether we have dined we say no in case our host has not begun his dinner; and then if the people there invite us to sit down, we accept without any further pressing at all, for on some occasions when we have shown some reticence about accepting we have had to pay for our deference by not being pressed any further, and have so kept inordinate fasts. In case dinner is in progress we say we have already dined and compliment our host on his dexterity in carving the fowl, the bread, the meat, or whatever else he happens to be carving. In order to sneak in a bite of it we go on to say: 'Why don't you let me be your chief waiter, Sir? You know, my lord the Duke (or Count or Marquis) of So-and-So (God guard him in heaven!) used to say to me: 'I would go without eating any time just to watch you carve!' Then we cut off the bits of the meat and finally say: 'How good it smells! It would really be quite an insult to the cook if I did not just taste it. How well turned it is! What wonderful seasoning!' And suiting our actions to our words we down a whole half plate of the meat under the pretext of *sampling* it. Down goes the turnip—just because it is such excellent turnip, and the pork just because it is such excellent pork, and so on. When this doesn't work we can always get a handout in the soup line at some monastery or other, but we are very particular not to be seen eating it out in the open. We hope, you see, to make the friars think we are eating more because of piety than from actual need.

"You really should see one of us," he continued, "at a gambling house, and watch how obsequiously we bring the candles and snuff them, how genteelly we bring in the chamber pots, and how skilfully we fix the cards and praise the winner's takings—and all for one wretched real.

"For our own purposes we know by heart the addresses of all the old secondhand shops; and, just as people elsewhere have fixed times during the day for prayers, so have we fixed hours for patching up our clothes. You should see us in the mornings. We are, of course, at war with the sun for showing up our patches, tatters, and stitches. At any rate, we spread our legs apart and watch to see from our shadows whether there are any tears or unravellings between our legs, and if there are we clip them off with the scissors. And since the wear and tear on our clothes between our legs is our biggest problem, we cut out scraps of cloth from the rear in order to cover up the front; but usually our backsides are in a very peaceful condition, for when there is no sword play on our part back there, they seem at times to be just 'felt.' Only our cloaks are in on the secret; and so we are very skittish when windy days come along; and we are also very careful about going up open stairs or getting on horseback. We make it a point to stand where the light is to our advantage, and we bow only from the ankles, because if we open our knees, all our openwork stares out. There is nothing on our bodies that at some time or other was not something else. Everything we have has an historical flavor about it. For example—look at this garment here. In the beginning it was a pair of pantaloons—the granddaughter of a cape and the great-granddaughter of an old cloak—its family history goes that far back. And it is expecting soon to be used to patch the bottom of my hose, or something of that sort. The interlining of my socks was at one time a kerchief, and before that a pillow sham, a shirt—the daughter of sheets. And finally we use our shreds and tatters for paper to write on, and then we make powder out of the paper and give new life to our shoes with it—I have, indeed, seen innumerable shoes reborn after such treatment. I need not tell you that at night we shy away from lights that might reveal our bald short cloaks and our beardless doublets, for there is no more nap on them than on a pebble. God's mercy has, you see, given us plenty of nap on our faces but none on our clothes. And we spend nothing on barbers, either. We always wait until one of our fellows has a heavy growth of hair and we then cut each other's hair, and by so doing carry out the instruction of Holy Gospel that men should come to each other's aid like unto good brothers. And we are careful not to intrude on one another's territory by visiting someone when he is entertaining people we know, even though our stomachs are, you might say, in heat.

"Once a month we feel it incumbent upon us to ride through the streets, even though it is only on a donkey, and we must also be seen at least once in that period riding in a coach, even though it is only on the chest in the back. And if we ever do chance to ride inside we take our places at the door and stick our necks way out, nodding and bowing to attract universal attention. We call to our friends and acquaintances, even though they happen to be looking elsewhere.

"If the desire to scratch ourselves overcomes us in the presence of ladies we have all sorts of ways of disguising what we really do. For example, if our thigh itches we talk about a soldier we once saw who was wounded down there and we then pretend to indicate the part of the body where the wound was given—and scratch like mad all the while. If we feel an urge in church to scratch our chests, why, we make movements with our arms more in keeping with the *santos* than with the *introibo*. And if our back starts itching we stand against the corner of a house, and moving up and down as if we were trying hard to see something, we scratch our fill.

"As for lying, I may say that the truth is an utter stranger to our mouths. We always manage to bring dukes and counts into our conversations, and sometimes we call them our friends, and at other times we say they are relatives of ours. We naturally make sure that those gentlemen aforesaid are either dead or distant. There is one thing we are always particularly sure to do and that is we never fall in love unless we get some reward out of it. Our code does not allow us to have any dealings with genteel ladies, no matter how charming they may be. We are therefore always on very good terms with the hostesses in restaurants who feed us, landladies who lodge us, and laundresses of big collars who do our laundry. Still, a man eats poorly and lives very badly even though he does have so many women indebted to him. This matter of indebtedness is something of a problem in itself; but, you know, by taking the girls on in shifts, you can somehow keep them all happy.

"Anyone looking at my boots would never suspect I wore no stockings under them; nor would anyone ever guess that this collar had no shirt to support it. Well, a gentleman may do without all those ordinary garments, but he can never get along without one of these big starched collars. Those are splendid adornments for one's person; and then after you try one of them in a variety of positions, you will find that it can also be used as food, for the starch in it is very nourishing. In brief, Licentiate, we are missing more things than the periods missed by a pregnant woman in nine months. One day we are well-off and on top of the world; the next we are in the poorhouse. At any rate, we manage to live; and, after all, anyone who succeeds in making ends meet is a king, no matter how little he really has."

I was so happy to hear about the entertaining gentleman's odd way of making a living that I let him ride on my donkey and, myself, walked on until we reached Rozas, where we stopped for the night.

My companion had dinner with me that evening. He had never a penny on him, and so I felt obliged to repay him for the way he had briefed me. I now thought I could see my way clear in many matters, and that included leading a life of knavery. Before we went to bed, I told him what my intentions were. He embraced me any number of times and said it had ever been his fond hope that his observations would impress a man who had such sound judgment as I had. He offered me his services and said he would help me find a home among the members of the swindle-crowd in Madrid. I accepted his offer, but took care not to tell him about the crowns I had on me. I limited myself to saying that I had only a hundred reals; and that, together with what I had done, and was doing, was sufficient to win his friendship.

I bought three strips of leather, and my companion tied up his trousers with them. We slept there that night, got up early the following morning, and were soon in Madrid.

CHAPTER XIV

What happened in Madrid between the time we arrived

there and nightfall

We entered the capital at ten that morning. We alighted at the home of Don Toribio's friends, and went up to the door and knocked. A little and very old lady answered the door. My companion asked for his friends, and the old creature replied that they had gone out "on business." The two of us were then alone until twelve, and he used the time to whet my appetite for the easygoing life. I listened all the while with the greatest attention. At twelve-thirty a ghostly phantom entered the place. He had on a baize outfit that reached to the ground, and it was more worn and threadbare than his recondite parts. My companion spoke to him in thieves' jargon, and as a result he gave me a big hug and placed himself at my service. We chatted a while and then he took out a glove, sixteen reals, and a letter which had garnered the latter for him (for it said that he had permission to beg for a poor woman). When he had emptied one glove he took out the other and then folded the two of them the way doctors do. I asked him why he did not put them on, and he replied that he couldn't—they both belonged to the same hand. This, he added, was the only possible way he had of sporting two gloves.

I noticed during all this that he was still bundled up, and in the ignorance of my novitiate I asked him the reason why he was always muffled up in his cape that way. He answered:

"My boy, I have a regular cathole right down my back and also a flannel patch and an oil spot. I stay bundled up this way to hide all that, and still get around."

He then opened up his cape, and I observed that underneath it there was a big bulk of something. I thought that it was his pantaloons, because it looked something like that; but when he decided to delouse himself and tucked up his frock, I saw the bulk was made up of two cardboard disks that he had somehow tied around his waist and fitted about his thighs to make it look as if he really had pantaloons on. But under his somber garb he actually had on neither shirt nor trousers. And so he actually had very few clothes to delouse. He went into the delousery and hung out a little sign like those placed on sacristies to keep people out, and it read "DELOUSER WITHIN." I thanked God most heartily when I stopped to think that even though He had not bestowed great wealth on some men, He had still been very liberal with His gifts of craft and cunning.

"That trip was pretty hard on my trousers," my companion said. "I find that they are now in need of repair."

He asked whether there was anything around he could use for patches. The old lady said there was not; and this in spite of the fact that she spent two days a week picking up bits of castoff cloth in the street, the way paper manufacturers do; and with that scavenging she managed to supply some of the terrible needs her gentlemen had. She went on to say that Don Lorenzo Iñiguez del Pedroso had had to stay in bed for two weeks because there was nothing to patch him up with.

We were engaged in all this when in came a fellow in riding boots and a brown outfit, and wearing a hat with the brim pulled up on both sides. He heard from the others there about my arrival and spoke to me very cordially. He took off his cloak—and who would ever have believed it?—he displayed a

doublet of brown stuff in front and white canvas in the back—
I should have said canvas sweat. I could not help laughing at
all this, and he said indulgently:

"You'll soon get used to it, and then you won't laugh. I'll
bet you don't know why I wear my hat brim fastened up like
this."

I said I supposed he did it to look dashing or perhaps because
it gave a better view that way.

"Not at all," says he. "It gives a worse view—to other people,
I mean. Which is the way I like it. The truth of the matter is
that I have no hatband, so when I pin it up this way no one
can tell whether my hat has a band around it or not."

And saying this, he produced twenty letters and a like number
of reals, and remarked that he had not been able to get rid of
the letters. The postage due on them was one real per letter—
and he had written them all himself. You see, he would put
on the outside any name he fancied—and the names he chose
belonged to people of importance. And then he would deliver
the letters and collect the postage due. This he did every month.

I found this trick quite a fascinating illustration of the kind
of life those fellows led.

Two more of them came in about then. One of them was
wearing a cloth doublet that reached half way down his
breeches, a cloak of the same stuff with the collar up so you
could not see the coarse linen, which was torn. His breeches
were of camlet—that is, all you could see of them. The rest was
of red baize. He was arguing with the other fellow, who was
wearing a Vandyke collar and not the big, fashionable starched
kind. He had on one of those belts worn diagonally from shoulder to hip, and it was adorned with powder flasks. All this in
lieu of cape. He was carrying a crutch, and one of his legs
was covered with rags, because though he had two legs himself,
his trousers had only one. He was playing soldier—and he had
been one, as a matter of fact, though a poor sort and on quiet
fronts. He was in the habit of recounting his extraordinary exploits, and assumed it was his prerogative to get in anywhere

he chose to. The fellow in the doublet and quasi pantaloons was saying:

"You owe me half of that—at least, a goodly share of it, and if you don't give it to me, I swear to God. . . ."

"Don't go swearing to God," the other one said; "for the minute we get home I won't be a cripple any longer, and I'll beat the hell out of you with this crutch."

Then followed the usual you-will's and I-won't and the customary you-lie's; and then they laid hold of each other—and at the first tugs their hands were full of each other's rags. We put an end to the fight and asked them what it had all been about. The soldier said:

"Don't you go playing around with me! You'll never even get half of it. Gentlemen, you must understand that today when I was at San Salvador a little boy came up to this wretched creature and asked him whether I was Lieutenant Juan de Lorenzana, and this fellow replied that I was, for he had seen that the child was carrying something he wished to deliver. He brought him over to me and, addressing me as 'Lieutenant', said: 'This lad here has something for you.' I caught on at once and said I was the officer in question. I accepted the message and with it twelve handkerchiefs. I sent off a reply to the boy's mother, who had obviously sent the stuff to someone by the name of Lorenzana. Now this scoundrel here is asking me for half of the take; but I had rather be torn to pieces than give it to him. My nose, and my nose alone, shall wear these handkerchiefs out."

The verdict was returned in favor of the defendant, but one reservation was made. He was forbidden to blow his nose in the handkerchiefs, and he was directed to deposit them with the old dame for the greater glory of the company, for she could make some collars and sleeve ends out of them that would cause people to think our members were wearing complete shirts. Nose blowing was forbidden in our order except in the air and with the assistance of the fingers.

And so this affair was brought to a happy close.

You should have seen us that night all sleeping in two beds—so bunched up together that we looked very much like tools in a box. There was not the slightest hint about having supper. Most of the community did not bother to undress—if, indeed, they could have—there was so little to take off; and so, dressed just as they had been all day, they may be said to have faithfully obeyed the precept that requires us to sleep at night with nothing on.

CHAPTER XV

In which the previous matter continues; and

of strange events

The Lord dawned a new day, and we all came to life.

By this time I was so much at home there that I felt we were all brothers—for bad things always have something smooth and easy-going about them.

You should have seen one of my friends putting on his shirt that morning. He tried twelve times—there were just twelve pieces to it. And he pronounced a prayer for each piece of shirt just the way a priest does when he is putting on the different parts of his vestment. One of them kept trying to get *his* leg down the leg of his pants, but he kept having difficulty getting his foot to come out in the right place. Another tried in vain for half an hour to work out a scheme for getting his doublet on; but he finally gave up.

When this preliminary stage of dressing was over, they all found needle and thread and began to exercise them in the attempt to sew up some of their tears. They had to assume some pretty strange postures to get at their innumerable holes. The old dame stood by, and handed them the assortment of many-colored rags and patches that the soldier had brought home.

When mendingtime was over (for such they called it), they milled about awhile giving each other the once-over and a final check. Then they prepared to go out. I asked them if they would mind planning a costume for me, and told them I could go as high as a hundred reals for one, for I very much wanted to be rid of my student's cassock.

"No, no," they said in one accord. "Put the money in the treasury and we'll dress him from the reserves. Then we can show him his diocese here in town. That will be his and his alone to pillage and exploit."

I accepted the plan, deposited my money, and in a very short jiffy they had turned my cassock into a thick mourning outfit; and cutting down my short cloak, they gave it a proper look. The leftovers were transferred onto an old redyed hat, and for additional decoration they applied some inkstand cotton to it. They took my collar and trousers away from me and gave me some of those trousers that you hook onto your doublet. My lower garment had slashes only in front, because the sides and back were made of chamois skin. My hose were only half hose, for they stopped four inches short of the knee, and the open territory there was bridged over by a tight boot on top of my red hose. My collar was of the big, fashionable, "open" kind; and open it really was—it was so ragged and torn.

This was the way they dressed me.

"The collar is a bit decrepit on the sides and in the back, so if anyone decides to look at you, be sure you make him look you straight in the eye, as a flower looks at the sun; and if two people chance to look at you from the sides, retire gracefully without turning your back; and just so no one can see what you look like in the rear, keep your hat pulled down on the back of your neck so that the brim will hide your neck and at the same time bare your brow. And if anyone asks you why you wear your hat that way, say that you like to have your face uncovered for all the world to see."

They then gave me a pouch containing some black and white thread, silk, twine, needles, a thimble, a knife, cloth, linen, satin, and other scraps of such stuff. Then they put a [tag] on my waistband and some flint and tinder in a leather pouch, saying:

"With these you may roam the world from end to end and have no need of kith or kin. Herein you have all the accouterments we ever need. Take them and guard them well."

They assigned me the quarter of San Luis as my particular bailiwick; and so, leaving the house with the others, I began my day; and in my novitiate they gave me as my sponsor in the racket the comrade who had brought me to them and converted me. This was very like what happens when a priest says mass for the first time.

We left the house at a slow pace. We had rosaries in our hands, and we proceeded to the diocese designated for me. We graciously greeted the people we met, and lifted our hats to the gentlemen. (We would have liked very much to lift their capes right off their backs.) We made our bows to the womenfolk, who always delight to be so greeted. To one person my sponsor would say: "I'm getting some money tomorrow." To another: "Can you give me one more day? The money changer keeps stalling." One of them asked him for his cape; and another, for his waistband. I very quickly came to the conclusion that he was so much a friend of his friends that he had nothing at all to call his own.

We moved on, zigzagging from one side of the street to the other to keep from running into his creditors. One of them asked him for the rent on his house; another, the rent for his sword; another, the rent for his sheets and shirts. I perceived that everything about this gentleman was as "rent" [as his garments were].

It happened that in the distance he spotted a man who was, he said, pressing him so much for a debt that he was practically gouging his eyes out. Now, to escape detection, my companion let his hair down from back of his ears—which made him look like a Nazarine—half Veronica, half Knight of the Fleece. Then he put a patch over one eye and began talking to me in Italian. The other fellow, who had been talking to an old lady—

and so had unwittingly given my companion just enough time to get his act ready—then came up (and I speak truly) moved round and round my friend like a dog getting ready to lie down. He made more signs of the cross than a faith healer and said:

"Lord Jesus! I'd have sworn that was the fellow. Well, 'when you've lost a belled [sheep], you hear bells in your sleep.'"

I stood there dying with laughter to see the figure cut by my companion. He went into a doorway to rearrange his hair and take off the patch.

"These are the trappings you need to get out of paying your debts," he said. "Reflect on what you have seen, for by and by you shall see innumerable things of this sort around here."

We moved on towards a street corner where for breakfast we got two slices of preserved fruit and some brandy. A lady pica-roon there let us have it free. She gave my friend and counsellor a nice welcome and then turned to me and said:

"With this you need not worry about food for the rest of the day. At least, with this for breakfast you won't exactly have to fast all day."

When I heard this I was greatly afflicted, and I let my stomach speak up for me. She answered:

"You seem to have little faith in the Order of the Famished. The Lord forgets neither rooks nor ravens, or notaries, either, for that matter. Will He therefore fail the feeble and the famished? How little stomach the man has!"

"Yes," I said; "and I fear I may have even less, and less in it."

We were about this when it struck twelve; and since I was new to these ways, my stomach was not at all satisfied with the preserved fruit, and I was just as hungry as if I had eaten nothing at all. When the sound of the clock reminded me of my empty condition, I turned to my friend and said:

"Brother, hunger is a hard novitiate. Man was made to eat good food and fill his crop, and yet you people have gone and put me on a fast. You perhaps do not feel your hunger as sharply as I feel mine, for you must have been brought up on it, just as King Mithridates of Pontus immunized himself against poison by taking a bit of it every day or so. So you must be more or less immune to hunger. I do not observe in a one of you any itch to exercise your jaws, so I have decided to do for myself whatever I can."

"God's body!" he said. "It is only twelve o'clock and you are in a hurry to *eat?* Your longings are, I must say, mightily punctual and peremptory. Well, they had better get used to running somewhat behind schedule. What you want to do? Eat like a beast all day long? None of *our* gentlemen has ever had the dysentery, I can tell you. Because our hunger is never relieved, we never have to relieve ourselves. I have told you that God forgets no one; but if you are in such a rush, then I am going to get some soup at San Jerónimo's, where the fat friars hang out; and I'll stuff myself there. If you want to go with me, then come along. If not—each to his adventures."

"Well then, good-by," I said. "My needs are not so small that they can easily be supplied by other people's leftovers. Let us then each follow his own course."

My friend was moving along stiffly, looking down at his feet. He took out a little box that contained some crumbs of bread (he carried it with him on purpose), and scattered them over his beard and clothes to make people think he had eaten. As for myself, I picked my teeth, shook the crumbs out of my beard and off my cloak to present some evidence that there had been a dinner—though the only ones who had really dined were my lice.

I could, of course, have fallen back on my gold crowns, but my conscience balked when it thought of letting me eat at my own expense and against the rules of our order, which prescribed that our insides must always be freebooters; but bit by bit I came to the conclusion that I must break my fast, and at any price.

By this time I had reached the corner of a street called San Luis, where a pastry maker did business. One of the browned eight-maravedí pies made its appearance before me, and the fragrant aroma issuing from the oven made me prick up my nostrils. I immediately assumed the stance of a pointer scenting game. And I fixed my burning gaze on that lush viand so intently that it simply shrivelled up, like a child transfixed by the evil eye. You can imagine the schemes I started cooking up in my head to get that sweet pie. Then again, I felt like breaking down and paying for it. It struck one just then, and I felt so distressed that I decided to go into a nearby restaurant. And while I was trying to decide for sure what I ought to do, God so ordered matters that I ran into an old acquaintance of mine by the name of Licentiate Flechilla, who came swishing down the street—a mass of spots, splashes, and pimples. He rushed over to me the minute he recognized me—and it was surprising he did recognize me, considering the way I looked. I embraced him and he asked me how I was.

"Oh, Licentiate!" I said. "I have so much to tell you. And, believe me, I am sorry to have to tell you that I am leaving town tonight, and I won't have time to have a nice long talk with you."

"I am certainly sorry to hear that," he replied. "If I were not in a hurry to keep a dinner engagement with my sister and her husband, I would certainly like to stop and chat with you."

"What! Doña Ana in town? I must put everything else out of my mind and go immediately and pay her my respects."

My eyes fairly danced with joy when I heard he had not eaten. I went along with him, and on the way told him about a little lady he had been very fond of at Alcalá. I said I knew where she was, and could give him an entrance to her house. He was quite taken by my offer (which was, of course, a pure fabrication to hold his interest). We continued talking in these terms until we reached his house. When I saw his sister and her husband, I protested to high heaven that I was their most humble servant. They took it for granted that I had been invited to dinner—otherwise, I would hardly have come at that time of day; and they said that if they had known they were to have such a guest they would have prepared for me properly. I seized the occasion and invited myself, saying I was almost one of the family and an old friend and that my feelings would be hurt if they insisted on treating me with the least bit of formality. We all sat down at table; and I managed to make my friend forget that he had really not invited me to dinner at all (it had not even crossed his mind to do so) by talking to him about his little lady. I whispered to him that she had asked about him—plus a host of similar lies. This made him feel a little more benevolently towards me when I began to engulf the food, for when the first course came—[it was a fruit course, as usual], I wreaked more havoc on it than a plague of fruit flies could have done. When the stew came, I quite unasham-edly downed almost every bit of it, in two gulps and in such fierce haste that it did not even pause at my teeth. As God is my father, I dispatched that meal posthaste and in less time than the earth in the cemetery of Nuestra Señora de la Antigua in Valladolid needs to devour bodies buried in it. My friends could not have helped observing my fierce gulping down of the broth, how I sopped the soup bowl bare, how I persecuted and pursued the bones, laid waste the meat, and then, half jokingly, lined my pockets with crusts of leftover bread. The table was cleared, and the Licentiate and I talked over our plans for going to see the little lady. I made it seem very easy for him. But while we were standing talking near the window, I pretended to hear someone calling me from the street.

"Are you calling me, ma'am?" I said. "Good. I'll be right down."

I begged to be excused and said I would be right back.

He has been waiting for me ever since. As far as I was con-cerned that party was over forever.

The Licentiate and I ran into each other any number of times after that, but I always apologized with innumerable lies. But that does not concern us here.

Well, I wandered on down the street. When I reached the Guadalajara Gate I sat down on one of those benches store-keepers place at the doors of their shops. It happened that just then I witnessed the arrival of two women of the sort who have only their faces to give as security. They were accom-panied by the usual old duenna and a little page, and they were muffled up so that only one eye was showing. They asked me whether there was any [sheer muslin] in stock. To start a conversation I made some bad puns on those words, and what had started as sheer muslin ended up as sheer nonsense.

I sensed that the liberty I had taken had given them some surety that they would be offered something there; so, since I had nothing to lose, I offered them anything they cared to ask for. They haggled about it, saying they could not take anything from a stranger. I said that it was a bit overbold of me to have offered to give them anything at all, but that I did hope they would do me the favor of accepting some Milan cloth which I would send them that evening by one of my pages. I pointed to a page with cowl off standing on the other side of the street waiting for his master, who was in another shop. And to make them think I was a man of parts and had many acquaintances I stood there doffing my hat to all the gentlemen and judges who went past; and although I knew not a one of them I pretended we were the very best of friends. They were very much impressed by all this—and even more so by the hundred gold crowns I took out of my store on the pretext of giving alms to a beggar who had just then asked me for something. Then they said that they felt they should be going, and excused themselves, reminding me that the page was to come very secretly. I spied a gold-encased rosary that the prettiest of the girls was wearing, and as if in jest I asked for it as a pledge that they would see me again on the following day. They hesitated about giving it to me; and then I offered them the hundred crowns as my own pledge. They told me where they lived, hoping thereby to fleece me even more. Having by now taken me into their confidence, they asked me where I lived, remarking that they could not receive a page at just any time of day, because they were people of importance. I took them down Calle Mayor and we turned into Carretas Street. I picked out the house that looked the biggest and most impressive to me. There was a coach without horses standing before the door. I told my friends that this was my house, and that coach and owner were at their service. I gave myself the name of Don Alvaro de Córdoba.

I recall now, too, that as we were leaving the shop I called to one of the pages and pretended to tell him to have my people wait for me there. At least, that is what I told the girls I said to him. But actually, I had inquired of him whether he happened to be a servant of my uncle the Comendador. And of course he said no. In that way I made use of other people's servants just the way a real gentleman would do.

Night came on—a dark one it was—and we repaired to our lodging. I went in and found the ragged soldier holding a big candle someone had given him during a funeral procession. He had just kept it and brought it home.

This fellow's name was Marguso, and he was a native of Olías [del Rey in the Province of Toledo]. He had played the part of a Captain in a play, and had fought with Moors—in a dance. He always told people from Flanders that he had been in China, and he told people from China that he had been in Flanders. He was always talking about [being in the field, but his only interest in fields was as a place to sow wild oats]. He was always talking about castles too, but he had never seen a castle—not even one on an ochavo-coin. He was fond of evoking the memory of Don Juan of Austria, and he made many references to the counsellor Luis Quijada, who, he said, had been a devoted friend of his. He liked to mention Turks, galleons, and great military men—but he got all his information from some popular songs written about such matters. The only naval encounter he had experienced was [with the lice and fleas around his umbilicus]. He knew absolutely nothing about the sea and when he spoke of Don Juan of Austria and Lepanto, he revealed that he had not the slightest idea about Lepanto being a strait, because he said Lepanto was a very valiant *Moor*.

We had some good times with him.

My companion now came home with his nose flattened out and his head all bandaged up. He was covered all over with blood, and he was dirty. We asked him what had happened, and he said he had gone for soup at San Jerónimo's, and that he had asked for a double portion, saying that it was for some worthy poor people. In order to give him what he had asked for, the people there had to take some away from the portion usually allotted to the other beggars. Well, the latter followed him and found him behind a door gulping it all down; and so they began to argue about whether it was right for him to take the soup out of *their* mouths and eat it all himself. The argument degenerated into a brawl, and he received a good number of welts and bruises on his poor head. They cudgeled him about the head with their pitchers, and his nose took a beating from a wooden bowl that one of his opponents made him smell a little too precipitously. They also took his sword away from him. The doorkeeper came out to see what all the noise was about, but he was unable to calm them down. My poor friend eventually saw himself in such great danger that he said: "I will return everything I have eaten." But even that was not enough to pacify the other beggars, because what they most resented was his being ashamed to be thought one of their company.

One of those run-down students who carry a basket to put alms in was present and said:

"Look at his rags! Just like a girl's rag doll, drabber than a pastry maker's shop during Lent, with more holes in him than a flute, and more splotches than a dappled mare, more spots and specks than jasper, more mending than [his ways need]! Why, you could have had a man in the blessed soup line who could be a bishop, and yet this Mr. Down-and-Out feels it below his dignity to eat with us. I myself have a Bachelor's degree from the University of Sigüenza."

The doorkeeper got in between them when he heard a little old man say that he came to get his handout even though he was a descendant of Gonzalo Fernández de Córdoba, the Great Captain.

I want to drop this matter here, because my companion had by this time finally got his bones safely free from that fierce and frightful fray.

CHAPTER XVI

In which the same matter is continued, until

we all finally ended up in jail

Merlo Díaz now came home, his waistband a very necklace of glasses and vases he had snitched from the wickets of some nuns who dispensed water. With little of the fear of the Lord in him, he simply kept his haul. But Don Lorenzo del Pedroso had outdone him. He came home with a very nice cape he had taken at a pool table, where he had left his own in exchange. The victim's [guardian angel must have been taking a nap at that time,] for our companion certainly left none on that shiny cape of his. This gentleman of ours had a neat habit of taking off his cape as if he intended to play, and then he would lay it with the others; and then, as if he had not been able to find anyone to play with him, he would go and get his cape; but he would take the best-looking one there, and then leave. He liked to play this trick at bowling and croquet games.

But all this was as nothing compared to the way Don Cosme looked when he came home. He was surrounded by a troop of boys with scrofula, malignant cankers, and leprosy—some disabled, some crippled. Our friend had chosen to be a faith healer and used some mysterious rituals and the prayers an old woman had taught him. He took in more than any of the rest of the crew, because he said there was nothing doing unless he could see that the patient had something bulky under his cape, or he could hear the jingling of coins in the sick man's pocket or the chirping of chickens and capons in the background. He had by these means laid waste half the kingdom. He made people believe anything he wished, for he was an absolute expert in the craft of lying. He was so wonderfully good at that art that he never once slipped and told the truth. He talked a lot about the Child Jesus; would enter people's homes with a *Deo gratias* on his lips, and a "May the Holy Spirit abide with you

all." He carried upon him all the appurtenances and parapher-
nalia of hypocrisy: a rosary of elephantine beads, and he would
see to it that people saw under his cape a piece of a scourge
splattered with blood (from his nose). When he scratched himself he pretended that it was because of the haircloth he was
supposed to be wearing, and not his fleas. His ravenous hunger
he pretended came from voluntary fasting. He recounted temp-
tations; and when he named the devil he would say: "God free
us and protect us." He would kiss the ground when he entered
a church; called himself unworthy. He never lifted his eyes to
women; but this static modesty did not exclude skirts. He thus
bore himself in such a manner that everybody in town was under
his orders—which was like being commanded by the devil himself. Besides being a gambler he was a cheat. He sometimes took
the Lord's name in vain—in vain. As for the women in his
life—well, he had six children already, and two saints' caretak-
ers pregnant. To put it briefly, if he did not exactly break all
the Ten Commandments, he certainly left them rather frac-
tured.

Then in came Polanco making a big noise and asking for his
brown "sack," his big cross, his long false beard and his bell.
He went about by night in this garb, saying: "Remember—ye
die; therefore do good to those souls that are already in
purgatory." With this, the alms came flowing in. When he saw
doors open he would go right inside the houses, and if no one
was present he would steal his fill; but if he was caught at it,
he would ring his bell and say: "Remember—ye die," etc., etc.

I learned all about these tricks and odd ruses during that
month.

Let us now return to the matter of that rosary. I showed it to
my friends, and they heartily applauded my ruse. The old lady
took it over and indicated she would sell it. She took it from
house to house saying it belonged to a poor young woman who
had been forced by hunger to put it up for sale. She had her lies
and tricks ready for every occasion. She wept at every step she
took, clasped her hands together, and most bitterly sighed. She
called everyone her son or daughter; and over a good waist,

jacket, underclothes, the usual skirts, and an outer skirt, she wore a sackcloth mantle that belonged to a hermit friend of hers out in the hills of Alcalá. She managed the congregation, gave us counsel, and covered up for us.

However, as the devil would have it (and he is never idle when his servants are concerned) it so happened that when she once went out to sell clothes someone recognized as his very own some of the goods she had, and called a bailiff, who forthwith arrested Mother Lepruscas—"Mother Ivyvine" we called her.

She immediately confessed her guilt, and revealed how we all lived, and referred to us as Gentlemen Plunderers. The bailiff deposited her in jail and then came over to our house, where he found us all. He had half a dozen constables with him—those ambulant hangmen—and he forthwith sent the whole lot of our Knaves' College to jail. Most pitiable was our plight.

CHAPTER XVII

A description of the jail; and what happened in it until

the time the old lady left it after she was lashed

and my friends were punished publicly,

and I was freed on bail

After we got there they put shackles on all of us and began to let us down into the dungeon. When I saw how things were going, I decided to use some of the money I had on me, and so I took out a doubloon and said to the jailor:

"Sir, let me tell you something secretly."

To encourage him to listen I let him have a glimpse of my doubloon; whereupon he drew me to one side.

"I beg Your Grace," I said, "to have mercy on an honest man."

I sought out his hands; and since his palms were used to such dates as that, he closed in on the money, saying:

"I will examine the illness and if it is not serious you will go down to the dungeon."

I caught on to his cover-up and made a humble reply. He left me outside while my companions were being let down into the dungeon.

I shall not tell you how much people laughed at us there at the jail and along the streets. The merriment was mostly provoked by our being tied together and shoved along, which showed up our patched and many-tinted, dappled persons. And of course whenever one of the constables tried to get hold of our clothes he found so little substance in them that he ended up by grasping our meat—and yet there was so little of that he could not hold on fast. Some of my companions presented to the constables the shreds and tatters of doublets and pantaloons; and when those officers of the law took the rope off of us it came loose flying many banners.

Finally they gave me as my bedroom what was called the Hall of Lineages, and provided me with a cot. You should have seen how some of my friends slept quite ensheathed and without taking off a stitch; others took the stitch off in a minimum jiffy. Some decided to gamble. And when they were through, the light was put out. We all forgot about our shackles.

The latrine was at the head of my bed. At midnight jailbird after jailbird came there to let loose a different kind of bird. When I first perceived those sounds I thought it was thunder, and began to cross myself and call on St. Barbara. But when I smelt the smells, I realized that it was thunder with a different background. [I saw I was to be present at a privy counsel.] It stank so terribly I thought I would die. Some had dysentery. . . . I finally worked up courage enough to ask them to transfer the receptacle somewhere else, and this provoked a discussion which led to a quarrel. I then took matters into my own hands . . . , and gave my opponent a clout in the snout. He tried to get up in a hurry and in doing so overturned the—starch. The whole company now woke up and came to life. We all started lashing away at each other in the dark. The stench was now so strong that everybody in the place woke up and started to shout. The jailor no doubt thought some of his vassals were escaping and came running up, accompanied by all his crew. He opened the room, brought in a light, and discovered what the trouble was. They all accused me, but I tried to get out of it by saying that all night long I had tried to advance into the realms of Morpheus but had been detained by so much action in the rear. The jailor seemed to think that I would give him another doubloon to keep from being sent down into the dungeon, and so he took matters in hand and ordered me to go down there. And I decided it would be better to go than to pinch my pouch more than I had already pinched it. So I was taken down below, and my friends there received me with shouting and joy.

I slept that night without protection. When the good Lord dawned His dawn we came out of the dungeon. We had no more than given one another the once-over when we were told to make arrangements for a cleanup (and not for Mary sans spot), or otherwise we would be lashed. I gave them six reals; and my companions, who had nothing to give, had to wait until night.

Among the occupants of the dungeon was a tall, one-eyed, bemustached fellow—a down-in-the-mouth creature, bent over from the lashes he had received. He had, with his pair of shackles and his chain, more iron about him than you could find in the Basque Provinces. He was called the Beast. He said his imprisonment had something to do with air; and I wondered whether he meant a bellows or a hornpipe or a fan. And when I asked him more about it, he said it was because of "something back there." I supposed he meant old delinquencies; but I later found out he was a sodomite. When the jailor scolded the Beast for some misbehavior, the latter would call him a hangman's butler and a general repository of errors. He had publicly confessed to his tendencies, and this caused us all to keep our back parts protected with a sort of dog collar with spikes on it—the kind mastiffs wear; and nobody dared make wind for fear it would remind him of the existence of those parts in which he was interested.

He had made friends with a fellow by the name of Robledo, nicknamed the Brute. He said he had been arrested for lavishness—but it was for the lavishness of movements his hands had engaged in while groping for things. He had been lashed more than a postboy's horse; and every hangman in existence had tried his hand on him. His face was all scarred; he had not a full complement of ears; and his nose had been slashed and sliced. These had been joined by four other men who were as wild for rapine as lions on the warpath. They were all shackled, for they had been condemned to the galleys. They said that soon they would be able to say they had served the King both on land and sea. You cannot imagine how joyfully they were waiting to do their bit.

All these, seeing that my companions could not pay their fee, decided to have them given a grand beating with a rope particularly designed for that sort of thing. Night came on and we were herded into the back pocket of the house. The light was put out, and I got under the bunk. Two of the others let out a whistle, and the others started to beat us. My good gentlemen, who saw the turn the affair had taken, piled up their starved carcasses—their carrion for mange and lice—into just one little crack in the bed. They were like nits on a hair or a nest of bedbugs. The blows rained down on the boards, but there was no other sound. Our opponents—the scoundrels—when they heard no complaining, began to throw bricks and some rubbish they had collected. That was really something. One of the missiles struck poor Don Toribio on the back of his neck and knocked him out. He began to shout that they were killing him; but the scoundrels kept him from being heard by singing and making a clatter with their ironwork. Don Toribio grabbed hold of the others and tried to get under them. This struggle caused their bones to rattle like the clappers beggars use to beg alms for hospitals. What few garments they had left all fell into tatters; not a shred was left intact. The blows now rained down so thick and fast that in no time at all Don

Toribio's head was simply covered with welts. He began to feel that he would never emerge alive from this bout, and was prepared to die just like another St. Stephen—though not exactly in the same odor. He begged to be let out, and promised to pay with every stitch of clothes he had. This promise was accepted, although some of the others were still after him. All beaten as he was, he got up and came over to me. Our other companions, who promised the same thing Don Toribio had promised, by now had their domes as heavily covered with tiles as with hair. They offered their clothes, as Toribio had done, for, they said, it was better to be in bed naked than bruised to death. Our opponents let us be; and on the following morning we were told to take our clothes off. Whereupon it was discovered that if they had put every stitch of them together there would not have been enough cloth to patch the sole of a sock. The poor fellows lay there all wrapped up in a thick woolen cloth that was used for delousing. They now began to realize how little protection the cloth offered them, because it was infested with lice as hungry as wolves. Some of the beasts were as big as Friesian horses; others could have attacked a bull by the ear. My friends got out from under the cloth, cursing their fortune and scratching themselves to death.

I got out of the dungeon, begging forgiveness for not keeping them very good company—and in truth it was the last company in the world I now wanted to keep. I oiled the jailor's palms with three eight-real coins; and, knowing as I did, who the notary in this case was, I sent a little picaroon to ask him to come and see me. He came, and I took him into another room and discussed the case with him. I told him I had a little money and asked him to keep it for me and to favor as much as he could the cause of a gentleman who by chance had been incriminated in this affair.

"Believe me, sir," he said, after he had swallowed my bait, "we are the ones who really control these affairs. And if a man does not want to be an honest man he can do much harm. I have sent more people to the galleys out of sheer whim than there are letters in an indictment. Just you rely on me and you can be sure I will get you safely out of all this."

With this he started to go, but turned back at the door to ask me for something for good old Diego García, the jailor, who needed to be kept quiet with a silver gag; and he reminded me too of the court reporter who might take care of the sentence for me. The notary then went on to say:

"A court reporter, sir, may arch his eyebrows, raise his voice, give a little tap with his shoe on the floor to attract the attention of a mayor whose wits are wandering (which they are most of the time), and make an accusation that would ruin a man."

I got the idea and added fifty reals to what I had already given him. To repay me he told me to straighten my collar up; and then he gave me two cures for a cold I had caught from the chill in the dungeon. Finally, looking at my shackles, he said:

"You will soon be rid of those, for the jailor will take them off for eight reals. He is a person who never does good unless he gets something out of it."

This observation pleased my fancy no end; and after he had gone I gave the jailor a crown, and he took my shackles off.

He let me come to his house. His wife was a whale; and his two daughters—daughters of the devil, they were—were scarecrows, idiots and whores in spite of the show they put on. The jailor's name, by the way, was Something-or-Other Blandones de San Pablo (Old Candlestick, they called him) and his wife's name was Doña Ana de Mora.

He once came home in a vile temper and refused to eat. His wife suspected something was wrong and went over to him— which made him all the madder—and he blurted out:

"Of course I'm mad. That scoundrel and thief, Almendros, the Billeter, told me when we were having some words about the rent, that you were not clean."

"Well!" cries his wife. "Does he think he is the one to scour me? You're no man, husband, or you would have plucked every hair out of his beard when you heard him say that. Do I call his servants to clean me up?" And turning to me, she continued: "He can never say I am Jewish the way he is, for one half of him is Ne'er-do-well and the other half is Jew. If I had been there, Señor Pablos, and had heard what that fellow said I would have reminded him that he had been brought to terms by the Inquisition. That's what I'd have done."

The jailor, much wrought up, said:

"Oh wife! I could not talk back because he said you were in the same boat. And when he said you were not clean, he didn't refer to your being dirty like a pig but to your refusing to eat one."

"So he said I was Jewish, did he! And you have the nerve to take it so calmly—you jellyfish. So that is what you think of the reputation of your wife Doña Ana de Mora—the granddaughter of Esteban Rubio and the daughter of Juan de Madrid, as God knows—and all the world."

"Did you say," I asked, "the daughter of Juan de Madrid?"

"The very daughter of Juan de Madrid of Auñón."

"I swear to God!" I said. "The scoundrel who said that is a Jew, a sodomite, and a cuckold, because Juan de Madrid, my lord (may he rest in heaven!) was my father's first cousin and I can certify to who and what he was. This matter concerns me personally. And if I get safely out of jail, I will give the lie a hundred times to the scoundrel who is maligning us. I have letters patent certifying their high standing in my town, and they are written in letters of gold."

The jailor and his wife were encouraged and delighted when they heard of the letters patent. But of course I did not have any such document. I did not even know who those people were. The jailor now wished to know in much greater detail about our family relationship. To keep from being caught in a lie, I pretended to be half out of my mind with wrath, and began vowing and swearing around. They tried to calm me down by saying that nothing further was going to be said about the whole thing; but every so often I would let myself be overcome and utter, as if out of the blue:

"Juan de Madrid! Well, they'll see whether the evidence I

have about him is any joking matter!" And: "Why, Juan de Madrid, the Elder, was married to Ana de Acebedo, the Fat." Then I would keep still for a while.

For all this the jailor fed me and gave me a bed at his house; and the notary, at the jailor's instigation, and bribed with my money, did so well that they put the old lady—the one who had taken care of my friends—on a donkey which they led by a halter down the streets for all to see. A town crier preceded her with the announcement: "This woman is being punished as a thief." The hangman beat out the rhythm on her back, as he had been ordered to do by the magistrates. They then brought out my companions and mounted them too, though they did not attach their beasts to halters. The poor fellows' heads and faces were bare. They were taken out to the stocks where their punishment would be corporal; and the poor things were so tattered and bare that they already reminded me of something corporal—a corporal who is watching his privates on parade. They were exiled for six years. I was let out on bail through the good graces of the notary. The court reporter did not neglect his duty either, because he spoke in a low voice, got things mixed up, and swallowed sentence after sentence after sentence.

CHAPTER XVIII

How I found lodgings; and of

my mishap there

I left the jail.

I was alone and without my friends; for, although they told me they were going to Seville (with the aid of charity), I did not care to go along with them.

I decided to try and find a place to stay, and found one. There was a young girl there—blond and fair, sharp-eyed, merry and meddlesome, and at times a bit forward and pert. She lisped a little too. She was afraid of mice, and she was very proud of her hands. She liked to show them off when she snuffed candles and dished up the food at the table. She would always go out of her way to point everything out. At church she would always clasp her hands before her, and in the street she was careful to point out the houses and tell who lived in them. When she reclined on a dais she was always fixing some pin or other in her headdress. She was handy at the pinching game called *pizpiri-gaña*, because it gave her so many opportunities to show off her hands. She would often yawn without any real desire to do so but only because the occasion gave her a chance to reveal her teeth, and she could also display her hands too while she was stifling her yawn. The household had after some time become so hand-conscious that even her parents were worn out from watching her handiwork.

They put me up very well there. They had planned to rent rooms to three lodgers—a Portuguese, a Catalan, and me. My new friends gave me a hearty welcome.

I was rather taken by the girl as possibly offering me some fun—and I was not disappointed to find her right there where I was living. I began to play up to her. I would tell stories around the house to amuse them—stories that I had carefully worked out so they would be entertaining. I brought them news and gossip about things that had never happened. I did all sorts of things for them—and they were things that didn't cost anything, you may be sure. I said I was a sorcerer and that I could make the house look as if it were on fire. They were so gullible they swallowed all the nonsense I fed them. I won them all over after a fashion, although I cannot say they were all exactly in love with me. My trouble was that I looked a bit shabby, although the jailor had done something to make me look somewhat less of a beggar than I had looked before. (I kept on going to his place, by the way, to get some nourishment.) At any rate, the people where I was staying did not treat me quite the way I would have liked.

To gain the reputation of being a man of wealth I decided to have some of my friends call at the house when I was not at home. The first one of them came by one day and asked for

Don Ramiro de Guzmán. I had decided to use that name, because my friends had pointed out that it cost nothing to change my name now and then, and that a new one might come in handy. My friend, then, asked for this Don Ramiro and said I was a rich business man who had had three negotiations with the King. The people there thought he must be looking for someone else by the name of Don Ramiro de Guzmán, for the person by that name who lived with them, they said, was of slight build and had an ugly face. Besides, he was poor and displayed more rags than moneybags. My friend replied that I was indeed the man he meant and said he could never for the glory of God ask for a greater income than what I had—more than two thousand ducats, he said it was. He told them several more lies that simply amazed them; and then he left with them a phony note for nine thousand crowns he had come to collect from me. He told them to see to it I got it. Mother and daughter believed the story of my supposed wealth and immediately decided I would be a good match for the girl.

I came home, pretending I knew nothing about all this. They gave me the note, saying:

"Wealth and love are two things people find it hard to hide, Señor Don Ramiro. Why have you tried to hide all this from us when you knew how very fond we are of you?"

I pretended to be put out because of that note, and went to my room. It was really very funny to watch them after they had come to the conclusion that I was a man of wealth. Anything I did after that was all right. They applauded everything I said. Nobody, they said, had as much wit as I did. When, therefore, I felt sure they were digesting the bait I had given them, I declared my intentions to the daughter. She was delighted, and flattered me nearly to death.

We went our ways. One night later on I thought I would fool them even more about my supposed wealth; and so I locked myself in my room, which was separated from theirs by only a thin wall, and took out fifty crowns and went to work counting them over and over. I kept on counting until I made my friends think I had at least six thousand crowns with me. When they realized I had (they thought) so much ready money on me they spared themselves no pains to wait on me and entertain me.

The Portuguese roomer went by the name of O Senhor Vasco de Meneses, a *fidalgo* of the order of Christus. He displayed a long baize cape, boots, a small collar and big mustachios. He was dying of love for Doña Berenguela de Robledo. He wooed her by just sitting and talking to her, and sighing more than a lay sister during a Lenten sermon. He sang very badly; and he was always at odds with the Catalan, who was the drabbest and most dreadfully wretched creature the Lord ever created. He ate only bi-daily—every other day, I mean; and the bread he ate was so hard that the most mordant tongue could hardly have softened it. He was always trying to show what a big, tough fellow he was; but he was really quite chicken about everything—except that he couldn't lay eggs. He certainly cackled like one. When the two of them saw that I was making progress, they took to saying bad things about me. The Portuguese said I was a lousy, down-at-the-heels picaroon, and the Catalan said I was a vile coward. I knew all about it too—I sometimes even overheard them at it, but I never felt particularly interested in answering them.

Finally the girl began to talk to me and answer my letters. I began those missives of mine in the usual fashion: "My boldness—your great beauty," etc., etc. I said I was her slave, and I signed below with a heart pierced by an arrow. We finally began to use the familiar form of address with each other.

In order to keep up the pretense that I was a man of quality I went out and rented a mule; then disguising my voice, and all bundled up, I came back to the house and asked for myself —"Señor Don Ramiro de Guzmán, Lord of Valcerrado and Velorete."

"Yes," the girl replied, "a gentleman by that name does live here. He is a rather smallish person."

I said that from her description I was sure that he was the man I was looking for, and I then asked her to be good enough to tell him that Diego de Solórzano, his sometime treasurer, was out collecting and had stopped by to pay his respects. Then I left.

When I came home a little later, I was received with the greatest joy in the world. They asked me why I had not told them I was the Lord of Valcerrado and Velorete, and gave me the message.

After that the girl went completely off the deep end—she was so greedy to get a rich husband; and so one night she arranged for me to come and talk to her. She told me to come down a passage that opened out on the roof, where, she said, I could find the window of her room.

The devil, who is a sly fellow, so arranged matters that when night came and I was anticipating my pleasure during the interview, I went to the passageway to get out on the roof; but it so happened that my foot slipped and I toppled over onto the roof of a notary who lived next door. I came down so hard I broke all the tiles. When the notary heard my fall he woke everybody up in his house—for he thought the sounds had been made by a thief. I may remark that of all people he was certainly the one most qualified to know what kind of noises a thief makes. When I saw him I tried to hide behind a chimney but that only increased his suspicion, and he and his brother and two servants began to rain down blows upon me. They managed to tie me up—and right before my lady's eyes, too. I could think of no way of getting loose. And the girl laughed heartily at all this, because she believed what I had told her about being able to do tricks and perform enchantments. She thought I was doing it all on purpose, and attributed my fall to necromancy; and so she kept calling to me to get up. "You have gone far enough," she said.

By now I was howling from all the blows I had received. But she still thought it was all a joke, and had become almost hysterical.

The notary now began to bring charges against me, and because he heard keys in my pocket, he insisted on writing down that I had passkeys; and even when I showed him they were not, he would still not back down. Passkeys they were. I told him I was Don Ramiro de Guzmán, and he just laughed heartily at that. I did not know what to do—all beaten up as I was, right in front of my lady, and arrested without cause. I knelt down before the notary, but I could say nothing that would soften his heart. All this took place up there on top of the house—which was not easy, for the notary was shouting his accusations in such a loud voice that it might have been said he was raising the roof. I was now ordered to go downstairs, and they lowered me through a window into a room that was used as a kitchen.

CHAPTER XIX

In which the previous matter is pursued; with

other events

I could not close my eyes all night long. I lay awake thinking how it had been my misfortune to have fallen not just on a roof but into the hands of a notary. And when I recalled the matter of the passkeys and how the notary had written it all down, I was reminded that in the hands of a notary a speck of suspicion becomes a mountain of guilt.

I spent the night scheming schemes. I thought once of appealing to Christ Himself; but when I thought how much He had borne from scribes and notaries, I did not dare. I tried any number of times to get free from my ropes; but the notary heard me every time and came and reknotted me up, for he was wider awake trying to magnify his lie than I was to get free.

He got up early the next morning while everybody but the witnesses were still in bed. He took up his strap and polished off my ribs again with it. He reprimanded me soundly for being a thief—as one who was, himself, thoroughly practiced in that vice. We were about this—he beating me and I feeling on the point of giving him some money (which is the only ointment that can soften such stones), when the Portuguese and the Catalan came in. They had been encouraged to come by the pleas my little lady had made them, for she at last realized that I had actually fallen and been beaten, and that it was no matter of enchantment at all. When the notary saw them talking to me he snatched up his pen to write down an accusation against them as accomplices in my crime. The Portuguese wouldn't take it and spoke right up to him, and not softly either. He said in Portuguese that he was a nobleman of the King's household and that I was a man of station too, and that the notary was a scoundrel for keeping me tied up.

The Portuguese began to undo me, and the notary at once started shouting: "You're helping him resist arrest!" And two of his aides—half-bailiff, half-scoundrel themselves—began to undo their capes and open their collars, as they always do when they pretend to be getting ready to start a fight (which, how-ever, never materializes). They called out for the King's help. My two friends finally got me untied; and the notary, seeing that no one would help him, said:

"I swear to God you can't do this to me. If you gentlemen were not who you are, it would cost you dear, I can tell you. Well, do something for these witnesses. I am not, myself, asking anything for my trouble."

I caught the drift. So I took out eight reals and gave them to him. I felt like returning him the blows he had given me. But in order not to confess publicly that I had received them from him, I left him as he was, and went off with my friends, thank-ing them for having rescued me.

I returned home, with my face all muffled up in welts and my back somewhat weary from beating.

The Catalan laughed heartily . . . ; and my two friends both said I was a fine, strapping fellow—though less strapping than strapped. I took considerable offense at these little quips. Whenever I dropped in to see them they would refer to beat-ings, and talk about boards and wood. When I saw that they had caught on to my lie about being rich and that I had become a laughingstock, I decided in my mortification to get out. And I had no intention of paying my board and room either, which by this time amounted to a considerable sum. I hoped to get my luggage out safely too. So I cooked up a scheme with my friend Brandalagas, a native of Hornillos, and two other friends of mine. They were to come on a certain night and arrest me.

They came that night at the appointed time, and informed the landlady that they were representatives of the Inquisition and suggested that she keep things quiet. The people at our house were scared to death. They thought, you see, that I was being taken prisoner because of the necromancy I had talked so much about. So they said nothing while I was being taken away. But when my friends started hauling out the baggage, the landlady's people said they deserved to keep that in lieu of the money I owed them. But my friends promptly said that those properties had been confiscated by the Inquisition. Well, the others had no desire to fool around with the Inquisition, so no one said a thing. They let me go without further ado, saying they had always feared it might turn out this way. They went and told the Catalan and the Portuguese what had just happened to me. Those two said that the people who had come to get me were demons, and that I had a familiar spirit. The Catalan and the Portuguese also convinced the others that I may have appeared to have considerable money, but in reality had none.

At any rate, I got away scot-free with all my clothes and with my board bill unpaid.

With the aid of my new friends I now decided to change my manner of dress and to wear fancy shoes and fashionable clothes. I felt the need of having a large stylish collar too. Nor did I forget how fashionable it was to have two pages. My friends encouraged me in all this by pointing out that with a new and flashy outfit I would certainly be able to make a good marriage. This sort of thing was quite common around Madrid, they said, and added that they would be glad to help me out and steer possibilities my way. Wretch that I was, I decided to follow their suggestions.

I don't know how many sales I visited. I bought my wedding

finery, and found out where horses could be rented, and then promptly acquired one for myself. The first day I could not find a lackey. I went out into the Calle Mayor, and stood in front of a saddler's shop, as one who contemplated buying something there.

Two men came up, each with two lackeys. They asked me whether I contemplated buying the silver trappings I was examining. I struck up a conversation with them, and by means of sallies and pleasantries, I managed to detain them there for a while. They eventually said they would like to go to the Prado and have a bit of fun; and I said that if they didn't mind I would like to go along with them. I instructed the shopkeeper there to direct my two pages and my lackey to catch up with me at the Prado. I described their livery for him. Then I got in between my two new friends, and off we went. It occurred to me that nobody could tell whose lackeys those two were, or which one of us did not have one. I began now to talk with great assurance about the equestrian sports at Talavera, and I also mentioned a white horse of mine which had a touch of blue in it. I referred in passing to a [roan] stallion I had, and remarked that I was expecting someone to bring it there to me. Whenever we came across a page or lackey on horseback I would have him stop, and then I would inquire whose horse he was riding. Then I would discourse knowingly about horses and finally ask whether the horse was for sale. I would have the page give the animal a turn or two in the street; and whether the bridle had some defect or not I would find one and suggest a way to fix it. And as my luck would have it, I found several occasions to show off like that.

My companions seemed terribly impressed, and I imagined they must be asking themselves who this run-down gentleman might be. One of them was wearing the insignia of a military order; and the other had on a diamond chain, which was both insignia and knight's cross. So I said I was on the look-out for good horses for myself and my cousin, because we intended to enter some contests.

When we reached the Prado I dismounted and started walking

around. I wore my cape thrown over my shoulder and held my hat in my hand. Everybody looked at me. Someone said: "I have seen him walking before." Another observed: "The rogue cuts a pretty figure, doesn't he?" I pretended to hear nothing and moved on.

My two acquaintances, who had come up to a coach occupied by several ladies, suggested I might like to have a little fun with them. I let the other two talk to the young ladies at their window, and, myself, engaged the mother and aunt in conversation at theirs. They were jolly old things—one of them was fiftyish, the other a little less so. I entertained them for a while with my sweet prattle (for, no matter how old a woman is, she always carries around with her more hopes than years). I promised them presents, and inquired about the status of the younger women. I was told that they were unmarried. You might have gathered that from their conversation. I uttered some more commonplaces; and said I hoped to see the girls properly "adjudicated." They liked that word "adjudicated" very much. They went on to ask me my business in Madrid. I said I had come there to get away from my parents, who were trying to marry me against my will to a foolish, ugly girl of no social consequence—but with a large dowry. "I, my ladies," says I, "would much rather have a neat little trick come to me as bare as she was born than to get a ponderous Jewess, for, thanks be to God, my estate is eventually going to bring me in four thousand ducats. And if I win a lawsuit I am engaged in at present, I shall have no further preoccupation about money, ever."

The aunt replied very quickly:

"How I do admire you for all that, sir! Never, never marry, unless it is with a woman you care for; and do see to it that she is of good social standing. I can assure you of one thing. I am not very rich, and yet I have several times refused to let my niece get married, even though she has had some very wealthy suitors—wealthy, yes, but they were just not gentlemen of quality. She has very little money—only six thousand ducats' dowry, but when it comes to family no one has a better pedigree."

"I can very well imagine that," I said.

The young girls had brought the first stage of the conversation to a close by asking my friends to take them to lunch. And my friends suddenly acted very much like the characters in the old ballad about the death of Alonso de Aguilar:

> *They looked at each other*
> *And tried to dissemble;*
> *Their faces turned white,*
> *Their beards 'gan to tremble.*

I saw that my way out would be to say I very much needed to have my pages go home and bring back some boxes I had there. They thanked me, and I then begged them to go to the "Country Club" the next day; and I also said I was sending along a picnic lunch. They accepted my invitation and told me where they lived, and asked where I lived. The coach then moved away, and my companions and I started for home. They seemed to have taken quite a liking to me because of the invitation I had extended to the ladies, and so asked me to have supper with them that night. I allowed myself to be urged a bit and then dined with them. I kept pretending I was trying to locate my servants, and swore I would dismiss them. At ten o'clock I said I had a little rendezvous and asked to be excused. And then, after we had made arrangements for meeting the next day at the "Country Club," I left them.

I left my rented horse with its owner and then proceeded on home. I found my companions there playing a card game called "reversi." I told them what had happened and the arrangements that had been made. We decided to spend two hundred reals on the picnic lunch we were going to send the ladies the next day. Then I went to bed, but I could not sleep a wink all night long, for I will confess that I spent the night thinking over what I would do with the dowry I expected to receive. I did not know whether it would be more profitable to buy a house or an annuity with it.

CHAPTER XX

In which the story continues; with further

noteworthy events and misfortunes

Dawn came, and we woke up and began to make arrangements about servants, silver and food for the party. I won't go into detail, but since money commands respect, I paid a certain gentleman's butler to let me use his silver and to get three other servants to help him serve the meal. I spent the rest of the morning getting everything ready, and that afternoon I rented my horse. I left for the "Country Club" at the appointed hour. My waistband was stuffed with papers that were supposed to be legal documents, and I unbuttoned six buttons on my doublet and let some other papers stick out there.

When I reached the place, the ladies and gentlemen had already arrived and were waiting for me. The ladies received me with a great show of affection and addressed me in the second person plural to show me what good friends we were. I had told them my name was Don Felipe Tristán; so for the rest of the day it was Don-Tristán-this, Don-Tristán-that. I told them right at the beginning that I had become so involved in some negotiations I was carrying on with His Majesty, and also in some matters connected with the finances of my estate, that for a while I had feared I might not be able to keep my appointment with them; and so I had really had to throw a luncheon together for them the best I could. The butler came up just then with his equipment, which included a table and some silver. My friends and the ladies could not keep from staring at me in complete silence. I directed the servants to move over to the summerhouse while the rest of us went to look at the ponds.

The older ladies positively melted over me; and I was happy to see the girls with their faces uncovered, for the one I was trying to trap into marrying me was the prettiest little thing I have ever seen in all my life. She was blond and white and carmine.

She had a small mouth, tiny teeth set tightly together, a fair nose, and big green eyes. She was tall and her hands were very pretty.

The other girl was much less restrained, and I suspected from the way she acted that she was not averse to kissing parties.

We went and looked over the ponds; and there I saw that my betrothed would have been in considerable peril in the days of Herod—she was so innocent. She just didn't *know*; but after all I am not interested in having a woman be a buffoon or a counsellor. If a woman is wise but ugly you might as well go to bed with Aristotle or Seneca—or a book, for that matter. I want my women properly fashioned for the arts and sciences of the bedroom.

As we approached the summerhouse we passed through a bower, and there the embellishments on my collar caught on a tree and were slightly torn. The girl came over and pinned me up with a silver pin; and her mother told me to send it to their house the next day for Doña Ana to mend. (Doña Ana was my girl's name.)

The meal itself turned out to be excellent, and there was an ample sufficiency of food, hot and cold, from entrées to dessert. The company was very merry; they were all very nice to me, and I was very nice to them. While the cloth was being removed, I observed that a gentleman accompanied by two servants was coming through the garden, and lo and behold! it was none other than my old friend Don Diego Coronel. He came over to us. He did not quite recognize me in that new outfit, so he simply stopped and stared at me. He spoke to the ladies and called them "cousin"—and went right on staring at me. I was busy talking to the butler, and my two friends at the party began talking to Don Diego, who was a friend of theirs. He asked them (as it later came to light) who I was, and they replied: "Don Felipe Tristán, a rich man of quality." I saw him cross himself. Finally, in front of them all, he came over to me and said: "I beg your pardon, but I swear that before I learned your name, I thought you were someone else, because you look just exactly like a servant I once had in Segovia by the name of

Pablos. He was the son of a barber." They all laughed heartily at this. I made a great effort not to blush and reveal my embarrassment, and so give myself away. I told him I would give anything to see that fellow, because any number of people had told me I resembled him. "Resemble?" he said. "Why, you are exactly like him in everything—build, speech, gestures—I've never seen the like! It is really incredible. Nothing like it was ever seen before." Then the mother and the aunt asked how it could be possible that so fine a gentleman could resemble so low a rogue—a barber's son. And to dispel any further suspicions, one of them said:

"I know Don Felipe—our host here—very well. He has entertained us royally at my husband's request. They were very good friends back on Ocaña."

I caught on, and said that I hoped, and would continue to hope, to be of service to them anywhere, as far as my possibilities would allow.

Don Diego apologized for having given me offense by calling me a barber's son, and said he was my servant.

"You will never believe it," he said; "but the fellow's mother was a witch, his father a thief, his uncle a hangman, and he is himself the lowest and most depraved person in all God's world."

You can imagine how I must have felt, hearing that insulting indictment with my own ears! I covered up my embarrassment, but I was simply burned up.

The conversation then shifted back to matters at hand.

My friends and I then said good-by, and Don Diego got into the coach with them. He asked them what had occasioned the picnic, and how I happened to be there; and both mother and aunt replied that I was heir to a considerable fortune and had an income of ever so many ducats. They further told him I wished to marry Doña Ana, and that if he knew all the facts he would realize it was a good match and would bring great honor to their family. They talked all this over until they reached their house, which was Arenal Street in the San Felipe region.

My friends and I went home as we had done previously. They

invited me to play cards, in the hope of fleecing me. I knew that, and sat down with them. They took out some marked cards. I lost one round, and then I won something like three hundred reals from them by using a trick I knew. And went home.

I found my friends there—Lucentiate Brandalagas and Pero López. They were in the process of working out some tricks with dice. When they saw me come in they were so eager to hear my story they stopped playing with the dice. I looked dejected and downcast. All I told them was that I had really been in a tight fix in the Don Diego affair. They comforted me and advised me not to give up my suit on any condition.

About then we heard that a game of lansquenet was going on at a neighboring druggist's. I had some proficiency at that card game—what with some tricks I knew, and marked cards. I decided to make a kill there, so I sent my friends on ahead. They entered the room where the game was being played and asked whether the people there would care to play with a Benedictine friar who had come to recuperate from a recent illness at some cousins' of theirs. He was said to be filthy with lucre. At this their greediness awoke and they cried out:

"Bring him over! Bring him over!"

"He is a grave person in the order," said Pero López, "and since he has come out, he enjoys conversing more than anything else."

"It doesn't matter," they called out. "Just bring him along."

"Well, you must promise not to bring anybody else in—just for the looks of the thing."

"Right!" said the host. "We promise."

They felt quite sure of their ground by this time—after having swallowed the lie.

My friends—now acolytes—returned. By that time I had on a Benedictine friar's habit (which I had got hold of somewhere or other), a pair of spectacles, a false beard that was well trimmed and convincing-looking, and a nightcap that hid my hair and gave me the appearance of a convalescent.

I came in in great humility and sat down, and the game began. They did well, and it was a case of three against one for a while; but I ended up after three hours with more than thirteen hundred reals. I gave out some gratuities, and with a "Praise be the Lord" I took my leave, charging them not to be shocked to see me playing cards, for I did it only for entertainment and for no other reason. The others had lost everything they had and sent themselves to the devil. My friends and I left.

We got home at 1:30 that morning and divided the spoils. Then we went to bed.

I was somewhat consoled by what had happened.

The next morning I got up and went out to rent a horse. I could not find one; which led me to believe that there were many others in the same boat I was in. I felt embarrassed to be seen walking, and all the more so now, after what had happened the day before. I went on toward San Felipe and finally came across a lackey holding the horse of an advocate who had gone in to mass. I gave the fellow four reals to let me have the horse while his master was at church so that I could take a turn or two on Arenal Street. I rode up and down the street without seeing anyone; and as I was going out the third time, Doña Ana appeared. Now, although I did not, of course, know that horse very well, and I was not a good rider either, yet when I saw my lady I decided to perform a few gallantries for her. I gave the horse a couple of blows with my rod and pulled him up sharply with the bridle. He reared up and kicked out a couple of times, and then started to run away—landing me on my ear in a puddle. When I saw myself in this state, and with an audience of children who had come up, I realized what a picture I must make in my lady's eyes, and so said:

"You bastard! I only wish you didn't come from such fine Arab stock. I had better stop taking all these chances. They told me he was tricky, and yet I *would* have it out with him."

The horse stopped and the lackey brought him back again. By this time Don Diego Coronel had come to the window. (He lived in the same house his cousins lived in.) When I saw him, I changed color. He asked me whether anything serious had happened. I said no, even though one of my legs was maimed.

The lackey was trying to hurry me up, because he was afraid his master might come from church and see him. I got on the horse, but I am so unlucky that at the very moment the boy was encouraging me to get going, his master (who was on the way to the palace) came up behind us, and recognizing his beast, lunged forward and began to give the lackey a drubbing, demanding of him why he had let anyone use his horse. And the worst part of it was that he then turned to me and told me in no uncertain terms to dismount—and on the double. All this was witnessed by my lady and Don Diego. No lashed culprit ever felt so ashamed. I felt very sad to see two misfortunes happen to me one right after the other. There was nothing for me to do but get down. The lawyer mounted and rode away. And I, to patch things up the best I could, stayed a while and, still in the street, chatted with Don Diego.

"I never in all my life rode such a wicked beast," I said. "I left my own peach-colored horse back at San Felipe. He is easy to handle either racing or at a trot. I was telling some people back there how easy it was for me to get him to race or come to a halt and they told me that the one that just threw me—the lawyer's—was a different sort. I thought I would like to give him a try. You have no idea how unmanageable he is—his haunches hard as rocks. With that miserable saddle he had on, it's a miracle he didn't kill me."

"It was indeed," said Don Diego. "But you do seem to have got a bad leg from it."

"That is right," I said. "And I had better go and get on my own horse."

The girl was satisfied with my explanation and was sorry for what had happened to me; but Don Diego was suspicious about what had happened between me and the lawyer, and that brought about my undoing—to say nothing of many other misfortunes that befell me. The beginning of the unleashing of my miseries started almost immediately. When I got home I found that good Licentiate Brandalagas and Pero López had rifled a chest where I kept the bag containing my legacy and the other money that I had earned, and had skipped out with everything I had, with the exception of the hundred reals I had on me. It knocked me cold. I had no idea what to do about it. I said to myself: "I had it coming to me for depending on ill-earned money. That goes just as easily as it comes. Poor old Pablos! What am I ever going to do!"

I didn't know whether I ought to try to find the thieves, or call the police. I gave up the second idea, for I knew that if my friends were arrested they would most certainly tell about the trick I played when I was dressed like a friar—and a few other little things of the sort. I would probably be sent to the gallows. And as for trying to find my friends—where in the world would I go?

I finally determined to stay put, so that I would not lose out on the marriage. I hoped the girl's dowry would make up for my losses. I felt now that I had better get the wedding over as fast as possible.

I had dinner and then rented a horse in the afternoon. I rode to my lady's street. And since I had no lackey with me—and I did not wish to be seen without one—I waited at the corner until someone who looked like a lackey should come along and seem to be accompanying me—without, of course, knowing he played that role. And I thought that when I had got to the other end of the street I could come back again with the help of a second passerby who should also unwittingly play that part.

I do not know whether my fraudulence was so utterly apparent that it could not have escaped Don Diego's eyes, or whether my story about the lawyer's horse had made him suspicious, or whether it was because he started trying to discover who I was and so spied on me—at any rate it happened that he worked so hard at it that in the most unheard-of way he found out who I really was. I had been pressing my lady's family rather hard to sign the final papers, and they, wishing to get the matter settled, kept after Don Diego so much that in his search for evidence about me he happened to run across Licentiate Flechilla (the one who had invited me to dine when I was still living with the penniless gentlemen). Flechilla was annoyed with me for not having come to see him again and told Don Diego how I had acted toward him that night of the dinner. He knew, you see, that I had been Don Diego's servant. He said he had seen me only two days before riding around somewhat ostentatiously on horseback. He said I had spoken to him about making a very rich marriage.

Don Diego hesitated no more. He ran into those two recent friends of mine—the ones with the insignia and chain—in the Puerta del Sol and told them what was going on and asked them to give me a sound beating that night when they saw me in the street. He said they could recognize me easily because I would be wearing his cape. They agreed to this, and as they were going down the street they met me; but they acted so innocently that I had never before felt them to be such good friends of mine as they seemed to be on that occasion. We talked over what we might do for entertainment until time for the Angelus bell. Then my two friends left and went on down the street, and Don Diego and I started off alone to San Felipe. As we were about to turn into La Paz Street, Don Diego said:

"By the life of Don Felipe! Would you mind trading capes with me? I have certain reasons for not being recognized in this district."

"I should be very happy to," said I.

I innocently took his cape and gave him mine. I offered myself to protect him from the rear, but he, having planned to lay mine waste, said it was essential to him to be alone. He suggested I move on; and I had no sooner done so when the devil so contrived matters that two fellows who were waiting for Don Diego to give him a beating at the request of some little lady, suddenly got up and started raining blows on my back and head. They had, of course, seen me wearing Don Diego's coat and had naturally supposed I was Don Diego. I began to shout, and from my voice and my looks they soon realized I was not the man they were after. They fled, leaving me and my welts alone in the street. I tried to hide the three or four big bumps I had received, and stayed there a while for fear of going along the street. Finally at twelve o'clock—the hour when I was accustomed to talk to my girl—I got there, and those two friends of Don Diego's, who were following his instructions, came up to me. One of them gave me two blows on my legs with a club and knocked me down, and then the other one came up and slashed my face from ear to ear. They took my cape and said to me as I lay there on the ground:

"This is a just reward for a lying, lowborn rascal like you."

At the time I really did not know what had happened or who my assailants were. From what had been said I suspected one of them might be the landlord I played my Inquisition trick on, or perhaps the jailor I had fooled, or my companions who had fled. I expected a slash from almost any quarter, and stood there utterly confused. But there was one person I never suspected, and that was Don Diego.

I kept calling for protection against cape-snatchers. The commotion brought the police. They propped me up, and when they saw my face was laid open from end to end and that I had no cape, they were unable to ascertain what had happened, and so promptly bustled me off for treatment. When the surgeon had managed to patch me up, the constables inquired about my lodgings and then took me to those premises.

Because of the beating I had received, my legs were too numb to support me; whereupon I was placed in a bed, and there I lay bewildered and pensive, with no money and a face that resembled a hoof, and a body that felt as if a herd of them had passed over it. I remained there for some time in great hurt, being neither capable of following my friends or of doing anything about the marriage. My dilemma was that neither could I leave Madrid nor could I stay there.

CHAPTER XXI

Concerning the hero's recovery and certain other

singular matters

The next morning I was greeted by the proprietress of the house, who was standing at the head of my bed. She was one of those old rosary-laden dames in the prime of life (just thirty-eight by her reckoning), with a face that bore no little resemblance to a prune dipped in paprika and flour—indeed, she had a corrugated, sallow-saffron countenance which was transversed by a snout that supported a pair of slots for eyes. Hanging from this ensemble was a veritable promontory of a jaw, which housed a wagging tongue. In a word, she lacked only a broom and she could have effected a change of life. She had something of a reputation in the vicinity, and she enhanced it from time to time with anyone who would. This good madam (for such was the case) was a connoisseur of physical pleasure and all the delights therewith connected. The townspeople knew her as Maude the Bawd, for she rented her house and served as entrepreneur for others. This establishment was never without a full complement of guests the whole year round. It was indeed an experience to see how Maude trained girls to appear in public with their faces properly covered. Maude would first point out those features which girls ought to leave as nature willed. For girls with pearly teeth (for example) she would advise continuous smiling—even in the face of adversity; for those blessed with beautiful hands, she counselled exhibition of them in all circumstances; and to those who had flaxen hair, Maude would suggest an occasional shake of the head and say that just a tuft of hair peeping from under the shawl would not be amiss. She advocated pretty little dances for damsels with alluring eyes because they would then have occasion to roll those orbs and flutter their lashes. So great was Maude's virtuosity in matters of cosmetics that a crow's husband would have mistaken his mate for a pigeon after she had made just one visit to Madame Maude's parlor. Among her various arts she knew the secret of bleaching hands and throats, polishing teeth, and removing unseemly fuzz. She had a brew aptly called "Herod," because it would kill babes in the womb and aid in miscarriage. But her talents were most visibly manifest in the arts of replacing maidenheads and restoring virginity.

I witnessed her exercise all these dexterities in the course of my eight days at her house. And as if this were not enough, she taught all the girls there how to extort money from the customers, and she taught the latter the science of murmuring sweet nothings to the former. In addition to these services, she gave counsel to young and old ladies alike concerning the most efficacious manner of profiting from occasions. She offered instruction in how to wheedle money, necklaces, and the like from gentlemen. She proudly pointed out her disciples, Mesdames Vidaña of Alcalá, Plañosa of Burgos, and Muñatones of Salamanca, as women highly skilled in the arts of deception.

I have dwelt on this, dear reader, so that you may commiserate with me in my ill fortune, and meditate upon the things she said to me. Madame Maude habitually spoke to me in proverbs. "A rolling stone gathers no moss, my son, and birds of a feather flock together, just as you can't squeeze blood out of a turnip. I don't know, nor do I understand, your way of life. You're a mere lad; it wouldn't surprise me if you had committed a few misdeeds here and there without realizing that even sleep moves us a few steps closer to the grave. I've lived a long, long time, and I should know. What difference does it make to me that you've lost a lot of opportunities without knowing where, or that you've frittered your time away—first, as a student, then as a rogue, then as a gentleman, and then running around in vulgar company. Tell me your friends, and I'll tell you who you are. To each his own. And bear in mind, my boy, that a bird in the hand is worth two in the bush. Now, go your way, and if women bother you, remember that in this area I'm the perennial dealer in that merchandise. And don't get yourself mixed up with any more vagrants and go taking

off after painted-up blonds and foxy redheads, because they'll
sleep with anyone. Let me tell you that you could have saved a
lot of money if you had been with me, since I'm certainly not
known to be a miser. What with my deceased and buried husbands, (God rest their souls!) I'll be sure to end up my days in
grand style, and that is why I don't press people like you for
the rent money unless I have to have it to get a few candles
and herbs."

Although not an apothecary, she commerced in drugs, and
if silver was applied to the palm of her hands, she could, it was
said, issue forth from her chimney at night to fulfill any bar-
gain.

When she had finished her monologue and sermon about the
rent (for, although she touched on this matter only at the end
of her discourse, it had been, however, the true purpose of the
harangue), I realized that I had no real reason to be surprised
at her visitation. She had, you see, not come before, except one
day when she called to tell me to pay no heed to some pernicious rumors to the effect that the police were going to ap-
prehend her for being a witch. She wanted to make it clear
that the woman in question was another Maude. With such an
abundance of Maudes in the world today, is there any wonder
that the poor old globe is considerably (if I may say so) "maud-
dled?" I shall never forget that day, because, while I was counting out her money, the devil conspired to have the police arrest the illustrious dame along with her mate for concubinage.
At the precise moment the officers entered my chamber, Maude
and I were sitting on the bed together. The police closed in on
us and with several lusty thwacks, threw me to the floor. Two
other policemen had arrested Maude on charges of being a
madam and a witch. Now, who would ever have thought that
about a woman who had led so exemplary a life as she had?
In all the bedlam and shouting, her lover (a fruiterer who was
in an inner room) made his escape. When the police saw him
and found out from one of the guests that I was not the real
culprit, they bolted out after the scoundrel and seized him,
leaving me all bruised and battered. But in spite of all my woes

I had to chuckle at the remarks the rogues made to the old dame. One of them looked her straight in the eye and said: "How well you shall look in a mitre, Mother! What a joy it will be to dedicate three thousand turnips to your service!" And another said: "the lord mayors have already chosen your feathers for you, so you can go to jail in grand style."

Finally they returned with the rogue, bound the two together, begged my forgiveness, and took their leave. I must confess that I was greatly relieved to see the good lady in the condition she was in. And so, I had no care but to get up and throw my orange at her—although, because of what one of the servants told me later, I had my doubts about their being able to keep her in prison—if the rumors I had heard about her flying and the like were really so.

I stayed on in the house for a week without being able to go out. The doctor took seven stitches in my face, and I had to have recourse to crutches as my only means of locomotion. With the medicine and room and board, my hundred reals were soon exhausted, and I found myself without funds. Thus it was that in order not to incur further expenses (since I had no capital), I elected to go out into the street on my crutches in order to effect the sale of a suit, and some doublets and collars, all of which were in good condition. With the money accruing therefrom, I bought an old leather jacket, a flaxen doublet, a somewhat shabby greatcoat (a bit on the large side), and some leggings and oversized shoes. With the hood of the greatcoat over my head, a rosary, the image of Christ in bronze hanging around my neck, and a few tremulous words and phrases I had learned from an old beggar who knew the art well, I began to exercise the profession of mendicant. I had seventy-nine reals left over, and I sewed them inside the doublet; and then I embarked upon the way of the petitioner of alms, relying on my glib tongue to be my support. I roamed about the streets for a week, moaning in a low and feeble voice, which I occasionally raised in supplication: "Alms, alms for the poor and destitute! Good Christian sir and servant of the Lord, take heed of my need." This was the line of my beseech-ment on ordinary days; but on festive occasions I altered my approach and said: "Oh faithful Christians and the Lord's devout: for love of the Mother of God, that most sublime Princess and Queen of the Angels, bestow some little charity on one who has been smitten lame by the hand of the Almighty." At this point I would hesitate for a moment—a matter, good reader, of the utmost importance, before adding: "Once when I was well and fit, I was working in a vineyard, and the poisoned air there fettered my limbs at an evil moment, praise be to God!" This never failed to bring me profit, and the money tinkled merrily in my cup. I would have earned more if an ill-faced lad with no arms and only one leg who worked the same streets as I did, had not crossed my path. He begged with less art but took in more money. He would shout in a rasping voice that invariably turned into a squeak: "Oh servants of Jeeeeesiss, do not forget those punished by God for their sins. Remember: a gift to the poor is a gift to the Savior." And then he would blurt out: "For the love of Jeeeeesiss. . . ." And with this he amassed a fortune. Being of an observant nature, I uttered Christ's name in the usual way no more, but prolonged and mispronounced it the way the other fellow did in order to call forth more piety. After I had changed my manner of petitioning, my capital swelled rapidly.

At night I slept on a surgeon's porch with a local indigent who was one of the greatest tricksters ever sanctioned by the Lord. He was exceedingly clever, and he was therefore more opulent than any of the rest of us. He had a great hernia. He concealed one arm and tied the other up with a sash in such a way that one hand appeared swollen and the other missing. To complete his act he cultivated a feverish look at all times. It was his custom to place himself in a supine position with the hernia on display as if it had been a melon. Once he had assumed this pose, he would ejaculate: "Take notice of my poverty and the curse God has doomed me to bear." If a woman passed by, he would say: "Oh most gracious lady, may God be in your heart." Many people came daily and left him small sums, even though his corner was out of their way, simply because he flattered them with great adroitness. A passing soldier was always addressed as "Good captain" and a plain, ordinary man as "Great sir." For those who happened to go by in a coach he was ready with "Your Grace," and to others he would say "Your Excellency," while a simple priest on muleback was always worth a hearty "Good Archdeacon." To come to the point, I may say that he was an archsycophant whose flexible style of begging was ever adjusted to the occasion and to the person. I developed a great friendship with him, and he told me the secret of his success. It was an arrangement he had made with three little boys who begged in the streets, stealing what they could. My master acted as custodian of their earnings. But that was not all, for he also shared the profits from the cup and arts of two other lads who roamed the vicinity. With such excellent advice from so experienced a teacher, plus the practical lessons he gave me, I developed a similar style. Since he purposely directed good people to my location, I had within the month acquired savings that amounted to two hundred reals. One day he divulged to me his most precious secret with the understanding that we were to work in cooperation. His plan, which seemed to me to be the greatest trick ever devised by a mendicant, was to (more or less) kidnap some four or five children and go about the streets heralding a description of them. On meeting the parents we would answer: "Yes sir, we found him at such-and-such an hour, and if we hadn't arrived just at that moment, a vehicle most certainly would have killed him. But rest assured that he is safe now at our house."

With the rewards we received I soon accumulated such wealth that I had a total sum of fifty crowns. By that time my legs were well, although still bandaged. I resolved to leave Madrid and take the road to Toledo, where I knew no one and no one knew me. I bought a beige suit, a collar, and a sword; and I took my leave of Valcázar (my companion referred to above), and at various inns tried to find a way to reach my destination.

CHAPTER XXII

Which relates how the hero became an actor, a poet, and

a suitor of nuns, whose virtues are briefly described

In a certain tavern I met a company of players on their way to Toledo. They were travelling in three coaches, and as God would have it, there happened to be among them an old friend of mine who had been a student with me at Alcalá. He had later deserted the academic world in order to join the company. I told him how much I needed to leave Madrid and go to Toledo. Because of the scar on my face, the fellow did not at first recognize me, and crossed himself as he spoke. At length I won his friendship with the aid of a little money, and he made room for me in his group.

Men and women were mixed together promiscuously. One of the ladies, a dancer who also played the serious part of queen, struck me as being exceedingly comely. But, as fortune would have it, her husband was seated at my side, and I—not aware of the gentleman's identity, and being at the same time carried away with the amorous intention of possessing the aforementioned damsel—I said to the husband: "Could you tell me how I might talk to that woman who is possessed of such marvellous beauty? I should like to tell her that I would enjoy spending twenty or thirty crowns in communion with her." "Well," says he, "it is hardly for me to say. I happen to be her husband. But (and I speak quite objectively) any money spent on her is money well spent, for there is no better or more enticing bit of flesh to be found in this broad world."

I found his reply most amusing. It was like that of an ignoramus who has imperfectly understood Saint Paul's precept concerning the possession of a wife: "Let those who have wives live as if they had none." So I availed myself of the opportunity, and essayed a conversation with the lady in question. She inquired about my livelihood and destination; and after great effort I was able to arrange a meeting between us as soon as we reached Toledo. When this difficulty had been dispatched, we passed the remainder of the journey in pleasant parlance.

By chance I happened to recite part of a play about Saint Alexis that I had learned as a child. My performance was so good that it awakened no little jealousy in some of the members of the company. My friend, to whom I had already related my misfortunes, asked me whether I would care to become a member of the troupe. He praised the actor's life so excellently that I pledged myself to work for two years with the director, partly from necessity and partly from desire for the damsel. I signed an agreement and received in return my daily allowance and my scripts. And so we reached Toledo. I was given three or four short plays to study and was assigned some old men's parts, which seemed to suit my voice very well. I took great pains to give a creditable performance in this my first play. It was set on a boat, as all of them are—a boat that was badly damaged and without provisions. I pronounced my lines with artistry, and addressed the audience as "Senate," asked for tolerance for the play's shortcomings, and begged for silence before making my exit. There was only gentle applause, but at least I knew I could act.

We presented a play composed by one of our own actors. I must confess that I was greatly astonished to learn that he was a poet, for I had always considered poets to be learned and wise men, and not mere laymen. But the truth is that nowadays every producer writes plays, and every player composes his farce about Moors and Christians. I recall that in the past, if no play by Lope or Alonso Ramón was to be had, the day was lost.

To be brief, the first day we presented the play, no one understood a word of it. We tried it again the second day, and as God would have it, it began with a war. I came on stage in armor, and luckily, I had a shield—because had it been otherwise, I most surely would have been pummeled to death with cucumbers, overripe quinces, stalks, and sundry other missiles. Such a commotion was never heard in all the world; and no play was ever compounded of so much nonsense as that one was. It was about a king of Normandy disguised as a hermit, who apparently had no idea about what was going on. With him were two lackeys whose only function was to provoke laughter. The plot was so involved that there was nothing to do but marry everybody to everybody else, and call it a day. The least I can say is that our talents were justly appreciated.

Afterwards, the entire company gave the egregious poet a very hard time. I, for one, advised him to be grateful for his escape and counselled him to profit from his errors. He swore up and down that the play was really not his, and that it had been built up with one act from one play and another act from a second, and was put together with brief emendations which he had himself made in the wretched thing. In his judgment its principal defect lay in faulty assembly. He then confessed that the fools who wrote plays were prompted by profit, and it was easier for them to avail themselves of any composition they could lay hands on rather than write one of their own. Affirming that no dramatist had ever done otherwise, he added that for three or four hundred reals any author would gladly expose himself to such risks, even though it entailed plagiarizing a work presented previously in the same city. And he went on to say: "We read them, add and subtract a few things, and then claim them as the fruits of our genius."

The scheme did not sound too bad to me, and I confess that I was really quite taken with the idea, for by nature I was inclined to writing poetry, and I had no mean acquaintance with the poets, especially Garcilaso. So with this in mind, I determined to try my hand at the art.

I henceforth spent my time performing the various duties connected with my profession, and within a month the audiences of Toledo had become used to calling me *Alonsito* (a name which I had assumed), and I was also called "The Cruel" —a sobriquet that proceeded from a role I had played to the delight of groundlings and the common herd.

I now had three suits, and there were several producers after me, trying to entice me away from the company. I now talked knowingly about the stage, criticised the famous, disapproved of Pinedo's style of acting, applauded Sánchez's repose, and said that Morales did a nice job. My advice was asked about stage decorations and special theater equipment. And if anyone wished an audition to read his play, I was the one who heard it.

In short, encouraged by the applause I had received, I made my début as a dramatist-poet with a ballad I had written, and then I did an interlude which wasn't bad. Later on I tried my hand at a full-length play, and so that no one could say it was not "divine" I wrote it about Our Lady of the Rosary. It began with music on the flageolets, and there were the usual souls in purgatory, and demons too. The latter entered chanting *bu, bu* and exited chanting *ri, ri*. (That was the style back then.) In my verses I used the name Satan, and discoursed on whether he fell from heaven, and all that sort of thing. The townspeople seemed to like it very much. My play was, to be brief, quite a success.

After that, I was terribly busy, what with lovers who wanted me to write eye- and eyebrow-poems for them. Others commissioned hair- and hand-poems. I had a different price for everything, even though I was willing to let some items go cheap because of certain competition I had. And how about carols? I was swamped by requests from sacristans and suitors of nuns. Blind men practically supported me with prayers—the ones I wrote for them at eight reals a piece, I mean. I also wrote one to the Just Judge about this time. It was resonant and sonorous, and called forth charitable reactions in hearers. I wrote this piece for a blind man who published it under his own name, and it became quite famous. It went like this:

> *Mother of the Human Word,*
> *Daughter of the heavenly Race,*
> *[Let my chaste heart be stirred],*
> *Lend me virginal grace. Etc., etc. . . .*

I was the first ever to introduce the idea of ending carols like sermons, with "grace in this world," and "glory in the next," as in this piece I wrote about a captive from Tetuán:

> Let us pray with all insistence
> To that high King which hath no dross
> That since He seeth our long persistence
> We shall not, earthly, suffer loss,
> Nor lose redemption through His cross.
> With lack of grace in this world ne'er perplexed,
> Grant us a crown of glory in the next.

I was doing famously at this line of work, and I was so well-off, that I almost aspired to be a producer myself. I had my house brushed up, and went about taverns buying up covers decorated with coats-of-arms. And my coats-of-arms were really more understandable than the King's, for his are always complicated; but mine were very easy to figure out—there were, you see, so many holes there, you could see right through them.

Something happened to me one day, and although it was very embarrassing to me, I am going to put it down here, anyway. I had repaired to the attic of my abode, while I was working on a play. I liked to work up there and so had a servant girl bring my food up to me. I had got into the habit of reciting out loud what I was writing—and right briskly too. Now the devil so brought it about that on one occasion the girl came up the dark, narrow stairs loaded down with dishes and a stew —and just at the moment I was busy writing a scene about a hunting party. As I composed my play I began shouting out in a very loud voice:

> "Oh hold, Oh hold the fiery bear,
> For he in pieces me doth tear,
> And after thee will promptly fare! . . ."

Well, the girl took it to be a real warning. She turned to flee and in her confusion, stepped on her skirt and rolled all the way down the stairs, spilled the stew, broke all the plates, and ran screaming into the street, crying out that a bear was killing a man. And although I immediately hurried down to her, the whole neighborhood had flocked around me to inquire about the bear. Even after I explained to them that it was all in a play I was writing and that the girl had simply misunderstood what was going on, they still would not quite believe it. I did not eat that day. My companions found out about my mishap, and the story was bruited about all over town. Many things like that happened to me while I persevered in the office of author-poet, and I continued to get into all sorts of trouble.

It so happened that our director ended up the way such fellows usually do. It was learned that things had gone well with him in Toledo, and some legal action was then taken against him, and he was clapped in jail. The company then broke up, and we went separate ways. Although my companions wanted me to get a new company together, I did not, to tell the truth, care to assume any such undertaking. My alliance with them had come about through sheer necessity, and nothing more. Now that I had some little capital and felt a bit secure, my only concern was to take some time out and have a good time. So I said good-by to them all, and they went their several ways.

Now, I thought I would get out of the precarious life I had led as an actor, but (if you will not take amiss what I am about to write down) I became what is known as a "grating-lover." I may explain this expression by saying that I aspired to be the father of the Antichrist, whose mother will be, it is said, a nun. In brief, I became a wooer of nuns. This all began when one of those ladies of religion, who had commissioned me to write some carols for her, rather took to me when she saw me in a Corpus play in which I played the part of St. John the Evangelist, from whom her order took its name. She showered me with favors and said her only regret was that I had turned out to be an actor (for I had made out to her that I was really the son of a great gentleman). She felt very bad about that. Finally I decided to write her the following

LETTER

"I have, Your Grace, abandoned the company of players I was in, not so much because I felt that such a step was to my advantage as because I knew it would be pleasing to yourself. And although I had been placed there for some time, no company, madam, can be good company to me that is not your own good company, for away from your presence I am most desolately alone. And now I shall be all the more yours the more I am able to live my own life. Advise me, dear lady, when you have visiting hours, and at that time I shall know when my happiness will begin"—etc., etc. . . .

One of those convent messengers took my letter to her. You cannot imagine how delighted the good nun was to hear of my new way of life. She answered my letter in the following

REPLY

"I must withhold my best wishes now rather than to have to *send* them to you; and I should regret to have to do that, were I not convinced that my good will and your profit are one and the same thing. You have, I think we may say, seen the light. Now all that is needed is perseverance—perseverance that will match the perseverance that I shall also have. I am afraid we shall not be receiving here today; but do not fail to appear at vespers, and we shall see each other then, and then hold colloquies at the window. Perhaps I shall be able to pull the wool over the abbess's eyes. And so, farewell."

I was very happy to get this note, for my nun was very bright and pretty to look at. I had dinner and then put on the clothes I wore when I played the part of gallant on the stage. I went straight to church, and prayed there, and at once began to try and spy out all the holes and crannies in the grating to see whether she had appeared. And so, as God willed it in His good hour, (though I rather think it must have been the Devil in his evil one), I at last heard the ancient signal: she began to cough. And then I began to cough; and the coughing that ensued sounded as if hell itself had opened up and was coughing its entrails to death. You might have thought that someone had scattered pepper all over the church.

I eventually got tired of coughing so much, and then I perceived that an old dame had appeared at the grating. She was all cough; and then I saw what had happened to me. To get involved in coughing at a convent is not without its dangers; for what is a sign of beckoning in the young is merely habit in the old. And you may think you are listening to the dulcet notes of a nightingale when you are really hearing the caw of a crow. I stayed there in the church until vespers began. I heard them all the way through. You may understand why nuns' wooers are called *solemn* lovers. It is because they are so intimately connected with *solemn vespers* at eventide. And in a way, their fate does have much of evening about it, for the day they hope for never, never dawns.

You can never imagine how many vespers I listened to; and at the end my neck was two yards longer than it had previously been—from my sheer stretching it out to see what was going on. I became a great friend of the sacristan and the acolyte, and I was even well received by the vicar, who was certainly a queer one—he walked about so stiffly you might have thought he ate spits for breakfast and inflexible arrows for dinner.

I went to the casements; but the courtyard was so small it would have been necessary to reserve seats there before twelve o'clock—just as if you had been going to the theater. The place was simply seething with devotees. Well, I managed to get in the best I could. The postures assumed by the wooers there was something to behold. Some of them simply froze and never batted an eye—just looked straight ahead, with one hand on their swords and the other on their rosaries, so that they looked very like stone statues on a tomb. Another kind would lift its arms and extend them and throw out its hands seraphically, as if being martyred. Another sort would stand there with mouth wider open than a demanding woman's, never uttering a sound and allowing the lady to strike up an acquaintance with his innermost portions as her gaze penetrated down his gullet. Another would press tight against the wall and become a heavy burden to the bricks, and stand as if trying to measure himself against the corner of the house. There was another kind that strode up and down as if they thought they could win their ladies over with only their gait—they showed off just like he-mules. And finally there were some who held billets-doux aloft, like hunters calling their falcons back. There was one crowd that I call the jealous crowd. They gathered in little clusters, laughing and looking at the girls. Others read verses and waved them about; an occasional one, to make his lady jealous, would walk up and down the clear space before the building holding hands with some woman. And another would talk to a servant who was in on the game and would pretend to bring him a message from another ladylove.

This is what went on down below; but what went on up above where the nuns were was well worth seeing too. The place where the interviews took place was a little tower so full of cracks and with so much openwork in its walls that at times it looked like a little perforated box people put sand in to blot letters with, and at other times it looked very much like a pomander box for putting scents in. All those little holes and crevices were peopled by numberless spying apparitions. The whole scene was a perfect hodgepodge of hands and feet. It reminded me of an old-fashioned Castilian Saturday dinner [when, as on Fridays, meat of the usual variety was not supposed to be eaten, although the eating of the heads, feet and miscellaneous parts of animals was allowed]. Well, that was just the way that scene looked to me—heads and feet and miscellaneous parts . . . but no brains. On one side, the place looked like a peddlar's wares on display—a rosary here, a handkerchief there, a glove here, a green ribbon there. Some of the nuns talked right out full and loud; others coughed. And still others made hissing sounds the way hat sellers do to attract the attention of customers. And the signals made by their fingers sticking through the holes in the grating looked like a lot of spiders scurrying about.

It is amazing to see how in the summertime they not only

bask themselves in the sun but go so far as to get scorched. It is something of a contrast to see the men so sunburnt and the women so bleached out. And with the humidity of winter some of us sprout watercress and other little glades on our persons. No snow falls to whiten us; no rains pass us by. And yet! we go through all this just to talk to a woman through a grating or a window as if we stood admiring the bones of a saint. If the beloved talks, it is all very much like falling in love with a thrush in a cage; if she is silent, it is very like being enamored of a picture. Or like two croquet balls that never quite collide. Their favors are fruitless—a brush of the fingers. They wedge their heads between bars and send their verbal caressings through diminutive casements; and all is clandestine. All speech is hushed and recondite. Why should they put up with the gruntings and scoldings of an old woman, a bossy portress, or a lying doorkeeper? And they try very hard to show their jealousy of the women in the outside world. They tell us their love for us is the one and only true love. And you cannot imagine the reasons they give to convince us of that.

I eventually ended up by calling the abbess "my lady," the vicar "father", and the sacristan, "brother." That sort of thing is quite likely to happen in the course of time to a man who is as far gone as I was. The doorkeepers began to get on my nerves by sending me away; and the nuns with their constant requests bothered me too. I began to realize that hell, which usually comes cheap, had begun to cost me a pretty penny. I saw that I was becoming the architect of my own perdition; and I realized that I was moving downward only from having exercised my sense of touch. When I talked to my lady I would try to keep the others there from hearing me and I would press my head so tightly against the bars that for three days afterwards I bore the imprint of iron on my brow. And I sounded like a priest saying the words of the Consecration; and everyone who saw me said: "You damned low-down wooer of nuns"—and several things worse.

Well, all these matters forced me to take stock of myself. I almost decided to give up my nun, even though it meant renouncing my sustenance; and I finally did make up my mind on the Day of St. John the Evangelist, because I then came to the conclusion that I knew what nuns were like. All I need to tell you, sir, is that the sisters there made themselves hoarse on purpose and instead of singing mass they moaned it. They never washed their faces, and they wore old rags; and the devotees of the Baptist sisters, to discredit this fiesta, brought stools to church instead of chairs and came accompanied by many picaroons from the cheap parts of town.

When I saw that some of the nuns in the name of one saint, and other nuns in the name of another saint, were giving their devotees pretty rough treatment, I inveigled my nun into giving me (to raffle off, I told her) fifty crowns' worth of needlework, some silk stockings, and pouches full of amber and sweets; and I forthwith went my way to Seville. . . . What the nun's sorrow and regret must have been, the pious reader may conjecture; but her sentiments were, I daresay, far more concerned with the property I had stolen from her than with my miserable self.

CHAPTER XXIII

AND THE LAST

My trip from Toledo to Seville was a prosperous one, for I was well trained in the arts of trickery. I had on me some dice that were loaded and designed falsely, and I had brought along some trick cards too. [The number of deceptions and frauds practiced with this sort of equipment is numberless, and I should like to warn the reader to be on guard against them at all times.*]

---

* The words in brackets are a feeble summary of about thirty lines in the original that are concerned with card games and sharper's tricks used in them. Américo Castro's 1927 edition has considerable commentary on this; but at the end of one long note, Professor Castro writes—I translate: "In spite of what has been written about the matter, we still know very little about these tricks. It is regrettable that no one has thought of making a

I reached Seville with all my jargon and tricks. I won enough money from my companions to pay for the rental on my mule; and I exploited innkeepers in the same fashion and made enough to pay for my food and lodging. I betook myself to the Moor's Inn, where I met an old schoolmate from Alcalá. His name was Mata but he thought it not resounding enough and so had renamed himself Matorral. He was a dealer in lives and the proprietor of slashes—and he was very well fitted for this latter occupation, for he was one mass of gashes and slashes, and he had them all classified so he could use them when it came time for his customers to choose the kind of gash he was to give their enemies. He used to say: "There is no teacher like one who has been well slashed." And he was right, for his face was a perfect leather jacket, and he was himself nothing but a big leather skin.

He asked me to come and have dinner with him and some of his friends. He said they would get me back home safely.

I went; and when we reached his inn, he said: "Come now: take yer cape off, and act big; for yer going to see the finest boys in Seville tonight; and so yer won't be taken for a sissy, muss up yer hair, slump over a bit, and let yer cape drag a little (the way we drag out our existence); screw up yer snout, gesture all over the place and when you talk pronounce your *h*'s like *j*'s and yer *j*'s like *h*'s: [for *Huelve* say 'Juelva' and for *Jarama* say 'Harama']. Don'cher forget."

He lent me a dagger that was as broad as a cutlass and as long as a sword (though in its modesty it would have refrained from so praising itself). "Here," said my friend: "drink half a gallon of this wine. Unless you are stinking with it they won't think you are a real he-man."

While we were about this (and I was getting giddy with my half gallon of wine) four of his friends came in weaving back

---

clear and methodical study of games of chance in the seventeenth century. . . ." It has been thought wise to summarize these obscure and difficult lines, which, even if they could be correctly deciphered, might not be very rewarding—and perhaps, after all the effort, they would still be incomprehensible to the modern English reader.

and forth and sporting four gouty shoes for faces. They did not use their capes to cover themselves with in the usual fashion but had them swathed around their middles. They wore their hats pushed high up on their foreheads and the skirts of their garments high up in front (like diadems). And they wore so many complex swords and daggers they looked like perfect hardware stores. The tips of their accouterments touched their right heels. Their eyes had a furtive look about them but they could look at you piercingly. Their mustaches were pointed like horns. . . . They gave us a greeting with their mouths, and then said to my friend in a petulant tone, excising their words: "Y'r suvv'nt." My guide replied: "Old chum!" And they sat down.

They tried to find out who I was but asked no verbal questions. One of them just looked at Matorrales and opened his mouth and then stuck out his lower lip in my direction. My guide answered silently by stroking his beard and looking down at the floor. At this they all got up and came forward and embraced me, and I embraced them—which amounted to my sampling four different brands of wine.

The supper hour arrived; and some rogues who worked for tough characters came in and waited on us. We sat down at the table, and the capers appeared. Then as a welcome to me they drank to my honor; and I never before realized I had so much of it until I saw them drinking to its health at such great length. Then in came the fish and meat, all thirsty and productive of more imbibing. A big tub filled with wine was there on the floor, and anyone who felt the urge to have a swig could bend down over it and drink his fill. I was amused by this little tank. Well, after two helpings not a one of them could tell the others apart. They started telling war stories; the air turned thick with their swearing. Every time they drank a toast, the bells tolled for twenty or thirty of their victims who had died without confession. They prescribed a thousand stabs for the Chief Magistrate of Seville. They then had a memorial service for Diego Tiznado, the Dark; and oblations were poured out on the ground [as the custom was], in memory of Escamilla, the

Bully. Some of the guests became tender and bewept poor unlucky Alonso Álvarez. My companion was also affected—the
clock-wheels in his head began to move in peculiar directions;
and he took up a loaf of bread and held it up to the light and
somewhat hoarsely said: "By this bread, which is the very face
of God, and by that light that issued from the angel's mouth,
let us, my friends, if you will, give the constable the same treatment tonight that he once gave poor dear old One-Eye."

A jarring shout now surged forth from them; and baring their
daggers they placed their hands on the edge of the tub and bent
down over it, saying:

"Just as we drink this wine, so shall we drink the blood of
anyone who plays tricks on us."

"And who is this Alonso Alvarez?" I asked. "Why do they
take his death so hard?"

"A tough customer he was," one replied; "and a fearless
scrapper. He was ready of hand and he was a good buddy.
Watch me! The devils are after me again."

At this we left the house in search of constables. I had let
myself succumb to the half-gallon of wine; and my senses were
by now acting so vinously that I barely realized what a dangerous situation I was in. We reached La Mar Street, where we
ran into the night watch. Our people immediately drew their
swords and attacked the newcomers. I did the same. Two of
the constables gave up their damned souls at the very first on-
slaught. The chief bailiff told his men to take to their heels,
and they ran up the street crying for help. We could not catch
them—they had too good a head start. We eventually ended
up by taking sanctuary in the cathedral, where we were sheltered from the rigors of justice. There we slept off the wine
that was fuming and spuming in our heads. When we came to,
I was amazed to realize that two constables had been killed
and the chief bailiff had actually fled—all because of the action
of the bunch of drunken thugs that we were.

We had a grand time there in the church, because a lot of
whores smelled out the presence of fugitives from justice and
came and took care of us—in a sense, they undressed outside

to help us keep dressed within. One of them by the name of La Grajal became quite fond of me. I, for my part, had already taken more of a liking to this way of life than any other I had ever had. And so I proposed to the girl to sail the sea of love with her until we died. I studied up on underworld balladry; and in a few days I was a very musical rabbi among my tough friends.

The police had not given up trying to get us out of our sanctuary. They continued to prowl around the doors of the cathedral. We were able, nevertheless, to get out and, disguised, prowl around, ourselves, after midnight.

When I realized that this sort of thing had been going on for a good long while and that Fortune was unrelenting in her castigations of me (though I never profited from the experience she offered—I am not sensible enough to do that—but continued to act from sheer weariness like an obstinate and jaded sinner)—when I had realized all this (I was saying), I decided to consult La Grajal about my future; and then I made up my mind to go to America with her to see whether I might, by changing worlds and countries, perhaps better my plight. But it turned out worse than ever for me, as you shall see, sir, in the second part. For a man may change his lifelong habitat, but it will do him no earthly good unless he likewise changes his lifelong habits.*

---

* No second part ever appeared.

FUENTE OVEJUNA

LOPE DE VEGA

Translated by Angel Flores and Muriel Kittel

DRAMATIS PERSONAE

QUEEN ISABELLA OF CASTILE
KING FERDINAND OF ARAGON
RODRIGO TÉLLEZ GIRÓN, *Maestre of the religious*
and military Order of Calatrava
FERNÁN GÓMEZ DE GUZMÁN, *Comendador Mayor*
of the Order of Calatrava
DON MANRIQUE
A JUDGE
TWO COUNCILMEN OF CIUDAD REAL
ORTUÑO ⎫
FLORES ⎭ *servants of the Comendador*
ESTEBAN ⎫
ALONSO ⎭ *Mayors of Fuente Ovejuna*
LAURENCIA ⎫
JACINTA ⎬ *peasant girls*
PASCUALA ⎭
JUAN ROJO, *Councilman of Fuente Ovejuna, a peasant*
ANOTHER COUNCILMAN OF FUENTE OVEJUNA
FRONDOSO ⎫
MENGO ⎬ *peasants*
BARRILDO ⎭
LEONELO, *Licentiate of Law*
CIMBRANOS, *a soldier*
A BOY
PEASANTS, MEN AND WOMEN
MUSICIANS   *Time:* 1476

ACT I

Hall of the MAESTRE OF THE ORDER OF CALATRAVA, *in Almagro.*

[*Enter the* COMENDADOR *and his servants,* FLORES *and* ORTUÑO.]

COMENDADOR: Does the Maestre know that I am here?

FLORES: He does, my lord.

ORTUÑO: The Maestre is becoming more mature.

COMENDADOR: Does he know that I am Fernán Gómez de Guzmán?

FLORES: He's only a boy—you mustn't be surprised if he doesn't.

COMENDADOR: Nevertheless he must know that I am the Comendador.

ORTUÑO: There are those who advise him to be discourteous.

COMENDADOR: That will win him little love. Courtesy is the key to good will, while thoughtless discourtesy is the way to make enemies.

ORTUÑO: If we but realized how it makes us hated and despised by everyone we would rather die than be discourteous.

FLORES: What a nuisance discourtesy is: among equals it's foolish and toward inferiors it's tyrannical. In this case it only means that the boy has not learned what it is to be loved.

COMENDADOR: The obligation he took upon himself when he accepted his sword and the Cross of Calatrava was placed on his breast should have been enough to teach him courtesy.

FLORES: If he has been prejudiced against you you'll soon find out.

ORTUÑO: Why don't you leave if you're in doubt?

COMENDADOR: I wish to see what he is like.

[*Enter the* MAESTRE OF CALATRAVA *and retinue.*]

MAESTRE: Pardon me, Fernán Gómez de Guzmán; I only just heard that you had come. Forgive me if I have kept you waiting.

COMENDADOR: I have just cause for complaint. Both my love for you and my rank entitle me to better treatment—for you are the Maestre of Calatrava and I your Comendador and your servant.

MAESTRE: I did not know of your welcome arrival—let me embrace you again.

COMENDADOR: You owe me a great deal; I have risked my life to settle your many difficulties. I even managed to persuade the Pope to increase your age.

MAESTRE: That is true, and by the holy cross which we both proudly bear on our breasts I shall repay you in love, and honor you as my own father.

COMENDADOR: I am satisfied that you will.

MAESTRE: What news of the war?

COMENDADOR: Listen carefully, and I will tell you where your duty lies.

MAESTRE: I am listening; tell me.

COMENDADOR: Maestre Don Rodrigo Téllez Girón, I need hardly remind you how your brave father resigned his high position as Maestre to you eight years ago, and appointed Don Juan Pacheco, the Grand Maestre of Santiago, to be your co-adjutor, nor how kings and comendadors confirmed and swore to his act, and the Pope [Pius II] * and his successor Paul agreed to it in their bulls; no, what I have come to tell you is this: now that Pacheco is dead and you, in spite of your youth, have sole control of the government, now is the time for you to take up arms for the honor of your family. Since the death of Henry IV your relatives have supported the cause of Don Alonso, King of Portugal, who claims the throne of Castile through his wife Juana. Ferdinand, the great prince of Aragon, makes a similar claim through his wife Isabella. But your relatives do not consider Ferdinand's rights to be as clear as those of Juana—who is now in your cousin's power. So I advise you to rally the knights of Calatrava in Almagro and to capture Ciudad Real, which stands on the frontier between Andalusia and Castile. You will not need many men, because the enemy can count only on their neighbors and a few noblemen who support Isabella and consider Ferdinand their legitimate king. It will be wonderful if you, Rodrigo, if you, a youth, can astonish those who say that

---

* Material which has been added for clarity has been placed in brackets throughout the play.

this cross is too heavy for your young shoulders. Emulate the counts of Urueña from whom you spring, and who from the height of their fame seem to be challenging you with the laurels they have won; emulate the marquises of Villena and those other captains who are so numerous that the wings of fame are not strong enough to bear them. Unsheathe your white sword, dye it red in battle till it matches the cross upon your breast. For I cannot call you the Maestre of the Red Cross as long as your sword is white: both the sword you bear and the cross you wear must be red. And you, mighty Girón, must add the crowning glory to the immortal fame of your ancestors.

MAESTRE: Fernán Gómez, you may be sure that I side with my family in this dispute, for I am convinced that they are right. And as I translate my conviction into action at Ciudad Real you will see me tearing the city walls down with the violence of a thunderbolt. I know that I am young—but do not think that my courage died with my uncle's death. I will unsheathe my white sword and its brilliance shall become the color of the cross, bathed in red blood.

But tell me, where do you live, and do you have any soldiers?

COMENDADOR: A few—but they are faithful and they will fight like lions. I live in Fuente Ovejuna, where the people are skilled in agriculture and husbandry rather than in the arts of war.

MAESTRE: And you live there, you say?

COMENDADOR: I do. I chose a house on my estate to stay in during these troubled times. Now see that all your people go into action with you—let no man stay behind!

MAESTRE: You shall see me today on horseback, bearing my lance on high.

[*Exeunt* COMENDADOR *and* MAESTRE.]

A *public square in Fuente Ovejuna.*

[*Enter* LAURENCIA *and* PASCUALA.]

LAURENCIA: I hoped he would never come back.

PASCUALA: I must say I thought you'd be more distressed at the news.

LAURENCIA: I hoped to God I'd never see him again.

PASCUALA: I have seen women just as adamant as you, Laurencia, if not more so—and yet, underneath, their hearts were as soft as butter.

LAURENCIA: Well, is there an oak tree as hard as I am?

PASCUALA: Be careful. No one should boast that he'll never thirst for water.

LAURENCIA: But I do. And I'll maintain it against the world. What good would it do me to love Fernán? Do you think I would marry him?

PASCUALA: Of course not.

LAURENCIA: Well then, I condemn infamy. Too many girls hereabouts have trusted the Comendador only to be ruined by him.

PASCUALA: All the same it will be a miracle if you escape him.

LAURENCIA: You don't understand, Pascuala. He has been after me for a month now, but he has only been wasting his time. His emissary, Flores, and that blustering fool Ortuño have come to show me a blouse, a necklace, a hat, and have told me so many wonderful stories about their lord and master that they have succeeded in frightening me but not in moving my heart.

PASCUALA: Where did they talk to you?

LAURENCIA: Down there by the brook, about six days ago.

PASCUALA: It looks as if they are trying to deceive you, Laurencia.

LAURENCIA: Deceive me?

PASCUALA: If not you, then the priest.

LAURENCIA: I may be a young chicken, but I'm too tough for His Highness. Pascuala, I would far rather put a slice of ham on the fire in the early morning and eat it with my homemade bread and a glass of wine stolen from my mother, and then at noon to smell a piece of beef boiling with cabbage and eat it ravenously, or, if I have had a trying day, marry an eggplant to some bacon; and in the evening, while cooking the supper, go and pick a handful of grapes from the vines (God save them from the hail) and afterwards dine on chopped meat with oil and pepper, and so happily to bed murmuring "Lead us not

into temptation"—I would much rather this than all the wiles
and tricks of scoundrels. For after all, all they want after giving
us so much trouble is their pleasure at night and our sorrow in
the morning.

PASCUALA: You are right, Laurencia, for as soon as they tire
of love they are more ungrateful than the sparrows are to the
peasants. In winter when the fields are frozen hard the sparrows
fly down from the roofs, and saying "Sweet Sweet," hop right
on to the dining table for crumbs, but as soon as the cold is
over and the fields are again in bloom they no longer come
down saying "Sweet Sweet," but stay hopping on the roof,
mocking us with their calls. Men are the same; when they need
us nothing can be sweeter than they—we are their life, their
soul, their heart, their all—but as soon as they tire of us their
sweetness disappears and their wooing phrases become a mock-
ery.

LAURENCIA: The moral of which is: trust no man, Pascuala.

PASCUALA: That's what I say.

[*Enter* MENGO, BARRILDO, *and* FRONDOSO.]

FRONDOSO: You are wrong, Barrildo, in this argument.

BARRILDO: Well never mind, here's somebody who will settle
the matter.

MENGO: Let's have an understanding before we reach them:
if I'm right, then each of you gives me a present as a reward.

BARRILDO: All right. But if you lose, what will you give?

MENGO: I'll give my boxwood rebec, which I value more than
a barn.

BARRILDO: That's fine.

FRONDOSO: Let's approach them. God bless you, fair ladies.

LAURENCIA: You call us ladies, Frondoso?

FRONDOSO: We want to keep up with the times. In these
days all bachelors are licentiates; the blind are one-eyed; the
cross-eyed merely squint; and the lame have only a sprained
ankle. The unscrupulous are called honest; the ignorant, clever;
and the braggart, brave. A large mouth is described as luscious,
a small eye as sharp. The pettifogger is called diligent; the
busybody, charming; the charlatan, sympathetic; the deadly

bore, gallant. The cowardly become valiant; the hard-headed, vivacious; coxcombs are comrades; fools, broad-minded; malcontents, philosophers. Baldness is identified with authority, foolish chatter with wit. People with tumors have only a slight cold, and those who are arrogant are circumspect; the shifty are constant; and the humpbacked, just slightly bent. This, in short —the enumeration could go on indefinitely—was the sort of thing I did in calling you ladies. I merely followed the fashion of the day.

LAURENCIA: In the city, Frondoso, such words are used in courtesy; discourteous tongues use a severer and more acrimonious vocabulary.

FRONDOSO: I should like to hear it.

LAURENCIA: It's the very opposite of yours. The serious-minded are called bores; the unfortunate, lucky; the even-tempered, melancholy; and anyone who expresses disapproval is hateful. Those who offer good advice are importunate; the liberal-minded are dull-witted; the just, unjust; and the pious, weak-kneed. In this language the faithful become inconstant; the courteous, flatterers; the charitable, hypocrites; and the good Christians, frauds. Anyone who has won a well-deserved reward is called fortunate; truth becomes impudence; patience, cowardice; and misfortune, retribution. The modest woman is foolish; the beautiful and chaste, unnatural; and the honorable woman is called . . . . But enough! This reply should be sufficient.

MENGO: You little devil!

LAURENCIA: What an elegant expression.

MENGO: I bet the priest poured handfuls of salt on her when he christened her.

LAURENCIA: What was the argument that brought you here, if we may ask?

FRONDOSO: Listen, Laurencia.

LAURENCIA: Speak.

FRONDOSO: Lend me your ear, Laurencia.

LAURENCIA: Lend it to you? Why, I'll give it to you right now.

FRONDOSO: I trust your discretion.

LAURENCIA: Well, what was the wager about?

FRONDOSO: Barrildo and I wagered against Mengo.

LAURENCIA: And what does Mengo claim?

BARRILDO: It is something that he insists on denying, although it is plainly a fact.

MENGO: I deny it because I know better.

LAURENCIA: But what is it?

BARRILDO: He claims that love does not exist.

LAURENCIA: Many people think that.

BARRILDO: Many people do, but it's foolish. Without love not even the world could exist.

MENGO: I don't know how to philosophize; as for reading, I wish I could! But I say that if the elements of Nature live in eternal conflict, then our bodies, which receive from them food, anger, melancholy, phlegm, and blood, must also be at war with each other.

BARRILDO: The world here and beyond, Mengo, is perfect harmony. Harmony is pure love, for love is complete agreement.

MENGO: As far as the natural world goes, I do not deny it. There is love which rules all things through an obligating inter-relationship. I have never denied that each person has love proportionate to his humour—my hand will protect me from the blow aimed at my face, my foot will protect me from harm by enabling me to flee danger, my eyelids will protect my eyes from threatening specks—such is love in nature.

PASCUALA: What are you trying to prove, then?

MENGO: That individuals love only themselves.

PASCUALA: Pardon me, Mengo, for telling you that you lie. For it is a lie. The intensity with which a man loves a woman or an animal its mate . . .

MENGO: I call that self-love, not love. What is love?

LAURENCIA: A desire for beauty.

MENGO: And why does love seek beauty?

LAURENCIA: To enjoy it.

MENGO: That's just what I believe. Is not such enjoyment selfish?

LAURENCIA: That's right.

MENGO: Therefore a person seeks that which brings him joy.

LAURENCIA: That is true.

MENGO: Hence there is no love but the kind I speak of, the one I pursue for my personal pleasure, and which I enjoy.

BARRILDO: One day the priest said in a sermon that there was a man named Plato who taught how to love, and that this man loved only the soul and the virtues of the beloved.

PASCUALA: You have raised a question which the wise men in their schools and academies cannot solve.

LAURENCIA: He speaks the truth; do not try to refute his argument. Be thankful, Mengo, that Heaven made you without love.

MENGO: Are you in love?

LAURENCIA: I love my honor.

FRONDOSO: May God punish you with jealousy.

BARRILDO: Who has won the wager then?

PASCUALA: Go to the sacristan with your dispute, for either he or the priest will give you the best answer. Laurencia does not love deeply, and as for me, I have little experience. How are we to pass judgment?

FRONDOSO: What can be a better judgment than her disdain?

[*Enter* FLORES.]

FLORES: God be with you!

PASCUALA: Here is the Comendador's servant.

LAURENCIA: His goshawk, you mean. Where do *you* come from, my good friend?

FLORES: Don't you see my soldier's uniform?

LAURENCIA: Is Don Fernán coming back?

FLORES: Yes, the war is over, and though it has cost us some blood and some friends, we are victorious.

FRONDOSO: Tell us what happened.

FLORES: Who could do that better than I? I saw everything. For his campaign against this city, which is now called Ciudad Real [Royal City], the valiant Maestre raised an army of two thousand brave infantry from among his vassals and three hundred cavalry from laymen and friars. For even those who belong to Holy Orders are obliged to fight for their emblem of the red cross—provided, of course, that the war is against the Moors. The high-spirited youth rode out to battle wearing a green coat embroidered with golden scrolls; the sleeves were fastened with six hooks, so that only his gauntlets showed beneath them. His horse was a dappled roan, bred on the banks of the Betis, drinking its waters and grazing on its lush grass. Its tailpiece was decorated with buckskin straps, the curled panache with white knots that matched the snowflakes covering its mane. Our lord, Fernán Gómez, rode at the Maestre's side on a powerful honey-colored horse with black legs and mane and a white muzzle. Over a Turkish coat of mail he wore a magnificent breast-and-back plate with orange fringes and resplendent with gold and pearls. His white plumes seemed to shower orange blossoms on his bronze helmet. His red and white band flashed on his arm as he brandished an ash tree for a lance, making himself feared even in Granada. The city rushed to arms; the inhabitants apparently did not come out to fight but stayed within the city walls to defend their property. But in spite of the strong resistance the Maestre entered the city. He ordered the rebels and those who had flagrantly dishonored him to be beheaded, and the lower classes were gagged and whipped in public. He remained in the city and is so feared and loved that people prophesy great things for him. They say that a young man who has fought so gloriously and punished so severely all in a short time must one day fall on fertile Africa like a thunderbolt, and bring many blue moons under the red cross. He made so many gifts to the Comendador and his followers that he might have been disposing of his own estate rather than despoiling a city. But now the music sounds. The Comendador comes. Welcome him with festivity, for good will is one of the most precious of a victor's laurels.

[*Enter the* COMENDADOR *and* ORTUÑO; MUSICIANS; JUAN ROJO, ESTEBAN, *and* ALONSO, *elders of the town.*]

MUSICIANS: [*Singing*]
Welcome, Comendador,
Conqueror of lands and men!

Long live the Guzmanes!
Long live the Girones!
In peacetime gracious,
Gentle his reasoning,
When fighting the Moors
Strong as an oak.
From Ciudad Real
He comes victorious,
Bearing to Fuente Ovejuna
Its banners in triumph.
Long live Fernán Gómez,
Long live the hero!

COMENDADOR: Citizens of Fuente Ovejuna, I am most grateful to you for the love you show me.

ALONSO: It is but a small part of the love we feel, and no matter how great our love it is less than you deserve.

ESTEBAN: Fuente Ovejuna and its elders, whom you have honored with your presence, beg you to accept a humble gift. In these carts, sir, we bring you an expression of gratitude rather than a display of wealth. There are two baskets filled with earthenware; a flock of geese that stretch their heads out of their nets to praise your valor in battle; ten salted hogs, prize specimens, more precious than amber; and a hundred pairs of capons and hens, which leave the cocks of the neighboring villages desolate. You will find no arms, no horses, no harnesses studded with pure gold. The only gold is the love your vassals feel towards you. And for purity you could find nothing greater than those twelve skins of wine. That wine could give warmth and courage to your soldiers even unclothed in the dead of winter; it will be as important as steel in the defense of your walls. I leave unmentioned the cheese and other victuals: they are a fitting tribute from our people to you. May you and yours enjoy our gifts.

COMENDADOR: I am very grateful to you for all of them. Go now and rest.

ESTEBAN: Feel at home in this town, my lord! I wish the reeds of mace and sedge that we placed on our doors to celebrate your triumphs were oriental pearls. You deserve such tribute and more.

COMENDADOR: Thank you, gentlemen. God be with you.

ESTEBAN: Singers, sing again.

MUSICIANS: [*Singing*]
              Welcome, Comendador,
              Conqueror of lands and men!

[*Exeunt* ELDERS *and* MUSICIANS.]

COMENDADOR: You two wait.

LAURENCIA: What is Your Lordship's pleasure?

COMENDADOR: You scorned me a few days ago, didn't you?

LAURENCIA: Is he speaking to you, Pascuala?

PASCUALA: I should say not—not to me!

COMENDADOR: I am talking to you, beautiful wildcat, and to the other girl too. Are you not mine, both of you?

PASCUALA: Yes, sir, to a certain extent.

COMENDADOR: Go into the house. There are men inside, so you need not fear.

LAURENCIA: If the elders accompany us—I am the daughter of one of them—it will be all right for us to go in too, but not otherwise.

COMENDADOR: Flores!

FLORES: Sir?

COMENDADOR: Why do they hesitate to do what I command?

FLORES: Come along, girls, come right in.

LAURENCIA: Let me go!

FLORES: Come in, girl, don't be silly.

PASCUALA: So that you can lock us in? No thank you!

FLORES: Come on. He wants to show you his spoils of war.

COMENDADOR: [*Aside to* ORTUÑO] Lock the door after them. [*Exit* COMENDADOR.]

LAURENCIA: Flores, let us pass.

ORTUÑO: Aren't you part of the gifts of the village?

PASCUALA: That's what you think! Out of my way, fool, before I . . .

FLORES: Leave them alone. They're too unreasonable.

LAURENCIA: Isn't your master satisfied with all the meat given him today?

ORTUÑO: He seems to prefer yours.

LAURENCIA: Then he can starve!

[*Exeunt* LAURENCIA *and* PASCUALA.]

FLORES: A fine message for us to bring! He'll swear at us when we appear before him empty-handed.

ORTUÑO: That's a risk servants always run. When he realizes the situation he'll either calm down or else leave at once.

Chamber of the Catholic Kings, in Medina del Campo.

[*Enter* KING FERDINAND OF ARAGON, QUEEN ISABELLA, MAN-RIQUE, *and* ATTENDANTS.]

ISABELLA: I think it would be wise to be prepared, Your Majesty—especially since Don Alfonso of Portugal is encamped there. It is better for us to strike the first blow than to wait for the enemy to attack us.

KING: We can depend on Navarre and Aragon for assistance, and I'm trying to reorganize things in Castile so as to ensure our success there.

ISABELLA: I'm confident your plan will succeed.

MANRIQUE: Two councilmen from Ciudad Real seek audience with Your Majesty.

KING: Let it be granted them.

[*Enter two* COUNCILMEN *of Ciudad Real.*]

1ST COUNCILMAN: Most Catholic King of Aragon, whom God has sent to Castile to protect us, we appear as humble petitioners before you to beg the assistance of your great valor for our city of Ciudad Real. We are proud to consider ourselves your vassals, a privilege granted us by a royal charter but which an unkind fate threatens to take away. Don Rodrigo Téllez Girón, famous for the valiant actions that belie his youth, and ambitious to augment his power, recently laid close siege to our city. We prepared to meet his attack with bravery, and resisted his forces so fiercely that rivers of blood streamed from our innumerable dead. He finally conquered us—but only because of the advice and assistance given him by Fernán Gómez. Girón remains in possession of our city, and unless we can remedy our disaster soon we will have to acknowledge ourselves his vassals against our will.

KING: Where is Fernán Gómez now?

2ND COUNCILMAN: In Fuente Ovejuna, I think. That is his native town and his home is there. But the truth is, his subjects are far from contented.

KING: Do you have a leader?

2ND COUNCILMAN: No, we have none, Your Majesty. Not one nobleman escaped imprisonment, injury, or death.

ISABELLA: This matter requires swift action, for delay will only work to the advantage of the impudent Girón. Furthermore the King of Portugal will soon realize that he can use him to gain entry to Extremadura, and so cause us much damage.

KING: Don Manrique, leave at once with two companies. Be relentless in avenging the wrongs this city has suffered. Let the Count of Cabra go with you. The Cordovan is recognized by everyone as a brave soldier. This is the best plan for the moment.

MANRIQUE: I think the plan is an excellent one. As long as I live, his excesses shall be curbed.

ISABELLA: With your help we are sure to succeed.

The countryside near Fuente Ovejuna.

[*Enter* LAURENCIA *and* FRONDOSO.]

LAURENCIA: You are very stubborn, Frondoso. I left the brook with my washing only half wrung out, so as to give no occasion for gossip—yet you persist in following me. It seems that everyone in town is saying that you are running after me and I after you. And because you are the sort of fellow who struts about and shows off his clothes, which are more fashionable and expensive than other people's, all the girls and boys in the countryside think there must be something between us. They are all waiting for the day when Juan Chamorro will put down his flute and lead us to the altar. I wish they would occupy their minds with things that are more their business—why don't they imagine that their granaries are bursting with red wheat, or that their wine jars are full of dregs? Their gossip annoys me, but not so much that it keeps me awake at night.

FRONDOSO: Your disdain and beauty are so great, Laurencia, that when I see you and listen to you I fear they will kill me. You know that my only wish is to become your husband: is it fair then to reward my love in this way?

LAURENCIA: I know no other way.

FRONDOSO: Can you feel no pity for my troubled mind, no sympathy for my sad condition when you know I cannot eat or drink or sleep for thinking of you? Is it possible that such a gentle face can hide so much unkindness? Heavens! you'll drive me mad.

LAURENCIA: Why don't you take medicine for your condition, Frondoso?

FRONDOSO: You are the only medicine I need, Laurencia. Come with me to the altar, and let us live like turtle doves, billing and cooing, after the church has blessed us.

LAURENCIA: You had better ask my uncle, Juan Rojo. I'm not passionately in love with you . . . but there is hope that I might be in time.

FRONDOSO: Oh—here comes the Comendador!

LAURENCIA: He must be hunting deer. Hide behind these bushes.

FRONDOSO: I will. But I'll be full of jealousy.

[*Enter the* COMENDADOR.]

COMENDADOR: This is good luck. My chase of the timid fawn has led me to a lovely doe instead.

LAURENCIA: I was resting a bit from my washing. By Your Lordship's leave I'll return to the brook.

COMENDADOR: Such disdain, fair Laurencia, is an insult to the beauty Heaven gave you; it turns you into a monster. On other occasions you have succeeded in eluding my desires—but now we are alone in these solitary fields where no one can help you. Now, with no one to witness, you cannot be so stubborn and so proud, you cannot turn your face away without loving me. Did not Salustiana, the wife of Pedro Redondo, surrender to me—and Martín del Pozo's wife, too, only two days after her wedding?

LAURENCIA: These women, sir, had had others before you, and knew the road to pleasure only too well. Many men have enjoyed *their* favors. Go, pursue your deer, and God be with you. You persecute me so that were it not for the cross you wear I should think you were the devil.

COMENDADOR: You little spitfire! [*Aside*] I had better put my bow down and take her by force.

LAURENCIA: What? . . . What are you doing? Are you mad? [*Enter* FRONDOSO, *who picks up the bow.*]

COMENDADOR: Don't struggle. It won't help you.

FRONDOSO: [*Aside*] I'll pick up his bow, but I hope I don't have to use it.

COMENDADOR: Come on, you might as well give in now.

LAURENCIA: Heaven help me now!

COMENDADOR: We are alone. Don't be afraid.

FRONDOSO: Generous Comendador, leave the girl alone. For much as I respect the cross on your breast, it will not stop me from aiming this bow at you if you do not let her go.

COMENDADOR: You dog, you peasant slave!

FRONDOSO: There's no dog here. Laurencia, go quickly now.

LAURENCIA: Take care of yourself, Frondoso.

FRONDOSO: Run . . .

[*Exit* LAURENCIA.]

COMENDADOR: What a fool I was to put down my sword so as not to frighten my quarry!

FRONDOSO: Do you realize, sir, that I have only to touch this string to bring you down like a bird?

COMENDADOR: She's gone. You damned, treacherous villain. Put that bow down, put it down, I say.

FRONDOSO: Put it down? Why? So that you can shoot me? No, love is deaf, remember, and hears nothing when it comes into its own.

COMENDADOR: Do you think a knight surrenders to a peasant?

Shoot, you villain, shoot and be damned, or I'll break the laws of chivalry.

FRONDOSO: No, not that. I'm satisfied with my station in life, and since I must preserve my life, I'll take your bow with me. [*Exit* FRONDOSO.]

COMENDADOR: What a strange experience! But I'll avenge this insult and remove this obstacle . . . . But to let him go! My God, how humiliating!

ACT II

The Plaza of Fuente Ovejuna.

[*Enter* ESTEBAN *and* 1ST COUNCILMAN.]

ESTEBAN: I don't think any more grain should be taken out of our community granaries, even though they are full right now. It's getting late in the year, and the harvest looks poor. I think it's better to have provisions stored up in case of emergency—though I know some people have other ideas.

1ST COUNCILMAN: I agree with you. And I've always tried to administer the land along such peaceable ways.

ESTEBAN: Well, let's tell Fernán Gómez what we think about it. We shouldn't let those astrologers, who are so ignorant of the future, persuade us that they know all the secrets that are only God's business. They pretend to be as learned as the theologians the way they mix up the past and the future—but if you ask them anything about the immediate present they are completely at a loss. Do they have the clouds and the course of the sun, the moon, and the stars locked up at home that they can tell us what is happening up there and what is going to bring us grief? At seed time they levy tax on us; give us just so much wheat, oats and vegetables, pumpkins, cucumbers, mustard . . . . Then they tell us someone has died, and later we discover it happened in Transylvania; they tell us that wine will be scarce and beer plentiful—somewhere in Germany; that cherries will freeze in Gascony, or hordes of tigers will prowl through Hircania. Their final prophecy is that whether we sow or not the year will end in December!

[*Enter the licentiate* LEONELO *and* BARRILDO.]

LEONELO: You won't be awarded the hickory stick to beat the other students with, for it's already been won by somebody else.

BARRILDO: How did you get on at Salamanca?

LEONELO: That's a long story.

BARRILDO: You must be a very learned man by now.

LEONELO: No, I'm not even a barber. The things I was telling you about happen all the time in the school I was at.

BARRILDO: At least you are a scholar now.

LEONELO: Well, I've tried to learn things that are important.

BARRILDO: Anyone who has seen so many printed books is bound to think he is wise.

LEONELO: Froth and confusion are the chief results of so much reading matter. Even the most voracious reader gets sick of seeing so many titles. I admit that printing has saved many talented writers from oblivion, and enshrined their works above the ravages of time. Printing circulates their books and makes them known. Gutenberg, a famous German from Mainz, is responsible for this invention. But many men who used to have a high reputation are no longer taken seriously now that their works have been printed. Some people put their ignorance in print, passing it off as wisdom; others inspired by envy write down their crazy ideas and send them into the world under the name of their enemies.

BARRILDO: That's a disgraceful practice.

LEONELO: Well, it's natural for ignorant people to want to discredit scholars.

BARRILDO: But in spite of all this, Leonelo, you must admit that printing is important.

LEONELO: The world got on very well without it for a good many centuries—and no Saint Jerome or Saint Augustine has appeared since we have had it.

BARRILDO: Take it easy, Leonelo. You're getting all worked up about this printing business.

[*Enter* JUAN ROJO *and another* PEASANT.]

JUAN ROJO: Four farms put together would not raise one dowry, if they're all like the one we've just seen. It's obvious that both the land and the people are in a state of chaos.

PEASANT: What's the news of the Comendador?—don't get excited now.

JUAN ROJO: How he tried to take advantage of Laurencia in this very field!

PEASANT: That lascivious brute! I'd like to see him hanging from that olive tree! . . .

[*Enter* COMENDADOR, ORTUÑO, *and* FLORES.]

COMENDADOR: Good day to you all!

COUNCILMAN: Your Lordship!

COMENDADOR: Please don't get up.

ESTEBAN: You sit down, my lord. We would rather stand.

COMENDADOR: Do sit down.

ESTEBAN: Honor can only be rendered by those who have it themselves.

COMENDADOR: Sit down, and let us talk things over calmly.

ESTEBAN: Has Your Lordship seen the hound I sent you?

COMENDADOR: Mayor, my servants are all amazed by its great speed.

ESTEBAN: It really is a wonderful animal. It can overtake any culprit or coward who is trying to escape.

COMENDADOR: I wish you would send it after a hare that keeps eluding me.

ESTEBAN: I'd be glad to. Whereabouts is this hare?

COMENDADOR: It's your daughter.

ESTEBAN: My daughter!

COMENDADOR: Yes.

ESTEBAN: But is she worth your while?

COMENDADOR: Intervene in my favor, Mayor, for God's sake.

ESTEBAN: What has she done?

COMENDADOR: She's determined to hurt me—while the wife

of a nobleman here in town is dying for an opportunity to see me.

ESTEBAN: Then she would do wrong—and you do yourself no good to talk so flippantly.

COMENDADOR: My, my, what a circumspect peasant! Flores, give him a copy of the *Politics* and tell him to read Aristotle.

ESTEBAN: My lord, the town's desire is to live peaceably under you. You must remember that there are many honorable persons living in Fuente Ovejuna.

LEONELO: Did you ever hear such impudence as this Comendador's?

COMENDADOR: Have I said anything to offend you, Councilman?

COUNCILMAN: Your pronouncements are unjust, my lord, and not worth uttering. It is unfair to try to take away our honor.

COMENDADOR: Honor? Do you have honor? Listen to the saintly friars of Calatrava!

COUNCILMAN: Some people may boast of the cross you awarded them, but their blood is not as pure as you may think.

COMENDADOR: Do I sully mine by mixing it with yours?

COUNCILMAN: Evil will sully it rather than cleanse it.

COMENDADOR: However that may be, your women are honored by it.

ESTEBAN: Such words are dishonorable.

COMENDADOR: What boors these peasants are! Ah, give me the cities, where nobody hinders the pleasures of lofty men. Husbands are glad when we make love to their wives.

ESTEBAN: They certainly should not be. Do you expect us to suffer such tribulations as readily? There is a God in the cities too, and punishment falls swiftly.

COMENDADOR: Get out of here!

ESTEBAN: Are you talking to us?

COMENDADOR: Get off the Plaza immediately. I don't want to see any of you around here.

ESTEBAN: We're going.

COMENDADOR: Not in a group like that . . .

FLORES: I beg of you to control yourself.

COMENDADOR: These peasants will gossip in groups behind my back.

ORTUÑO: Have a little patience.

COMENDADOR: I marvel that I have so much. Let each man go alone to his own house.

LEONELO: Good Heavens! Will the peasants stomach that?

ESTEBAN: I'm going this way.

[*Exeunt* PEASANTS.]

COMENDADOR: What do you think of those fellows?

ORTUÑO: You don't seem to be able to hide your emotions, yet you refuse to sense the ill feeling around you.

COMENDADOR: But are these fellows my equals?

FLORES: It's not a question of equality.

COMENDADOR: Is that peasant to keep my bow unpunished?

FLORES: Last night I thought I saw him by Laurencia's door and I gave him a slash from ear to ear—but it was someone else.

COMENDADOR: I wonder where that Frondoso is now?

FLORES: They say he's around.

COMENDADOR: So that's it. The villain who tried to murder me is allowed to go about scot-free.

FLORES: Don't worry. Sooner or later he'll fall into the snare like a stray bird, or be caught on the hook like a fish.

COMENDADOR: But imagine—a peasant, a boy, to threaten me with my own crossbow, me, a captain whose sword made Cordova and Granada tremble! Flores, the world is coming to an end!

FLORES: Blame it on love.

ORTUÑO: I suppose you spared him for friendship's sake.

COMENDADOR: I have acted out of friendship, Ortuño, else I should have ransacked the town in a couple of hours. However, I plan to withhold my vengeance until the right moment arrives. And now—what news of Pascuala?

FLORES: She says she's about to get married.

COMENDADOR: Is she going to that length?

FLORES: In other words, she's sending you to where you'll be paid in cash.

COMENDADOR: What about Olalla?

ORTUÑO: Her reply is charming.

COMENDADOR: She's a gay young thing. What does she say?

ORTUÑO: She says her husband follows her around all the time because he's jealous of my messages and your visits, but as soon as she manages to allay his fears you'll be the first to see her.

COMENDADOR: Fine! Keep an eye on the old man.

ORTUÑO: You'd better be careful.

COMENDADOR: What news from Inés?

FLORES: Which Inés?

COMENDADOR: The wife of Antón.

FLORES: She's ready when you are. I spoke to her in her backyard, through which you may go whenever you wish.

COMENDADOR: Easy girls I love dearly and repay poorly. Flores, if they only knew their worth! . . .

FLORES: To conquer without a struggle nullifies the joy of victory. A quick surrender impairs the pleasure of love making. But, as the philosophers say, there are women as hungry for men as form is for matter, so you shouldn't be surprised if things are the way they are.

COMENDADOR: A man who is maddened by love congratulates himself when girls fall easily to him, but later he regrets it. For however much we desire things we soon forget them, even the most thoughtful of us, if we have gotten them cheaply.

[*Enter* CIMBRANOS, *a soldier.*]

CIMBRANOS: Is the Comendador here?

ORTUÑO: Don't you see him before you?

CIMBRANOS: Oh, valiant Fernán Gómez! Change your green cap for your shining helmet, and your cloak for a coat of mail! For the Maestre of Santiago and the Count of Cabra are attacking Rodrigo Girón, and laying siege to Ciudad Real in the name of the Queen of Castile. All that we won at so much cost in blood and men may soon be lost again. Already the banners of Aragon with their castles, lions and bars, can be seen above the high towers of the city. Though the King of Portugal has paid homage to Girón, the Maestre of Calatrava may have to return to Almagro in defeat. Mount your horse, my lord, your presence alone will force the enemy back to Castile.

COMENDADOR: Stop. That's enough. Ortuño, order a trumpet to sound at once in the Plaza. Tell me, how many soldiers do I have?

ORTUÑO: Fifty, I believe, sir.

COMENDADOR: Order them to horse.

CIMBRANOS: Ciudad Real will fall to the King if you do not hurry.

COMENDADOR: Never fear, that shall not happen!

[*Exeunt all.*]

Open country near Fuente Ovejuna.

[*Enter* MENGO, LAURENCIA, *and* PASCUALA, *running.*]

PASCUALA: Please don't leave us.

MENGO: Why? What are you afraid of?

LAURENCIA: Well, Mengo, we prefer to go to the village in groups when we don't have a man to go with us. We're afraid of meeting the Comendador.

MENGO: What a cruel and importunate devil that man is.

LAURENCIA: He never stops pestering us.

MENGO: I wish God would strike him with a thunderbolt and put an end to his wickedness.

LAURENCIA: He's a bloodthirsty beast that poisons and infects the whole countryside.

MENGO: I hear that in trying to protect you, here in the meadow, Frondoso aimed his crossbow at the Comendador.

LAURENCIA: I used to hate men, Mengo, but since that day I've looked at them with different eyes. Frondoso acted so gallantly! But I'm afraid it may cost him his life.

MENGO: He'll be forced to leave the village.

LAURENCIA: I keep telling him to go away, although I love him dearly now. But he answers all such counsel with anger and contempt—and all the while the Comendador threatens to hang him by the feet.

PASCUALA: I'd like to see that Comendador carried off by the plague!

MENGO: I'd rather kill him with a mean stone. By God, if I threw a stone at him that I have up at the sheepfold, it would hit him so hard it would crush his skull in. The Comendador is more vicious than that old Roman, Sabalus.

LAURENCIA: You mean Heliogabalus, who was more wicked than a beast.

MENGO: Well, Galván or whoever it was—I don't know too much about history—the Comendador surpasses him in wickedness. Can anyone be more despicable then Fernán Gómez?

PASCUALA: No one can compare with him. You'd think he'd sucked his cruelty from a tigress.

[*Enter* JACINTA.]

JACINTA: If friendship means anything, in God's name help me now!

LAURENCIA: What's happened, Jacinta, my friend?

PASCUALA: Both of us are your friends.

JACINTA: Some of the Comendador's attendants are trying to take me to him. They're on their way to Ciudad Real, but they're acting more like villains than soldiers.

LAURENCIA: May God protect you, Jacinta! If the Comendador is bold with you he'll be cruel to me.

[*Exit* LAURENCIA.]

PASCUALA: Jacinta, I'm not a man, so I can't defend you.

[*Exit* PASCUALA.]

MENGO: But I have both strength and reputation. Stand beside me, Jacinta.

JACINTA: Have you any arms?

MENGO: Yes, those that Nature gave me.

JACINTA: I wish you were armed.

MENGO: Never mind, Jacinta. There are plenty of stones around here.

[*Enter* FLORES *and* ORTUÑO.]

FLORES: So you thought you could get away from us, did you?

JACINTA: Mengo, I'm dead with fear.

MENGO: Gentlemen, this is a poor peasant girl . . .

ORTUÑO: Oh, have you decided to defend young women?

MENGO: I'm merely asking for mercy. I'm her relative, and I hope to be able to keep her near me.

FLORES: Kill him off!

MENGO: By God, if you make me mad and I take out my sling, your life will be in danger!

[*Enter the* COMENDADOR *and* CIMBRANOS.]

COMENDADOR: What's all this? Do I have to get off my horse for some petty quarrel?

FLORES: You ought to destroy this miserable village for all the joy it brings you. These wretched peasants have dared to challenge our arms.

MENGO: My lord, if injustice can move you to pity, punish these soldiers who in your name are forcing this girl to leave her husband and honest parents. Grant me permission to take her home.

COMENDADOR: I will grant them permission to punish you. Drop that sling!

MENGO: My lord!

COMENDADOR: Flores, Ortuño, Cimbranos, tie his hands with it.

MENGO: Is this your justice?

COMENDADOR: What do Fuente Ovejuna and its peasants think of me?

MENGO: My lord, how have I or Fuente Ovejuna offended you?

FLORES: Shall I kill him?

COMENDADOR: Don't soil your arms with such trash. Keep them for better things.

ORTUÑO: What are your orders?

COMENDADOR: Flog him. Tie him to that oak tree and beat him with the reins.

MENGO: Pity, my lord, have pity, for you are a nobleman!

COMENDADOR: Flog him till the rivets fall from the leather.

MENGO: My God. For such ugly deeds, uglier punishments!

[*Exeunt* MENGO, FLORES, *and* ORTUÑO.]

COMENDADOR: Now my girl, why were you running away? Do you prefer a peasant to a nobleman?

JACINTA: Can you restore the honor which your attendants have taken from me in bringing me to you?

COMENDADOR: Do you mean to say your honor has been lost because I wanted to take you away?

JACINTA: Yes. For I have an honest father who, if he does not equal you in birth, surpasses you in virtue.

COMENDADOR: All these troubles around this village, where peasants defy their betters, scarcely help to soothe my temper. Come along here now!

JACINTA: With whom?

COMENDADOR: With me.

JACINTA: You had better think over what you're doing.

COMENDADOR: I have thought it over, and it's so much the worse for you. Instead of keeping you for myself, I shall give you to my whole army.

JACINTA: No power on earth can inflict such an outrage on me while I live.

COMENDADOR: Get a move on now, girl.

JACINTA: Sir, have pity!

COMENDADOR: There is no pity.

JACINTA: I appeal from your cruelty to divine justice.

[*Exit* COMENDADOR, *hauling her out.*]

Esteban's *house.*

[*Enter* LAURENCIA *and* FRONDOSO.]

LAURENCIA: Are you not aware of your danger, that you dare to come here?

FRONDOSO: My daring is proof of my love for you. From that hill I saw the Comendador riding away, and since I have complete confidence in you all my fear left with him. I hope he never comes back!

LAURENCIA: Don't curse him—for the more one wishes a person to die the longer he lives.

FRONDOSO: In that case may he live a thousand years, and so by wishing him well let's hope his end will be certain. . . . Tell me, Laurencia, has my fondness for you affected you at all? Is my loyalty safely entrusted? You know that the entire village thinks we are made for each other. Won't you forget your modesty and say definitely yes or no?

LAURENCIA: My answer to you and to the village is—yes!

FRONDOSO: I could kiss your feet for such an answer! You give me new life . . . let me tell you now how much I love you.

LAURENCIA: Save your compliments and speak to my father, Frondoso, for that's the important thing now. Look, there he comes with my uncle. Be calm and confident, Frondoso, for this meeting will determine whether I'm to be your wife or no.

FRONDOSO: I put my trust in God.

[LAURENCIA *hides herself. Enter* ESTEBAN *and the* COUNCILMAN.]

ESTEBAN: The Comendador's visit has aroused the whole town. His behavior was most regrettable, to say the least. Everybody was shocked, and poor Jacinta is bearing the brunt of his madness.

COUNCILMAN: Before long Spain will be rendering obedience to the Catholic Kings, as they are called. The Maestre of Santiago has been appointed Captain General, and is already coming on horseback to free Ciudad Real from Girón. . . . I'm very sorry about Jacinta, who is an honest girl.

ESTEBAN: The Comendador also had Mengo flogged.

COUNCILMAN: Yes. His flesh is blacker than ink or a black cloth.

ESTEBAN: Please, no more—it makes my blood boil when I think of his disgusting behavior and reputation. What good is my Mayor's staff against that?

COUNCILMAN: It was his servants who did it. Why should you be so upset?

ESTEBAN: Shall I tell you something else? I have been told that one day Pedro Redondo's wife was found down there in the depth of the valley. He had abused her and then turned her over to his soldiers.

COUNCILMAN: Listen, I hear something. . . . Who's there?

FRONDOSO: It is I, Frondoso, waiting for permission to come in.

ESTEBAN: You need no permission, Frondoso, to enter my house. You owe your life to your father, but your upbringing to me. I love you like my own son.

FRONDOSO: Sir, trusting that love, I want to ask a favor. You know whose son I am.

ESTEBAN: Did that crazy Fernán Gómez hurt you?

FRONDOSO: Not a little.

ESTEBAN: My heart told me so.

FRONDOSO: You have shown me so much affection that I feel free to make a confession to you. I love Laurencia, and wish to become her husband. Forgive me if I have been too hasty. I'm afraid I've been very bold.

ESTEBAN: You have come just at the right moment, Frondoso, and you will prolong my life, for this touches the fear nearest my heart. I thank God that you have come to save my honor, and I thank you for your love and the purity of your intentions. But I think it only right to tell your father of this first. As soon as he approves I will give my consent too. How happy I shall be if this marriage takes place.

COUNCILMAN: You should ask the girl about him before you accept him.

ESTEBAN: Don't worry about that. The matter is settled; for they discussed it beforehand, I'm sure. If you like, Frondoso, we might talk about the dowry, for I'm planning to give you some *maravedíes*.

FRONDOSO: I'm not concerned about that. I don't need a dowry.

COUNCILMAN: You should be grateful that he doesn't ask you for it in wineskins.

ESTEBAN: I'll ask Laurencia what she would like to do and then let you know.

FRONDOSO: That's fair. It's a good idea to consult everybody concerned.

ESTEBAN: Daughter! . . . Laurencia!

LAURENCIA: Yes, father.

ESTEBAN: You see how quickly she replies. Laurencia, come here a minute. What would you say if your friend Gila were to marry Frondoso, who is as honest a young man as one could find in Fuente Ovejuna?

LAURENCIA: Is Gila thinking of getting married?

ESTEBAN: Why yes, if someone can be found who would be a worthy match for her.

LAURENCIA: My answer is yes.

ESTEBAN: I would say yes too—except that Gila is ugly, and it would be much better if Frondoso became your husband, Laurencia.

LAURENCIA: In spite of your years, you are still a flatterer, father.

ESTEBAN: Do you love him?

LAURENCIA: I am fond of him, and he returns my affection, but you were saying . . .

ESTEBAN: Shall I say yes to him?

LAURENCIA: Yes, say it for me, sir.

ESTEBAN: I? Well, then I have the keys. It's settled then. Let's go to his father.

COUNCILMAN: Yes, let's go.

ESTEBAN: What shall we tell him about the dowry, son? I can afford to give you 4000 *maravedíes*.

FRONDOSO: Do you want to offend me, sir?

ESTEBAN: Come, come, my boy, you'll get over that attitude in a day or two. Even if you don't need it now, a dowry will come in handy later on.

[*Exeunt* ESTEBAN *and* COUNCILMAN.]

LAURENCIA: Tell me, Frondoso, are you happy?

FRONDOSO: Happy? I'm afraid I'll go crazy with so much joy and happiness. My heart is so overflowing that my eyes are swimming with joy when I look at you, Laurencia, and realize that you, sweet treasure, will be mine.

[*Exeunt* LAURENCIA *and* FRONDOSO.]

Meadow near Ciudad Real.

[*Enter the* MAESTRE, *the* COMENDADOR, FLORES, *and* ORTUÑO.]

COMENDADOR: Fly, sir! There's no hope for us.

MAESTRE: The walls were weak and the enemy strong.

COMENDADOR: They have paid dearly for it, though, in blood and lives.

MAESTRE: And they will not be able to boast that our banner of Calatrava is among their spoils. That alone would have been enough to honor their enterprise.

COMENDADOR: Your plans are ruined now, Girón.

MAESTRE: What can I do if Fate in its blindness raises a man aloft one day only to strike him down the next?

VOICES BACKSTAGE: Victory for the Kings of Castile!

MAESTRE: They're decorating the battlements with lights now, and hanging out pennants of victory from the windows in the high towers.

COMENDADOR: They do that because they have paid heavily in blood—it's really more a sign of tragedy than a celebration.

MAESTRE: Fernán Gómez, I'm going back to Calatrava.

COMENDADOR: And I to Fuente Ovejuna. Now you have to think of either defending your relatives or paying homage to the Catholic King.

MAESTRE: I'll write to you about my plans.

COMENDADOR: Time will tell you what to do.

MAESTRE: Ah, years full of the bitterness of time's betrayals! [*Exeunt.*]

A *meadow near Fuente Ovejuna.*

[*Enter the wedding train:* MUSICIANS, MENGO, FRONDOSO, LAU-RENCIA, PASCUALA, BARRILDO, ESTEBAN, *and* JUAN ROJO.]

MUSICIANS:

[*Singing*]
Long live the bride and groom!
Many long and happy years to them.

MENGO: It has not been very difficult for you to sing.

BARRILDO: You could have done better yourself, couldn't you?

FRONDOSO: Mengo knows more about whippings now than songs.

MENGO: Don't be surprised if I tell you that there's someone in the valley to whom the Comendador . . .

BARRILDO: Don't say it. That brutal assassin has assailed everyone's honor.

MENGO: It was bad enough for a hundred soldiers to whip me that day when all I had was a sling. It must have been unbearable for that man to whom they gave an enema of dye and herbs—I won't mention his name, but he was an honorable man.

BARRILDO: It was done in jest, I suppose . . .

MENGO: This was no joke. Enemas are desirable sometimes, but I would rather die than undergo one like that.

FRONDOSO: Please sing us a song—if you have anything worth listening to.

MENGO:

> God grant the bride and groom long life
> Free from envy and jealous strife,
> And when their span of years is past,
> May they be united at the last.
> God grant the bride and groom long life!

FRONDOSO: Heaven curse the poet who conceived such a poem!

BARRILDO: It was rather a sloppy job.

MENGO: This makes me think of something about the whole crew of poets. Have you seen a baker making crullers? He throws the pieces of dough into the boiling oil until the pot is full. Some buns come out puffed up, others twisted and funnily shaped, some lean to the left, others to the right, some are well fried, others are burnt. Well, I think of a poet composing his verses in much the same way that the baker works on his dough. He hastily throws words into his pot of paper, confident that the honey will conceal what may turn out ridiculous or absurd. But when he tries to sell his poem no one wants it and the confectioner is forced to eat it himself.

BARRILDO: Stop your foolishness now, and let the bride and groom speak.

LAURENCIA: Give us your hands to kiss.

JUAN ROJO: Do you ask to kiss my hand, Laurencia? You and Frondoso had better ask to kiss your father's first.

ESTEBAN: Rojo, I ask Heaven's blessing on her and her husband for ever.

FRONDOSO: Give us your blessing, both of you.

JUAN ROJO: Let the bells ring, and everyone celebrate the union of Laurencia and Frondoso.

MUSICIANS:

> [*Singing*]
> To the valley of Fuente Ovejuna
> Came the maid with the flowing hair.
> A knight of Calatrava
> Followed her to the valley here.
> Amid the shrubs she hid herself,
> Disturbed by shame and fear.
> With the branches she covered herself,
> Feigning she had not seen him,
> But the knight of Calatrava drew near:
> "Why are you hiding, fair maiden,
> Know you not that my keen desire
> Can pierce the thickest wall?"
> She made curtains of the branches
> Confused by shame and fear.
> But love passes sea and mountain:
> "Why are you hiding, fair maiden,
> Know you not that my keen desire
> Can pierce the thickest wall?"

[*Enter the* COMENDADOR, FLORES, ORTUÑO, *and* CIMBRANOS.]

COMENDADOR: Silence! You will all remain quietly where you are.

JUAN ROJO: This is not a game, my lord, and your orders will be obeyed. Won't you join us? Why do you come in such a bellicose manner? Are you our conqueror? But what am I saying . . .

FRONDOSO: I'm a dead man. Heaven help me!

LAURENCIA: Quickly, Frondoso, escape this way.

COMENDADOR: No. Arrest him, and tie him up.

JUAN ROJO: Yield to them, my boy, and go quietly to prison.

FRONDOSO: Do you want them to kill me?

JUAN ROJO: Why?

COMENDADOR: I am not a man to murder people without reason. If I were, these soldiers would have run him through by now. I'm ordering him to be taken to jail where his own father will pronounce sentence on him.

PASCUALA: Sir, a wedding is in progress here now.

COMENDADOR: What is that to me? Is he the only person in town who counts?

PASCUALA: If he offended you, pardon him, as becomes your rank.

COMENDADOR: Pascuala, it is nothing that concerns me personally. He has offended the Maestre Téllez Girón, whom God preserve. He acted counter to his orders and his honor, and must be punished as an example. Otherwise others may rebel too. Don't you know that one day this boy aimed a crossbow at the very heart of the Comendador, Mayor? Loyal vassals you are indeed!

ESTEBAN: As his father-in-law I feel I must come to his defence. I think it only natural that a man, especially a man in love, should challenge you for trying to take away his girl—what else could he do?

COMENDADOR: You are a fool, Mayor.

ESTEBAN: In your opinion, my lord!

COMENDADOR: I had no intention of taking away his girl—for she was not his.

ESTEBAN: You had the thought, and that is enough. There are kings in Castile who are drawing up new rules to prevent disorder. And they will do wrong if, after the wars, they tolerate in the towns and country districts such powerful men wearing those huge crosses on their chests. Those crosses were meant for royal breasts, and only kings should wear them.

COMENDADOR: Wrest the mayor's staff from him!

ESTEBAN: Take it, sir, it is yours to keep.

COMENDADOR: I'll strike him with it as if he were an unbroken horse.

ESTEBAN: You are my lord, and I must bear it: strike, then.

PASCUALA: Shame on you! Striking an old man!

LAURENCIA. You strike him because he is my father—what injury do you avenge in this way?

COMENDADOR: Arrest her, and let ten soldiers guard her.

[*Exeunt* COMENDADOR *and his men.*]

ESTEBAN: May Heaven visit justice upon him!

[*Exit* ESTEBAN.]

PASCUALA: The wedding has become a mourning.

[*Exit* PASCUALA.]

BARRILDO: Is there not one of us who can speak?

MENGO: I've already had a sound whipping and I'm covered with wales—let someone else anger him this time.

JUAN ROJO: Let us all take counsel.

MENGO: I advise everybody to keep quiet. He made my posterior look like a piece of salmon.

[*Exeunt all.*]

ACT III

A *room in the Town Hall of Fuente Ovejuna.*

[*Enter* ESTEBAN, ALONSO, *and* BARRILDO.]

ESTEBAN: Has everybody come to the meeting?

BARRILDO: Some people are absent.

ESTEBAN: Then our danger is more serious.

BARRILDO: Nearly all the town has been warned.

ESTEBAN: With Frondoso imprisoned in the tower, and my daughter Laurencia in such peril, if God, in his mercy, does not come to our help . . .

[*Enter* JUAN ROJO *and the* COUNCILMAN.]

JUAN ROJO: What are you shouting about, Esteban? Don't you know secrecy is all important now?

ESTEBAN: I wonder I'm not shouting even louder!

[*Enter* MENGO.]

MENGO: I want to join in this meeting.

ESTEBAN: With tears streaming down my beard, I ask you, honest farmers, what funeral rites can we give to a country without honor—a country that is lost? And if our honor is indeed lost, which of us can perform such rites, when there is not one among us who has not been dishonored? Answer me now, is there anyone here whose life, whose deep life of honor, is still intact? Are we not all of us in mourning for each other now? If all is lost, what is there to wait for? What is this misfortune that has overtaken us?

JUAN ROJO: The blackest ever known. . . . But it has just been announced that the Kings of Castile have concluded a victorious peace, and will soon arrive in Cordova. Let us send two Councilmen to that city to kneel at their feet and ask their help.

BARRILDO: But King Ferdinand, who has conquered so many enemies, is still busy making war, and will not be able to help us now while he's in the midst of battles. We must find some other way out.

COUNCILMAN: If you want my opinion, I suggest we leave the town.

JUAN ROJO: But how can we do that on such short notice?

MENGO: If I understand the situation at all, this meeting will cost us a good many lives.

COUNCILMAN: The mast of patience has been torn from us, and now we are a ship driven before a storm of fear. They have brutally abducted the daughter of the good man who rules our community, and unjustly broken the staff of office over his head. What slave was ever treated worse?

JUAN ROJO: What do you want the people to do?

COUNCILMAN: Die, or give death to the tyrants, for we are many and they are few.

BARRILDO: What? Raise our weapons against our lord and master!

ESTEBAN: Except for God, the King's our only lord and master, not these inhuman, barbarous men. If God is behind our rightful anger, what have we to lose?

MENGO: Let us be a little more cautious. I'm here to speak for the humblest peasants who always have to bear the brunt of any trouble—and I want to represent their fears prudently.

JUAN ROJO: Our misfortunes have prepared us to sacrifice our lives, so what are we waiting for? Our houses and vineyards have been burned down. They are tyrants and we must have our revenge.

[*Enter* LAURENCIA, *her hair dishevelled.*]

LAURENCIA: Let me come in, for I sorely need the advice of men! Do you know me?

ESTEBAN: God in Heaven, is that my daughter?

JUAN ROJO: Don't you recognize your Laurencia?

LAURENCIA: Yes, I am Laurencia, but so changed that looking at me you still doubt it.

ESTEBAN: My daughter!

LAURENCIA: Don't call me your daughter!

ESTEBAN: Why not, my dear? Why not?

LAURENCIA: For many reasons—but chiefly because you let me be carried off by tyrants, by the traitors who rule over us, without attempting to avenge me. I was not yet Frondoso's wife, so you cannot say my husband should have defended me; this was my father's duty as long as the wedding had not been consummated; just as a nobleman about to purchase a jewel need not pay for it if it is lost while still in the merchant's keeping. From under your very eyes, Fernán Gómez dragged me to his house, and you let the wolf carry the sheep like the cowardly shepherd you are. Can you conceive what I suffered at his hands?—the daggers pointed at my breast, the flatteries, threats, insults, and lies used to make my chastity yield to his fierce desires? Does not my bruised and bleeding face, my dishevelled hair tell you anything? Are you not good men?—not fathers and relatives? Do your hearts sink to see me so grievously betrayed? . . . Oh, you are sheep; how well named the village of Fuente Ovejuna [Sheep Well]. Give me weapons and let me fight, since you are but things of stone or metal, since you are but tigers—no, not tigers, for tigers fiercely attack those who steal their offspring, killing the hunters before they can escape. You were born timid rabbits; you are infidels, not Spaniards. Chicken-hearted, you permit other men to abuse your women. Put knitting in your scabbards—what need have you of swords? By the living God, I swear that your women will avenge those tyrants and stone you all, you spinning girls, you sodomites, you effeminate cowards. Tomorrow deck yourselves in our bonnets and skirts, and beautify yourselves with our cosmetics. The Comendador will hang Frondoso from a merlon of the tower, without let or trial, and presently he will string you all up. And I shall be glad—you race of half-men—that this honorable town will be rid of effeminates, and the age of Amazons will return, to the eternal amazement of the world.

ESTEBAN: Daughter, I will not stay to hear such names. I shall go now, even if I have to fight the whole world.

JUAN ROJO: I will go with you, in spite of the enemy's power.

COUNCILMAN: We shall die together.

BARRILDO: Let us hang a cloth from a stick to fly in the wind, and death to the traitors.

JUAN ROJO: What shall our orders be?

MENGO: To kill the Comendador without order. To rally the whole town around us: let us all agree to kill the tyrants.

ESTEBAN: Take with you swords, lances, crossbows, pikes, and sticks.

MENGO: Long live the Kings, our only lords and masters!

ALL: Long live the Kings!

MENGO: Death to the traitor tyrants!

ALL: Death to the tyrants!

[*Exeunt all but* LAURENCIA.]

LAURENCIA: Go—God will be with you! Come, women of the town, your honor will be avenged—rally round me!

[*Enter* PASCUALA, JACINTA, *and* OTHER WOMEN.]

PASCUALA: What is happening? What are you shouting about?

LAURENCIA: Can't you see how they're on their way to kill Fernán Gómez? Every man, boy, and child is rushing furiously to do his duty. Is it fair that the men alone should have the glory of a day like this, when we women have the greater grievances?

JACINTA: Tell us your plans then.

LAURENCIA: I propose that we all band together and perform a deed that will shake the world. Jacinta, your great injury will be our guide.

JACINTA: No more than yours.

LAURENCIA: Pascuala, you be our standard bearer.

PASCUALA: I'll be a good one. I'll put a cloth on a lance and we'll have a flag in the wind.

LAURENCIA: There's no time for that. We'll wave our caps for banners.

PASCUALA: Let's appoint a captain.

LAURENCIA: We don't need one.

PASCUALA: Why not?

LAURENCIA: Because when my courage is up, we don't need any Cids or Rodamontes.

[Exeunt all.]

Hall in the castle of the COMENDADOR.

[*Enter* FRONDOSO, *his hands tied,* FLORES, CIMBRANOS, OR-TUÑO, *and the* COMENDADOR.]

COMENDADOR: I want him hung by the cord that binds his wrists, so that his punishment may be the more severe.

FRONDOSO: How this will add to your descendants' honor, my lord!

COMENDADOR: Hang him from the highest merlon.

FRONDOSO: It was never my intention to kill you.

FLORES: Do you hear that noise outside?

[*Alarum.*]

COMENDADOR: What can it be?

FLORES: It looks as if the villagers are planning to stay your sentence, my lord.

ORTUÑO: They are breaking down the doors!

[*Alarum.*]

COMENDADOR: The door of my house? The seat of the Commandry?

FRONDOSO: The whole town is here!

JUAN ROJO: [*Within*] Break them down, smash them in, burn, destroy!

ORTUÑO: It's hard to stop a riot once it gets started.

COMENDADOR: The town against me!

FLORES: And their fury has driven them to tear down all the doors.

COMENDADOR: Untie him. And you, Frondoso, go and calm down the peasant mayor.

FRONDOSO: I'm going, sir—love has spurred them to action. [*Exit* FRONDOSO.]

MENGO: [*Within*] Long live Ferdinand and Isabella, and down with the tyrants!

FLORES: In God's name, my lord, don't let them find you here.

COMENDADOR: If they persist—why, this room is strong and well protected. They will soon turn back.

FLORES: When villages with a grievance decide to rise against their rulers they never turn back until they have shed blood and taken their revenge.

COMENDADOR: We'll face this mob with our weapons, using this door as a portcullis.

FRONDOSO: [*Within*] Long live Fuente Ovejuna!

COMENDADOR: What a leader! I'll take care of his bravery!

FLORES: My lord, I marvel at yours.

[*Enter* ESTEBAN *and the* PEASANTS.]

ESTEBAN: There's the tyrant and his accomplices! Long live Fuente Ovejuna, death to the tyrants!

COMENDADOR: Wait, my people!

ALL: Wrongs never wait.

COMENDADOR: Tell me your wrongs, and, on a knight's honor, I'll set them right.

ALL: Long live Fuente Ovejuna! Long live King Ferdinand! Death to bad Christians and traitors!

COMENDADOR: Will you not hear me? It is I who address you, I, your lord.

ALL: Our lords are the Catholic Kings.

COMENDADOR: Wait.

ALL: Long live Fuente Ovejuna, and death to Fernán Gómez!

[*Exeunt all. Enter* LAURENCIA, PASCUALA, JACINTA, *and* OTHER WOMEN, *armed.*]

LAURENCIA: You brave soldiers, no longer women, wait here in this place of vantage.

PASCUALA: Only women know how to take revenge. We shall drink the enemy's blood.

JACINTA: Let us pierce his corpse with our lances.

PASCUALA: Agreed.

ESTEBAN: [*Within*] Die, treacherous Comendador!

COMENDADOR: I die. O God, in Thy clemency, have mercy on me!

BARRILDO: [*Within*] Here's Flores.

MENGO: Get that scoundrel! He's the one who gave me a thousand whippings.

FRONDOSO: [*Within*] I shan't consider myself avenged until I've pulled out his soul.

LAURENCIA: There's no excuse for not going in.

PASCUALA: Calm yourself. We had better guard the door.

BARRILDO: [*Within*] I am not moved. Don't come to me with tears now, you fops.

LAURENCIA: Pascuala, I'm going in; I don't care to keep my sword in its scabbard.

[*Exit* LAURENCIA.]

BARRILDO: [*Within*] Here's Ortuño.

FRONDOSO: [*Within*] Slash his face!

[*Enter* FLORES, *fleeing, pursued by* MENGO.]

FLORES: Pity, Mengo! I'm not to blame!

MENGO: O no? Not for being a pimp, you scoundrel, not for having whipped me?

PASCUALA: Mengo, give him to us women, we'll . . . . Hurry, Mengo!

MENGO: Fine, you can have him—no punishment could be worse!

PASCUALA: We'll avenge the whippings he gave you.

MENGO: That's fine!

JACINTA: Come on, death to the traitor!

FLORES: To die at the hands of women!

JACINTA: Don't you like it?

PASCUALA: Is that why you're weeping?

JACINTA: Die, you panderer to his pleasures!

PASCUALA: Die, you traitor!

FLORES: Pity, women, *pity!*

[*Enter* ORTUÑO, *pursued by* LAURENCIA.]

ORTUÑO: You know I have had nothing at all to do with it . . .

LAURENCIA: I know you! Come on, women, dye your conquering weapons in their vile blood.

PASCUALA: I'll die killing!

ALL: Long live Fuente Ovejuna! Long live King Ferdinand!

[*Exeunt all.*]

Room of the Catholic Kings, at Toro.

[*Enter* KING FERDINAND, QUEEN ISABELLA, *and the* MAESTRE DON MANRIQUE.]

MANRIQUE: We planned our attack so well that we carried it out without any setback. There was little resistance—even if they had tried to organize any, it would have been weak. Cabra has remained there to guard the place in case of counterattack.

KING: That was a wise decision, and I am glad that he is in charge of operations. Now we can be sure that Alfonso, who is trying to seize power in Portugal, will not be able to harm us. It is fortunate that Cabra is stationed there and that he is making a good show, for in this way he protects us from any danger and, by acting as a loyal sentinel, works for the good of the kingdom.

[*Enter* FLORES, *wounded.*]

FLORES: Catholic King Ferdinand, upon whom Heaven has

bestowed the Crown of Castile, excellent gentleman that you are—listen to the worst cruelty that a man could ever behold from sunrise to sunset.

KING: Calm yourself!

FLORES: Supreme Sovereign, my wounds forbid me to delay in reporting my sad case, for my life is ebbing away. I come from Fuente Ovejuna, where, with ruthless heart, the inhabitants of that village have deprived their lord and master of his life. Fernán Gómez has been murdered by his perfidious subjects, indignant vassals who dared attack him for but a trivial cause. The mob called him tyrant and inflamed by the power of the epithet, committed this despicable crime: they broke into his house and having no faith that he, a perfect gentleman, would right all their wrongs, would not listen to him, but with impatient fury pierced his chest which bore the cross of Calatrava with a thousand cruel wounds and threw him from the lofty windows onto the pikes and lances of the women in the street below. They carried him away, dead, and competed with one another in pulling his beard and hair, and recklessly slashing his face. In fact their constantly growing fury was so great, that some cuts went from ear to ear. They blotted out his coat-of-arms with their pikes and loudly proclaimed that they wanted to replace it with your royal coat-of-arms since those of the Comendador offended them. They sacked his house as if it were the enemy's and joyfully divided the spoils among themselves. All this I witnessed from my hiding place, for my cruel fate did not grant me death at such a time. Thus I remained all day in hiding until nightfall, when I was able to slip away furtively to come to render you this account. Sire, since you are just, see that a just punishment is administered to the brutal culprits who have perpetrated such an outrage.

KING: You may rest assured that the culprits will not go without due punishment. The unfortunate event is of such magnitude that I am astonished; I will send a judge to investigate the case and punish the culprits as an example to all. A captain will accompany him for his protection, for such great offence requires exemplary punishment. In the meantime your wounds will be cared for.

[*Exeunt* ALL.]

The countryside.

[*Enter* PEASANTS, *both men and women, with* FERNÁN GÓMEZ' *head on a lance.*]

MUSICIANS: [*Singing*]
                Long live Isabella and Ferdinand
                And death to the tyrants!

BARRILDO: Sing us a song, Frondoso.

FRONDOSO: Here goes, and if it limps let some critic fix it.
                Long live fair Isabella
                And Ferdinand of Aragon.
                He is made for her
                And she is meant for him.
                May St. Michael guide them
                To Heaven by the hand . . .
                Long live Isabella and Ferdinand
                And death to the tyrants!

LAURENCIA: Now it's your turn, Barrildo.

BARRILDO: Listen to this, for I've been working on it.

PASCUALA: If you say it with feeling, it's going to be good.

BARRILDO: Long live the famous kings
                For they are victorious.
                They'll be our lords
                Happy and glorious.
                May they conquer always
                All giants and dwarfs . . .
                And death to the tyrants!

MUSICIANS: [*Singing*]
                Long live Isabella and Ferdinand
                And death to the tyrants!

LAURENCIA: Now it's your turn, Mengo.

FRONDOSO: Yes, Mengo.

MENGO: I'm a most gifted poet, you know.

PASCUALA: You mean a poet with a bruised backside.

MENGO: I was whipped on a Sunday morning
My back still feels the pain
But the Christian Kings are coming
There'll be no tyrants here again.

MUSICIANS: Long live the Kings!

ESTEBAN: Take away that head!

MENGO: He has the face of one who has been hanged.

[JUAN ROJO *brings in a scutcheon with the royal arms.*]

COUNCILMAN: The scutcheon has arrived.

ESTEBAN: Let's see it.

JUAN ROJO: Where shall we place it?

COUNCILMAN: Here, in the Town Hall.

ESTEBAN: What a beautiful scutcheon!

BARRILDO: What joy!

FRONDOSO: A new day is dawning for us, and that's our sun.

ESTEBAN: Long live Castile and Leon
And the bars of Aragon.
Down with tyranny!

People of Fuente Ovejuna, listen to the words of an old man whose life has been blameless. The Kings will want to investigate what has happened, and this they will do soon. So agree now among yourselves on what to say.

FRONDOSO: What is your advice?

ESTEBAN: To die saying Fuente Ovejuna and nothing else.

FRONDOSO: That's fine! Fuente Ovejuna did it!

ESTEBAN: Do you want to answer in that way?

ALL: Yes.

ESTEBAN: Well then, I'd like to play the role of questioner—let's rehearse! Mengo, pretend that you are the one being grilled.

MENGO: Can't you pick on someone else, someone more emaciated?

ESTEBAN: But this is all make believe.

MENGO: All right, go ahead!

ESTEBAN: Who killed the Comendador?

MENGO: Fuente Ovejuna did it!

ESTEBAN: You dog, I'm going to torture you.

MENGO: I don't care—even if you kill me.

ESTEBAN: Confess, you scoundrel.

MENGO: I am ready to confess.

ESTEBAN: Well, then, who did it?

MENGO: Fuente Ovejuna.

ESTEBAN: Bind him tighter.

MENGO: That will make no difference.

ESTEBAN: To hell with the trial then!

[*Enter the* COUNCILMAN.]

COUNCILMAN: What are you doing here?

FRONDOSO: What has happened, Cuadrado?

COUNCILMAN: The questioner is here.

ESTEBAN: Send him in.

COUNCILMAN: A captain is with him.

ESTEBAN: Who cares? Let the devil himself come in: you know your answer.

COUNCILMAN: They are going around town arresting people.

ESTEBAN: There's nothing to fear. Who killed the Commendador, Mengo?

MENGO: Who? Fuente Ovejuna.

[*Exeunt all.*]

Room of the MAESTRE OF CALATRAVA, *at* Almagro.

[*Enter the* MAESTRE *and a* SOLDIER.]

MAESTRE: What a horrible thing to have happened! Melancholy was his end. I could murder you for bringing me such news.

SOLDIER: Sir, I'm but a messenger. I did not intend to annoy you.

MAESTRE: That a town should become so fierce and wrathful, that it would dare to do such a thing! It's incredible! I'll go there with a hundred men and raze the town to the ground, blotting out even the memory of its inhabitants.

SOLDIER: Calm yourself, sir. They have given themselves up

to the King and the most important thing for you is not to
enrage him.

MAESTRE: How can they give themselves up to the King?
Are they not the vassals of the Comendador?

SOLDIER: That, sir, you'll have to thrash out with the King.

MAESTRE: Thrash it out? No, for the King placed the land
in his hands and it is the King's. He is the Sovereign Lord and
as such I recognize him. The fact that they have given themselves up to the King soothes my anger. My wisest course is to
see him, even if I am at fault. He will pardon me on account
of my youth. I am ashamed to go—but my honor demands that
I do so and I shall not forget my dignity.

[*Exeunt the* MAESTRE *and* SOLDIER.]

Public square.

[*Enter* LAURENCIA.]

LAURENCIA:

> Loving, to suspect one's love will suffer pain
> Becomes an added suffering of love;
> To fear that pain great harm to him may prove
> Brings new torture to the heart again.
>
> Devotion, watching eagerly, would fain
> Give way to worry, worm of love;
> For the heart is rare that does not bend or move
> When fear his threat on the belov'd has lain.
>
> I love my husband with a love that does not tire;
> But now I live and move beneath
> The fear that fate may take away his breath.
> His good is all the end of my desire.
>
> If he is present, certain is my grief;
> If he is absent, certain is my death.

[*Enter* FRONDOSO.]

FRONDOSO: Laurencia!

LAURENCIA: My dear husband! How do you dare to come
here?

FRONDOSO: Does my loving care for you give you such worries?

LAURENCIA: My love, take care of yourself. I am afraid something may happen to you.

FRONDOSO: It would displease God, Laurencia, if I made you unhappy.

LAURENCIA: You have seen what has happened to your friends and the ferocious rage of that judge. Save yourself, and fly from danger!

FRONDOSO: Would you expect cowardice from me? Do not advise me to escape. It is inconceivable that in order to avoid harm I should forgo seeing you and betray my friends and my own blood at this tragic moment.

[*Cries within.*]

I hear cries. If I am not mistaken, they are from someone put to the torture. Listen carefully!

[THE JUDGE *speaks within, and is answered.*]

JUDGE: Tell me the truth, old man.

FRONDOSO: Laurencia, they are torturing an old man!

LAURENCIA: What cruelty!

ESTEBAN: Let me go a moment.

JUDGE: Let him go. Now, tell me, who murdered Fernán?

ESTEBAN: Fuente Ovejuna killed him.

LAURENCIA: Father, I will make your name immortal!

FRONDOSO: What courage!

JUDGE: Take that boy. Pup, speak up! I know you know. What? You refuse? Tighten the screws.

BOY: Fuente Ovejuna, sir.

JUDGE: By the life of the King, I'll hang the lot of you, you peasants, with my own hands! Who killed the Comendador?

FRONDOSO: They're racking the child, and he answers that way . . .

LAURENCIA: What a brave village!

FRONDOSO: Brave and strong.

JUDGE: Put that woman, over there, in the chair. Tighten it up!

LAURENCIA: He's blind with rage.

JUDGE: You see this chair, peasants, this means death to you all! Who killed the Comendador?

PASCUALA: Fuente Ovejuna, sir.

JUDGE: Tighter!

FRONDOSO: I hadn't imagined . . .

LAURENCIA: Pascuala will not tell him, Frondoso.

FRONDOSO: Even the children deny it!

JUDGE: They seem to be delighted. Tighter!

PASCUALA: Merciful God!

JUDGE: Tighter, you bastard! Are you deaf?

PASCUALA: Fuente Ovejuna killed him.

JUDGE: Bring me someone a bit bigger—that fat one, half stripped already!

LAURENCIA: Poor Mengo! That must be Mengo!

FRONDOSO: I'm afraid he'll break down.

MENGO: Oh . . . Oh . . .

JUDGE: Give it to him!

MENGO: Oh . . .

JUDGE: Need any help?

MENGO: Oh . . . Oh . . .

JUDGE: Peasant, who killed the Comendador?

MENGO: Oh . . . I'll tell, sir . . .

JUDGE: Release him a bit.

FRONDOSO: He's confessing!

JUDGE: Now, hard, on the back!

MENGO: Wait, I'll tell all . . .

JUDGE: Who killed him?

MENGO: Sir, Fuente Ovejuna.

JUDGE: Did you ever see such scoundrels? They make fun of pain. The ones I was surest of lie most emphatically. Dismiss them: I'm exhausted.

FRONDOSO: Oh, Mengo, God bless you! I was stiff with fear—but you have rid me of it.

[*Enter* MENGO, BARRILDO, *and the* COUNCILMAN.]

BARRILDO: Long live Mengo!

COUNCILMAN: Well he may . . .

BARRILDO: Mengo, bravo!

FRONDOSO: That's what I say.

MENGO: Oh . . . Oh . . .

BARRILDO: Drink and eat, my friend . . .

MENGO: Oh . . . Oh . . . What's that?

BARRILDO: Sweet cider.

MENGO: Oh . . . Oh . . .

FRONDOSO: Something for him to drink!

BARRILDO: Right away!

FRONDOSO: He quaffs it well! That's better, now.

LAURENCIA: Give him a little more.

MENGO: Oh . . . Oh . . .

BARRILDO: This glass, for me.

LAURENCIA: Solemnly he drinks it!

FRONDOSO: A good denial gets a good drink.

BARRILDO: Want another glass?

MENGO: Oh . . . Oh . . . . Yes, yes.

FRONDOSO: Drink it down; you deserve it.

LAURENCIA: A drink for each turn of the rack.

FRONDOSO: Cover him up, he'll freeze to death.

BARRILDO: Want some more?

MENGO: Three more. Oh . . . Oh . . .

FRONDOSO: He's asking for the wine . . .

BARRILDO: Yes, there's a boy, drink deep. What's the matter now?

MENGO: It's a bit sour. Oh, I'm catching cold.

FRONDOSO: Here, drink this, it's better. Who killed the Comendador?

MENGO: Fuente Ovejuna killed him . . .

[*Exeunt* MENGO, BARRILDO, *and the* COUNCILMAN.]

FRONDOSO: He deserves more than they can give him. But tell me, my love, who killed the Comendador?

LAURENCIA: Little Fuente Ovejuna, my dear.

FRONDOSO: Who did?

LAURENCIA: You bully, you torturer! I say Fuente Ovejuna did it.

FRONDOSO: What about me? How do I kill *you*?

LAURENCIA: With love, sweet love, with lots of love.

Room of the Kings, at Tordesillas.

[*Enter the* KING *and* QUEEN.]

ISABELLA: I did not expect to find you here, but my luck is good.

KING: The pleasure of seeing you lends new glory to my eyes. I was on my way to Portugal and I had to stop here.

ISABELLA: Your Majesty's plans are always wise.

KING: How did you leave Castile?

ISABELLA: Quiet and peaceful.

KING: No wonder, if you were the peacemaker.

[*Enter* DON MANRIQUE.]

MANRIQUE: The Maestre of Calatrava, who has just arrived, begs audience.

ISABELLA: I wanted very much to see him.

MANRIQUE: I swear, Madame, that although young in years, he is a most valiant soldier.

[*Exit* DON MANRIQUE, *and enter the* MAESTRE.]

MAESTRE: Rodrigo Téllez Girón, Maestre of Calatrava, who never tires of praising you, humbly kneels before you and asks your pardon. I admit that I have been deceived and that, ill-advised, I may have transgressed in my loyalty to you. Fernán's counsel deceived me and for that reason I humbly beg forgiveness. And if I am deserving of this royal favor, I pledge to serve you from now on; in the present campaign which you are undertaking against Granada, where you are now going, I promise to show the valor of my sword. No sooner will I unsheathe it, bringing fierce suffering to the enemy, than I will hoist my red crosses on the loftiest merlon of the battlements. In serving you I will employ five hundred soldiers, and I promise on my honor nevermore to displease you.

KING: Rise, Maestre. It is enough that you have come for me to welcome you royally.

MAESTRE: You are a consolation to a troubled soul.

ISABELLA: You speak with the same undaunted courage with which you act.

MAESTRE: You are a beautiful Esther, and you a divine Xerxes.

[*Enter* MANRIQUE.]

MANRIQUE: Sir, the judge you sent to Fuente Ovejuna has returned and he asks to see you.

KING: [*To the* MAESTRE] Be the judge of these aggressors.

MAESTRE: If I were not in your presence, Sire, I'd certainly teach them how to kill Comendadores.

KING: That is no longer necessary.

ISABELLA: God willing, I hope this power lies with you.

[*Enter* JUDGE.]

JUDGE: I went to Fuente Ovejuna, as you commanded, and carried out my assignment with special care and diligence. After due investigation, I cannot produce a single written page of evidence, for to my question: "Who killed the Comendador?" the people answered with one accord: "Fuente Ovejuna did it." Three hundred persons were put to torture, quite ruthlessly, and I assure you, Sire, that I could get no more out of them than this. Even children, only ten years old, were put to the rack, but to no avail—neither did flatteries nor deceits do the least good. And since it is so hopeless to reach any conclusion: either you must pardon them all or kill the entire village. And now the whole town has come to corroborate in person what they have told me. You will be able to find out from them.

KING: Let them come in.

[*Enter the two* MAYORS, ESTEBAN *and* ALONSO, FRONDOSO, *and* PEASANTS, *men and women.*]

LAURENCIA: Are those the rulers?

FRONDOSO: Yes, they are the powerful sovereigns of Castile.

LAURENCIA: Upon my faith, they are beautiful! May Saint Anthony bless them!

ISABELLA: Are these the aggressors?

ESTEBAN: Fuente Ovejuna, Your Majesty, who humbly kneel before you, ready to serve you. We have suffered from the fierce tyranny and cruelty of the dead Comendador, who showered insults upon us—and committed untold evil. He was bereft of all mercy, and did not hesitate to steal our property and rape our women.

FRONDOSO: He went so far as to take away from me this girl, whom Heaven has granted to me and who has made me so blissful that no human being can compete with me in joy. He snatched her away to his house on my wedding night, as if she were his property, and if she had not known how to protect herself, she, who is virtue personified, would have paid dearly, as you can well imagine.

MENGO: Is it not my turn to talk? If you grant me permission you will be astonished to learn how he treated me. Because I went to defend a girl whom his insolent servants were about to abuse, that perverse Nero handled me so roughly that he left my posterior like a slice of salmon. Three men beat my buttocks so relentlessly that I believe I still bear some wales. To heal my bruises I have had to use more powders and myrtle-berries than my farm is worth.

ESTEBAN: Sire, we want to be your vassals. You are our King and in your defense we have borne arms. We trust in your clemency and hope that you believe in our innocence.

KING: Though the crime is grave, I am forced to pardon it since no indictment is set down. And since I am responsible for you, the village will remain under my jurisdiction until such time as a new Comendador appears to inherit it.

FRONDOSO: Your Majesty speaks with great wisdom. And at this point, worthy audience, ends the play FUENTE OVEJUNA.

THE TRICKSTER OF SEVILLE
AND THE GUEST OF STONE

TIRSO DE MOLINA

Translated by Roy Campbell

DRAMATIS PERSONAE

Don Juan	First Servant at Inn
Catalinón	Soldier
Don Gonzalo	Gaseno
King Alfonso of Castile	Servant to Octavio
Don Pedro	Belisa
Anfriso	Fabio
Marquis de la Mota	Coridon
Don Diego Tenorio	Servant to King Alfonso
King of Naples	Second Servant at Inn
Felisa	Servant Woman
Isabel	Doña Anna
Thisbe	Aminta
Duke Octavio	A Country Maid
Patricio	Musicians
Ripio	

ACT I

Palace in Naples.

[*Enter* DON JUAN *and* ISABEL.]

DON JUAN: Now, Isabel, dear Duchess, it's time I went;
The Palace is all darkness, heaven sent,
The hour is late: one kiss, ah so!
Goodnight now; show me the way to go.

ISABEL: Here, Duke Octavio, this way out is safest.

DON JUAN: Once more, dear Duchess, let me swear my troth.

ISABEL: Then may I glory in each flattering oath,
Promise, and tender wish—when they come true!

DON JUAN: You shall, my love.

ISABEL: I'll go and fetch a light.

DON JUAN: Why?

ISABEL: To convince my soul of this delight.

DON JUAN: I'll smash the lamp in pieces if you do!

ISABEL: Why, heavens! Man! In God's name who are you?

DON JUAN: Who, I? I am a man without a name.

ISABEL: And not the Duke?

DON JUAN: No.

ISABEL: Help! The Palace Guard!

DON JUAN: Come, Duchess, take my hand. Don't scream so
hard.

ISABEL: Villainous fiend, let go my hand, for shame!

SOLDIER: [*Backstage*] The Duchess calls. Sound the alarm
and wake the king.

ISABEL: Help! Soldiers, Guards, and servants of the King!

[*Enter the* KING OF NAPLES *carrying a candle in a candle-holder.*]

KING OF NAPLES:
Who's there?

ISABEL: [*Aside*] The King of Naples, alas!

DON JUAN: Why can't you see—
A man here with a woman? Her and me.

KING: [*Aside*] Prudence in this would seem the better
plan.

        [*Aloud*] Call out the Palace Guard! Arrest this man!

ISABEL: [*Covering her face*] Oh, my lost honor!

[*Enter* DON PEDRO TENORIO, *Ambassador of Spain, and* SOLDIER.]

SOLDIER: Don Pedro! Sir, over here's the bother!

DON PEDRO: From the King's rooms, cries
and shouting? Sire, from what did this arise?

KING: Don Pedro, you take charge of this arrest.
Be shrewd, and yet be prudent in your quest.
Seize and identify this muffled pair
In secret. Harm may come of this affair.
For if it proves as it appears to me,
The scandal will be less—the less I see.

[*Exit* KING.]

DON PEDRO: Seize him at once!

DON JUAN: Come, which of you will dare?
I'm due to lose my life and much I care!
But I shall sell it dear. And some will pay!

DON PEDRO: Kill him at once!

DON JUAN: Now, don't be led astray.
I'm resolute to die. For not in vain
Am I a noble cavalier of Spain,
And of her Embassy. That being known,
Each one of you must fight with me alone.
Such is the law.

DON PEDRO: Go, all of you, in there:
And take the woman. Leave him to my care.

SOLDIER: Come, Duchess, you heard our orders given;
Let us escort you to where you may be hidden.

[*Exeunt* ISABEL *and* SOLDIER.]

DON PEDRO: And now that we two are alone at length,
Let's test this vaunted valor and this strength.

DON JUAN: Although, dear Uncle, I've enough of both,
To use them on yourself I'm something loth.

DON PEDRO: Say who you are!

DON JUAN: [*Unmasking himself*] I shall. Your nephew, sir.

DON PEDRO: [*Aside*] My heart! I fear some treason is astir.
             [*Aloud*] What's this you've done, base enemy.

                                                   How is it
             That in this guise you come to such a visit?
             Tell me at once, since I must kill you here.
             Quick! Out with it at once! And be sincere!

DON JUAN: My Uncle and my lord, I'm still a lad,
             As you were once. Such youthful loves you had.
             Then don't blame me that I too feel for beauty.
             But since you bid me tell it as a duty:
             In this disguise I cheated Isabel
             (Who took me for another man) and, well,

DON PEDRO: Enjoyed her— How could you so?
             Don't answer me, if you can't speak more low.

DON JUAN: [*In a lower voice*] Pretending I was Duke Octavio.

DON PEDRO: What! Say no more! Enough!
             [*Aside to himself*]   If the King learns
             The truth, I'm lost. Oh, by what twists and turns
             Can I escape so dangerous a maze?
             [*Aloud*] Say, villain, was it not enough to raise,
             With treachery and violence, such shame,
             And with another great and noble dame,
             Back home, in Spain—but you repeat the crime
             With one that is of *princely* rank this time
             In the King's palace? May God punish you!
             Your father, from Castile had shipped you through
             Safely to Naples' hospitable strand,
             Who might have hoped for better at your hand
             Than, in return, have such shame heaped upon her
             The greatest of her ladies to dishonor.
             But here we're wasting time with this delay.
             Think, what to do, and how to get away.

DON JUAN: Pardon for this offence I can't implore.
             It would be insincere: and what is more—
             Unmanly. My blood's yours—for you to take.
             Come, let it out, and let me pay my stake.
             Here at your feet, my Uncle and my lord,

I offer you my lifeblood and my sword.

DON PEDRO: Curse you! Get up and fight! Prove you're a man!
This meek humility has spoilt my plan.
To slaughter in cold blood I never could.
Would you dare jump that balcony?—You could?

DON JUAN: Your favor gives me wings. I surely can. [*Opens window*]

DON PEDRO: Then down you go! Seek hiding in Milan,
Or Sicily.

DON JUAN: Why, soon enough!

DON PEDRO: You swear?

DON JUAN: Oh surely!

DON PEDRO: You'll be hearing from me there
The consequences of this sad affair.

DON JUAN: A pleasant one for me, you must consent.
Though I may be to blame, I'm well content.

DON PEDRO: You're led astray by youth. Quick, jump the railing.

DON JUAN: And now, for Spain, how happily I'm sailing!

[*Exit* DON JUAN *and enter* KING.]

KING: Don Pedro! The villain's gone!

DON PEDRO: I tried to execute your orders, Sire,
As well as your strict justice would require.
The man . . .

KING: Is dead?

DON PEDRO: No, he escaped the sword
And the fierce thrusts of it.

KING: How?

DON PEDRO: Thus, my lord.
You'd hardly told your orders, when, without
More said, he gripped his sword and wheeled about
Winding his cape around his arm, and so
Ready to deal the soldiers blow for blow,
And seeing death too near for hope of pardon,
Leaped desperately down into the garden
Over this balcony. Followed by all,
They found him agonizing from his fall,
Contorted like a dying snake; but when

They shouted, "Kill him!", turning on the men
With such heroic swiftness, he upstarted
As left me in confusion, and departed.
Isabel, whom I name to your surprise,
Says it was the Duke Octavio in disguise,
Who by his treachery enjoyed her.

KING: What!

DON PEDRO: I say what she confessed upon the spot.

KING: Poor Honor! If by you our value stands
Why are you always placed in women's hands
Who are all fickleness and lightness. [*Calls*] Here!

[*Enter* SOLDIER.]

SOLDIER: Sire!

KING: Bring me the woman now. Let her appear.

DON PEDRO: The Guards are bringing her already, Sire.

[*Enter* GUARDS *with* ISABEL.]

ISABEL: [*Aside*] How shall I dare to face the King?

KING: Retire.
And see the doors are guarded.

SOLDIER: We will, Sire.

[*Exit* SOLDIER.]

KING: Woman, say,
What force of fate, what angry planet, pray,
Makes you defile my palace and my board
With your lascivious beauty.

ISABEL: Oh, my lord . . .

KING: Be silent, for your tongue can never cleanse
Or gild the glaring fact of your offence.
Was it the Duke Octavio?

ISABEL: My lord . . .

KING: Can nothing cope with Love—guards within call,
Locks, bolts, and bars, and battlemented wall—
That he, a babe, can penetrate all these?
Don Pedro, on this very instant, seize
That woman: place her prisoner in some tower.
Arrest the Duke as well: once in my power
I'll have him make amends for this disgrace.

ISABEL: My lord, but once upon me turn your face!

KING: For your offences when my back was turned,
By the same back you are now justly spurned.

DON PEDRO: Come, Duchess.

ISABEL: [*Aside*]   Though I know I am to blame
Beyond excuse, it will decrease the shame
If Duke Octavio's forced to save my name.

KING: Don Pedro, I charge you, go arrest
The Duke, once he awakes from rest.

[*Exeunt all and enter the* DUKE *and* RIPIO, *his servant.*]

RIPIO: You're bright and early, Duke Octavio!
Did you sleep well, sir?

OCTAVIO: No sleep or rest
With love so fiercely burning in my breast!
For since Love is a child, he is not eased
With softest sheets, nor yet with ermine pleased.
He lies down sleepless; long before the day
Already longing to be up and play.
And, like a child, he plays, and keeps on playing.
The thoughts of Isabela keep me straying,
Ripio, in the doldrums of despair,
For since she lives within my soul, my body
Goes suffering with a load of anxious care
To keep her honor safe, whether I'm present
Or absent.

RIPIO: Sir, I find your love unpleasant.

OCTAVIO: What's that, you dolt?

RIPIO: I find it very wrong
To love as you do. Would you like to learn
The reason why I do?

OCTAVIO: Yes: come along!

RIPIO: You're certain that she loves you in return?

OCTAVIO: Of course, you idiot!

RIPIO: And you love her too?

OCTAVIO: Yes.

RIPIO: Why, what an idiot would I be
To lose my reason for a dame,

           If I loved her, and she loved me.
           Now, did she not return your flame,
           Then you might well keep such a coil;
           Adore, and flatter her and spoil
           And wait till she rewards your toil:
           But when you mutually adore
           And neither in your faith miscarry,
           What difficulty is there more—
           What is preventing that you marry?

OCTAVIO: Such weddings are for lackeys, slaves,
           And laundry wenches.

RIPIO: Well what's wrong
           With a fine laundry girl who loves,
           And sings and washes all day long?
           One who defends, and then offends,
           And spreads her linen out to see
           And is obliging to her friends—
           Is good enough for such as me!
           There are no kinder people living
           Than those who give for giving's sake.
           If Isabel is not for *giving*,
           Then see if she knows how to *take*.

    [*Knock on door.*]
           Come in.
    [*Door opens, enter* SERVANT.]

SERVANT: Don Pedro, the Ambassador of Spain has, even
                                       now,
           Dismounted here. He wears a stormy brow,
           Insisting, with a fierce and angry zest,
           To speak to you. I fear it means arrest.

OCTAVIO: Arrest? For what? Go, show His Lordship in.

SERVANT: This is the way, sir. I knew
           The Duke would be ready to receive you.

    [*Enter* DON PEDRO.]

DON PEDRO: His conscience must be clear, who so can win
           So late a sleep.

OCTAVIO: But when such men as you,

Your Excellency, come, as now you do,
To honor and to favor such as me—
It's wrong to sleep at all. My life should be
An endless vigil. But what could befall
To bring you, at such hours, on such a call?

DON PEDRO: The King sent me.

OCTAVIO: Well if the King's kind thought
Bend to me thus, I reck my life as naught,
To serve my liege; and would not count the cost
If in the cause of honor it were lost.
Tell me, my lord, what planet of good cheer;
What stroke of goodly fortune brought you here
To say I am remembered by the King?

DON PEDRO: For you, Your Grace, a most unhappy thing!
I am the King's Ambassador. I've brought
An embassy from him.

OCTAVIO: Yes, so I thought.
That doesn't worry me. Say on. What is it?

DON PEDRO: It is for your arrest I make this visit,
Sent from the King: do not resist the laws.

OCTAVIO: For my arrest he sent you? For what cause?
Tell me my crime!

DON PEDRO: You ought to know far more
Than I do: for I'm not entirely sure.
Though I may be mistaken, here's my thought,
If not my own belief, why you are sought.
Just when the giant negroes fold their tents
Of darkness, like funereal cerements,
And furtively before the dusky glow
Run jostling one another as they go,
I, with His Majesty, while talking late
Of certain treaties and affairs of State,
(Antipodes of sunlight are the Great)
Heard then a woman's scream ("Help! Help!")
                              resound
Through all the halls and corridors around.
And, as we all rushed forth to these alarms,

Found Isabel there, clasped with all her charms
By some most powerful man, in lustful arms.
Who ever it could be aspired so high—
Giant, or monster of ambition—I
Was ordered to arrest him. Held at bay,
I vainly strove to wrest his arms away.
And well I could believe it was the Fiend
Taking a human form, for, ably screened
In dust and smoke, the balcony he leapt
Down to the roots of the vast elms that swept
The palace roof. The Duchess I assisted,
Who, in the presence of us all, attested
It was yourself who, husband-like, had known her.

OCTAVIO: What's that you say?

DON PEDRO: Why, man, the whole world over,
It is notorious to the public gaze
That Isabel, yes, in a thousand ways
Has . . .

OCTAVIO: Say no more! Have mercy! Do not tell
So vile a treachery of Isabel.
[*Aside*] But say this were but caution on her part.
[*Aloud*] Go on; say more: speak out! [*Aside*] But
                              if the dart
Is poisoned that you're shooting at my heart,
Impervious to the scandal may I prove—
Unlike those gossips whom their own ears move,
Conceiving there, to give birth through their lips.
Could it be true my lady could eclipse
The memory of me, to deal me doom!
Yes: those who dream too brightly, wake in gloom.
Yet in my heart I have no doubt. It seems
These happenings are naught but evil dreams,
That, so to give more impulse to my sighs,
Entered my understanding in disguise.
[*Aloud*] Don Pedro, could it be that Isabel
Deceived me? That my heart in ambush fell,
And so my love was cheated? That can't be . . .

Why, the whole thing's impossible . . . that she . . .
Oh Woman! What a dreadful law is cloaked
In that word *honor!* . . . Whom have I provoked
To this foul trick? . . . Am I not honor-bound?
A man in Isabela's arms was found
Within the palace . . . . Have I lost my mind!

DON PEDRO: Just as it's true that birds live in the wind,
Fish in the wave, in keeping with their kind;
That all things have five elements to share;
That blessed souls in glory know no care;
That staunchness is in friends, in foes is treason;
In night is gloom, in day is light—so Reason
And Truth are in the very words I say.

OCTAVIO: Sir! My own belief will scarce obey.
And there's no thing that could astound me more—
That she, whom I as constant did adore,
Should prove no more than woman! More to know
I do not want, since it disgusts me so.

DON PEDRO: Well since you seem so prudent. Take your pick
Of the best means . . .

OCTAVIO: I would escape: and quick!
That's my best remedy.

DON PEDRO: Then go with speed.

OCTAVIO: Spain then will be my harbor in my need.

DON PEDRO: Here, by this garden door, evade the guard.

OCTAVIO: Ah, feeble reed! Ah, weathercock unstable!
Only on yourself you've turned the table,
Rousing my wrath to flee my native land
And seek my fortunes in a foreign strand.
Farewell, my country! Madness, death, and Hell—
Another, in the arms of Isabel!

[*Exeunt all.*]

Seashore.

[*Enter* THISBE, *with a fishing rod.*]

THISBE: Of all whose feet the fleeting waters
Kiss (as the breezes kiss the rose

And jasmine): of the fishers' daughters
And longshore maidens—of all those,
I Thisbe am the only one exempt
From Love; the only one who rules
In sole, tyrannical contempt
The prisons which he stocks with fools.
Here where the slumbrous suns tread, light
And lazy, on the blue waves' trance,
And wake the sapphires with delight
To scare the shadows as they glance;
Here by white sands, so finely spun
They seem like seeded pearls to shine,
Or else like atoms of the sun
Gilded in heaven—by this brine,
Listening to the birds, I quarter,
And to their amorous plaintive moans
And the sweet battles which the water
Is waging with the rocks and stones.
With supple rod that bends and swishes
And seems to stoop with its own weight,
I snare the little, silly fishes
That lash the sea, and scarce can wait.
Or else with casting net, deep down,
I catch as many as may live
Within the many-steepled town
Of conch shells. I could not be gladder
Than with this freedom I enjoy;
I, whom the poison-darting adder
Of Love did never yet annoy.
And when a thousand lovelorn hearts
Pour forth their bitter plaints forlorn,
I am the envy of these parts
Whose tragedies I laugh to scorn.
A thousand times, then, am I blest,
Love, since you never cursed my lot,
But left me tranquil in my nest
And scatheless in my humble cot.

It's just an obelisk of thatch
That crowns my dwelling with its cone,
Though no cicadas it may catch,
Attracting turtledoves alone.
My virtue is preserved in straw
Like ripening fruit, or glass, that's packed
In hay, as by the self-same law,
In order to arrive intact.
Of all the fisherfolk around
Whom Tarragona's guns defend
From pirates in the Silver Sound—
I am the one they most commend;
Impitiable to their moan
Am I, as granite to the wave,
And to their prayers a reef of stone.
Anfriso to whom Heaven gave,
In soul and body, wondrous gifts—
Measured in speech, in action brave,
Resourceful in the direst shifts,
Modest, long suffering of disdain,
Generous, valiant, tough as leather—
Has hung around my hut in vain,
Haunting my caves in every weather,
Night after night, in wind or rain,
Till with his health and youth together
He gave the dawn its blush again.
Then also, with the fresh green boughs
Which he had hacked from elm trees down,
He loved to deck my straw-built house
Which wears his flattery like a crown.
And then beneath the midnight stars
Each evening he would come to woo me
With tambourines and soft guitars—
But all of that meant nothing to me.
Because in tyrannous dominion
I live—the empress of desire—
And love to clip Love's rosy pinion

And of his Hell to light the pyre.
The other girls for him go sighing,
Him, whom I murder with disdain.
For such is Love: still to be dying
For those who hate, and cause you pain.
In such contentment I employ
Without a care, each youthful year,
And any folly that I hear
Serves but to make me loth and coy,
And, like the wind, to disappear.
My only pleasure, care, and wish
Is forth to cast my trace and hook
To every breeze, and give the fish
My baited line.
     But as I look,
Two men have dived from yonder boat
Before the waves can suck it down.
It strikes the reef, and keeps afloat;
But now its poop begins to drown.
It sinks, releasing to the gale
Its topsail which finds there its home;
A kite upon the winds to sail,
One with the spindrift and the foam.
A madman in a topsail dwells . . .

DON JUAN: [*Backstage*] Help, I am drowning! Save my life!
THISBE: A man, borne on the rising swells
And bravely with the seas at strife,
Upon his back his comrade saves
As once Aeneas bore Anchises,
And, strongly cleaving through the waves,
Subdues them as he falls and rises.
But on the beach there's no one standing
To lend a hand, or pull them clear.
Anfriso! here are wicked men landing!
Tirso, Alfred!—Can't you hear?
But now miraculously come
Through the white surf, they step ashore—

Quite out of breath the man who's swum,
But still alive the one he bore.

[*Enter* CATALINÓN, *carrying* DON JUAN *in his arms—both are soaking wet.*]

CATALINÓN: Oh for the gift of Cana's wine!
The sea with too much salt is flavored.
By all who swim to save their lives
Freely it may be quaffed and savored.
But deep down there is doom and slaughter
Where Davy Jones lives soused in brine.
Strange, that where God put so much water
He should forget to mix the wine.
Master! It seems he's frozen quite.
Master! What if he should be drowned?
It was the sea that caused the trouble.
What if with me the fault be found?
Bad luck to him who planted pine
As masts upon the sea to grow
And who its limits would define
With measures made of wood. Ah, no!
Cursèd be Jason and his Argo,
And Typhis, cursèd may he be,
Forever, under God's embargo!
Catalinón, unhappy me!
What can I do?

THISBE: Why in such trouble,
Good man; why is your life so rough?

CATALINÓN: Ah, fishermaid, my ills are double
And my good luck is not enough.
I see, to free me from his service,
My master's lifeless: is he not?

THISBE: Oh no indeed! He's breathing yet.
Those fishermen in yonder cot—
Go call them here.

CATALINÓN: Would they agree?

THISBE: At once! This noble—who is he?

CATALINÓN: Son of the King's High Chamberlain

Expecting very soon to be
Raised to a Count within a week
In Seville, by His Majesty.
That's if the King and I agree.

THISBE: What is his name?

CATALINÓN: Don Juan Tenorio.
And I am Catalinón, his servant . . .

THISBE: Then call my people.

CATALINÓN: Yes, I'll go.

[*Exit* CATALINÓN. THISBE *holds* DON JUAN *in her arms.*]

THISBE: Noble young man, so handsome, gay,
And exquisite! Wake up, I say.

DON JUAN: Where can I be?

THISBE: Safe from all harms
Encircled by a woman's arms.

DON JUAN: I live, who perished in the sea,
Only and utterly in thee:
And now I lose all doubt to find
Heaven about me is entwined
After the Hell that was the ocean.
A frightful whirlwind wrecked my fleet
And swept me with its fierce commotion
To find a harbor at your feet.

THISBE: A lot of breath you have to waste
For one who nearly lost it all,
If after such a storm you haste
To raise a tempest and a squall.
But if the sea of storms is full
And waves are cruel in their hate,
It must be little ropes that pull
To make you talk at such a rate.
Beyond all doubt you must have taken
Salt water in above your ration—
More than you'd need to salt your bacon.
You talk in such a saucy fashion—
Quite eloquent enough, I'd say,
Lying as dead upon the beach,

With all your senses well in reach.
You seem the wooden horse of Greece
Washed at my feet for vengeance dire,
Seemingly full of cold sea water,
But pregnant with deceitful fire.
And if, all wet, you can ignite,
What won't you burn when you are dry?
You promise heat, and fire, and light,
Please God, it will not prove a lie!

DON JUAN: Ah, would to God, dear country maid,
I had been swallowed by the main
So in my senses to remain
And not to lunacy betrayed
For love of you. The sea could harm me
Drowned between silver waves and blue
That roll forever out of view—
But with fierce fire it could not char me.
You share the quality that flashes
In the great sun, like whom you show,
Though seeming cold and white as snow,
Yet you can burn a man to ashes.

THISBE: The frostier seems your desire
All the more flame you seem to hold
That from my own kindles its fire.
Please God, it was not lies you told!

DON JUAN: Hush! We are interrupted, see.

THISBE: Others must come between you and me.

[*Enter* CATALINÓN *with* ANFRISO *and* CORIDON, *fishermen.*]

CATALINÓN: They have all come.

THISBE: Your master's living.

DON JUAN: But only by your presence giving
The breath I yielded.

CORIDON: Thisbe, what's your will?

THISBE: Anfriso, Coridon, my friends . . .

CORIDON: We seek to gratify you still,
By every means, to all your ends.
And so your orders, Thisbe, tell,

Out of those lips of fresh carnation,
To us who, in your adoration,
Would see that all for you goes well,
And ask no more than thus to be:
To dig the earth, to plough the sea,
To trample air, or wind, or fire
To satisfy your least desire.

THISBE: [*Aside*] How stupid used to seem to me
Their vows, and how they used to jar!
But, now in very truth, I see
How far from flattery they are.
[*To the Fishermen*]
My friends, as I was fishing here
Upon this rock, I saw a barque
Sink in the waves. Two men swam clear.
I called for help, but none would hark.
It seemed that none of you could hear,
But one of them lay lifeless here—
Brought on the back of this brave fellow—
A nobleman, who, on the yellow
Sands, lay as though upon his bier,
Very near swamped by wave and tide,
And so I sent his man to guide
And call you, to revive him here.

ANFRISO: Well now we've all arrived. You say
Your orders, though it's not the way
I usually expect from you.

THISBE: Now to my hut we'll gently take him
Where with the gratitude that's due,
His clothing we'll repair, and make him
His rock-torn garments clean and new:
This bread of kindness that we break him
Will please my dear old father too.

CATALINÓN: [*Aside*] Her beauty is superb indeed.

DON JUAN: Come, listen here!

CATALINÓN: I am all heed . . .

DON JUAN: If here they ask you who I am

You do not know—or care a damn!

CATALINÓN: D'you try to tell me what to do?
Even here? Have I to learn from you?

DON JUAN: Why for her love I'm almost dying.
I'll have her now, then scamper flying—

CATALINÓN: But what d'you mean?

DON JUAN: Be dumb! and follow me!

CORIDON: Anfriso, in an hour the fête will be.

ANFRISO: Come on, it's an occasion for good wine,
Sliced melons, and slashed bunches from the vine.
[Aside] Slices, or cudgel blows, I see it fine!

DON JUAN: I'm dying, Thisbe.

THISBE: Yet you talk, and talk!

DON JUAN: You see, yourself, I scarce can move or walk.

THISBE: You speak too much!

DON JUAN: But you perceive my trend.

THISBE: Please God, it be not lies from end to end.

[Exeunt all.]

Palace of KING ALFONSO XI.

[Enter DON GONZALO de Ulloa and KING ALFONSO.]

SERVANT TO KING ALFONSO:
Make way for His Highness, King Alfonso of Cas-
tile and his Lord Commander, Don Gonzalo de
Ulloa . . .

KING: How did your Embassy succeed, my Lord Commander?

DON GONZALO:
. . . There I found your cousin, King
Don John, preparing, arming, and reviewing
Some thirty vessels of his fleet in Lisbon.

KING: Bound whither?

DON GONZALO:
They said Goa; but I guess
It is some closer quarry, like Tangiers
Or Ceuta, which they may besiege this summer.

KING: May God on high reward and help the zeal
With which he arms His glory. You and he—
Upon what general points did you agree?

DON GONZALO:
My lord, he asks for Serpa, Olivenza,
Mora and Toro: in return for these
He'll give you Villaverde, Mertola,
Herrera, and the districts round about,
Which lie between Castile and Portugal.

KING: At once confirm the contract, Don Gonzalo.
But what about your journey? You return
Both tired and out of pocket, I presume?

DON GONZALO:
To serve you, Sire, no hardship is too much.

KING: What's Lisbon like? A good place?

DON GONZALO:
                                   In all Spain,
It is the largest city. If you'd like it
I'll paint a picture of it in the air.

KING: I'd like to hear it: someone fetch a chair.

SERVANT: A chair! Here, Sire.

DON GONZALO:
Why Lisbon is the world's eighth wonder!
Cleaving the heart of her asunder
To travel half the breadth of Spain,
The sumptuous Tagus swirls its train
And through the ranges rolls its thunder
To enter deep into the main
Along the sacred wharves of Lisbon
Of which it laves the Southern side.
But just before its name it loses
And its own course, into the tide,
It makes a port in the sierras
Where ships of all the navies ride
That can be numbered in this world;
Where like the pikes of massed battalions
The masts of caravels and galleons,

Dhows, galleys, schooners, barques and sloops
Of Indians, Norsemen, or Italians,
In such innumerable troops
Are mustered upon either hand—
They seem to form a pine-wood city
Which Neptune rules—for miles inland!
Up on the side where sets the sun,
Guarding the port on either hand
Of where the Tagus makes its entry,
With many a grimly-snouted gun—
One called Cascais and one Saint John,
Two fearsome fortresses keep sentry
The navies of the world to stun—
The mightiest strongholds on this Earth!
Just half a league along this firth
Is Belén, convent of Jerome—
The Saint whose guardian was a lion
And for his emblem chose a stone—
Where Catholic and Christian princes
Are keeping their eternal home.
After this most astounding fabric,
Beyond Alcántara, you sally
A league, to reach Jabrega's convent
Which fills the center of a valley
That is encircled by three slopes.
Here, with his paintbrush, would Apelles
Have to renounce his proudest hopes.
For, seen from far, there seem to be
Clusters of pearls hung from the sky,
Within whose vast immensity
The Romes would seem to multiply
In labyrinths of convents, churches
With streets and pathways winding by
To many a vast estate and mansion,
Extending to the sea and sky,
And on, in infinite expansion,

Through empires, sowing deathless seeds
Wherever thought of man can fly,
In buildings, arts and letters, deeds
Of glory, feats of arms, and high
Impartial rectitude of law . . .
But reaching nearest to the sky
And towering over all I saw,
Outrivalling the pen and sword,
The summit of her Christian Pity,
And most of all to be adored—
The peak of this Imperial city
Is in her vast Misericord!
The thing most worthy of amaze
That in this glorious pile I found,
Was that, from its high top, the gaze
For seven leagues could sweep its rays
On sixty villages all round,
And each of them the sea, through bays,
Could reach, and at their doors were found
One of these ports is Olivelas,
A convent where myself I counted
Eight hundred cells: the blessed nuns
To full twelve hundred souls amounted.
Lisbon just hereabouts contains
Full fifteen hundred parks and halls—
The sort that here in Andalusia
The populace "sortijo" calls,
And each with poplar groves and gardens,
Surrounded, too, with stately walls.
Right in the center of the city
Rossío lies, a noble square,
Well paved, with statues, lawns, and fountains.
A century ago, just there,
The sea was lapping cold and green
But thirty thousand houses now,
From sea to city, intervene:

Where fishing yawls were wont to plough
A mighty township stands between;
The sea has lost its bearings here
And gone to rage in other parts:
For here they call it "New Street" where
The treasure of the East imparts
Grandeur and Wealth, in such a wise
That there's one merchant counts his treasure
(So the King told me) not in coins,
But in the old two-bushel measure
We use for fodder for our mules.
Terrero, so they call the place
Where-from the Royal Household rules,
Collects a countless shoal of boats
Constantly grounded in its port
From France and England.
                              The Royal Court
Whose hands the passing Tagus kisses,
Derives its name from its foundation
By him who conquered Troy—Ulysses:
And worthy such a derivation,
Ulissibona was its name
As spoken by the Roman nation:
Lisbon's a shortening of the same.
The City Arms are represented
By a great sphere, on which displayed
Are the red wounds that Don Alonso
Got in the terrible Crusade.
In the great Arsenal you spy
All kinds of vessels, among which
Those of the Conquest tower so high
That, looked at from the ground below,
Their mastheads seem to touch the sky.
It struck me as most excellent
That citizens, while they're at table,
Can buy great loads of living fish

And most, from their own doors, are able
To catch as many as they wish,
Since from the nets in which they flounder
It's scarce a stone's throw to the dish.
Each afternoon a thousand laden
Vessels are docked, each by its shed,
With divers merchandise and common
Sustenance—oil, and wine, and bread;
Timber, and fruits of all variety,
With ice, that's carried on the head
And cried by women through the street
(They fetch it from the peaked Estrella's
Remote sierra, for the heat).
I could go on like this forever
The city's marvels to repeat
But it would be to count the stars;
Number the sands, and grains of wheat.
Of citizens two hundred thousand
It boasts: and, what is more, a king
Who kisses both your hands and wishes
You all success in everything!

KING: I couldn't have enjoyed so much
Seeing the town in all its grandeur
As thus by your creative touch
To have it brought before my eyes.
By the way, have you children?

DON GONZALO: Sire
I have one daughter. She is such a beauty
That Nature in her features may admire
And marvel at herself.

KING: Then let me give her
In marriage, from my hand endowered.

DON GONZALO: My lord,
Your will is mine. But who is it you've chosen?

KING: Although he is not here, he's a Sevillian—
Don Juan Tenorio is the young man's name.

DON GONZALO:
>
> I'll go and tell the news to Doña Anna,
> My daughter.

KING: Go at once, Gonzalo. Yes:
> And let me have the answer very soon.

> [*Exeunt all.*]

Seashore.

> [*Enter* DON JUAN *and* CATALINÓN.]

DON JUAN: Now go and get those horses ready
> Since they are stabled close at hand.

CATALINÓN: Although I'm only just your servant,
> Catalinón, please understand,
> Of decencies I am observant.
> People don't say before my nose
> Nor even yet behind my back:
> "Catalinón is one of those . . . ."
> Bad names don't fit me. That's a fact.

DON JUAN: While all these jolly fishers squander
> The hours in revel, fix these horses!
> Galloping hoofs, in such a quandary,
> . . . have always been my best recourses.

CATALINÓN: But surely, sir, you won't abuse her,
> Who saved your life?

DON JUAN: As a seducer
> You've always known me. Why, then, ask me,
> And with my own true nature task me?
> Not only that! Her hut I'll fire
> To daze their minds while we retire.

CATALINÓN: Too well I know you are the scourge
> Of womankind.

DON JUAN: I'm on the verge
> Of dying for her. She's so good.

CATALINÓN: How generously you repay
> Your entertainment.

DON JUAN: Understood.

Aeneas paid in the same way
The Queen of Carthage, you poor dolt!

CATALINÓN: The way you tempt the thunderbolt!
Those who cheat women with base sham—
In the long run, their crime will damn
After they're dead. You'll find out when!

DON JUAN: Well on the credit side I am
If you extend my debt till then;
And stretch my credit out so lengthy
You'll wait till death to punish me.
No wonder you're nicknamed "The long one."

CATALINÓN: Follow your bent. I'd sooner be
Catalinón, than you, in what
Pertains to cheating women. See!
The poor unhappy soul draws near.

DON JUAN: Saddle those horses, do you hear?
And get them ready, now, for dodging.

CATALINÓN: [*Going*] Poor trustful creature, O how dear
We've paid you for our board and lodging!

[*Enter* THISBE.]

DON JUAN: Thisbe, my sweet, come over here.
Why so sad, there's nothing you should fear.

THISBE: When I am not with you I seem without
Myself.

DON JUAN: Such a pretence I beg to doubt.

THISBE: Why so?

DON JUAN: If you loved me, you'd ease my soul.

THISBE: I'm yours.

DON JUAN: If you were truly mine heart-whole,
How could you kill me thus, and make me wait?

THISBE: It is love's punishment at last I've found,
In you, and that's what makes me hesitate.

DON JUAN: If, my beloved, I live solely in you
And ever so to serve you will continue,
And give my life for you, why do you tarry
Since I shall be your husband? Yes, we'll marry.

THISBE: Our birth is too unequal.

DON JUAN: Love is King
And under him he matches everything.
Silk with sackcloth, and lace with corduroy.

THISBE: I almost could believe you in my joy . . .
If men were not such cheats.

DON JUAN: With your least wish,
You trawl me in your tresses like a fish.

THISBE: And I bow down beneath the hand and word
Of husband.

DON JUAN: Here I swear, oh peerless eyes
Where he who looks within them swoons and dies!
—To be your husband!

THISBE: Darling, save your breath,
But oh remember God exists—and Death.

DON JUAN: [*Aside*] Well on the credit side I seem to be
If it's till death you'll keep on trusting me!
[*Aloud*] While God gives life, I'll be a slave to you,
And here's my hand and word to prove it's true.

THISBE: Now to repay you I shall not be coy.

DON JUAN: I cannot rest within myself for joy.

THISBE: Come; in my cabin Love has built his nest
And there forever we shall be at rest.
Come in between these reeds, my love, and hide.

DON JUAN: But how on earth am I to get inside?

THISBE: I'll show you.

DON JUAN: With your glory, dearest bride,
You've lit my soul.

THISBE: May that compel you, love,
To keep your word; if not—may God above
Chastise you.

DON JUAN: [*Aside*]   Well in credit I must be
If not till death my reckoning: lucky me!

[*Exeunt. Enter* CATALINÓN, CORIDON, ANFRISO, FELISA *and*
MUSICIANS.]

CATALINÓN: So my mask's in. Poor simple creature;

	That pretty cabin will soon be
	Not such a homely feature.
CORIDON:	Come on all, come on.
CATALINÓN:	And now the other rustics come,
	Her friends Coridon, Felisa and Anfriso,
	Intent on simple dance and song
	Which means the scourge cannot be long
	And I must have the horses ready . . .
CORIDON:	Call Thisbe, and the other folk
	So that the guest alone may see
	Our retinue.
FELISA:	This is her cot.
ANFRISO:	No better piece of ground could be
	For dancing, than this very spot.
	Then call her out to join our glee.
CORIDON:	Now, steady on! for can't you see
	She's occupied with other guests.
	There's going to be some jealousy—
	Enough to fill a thousand breasts.
ANFRISO:	Thisbe is envied far and wide.
FELISA:	Let's sing a little to betide
	Her coming: since we want to dance.
ANFRISO:	[*Aside*] How can one's cares find peace and quiet
	When jealousy within runs riot
	And on our revel glares askance.
THE SONG:	The girl went out to fish, she thought,
	Casting her net among the shoals,
	But there instead of fish she caught
	A thousand lovesick souls.
THISBE:	Fire, oh fire! I'm burning, burning!
	My cabin burns, my flames and sighs.
	Oh, sound the tocsin, friends, I'm turning
	The water on, from my own eyes!
	My poor hut seems another Troy
	Since Love, eternally at war,
	For want of cities to destroy
	Must fire the cabins of the poor.

Fire, oh fire, and water, water!
Have pity, Love, don't scorch my sprite!
Oh wicked cabin, scene of slaughter,
Where honor, vanquished in the fight,
Bled crimson, vilest robber's den!
And shelter of my wrongs I mourn!
O traitor guest, most curst of men!
To leave a girl, betrayed, forlorn.
You were a cloud drawn from the sea
To swamp and deluge me with tears!
Fire, oh fire! and water! water!
Diminish, Love, the flame that sears
My soul. I was the one that ever
Made fun of men and cheated them.
Then came a cavalier to sever
The thread, and, by base stratagem
Destroyed and killed my honor dead;
By swearing marriage as his bait,
Enjoyed me, and profaned my bed,
And heartless left me to my fate.
Oh follow, follow him, and bring
Him back to me. But no—do not!
I'll take it even to the King
And ask him to avenge my lot.
Fire, oh fire! and water! water!
Have mercy, Love and grant me a quarter.

[*Exit* THISBE.]

CORIDON: Follow that fiendish cavalier.

ANFRISO: In silence I must bear my lot.
But I'll avenge me, never fear,
Against this thankless, misbegot,
Impostor of a cavalier.
Come let us catch him in the rear
Because he flees in desperate plight,
And who knows whether, far or near,
He may contrive more harm.

CORIDON: It's right

> That pride should finish, thus, in mire.
> And such proud confidence should bite
> The dust at last.

THISBE: [*Backstage*]   Oh fire! Oh fire!

ANFRISO: She's thrown herself into the sea.

CORIDON: Thisbe! Don't do it! Stop! Retire!

THISBE: [*Backstage*] Fire! Oh, fire! and water, water!
> O spare me, Love! Your furnace dire;
> Have pity on a poor man's daughter!

ACT II

Palace of the KING *in Seville.*

[*Enter* KING ALFONSO *and* DON DIEGO.]

KING: Don Diego Tenorio, you astound with what you
> say.

DON DIEGO: My lord, King of Castile, I know it's true.
> This letter's just arrived here from my brother,
> Your own Ambassador. They caught him with
> A noble beauty in the King of Naples' own quar-
> ters.

KING: What sort of Lady?

DON DIEGO: The Duchess Isabel.

KING: But what temerity! Where is he now?

DON DIEGO: From you, my liege, I can't disguise the truth—
> He's just arrived in Seville, with one servant.

KING: You know, Tenorio, I esteem you highly.
> I'll get particulars from the King of Naples
> And then we'll match your boy with Isabel
> Relieving Duke Octavio of his woes,
> Who suffers innocently. But, on this instant,
> Exile Don Juan from the town.

DON DIEGO: My lord
> Where to?

KING: He must leave Seville for Lebrija

Tonight; at once: and let him thank your merit
His sentence is so light. Meanwhile determine
What can be told Don Gonzalo de Ulloa.
For now the thought of marriage with his daughter
Is quite beyond the question.

DON DIEGO: Well, my liege,
I hope that your commands will be to honor
The lady in some other way as worthy
The child of such a father.

KING: Here's a plan
That will absolve me from Gonzalo's anger:
I'll make him Majordomo of the palace.

[*Enter* SERVANT.]

SERVANT: A noble, Sire, has just come from abroad—
Who says he is the Duke Octavio.

KING: The Duke Octavio?

SERVANT: Yes, my lord.

KING: Let him enter.

SERVANT: You are to enter, please.

[*Enter* DUKE OCTAVIO *in travelling clothes.*]

OCTAVIO: A miserable pilgrim and an exile
Offers himself, great monarch, at your feet,
Forgetting all the hardships of his journey
In your great presence.

KING: Duke Octavio!

OCTAVIO: I have come fleeing from the fierce pursuit
Of a demented woman—the result
Of the unconscious fault of some philanderer—
For which I have to seek your royal feet.

KING: Already, Duke, I know your innocence.
I've written to the King my vassal, also,
Restoring your estate, and any damage
You might have suffered owing to your absence.
I'll marry you in Seville (if you like,
And she agrees) to one beside whose beauty
Isabel's would seem ugly, even were she
An angel. Don Gonzalo of Ulloa

          The Grand Commander of Calatrava,
          Whom pagan Moors praise highly with their ter-
                                             ror—
          For always cowards are flatterers and praisers—
          Has a young daughter, whose outstanding virtue's
          A dowry in itself (I count it second
          To Beauty)—and a living marvel too!
          She is the sun, the star of all Castile,
          And it is she I wish to be your wife.

OCTAVIO: The very undertaking of this voyage
          Was worth while, Sire, just for this thing alone,
          That I should know and do what gives you pleas-
                                          ure.

KING: Don Diego, please see that the Duke is entertained
                                      and lodged
          Down to his least requirement.

OCTAVIO: O my lord!
          The man who trusts in you wins every prize,
          You're first of the Alfonsos, though Eleventh!

[*Exeunt* KING *and* DON DIEGO. *Enter* RIPIO.]

RIPIO: What's happened?

OCTAVIO: O, Ripio, all my toil's rewarded well.
          I told the King my wrongs. He honored me.
          Caesar was I with the Caesar. As you see
          I came, I saw, I conquered: and as well
          He's going to marry me from his own palace,
          And make the King of Naples understand,
          And so repeal the law by which I'm banned.

RIPIO: With real good reason do they call this King
          The benefactor of Castile. And so
          He's offered you a wife?

OCTAVIO: Yes, a friend, a wife
          And one from Seville. Seville breeds strong men
          And bold ones; also strapping women too.
          A dashing style within a veiling mantle,
          Which covers a pure sun of dazzling beauty—
          Where do you see such things except in Seville?

I am so happy, it was worth my troubles.

RIPIO: Quick, Sire, come over here into this shadow.

OCTAVIO: Why we have no cause to hide.

RIPIO: Look, have you not spied
Don Juan Diego and his servant-shadow.

[*Enter* DON JUAN *and* CATALINÓN.]

CATALINÓN: Wait, sir, there is the injured Duke,
The Sagittary of Isabel—
Rather, I'd say, her Capricorn.

DON JUAN: We just pretend, or hide.

CATALINÓN: You must flatter those you sell.

DON JUAN: I went from Naples in such haste
Upon the summons of the King,
I had no time to say good-by,
Octavio.

OCTAVIO: For such a thing
I hold you blameless. [*Aside*] So we two
Today have met in Seville.

DON JUAN: Who
Would think I would see you in Seville
Where I would serve you if I may
At your commands in every way?
You leave good things behind; for Naples
Is good: but only Seville's worth
Exchanging for so fine a city
Of all the cities on this earth.

OCTAVIO: If you had told me that in Naples
Before I ever came this way,
I would have laughed the thought to scorn
But now I credit what you say.
I would go further still, and add:
Your praise falls short, a good long way.
But who's that coming over there?

DON JUAN: The Marquis de la Mota; now
I'll have to be discourteous . . .

OCTAVIO: If ever you should need my sword,
I'm at your service, my good lord.

CATALINÓN: [*Aside*] And if he wants another dame,
             Too, to dishonor in your name . . .
             I suppose you're at his service just the same.

DON JUAN: I'm very pleased at meeting you
             But if you would excuse my haste—

OCTAVIO: I am your friend; until next time, good-by, my lord.

    [*Exeunt* OCTAVIO *and* RIPIO. *Enter the* MARQUIS DE LA
    MOTA.]

CATALINÓN: [*Aside*] Here comes another friend and fool!

MARQUIS: All day I've been upon your track
             But couldn't find you anywhere.
             How strange you should be safely back
             And your old friend be in despair
             Of finding you!

DON JUAN: For heaven's sake!
             That seems a lot of fuss to make.
             What news in Seville?

MARQUIS: The whole court
             Has changed.

DON JUAN: What women? Any sport?

MARQUIS: Of course.

DON JUAN: Inés?

MARQUIS: She has retired
             To Vejer.

DON JUAN: Oh, she's time-expired!
             And Constance?

MARQUIS: She's in sorry plight
             Moulting—both hair and eyebrows too!
             A Portuguese said she was *old*
             And she thought he meant *pretty*.

DON JUAN: True!
             Our word for "lovely to behold"
             Is like the Portuguese for "old."
             And Theodora?

MARQUIS: Why this Summer
             She cured herself of the French ill
             That seemed about to overcome her,

Sweating it out in streams, until
She is grown so tender and polite
She pulled a tooth for me, and quite
Surrounded me with heaps of flowers.

DON JUAN: And what of Julia Candlelight?
Does she still sell herself for trout?

MARQUIS: For stale salt cod, I have no doubt.

DON JUAN: How's Cantarranas, the old slum?

MARQUIS: Why, crawling with the same old scum!

DON JUAN: Are those two sisters still on view?

MARQUIS: Yes and that monkey of Tolú,
The Celestina, their old dame,
Who read them scriptures on the game.

DON JUAN: Oh, her! Beelzebub's old sow!
How is the elder of them now?

MARQUIS: She's spotless, and reformed at last,
And has a saint for whom to fast.

DON JUAN: A single lover, and no share?

MARQUIS: She's firm and faithful as she's fair.

DON JUAN: The other?

MARQUIS: Leads a livelier dance
And never yet would miss her chance.

DON JUAN: What jokes or scandals have you played?
What harlots have you left unpaid?

MARQUIS: De Esquivel and I both made
A cruel fraud last night. Tonight
We've got a better hoax in sight.

DON JUAN: I'll come with you too. Have you news
About Terrero, where I've got
Two nest eggs hatching in a plot?

MARQUIS: Don't speak about Terrero, where
My heart is buried deep in care.

DON JUAN: How so?

MARQUIS: I love one that is not
Attainable.

DON JUAN: The girl, does she
Reject you?

MARQUIS: No she favors me
And loves me.
DON JUAN: Who is it?
MARQUIS: My cousin,
Anna, who has arrived here newly.
DON JUAN: Where has she been?
MARQUIS: In Lisbon with
The Embassy.
DON JUAN: Good-looking?
MARQUIS: Truly
She's Nature's masterpiece; in her
Nature has strained her powers.
DON JUAN: Such beauty?
By God I'd like to see her!
MARQUIS: Yes.
You'll see in her the greatest beauty
The King has seen in all his State.
DON JUAN: Get married then: since it's your fate.
MARQUIS: The King's betrothed her to some other.
DON JUAN: But she accepts it that you love her?
MARQUIS: Yes, and she writes me daily too.
CATALINÓN: [*Aside*] Keep your mouth shut, or you'll be sorry.
Spain's greatest trickster marks his quarry.
DON JUAN: Who, then, more satisfied than you?
MARQUIS: I've come to see what resolution
Is taken on the lady's fate.
DON JUAN: Yes go and see,
And here I'll wait
For your return.
MARQUIS: I'll come back soon.
    [*Exeunt* MARQUIS *and* SERVANT.]
CATALINÓN: [*To the other* SERVANT]
Mister Round or Mister Square,
Good-by.
SERVANT: Oh! Good-by.
DON JUAN: Now we're alone,
Shadow the Marquis, keep his track.

He went into the palace there;
See where he goes, and then come back.

[*Exit* CATALINÓN.]

SERVANT WOMAN:
[*In window*] Who am I speaking to?

DON JUAN: Who called me?

SERVANT WOMAN: Now sir,
I have seen you are a good friend of the Marquis,
Prudent and courteous; take this note, and give it
Into the Marquis' hands: for it contains
The happiness and honor of a lady.

DON JUAN: As I'm a gentleman, and his good friend,
I swear to give it to him.

SERVANT WOMAN: Stranger, thanks.
Good-by.

[*Exit* SERVANT WOMAN.]

DON JUAN: The voice has gone, and I'm alone.
Doesn't it seem like magic what has passed
This minute? That this letter should arrive
As if the wind were carrier to my thoughts
And luck my letter box! Why this must be
A letter to the Marquis from the lady
His speeches so endeared to me. In Seville
I'm called the Trickster; and my greatest pleasure
Is to trick women, leaving them dishonored.
As soon as I have left this little square
I'll open this and read it. Idle caution!
It makes me want to laugh outright. The paper's
Open already. And it's plain it's hers,
For there's her signature, and here it says
"My unkind father secretly has forced me
To marry. I cannot resist. I doubt
If I can go on living: since it's Death
That he has given me. If you respect
My will and my dear love of you, then show it
This once. For just to see how I adore you,
Come to my door this evening at eleven

And you will find me waiting, and it open,
So to enjoy the very crown of love.
Wear for a signal (that the maids may know it
And let you in) a cape of crimson color.
My love I trust in you; farewell; Your own
Unhappy love." Why it's as good as done!
Oh, I could roar with laughter! I'll enjoy her
By the same trick that limed the other one,
Isabel, back in Naples.

[*Enter* CATALINÓN.]

CATALINÓN: Here's the Marquis
Returning now.

DON JUAN: Tonight the two of us
Have lots to do.

CATALINÓN: You've some new swindle!

DON JUAN: This one's a wonder!

CATALINÓN: Well, I disapprove.
You claim that we'll escape being caught out.
But those who live by cheating must be cheated
In the long run.

DON JUAN: You've turned a bloody preacher,
Have you, you cheeky knave?

CATALINÓN: Right makes men brave!

DON JUAN: Yes! and fear makes men cowards, just like you.
You earn by serving. If you'd always earn,
Act always on the spot: he who *does* most
Wins most.

CATALINÓN: And those who say and do the most
Collide with things the most, and come to grief.

DON JUAN: But now I'm warning you: so, for the last
Time, listen, for I shan't warn you again!

CATALINÓN: Well . . . yes, from now, whatever you command
I'll do; as if you were helped on both sides
Both by a tiger and an elephant.

DON JUAN: Quiet! here's the Marquis.

CATALINÓN: Must he be the victim?

[*Enter the* MARQUIS DE LA MOTA.]

DON JUAN: Out of this casement, Marquis, someone gave me
A very courteous message for yourself.
I could not see who gave it but the voice
Was of a woman: and she said at twelve
You are to go in secret to the door,
Which at that hour will be open to you:
And you must wear a cape of crimson color
So that the maids will know you.

MARQUIS: What?

DON JUAN: This message
Was passed me at the window here without
My seeing who it was who whispered it.

MARQUIS: This message has restored my life, dear friend.
May God reward you for it without end!

DON JUAN: I haven't got your cousin here inside,
So why should your embraces be applied
To one so worthless.

MARQUIS: You delight me so
That I am quite outside myself, I know.
Oh Sun, go down!

DON JUAN: It slopes towards its setting.

MARQUIS: Come, friends. Come, night. My reason I'm for-
                           getting—
I'm mad with joy.

DON JUAN: One sees that quite all right!
You'll reach the peak at twelve o'clock tonight!

MARQUIS: Crown of my very soul! My heart's delight
Who are to crown my loving faith tonight!

CATALINÓN: [*Aside*] Dear Christ! I would not even bet a dozen
Bad ha'pennies on that beloved cousin.

MARQUIS: [*Going*] Come, friends. Ah sun go down.

DON JUAN: [*Laughs*] At twelve he'll be too late.

    [*Enter* DON DIEGO.]

DON DIEGO: Don Juan!

CATALINÓN: Your father calls you.

DON JUAN: At your orders.

DON DIEGO: I'd like to see you far better behaved,

Good-natured, with a better reputation.
Can it be possible you wish to kill me
With your behaviour?

DON JUAN: Why in such a state?

DON DIEGO: For your behaviour and your madness now
The King has bade me ban you from the city,
For he is justly angered by a crime
Which, though you hid it from me, *he* has heard
of

In Seville here—a crime so grave and evil
I scarcely dare to name it! Make a cuckold
Of your best friend and in the royal palace!
May God reward you as your sins deserve.
Listen, for though it now appears that God
Puts up with you, consenting to your crimes—
That punishment is certain—and how fearful
For those who have profaned his name in vows!
His justice is tremendous after death!

DON JUAN: What, after death? How long you give me credit!
A long, long time, before I need repentance.

DON DIEGO: It will seem short when you receive your sentence.

DON JUAN: And now what would His Highness with myself?
Will it be for a long, long time as well?

DON DIEGO: Until you have repaired the august insult
Done to the Duke Octavio, and appeased
The scandals you have caused with Isabel,
You have to live in exile in Lebrija;
The King requires that you retire there instantly.
The sentence is too light for such a crime.

CATALINÓN: [*Aside*] And if he also knew about the case,
Of that poor fisher girl, the good old man
Would be far angrier.

DON DIEGO: Since no punishment,
Nor anything I say or do, affects you—
[*Going*] Your chastisement I here confide to God.

CATALINÓN: The dear old man was quite affected.

DON JUAN: Tears are well suited to old age.
              Well now the night is closing down,
              We'll seek the Marquis. Come, my page.
CATALINÓN: And now you will enjoy his bride.
DON JUAN: This ought to be a famous jest.
CATALINÓN: Pray God that we come out of it
              Alive.
DON JUAN: Now! Now!
CATALINÓN: I think the best
              Way to describe you, sir, would be
              The locust, to whom dames are grass;
              And that by public proclamation
              Whenever you're about to pass,
              Towns should be warned: "Here comes the plague
              Of women in a single man
              Who is their cheater and betrayer—
              The greatest trickster in all Spain."
DON JUAN: You've given me a charming name.

Street of Seville at night.

     [*Enter* MARQUIS *with* MUSICIANS.]
MUSICIANS: [*Singing*]
                  To him who waits a promised pleasure
                  Delay is like despair to measure.
MARQUIS: May never break of day destroy
              The night in which I take my joy.
              [*Aside*]   It appears
              The poet speaks to me. [*Aloud*] Who's there?
DON JUAN: Friend!
MARQUIS: It's Don Juan?
DON JUAN: The Marquis, you?
MARQUIS: Who other would it be?
DON JUAN: I knew
              You by the colored cape you wear.
MARQUIS: Sing, gentlemen, since Don Juan's come here too.

MUSICIANS: [*Singing*]
To him who waits a promised pleasure
Delay is like despair to measure.

DON JUAN: Whose house is that you gaze at so?

MARQUIS: Why Don Gonzalo de Ulloa's.

DON JUAN: Where shall we go?

MARQUIS: To Lisbon.

DON JUAN: How,
Being in Seville?

MARQUIS: Don't you know?
And do you wonder that the worst
Of Portugal live on the first
And best of Spain, right here and now.

DON JUAN: Where do they live?

MARQUIS: Why in the Street
Called "of the Serpent."

DON JUAN: You run along there while you can.
I have to play a scurvy joke.

MARQUIS: I'm being shadowed by a man—
Some pimp, or bravo . . .

DON JUAN: Leave him to me . . . .
I shan't let him escape, you'll see.

MARQUIS: Around your arm, then, wrap this crimson cloak
The better so to deal your stroke.

DON JUAN: A good idea; then come and show
The house to which I have to go.

MARQUIS: Now, while you carry out the plan,
Alter your voice and talk as though
You were indeed some other man.
D'you see that window there?

DON JUAN: I do.

MARQUIS: Then go to it, and whisper there
"Beatrice," and then pass right through.

DON JUAN: What sort of woman?

MARQUIS: Soft and pink.

CATALINÓN: Some water-cooling jar, I think.

MARQUIS: I'll wait for you at Gradas stair.

DON JUAN: Till then, dear Marquis! I'll be there.

CATALINÓN: Now whither bound?

DON JUAN: Shut up, you dolt.
I go to where my jest is played.

CATALINÓN: Nothing escapes you unbetrayed.

DON JUAN: I adore cheating.

CATALINÓN: Pass your cape,
Then, to the bull.

DON JUAN: Not so! The hornèd
Beast has passed his cape to *me*.
The girl will have to think I'm he!

CATALINÓN: That's certifying by mistake
(And the whole world is in the take).

MUSICIANS: [*Singing*]
               When one awaits a promised pleasure
               Delay is like despair to measure.

CATALINÓN: I like this hardly at all,
Standing here outside the house of Doña Anna;
I feel my master's heading for a fall
This trick though in his manner . . .

DOÑA ANNA: [*Backstage*] Help! Help!

CATALINÓN: A call!
The cat's escaped the bag . . .

DOÑA ANNA: [*Backstage*] False friend, you're not the Marquis—
You have tricked me!

DON JUAN: [*Backstage*] I'll tell you who I am.

DOÑA ANNA: [*Backstage*]   False enemy!
You lie! You lie!

     [*Enter* DON GONZALO.]

CATALINÓN: Here comes her father, sword already drawn
To break the doorway in.

DON GONZALO:
          I hear my daughter, Doña Anna's voice.

DOÑA ANNA: [*Backstage*] Will nobody kill this false traitor here,
The murderer of my honor?

DON GONZALO:

> Can such effrontery exist? She said
> "My honor murdered." Then, alas for me!
> Her venal tongue is like a bell to clamor
> Our sad disgrace to all.

DOÑA ANNA: [*Backstage*]   Kill him!

CATALINÓN: Here too escapes Don Juan, jumping
> From the balcony; as usual he will get a bumping.

[*Enter* DON JUAN.]

DON JUAN: Who's this?

DON GONZALO:

> The closed and fallen barbican is here
> Of the strong fortress of my honor, which,
> Base traitor, you have falsely undermined,
> Though there my life was warden.

DON JUAN: Let me pass!

DON GONZALO:

> Pass? You shall pass the point of this bare sword.

DON JUAN: You'll die for this.

DON GONZALO: That is no matter.

DON JUAN: Look,
> I'll have to kill you.

DON GONZALO: Die yourself, base traitor.

DON JUAN: [*Thrusts him with sword*] This is the way I die.

CATALINÓN: [*Aside*]   If I get free,
> Then no more feasts and scurvy tricks for me!

DON GONZALO:

> He's given me my death.

DON JUAN: You took your life
> By being rash.

DON GONZALO: What use was it to me?

DON JUAN: Come, Catalinón, let us run.

[*Exeunt* DON JUAN *and* CATALINÓN.]

DON GONZALO:

> My frozen blood you've swelled
> With fury. I am dead. I can expect
> No better thing. My fury will pursue you.

You are a traitor, and a traitor is
A traitor because he is first of all a coward.

[DON GONZALO's *body is removed from the stage. Enter*
MARQUIS *with* MUSICIANS.]

MARQUIS: Now midnight will be striking soon:
Don Juan's surely very late.
How hard a thing it is—to wait.

[*Enter* DON JUAN *and* CATALINÓN.]

DON JUAN: Is that the Marquis?

MARQUIS: You're Don Juan?

DON JUAN: I am. Here, take your cape.

MARQUIS: Your pranks? . . .

DON JUAN: . . . Have had a most funereal end
In death.

CATALINÓN: O flee from the dead man!

MARQUIS: Tell me, whom did you trick, my friend?

CATALINÓN: [*Aside*] You are the latest victim, thanks
To him.

DON JUAN: This prank has cost most dear.

MARQUIS: Don Juan, the whole debt I'll clear . . .
Because the girl will be complaining
Of me . . .

DON JUAN: The stroke of twelve draws near.

MARQUIS: May never break of day destroy
The night in which I take my joy.

DON JUAN: Farewell then, Marquis!

CATALINÓN: What a treat
Awaits the wretch!

DON JUAN: Let's run!

CATALINÓN: My feet
Than wings of eagles feel more fleet.
Twelve begins to strike.

[*Exeunt* DON JUAN *and* CATALINÓN.]

MUSICIANS: [*Singing*]
When one awaits a promised pleasure
Delay is like despair to measure.

MARQUIS: Now you can all go home. I'll go

　　　　　　　　　Alone.

SERVANT:　　　　　　God made the night for sleeping.
　　[*Exeunt* MUSICIANS *and* SERVANTS.]

SERVANT WOMAN:
　　　　　[*Backstage*] Was ever such a sight of woe? . . .
　　　　　Alas! How pitiless a blow! . . .

MARQUIS:　　God shield me! I hear cries and weeping
　　　　　Resounding from the castle square.
　　　　　At such an hour what could it be?
　　　　　Ice freezes all my chest. I see
　　　　　What seems another Troy aflare,
　　　　　For torches now come wildly gleaming
　　　　　With giant flames like comets streaming,
　　　　　And reeking from their pitchy hair,
　　　　　A mighty horde of tarry hanks.
　　　　　Fire seems to emulate the stars
　　　　　Dividing into troops and ranks.
　　　　　I'll go and find out . . .

　　[*Enter* DON DIEGO *and* GUARDS *with torches.*]

DON DIEGO:　　　　　　　　Who goes there?

MARQUIS:　　One who would know of this affair,
　　　　　And why there's such a hue and cry.

DON DIEGO:　Bind him!

MARQUIS:　　[*Drawing his sword*] What? Me? I'd sooner die!

DON DIEGO:　Give me your sword. The greatest valor
　　　　　Is speech without recourse to steel.

MARQUIS:　　And is it thus that you would deal
　　　　　With me, the Marquis de la Mota?

DON DIEGO:　Your sword! Whatever you may feel,
　　　　　The King has ordered your arrest!

MARQUIS:　　Ye Gods!

　　[*Enter* KING *and retinue.*]

KING:　　　Through Spain from east to west
　　　　　See that he can't escape; as well,
　　　　　In Italy (for who can tell
　　　　　If he should get there?). Start the quest.

DON DIEGO: He is here . . .

MARQUIS: Then, Sire, I'm apprehended
Truly, by your own orders; why?

KING: Take him, and have his head suspended
Upon a rampart near the sky.
You dare to stand before my eye?

MARQUIS: [*Aside*] The glories of tyrannic passion
Always so light in passing, by
The future weights on such a fashion,
The fetters make you wilt and die.
Well said the sage " 'twixt lip and beaker
There's many a slip." What stuns me more
Is the King's wrath as vengeance-wreaker.
[*Aloud*] I can't make out what crime it's for.

DON DIEGO: Who should know better than yourself?

MARQUIS: Me?

DON DIEGO: Come!

MARQUIS: What strange confusion!

KING: Charge him,
And cut his head off before day.
For the Commander—don't deny him
Solemnity and grave display,
Such as men grant to royal or sacred
Persons. The funeral must be grand.
The sepulchre of bronze and stone—
With Gothic letters, see it planned
Proclaiming vengeance is at hand.
In his last words, let it be shown.
And where has Doña Anna gone?

DON DIEGO: She's gone to sanctuary at the
Convent of our lady the Queen.

KING: This loss is grave, for such a Captain
Has Calatrava seldom seen.

[*Exeunt all.*]

The Countryside.

[*Enter* PATRICIO, AMINTA, GASENO, BELISA, SHEPHERDS, MUSICIANS.]

PATRICIO: Oh good Belisa, Aminta my bride—
    Will she soon be by my side?

BELISA: Patricio, have patience.
    The wedding feast seems quite prepared
    And first there must be shared
    The food amongst us; is that not so,
    Good friend Gaseno?

GASENO: Yes indeed, and we must say
    Our prayer to this fine day.
      [*Singing*]

PATRICIO,
GASENO and
BELISA
    Brightly April's sun shines over
    The orange-flowers and scented clover,
    But though she serves him as a star—
    Aminta shines out lovelier far.

PATRICIO: Upon this carpet made of flowers,
    When the red earth seems turned to snow,
    The sun exhausts his dazzling powers
    And freshens to his dawning glow.
    Come, let us sit, for such a place
    Invites us with its charm and grace.

BELISA: Look, here comes an important stranger.

[*Enter* CATALINÓN.]

CATALINÓN: Good people all, for your espousal
    More guests have come to the carousal.

GASENO: Let everybody be invited.
    I hope that all will be delighted.
    Who's coming?

CATALINÓN: Don Juan Tenorio.

GASENO: The old one?

CATALINÓN: No! I mean the young.

GASENO: He must be something of a blade!

PATRICIO: [*Aside*] I take this omen very hard,
    That being a cavalier and young,

It brings on envy . . . takes off lustre.
[*Aloud*] Who gave him notice of our muster?

CATALINÓN: He heard of it along the road.

PATRICIO: [*Aside*] That to the Devil must be owed.
But why anticipate the load?
[*Aloud*] Then come to my sweet wedding night
All those who wish to dance and dine,
[*Aside*] Except that one of them's a Knight—
I take that as an evil sign.

GASENO: Let the Colossus be invited
From Rhodes, the Pope, and Prester John,
With Don Alfonso the Eleventh,
His court, and all who follow on.
Mountains of bread for our espousal
Are heaped, with wine in mighty rivers
That overflows for your carousal
In Taguses and Guadalquivirs.
Babels and Babylons of ham;
Thrushes and quails in timid flocks
Are here, your bulging sides to cram—
With tender doves and basted cocks.
To Dos Hermanos, welcome here;
Bring in the noble cavalier
To honor these white hairs of mine!

BELISA: [*Respectfully*] Son of the Chancellor . . .

PATRICIO: [*Aside*] A sign
Of evil is this guest of mine;
For they must place him by my bride.
No more in feasting am I zealous
Since heaven dooms me to be jealous,
To love, to suffer, and abide.

BELISA: Come all, follow me in:
There sits the bride.
The room has been
Most gaily decked:
Leave room by her side.

[*Enter* DON JUAN.]

DON JUAN: I heard by chance there was a marriage feast
               When I was passing by this village here,
               And so I've come to revel in it too,
               Being so lucky as to pass just then.

GASENO: Your Lordship comes to honor and ennoble it.

PATRICIO: [Aside] And I, who am its host and master, say,
               Within me, that you come in evil hour.

GASENO: Won't you make room there for the cavalier?

DON JUAN: With your permission, I will sit just here.
               [*Sits next to the bride*]

PATRICIO: If you sit down before me, sir, you'll seem
               The bridegroom.

DON JUAN: If I were, I could choose worse!

GASENO: He *is* the bridegroom.

DON JUAN: Oh, I beg your pardon
               For my mistake.

CATALINÓN: [Aside]   Oh, poor unhappy bridegroom!

DON JUAN: [Aside, to CATALINÓN] He seems annoyed.

CATALINÓN: I'm quite aware of that,
               But if he has to serve you for a bull,
               What does it matter if he seems annoyed?
               I would not give one horn toss for his wife
               Nor for his honor. Poor unhappy man
               To fall into the hands of Lucifer.

DON JUAN: Can it be possible I am so lucky?
               I'm almost feeling jealous of your husband.

AMINTA: You seem to flatter me.

PATRICIO: [Aside]   Well it is said,
               "A great one at a wedding brings bad luck."

GASENO: Come let us eat and drink a while
               So that Your Lordship, while we dine,
               May rest himself.

DON JUAN: [*Takes* AMINTA's *hand*]
                      Why hide your hand?

AMINTA: It's mine.

GASENO: Let's go.

AMINTA: Strike up the song again.

DON JUAN: What do you make of it?

CATALINÓN: I fear a vile
Death at the hands of those same sturdy peasants

DON JUAN: What lovely eyes and spotless hands—
They're burning me with flaming brands.

CATALINÓN: It's you that brand her with your mark
And put her out to winter grazing—
Four little lambs, with this one.

DON JUAN: Mark
How all of them at me are gazing.

PATRICIO: It is an evil-boding thing—
A noble at my wedding.

GASENO: [*Keeping up appearances*] Sing!
Come, all must sing!

PATRICIO: God! I feel as if I'm dying.

CATALINÓN: [*Aside*] They sing now, who will soon be crying
[*Exeunt all.*]

ACT III

The Countryside.

[*Enter* PATRICIO, *pensive.*]

PATRICIO: Jealousy, timepiece of our cares, who strike
Fierce torments and alarms at every hour;
Torments with which you kill, although you give
Disjointed blows: cease from tormenting me,
Since it's absurd that if Love gives me life,
You should give death.—What do you wish of me,
Sir Cavalier, that you torment me so?
Well did I say, seeing him at my wedding:
"An evil omen." Was it not well done
That he should sit beside my bride, not letting
Me even put my hand in my own plate;
Because each time I tried to do so, he
Would brush it off exclaiming "What ill breed-
                                            ing!"

As for that other rogue, he'd say "You don't
Eat that?" And then he'd snatch it from my plate,
Saying that I was wrong not to enjoy it.
I am ashamed. This wedding was a jest
And not a marriage. None will suffer me,
Or let me pass among them. Now he's supped
With both of us, I suppose he has to come
To bed with us, and when I take my wife,
To chide me, "What ill breeding! What ill breed-
ing!"
He's coming now. I can't resist. I'll hide—
But that can't be, since he has seen me now.

[*Enter* DON JUAN.]

DON JUAN: Patricio.

PATRICIO: Yes, my lord.

DON JUAN: It's just to tell you—

PATRICIO: [*Aside*] What can it be but more ill luck for me?

DON JUAN: It's just to tell that I lost my soul
Some hours ago to our Aminta and
Enjoyed . . .

PATRICIO: Her honor?

DON JUAN: Yes.

PATRICIO: [*Aside*]   A certain proof
Is all that I've just seen. Did she not love him,
He never would have ventured to her house.
[*Aloud to* DON JUAN] She's only proved a woman,
after all.

DON JUAN: Aminta, in the end, grew jealous; desperate,
In fact, thinking herself forgotten by me,
And being married to another man.
And so she wrote this letter sending for me,
And in return I promised to enjoy
That which our souls had promised long ago.
Well, that's how things stand. Give your life a
chance,
For ruthlessly I'll kill whoever stops us.

PATRICIO: Why, if you leave it to my choice, I'll further

Your wishes. For when rumor breathes abroad,
Honor and woman suffer worst of all.
And women in the general opinion
Will always lose more than they gain. For women
Are tested, just as bells are, by their sound.
And it is known how reputation suffers
When in the common speech a woman's name
Rings with the sound of a cracked bell. Since you
Subdue me, I no longer want the bliss
That love commanded me to take. A woman
Half good, half bad, is like a piece of gold
Seen in the twilight. For a thousand years
Enjoy her, sir! I'd sooner die unhoodwinked
Than live the dupe of others. [*He leaves*]

DON JUAN: Through his honor
I conquered him, for always, with these peasants,
They hold their honor in both hands, and look
To their own honor first. For honor
Was forced, by so much falsity and fraud,
To leave the city for the countryside.
But now, before I work the final damage,
I shall pretend to remedy it too.
I'll go and talk to her old father; and get him
To authorise the deed against his will.
Oh stars of morning give me luck in this
Deception: since you keep the payment due
In death, for such a long, long time ahead.

[*Enter* GASENO.]

GASENO: Sir Cavalier, the honor you perform is very great.
Marriage to my daughter—I can hardly wait
To tell the girl.

DON JUAN: There's no hurry.

GASENO: Let me keep you company
So as I may congratulate my daughter.

DON JUAN: Oh, there'll be time enough for that tomorrow.

GASENO: Yes, you are right. I offer my own soul
Together with the girl.

DON JUAN: Rather, my bride. Good-by, Gaseno . . .

GASENO: Honored Sir, good-by.

[*Exit* GASENO.]

DON JUAN: Catalinón, go saddle up.

CATALINÓN: For when?

DON JUAN: For dawn, and when the sun, half dead with
                                       laughter,
    Rises to see the hoax.

CATALINÓN: There in Lebrija
    There is another bridal that awaits us.
    For God's sake hasten with the one in hand.

DON JUAN: But this will be the greatest hoax of all!

CATALINÓN: I only hope we come out safely from it.

DON JUAN: Seeing my father is Chief Justice and
    The King's most private friend, what can you fear?

CATALINÓN: God is accustomed to take vengeance on
    Those who use privacy merely to deprive.
    And often, when there's gambling on, spectators
    Are apt to lose as badly as the gamblers.
    I've long been a spectator of your gambles,
    And for this office I would dread to be
    Struck by the thunderbolt to dust and cinders,
    When it gets you.

DON JUAN: Go, saddle up those horses,
    Tomorrow night I have to sleep in Seville.

CATALINÓN: In Seville?

DON JUAN: Yes.

CATALINÓN: What are you saying? Look
    At what you've done, master: and look how short
    Even the longest life is until Death,
    And there's a Hell behind the gates of Death.

DON JUAN: If you concede me such a long, long time
    You'll be deceived . . .

CATALINÓN: Listen, my lord.

DON JUAN: Get out!
    You bore me.
    Thus I'm going to lay my trap.

Love guides me to my joy. None can resist him.
I've got to reach her bed.

[*Exit* DON JUAN.]

GASENO'S *house in Dos Hermanos.*

[*Enter* BELISA *and* AMINTA.]

BELISA: See, where your bridegrom comes, Aminta. Come,
             Enter and strip.

AMINTA: Of this unhappy wedding,
             I don't know what to think. For my Patricio
             All day was bathed in melancholy tears.
             All's jealousy and wild confusion. What
             A terrible misfortune!

BELISA: But why are you so sad?

AMINTA: Leave me, for I am all confusion,
             Since Shamelessness was made a Knight of Spain.
             Evil befall the knight that lost me my
             Good husband.

BELISA: Quiet! For I think he's coming.
             Let no one tread the floor of so robust
             A bridegroom.

AMINTA: Now farewell, my dear Belisa.

BELISA: You will appease his anger in your arms.

AMINTA: May it please heaven my sighs may seem endear-
                                                         ments
             And these poor tears appear to him caresses.

DON JUAN: [*Outside*] Aminta!

AMINTA: Who
             Calls for Aminta: Is it my Patricio?

DON JUAN: I'm not Patricio. No.

AMINTA: Then, who?

DON JUAN: [*Coming in*]   Look slowly,
             And you'll see who I am.

AMINTA: Why, sir, I'm lost—
             With you outside my bedroom at these hours!

DON JUAN: Such are the hours that I am wont to keep.

AMINTA: Return, or I shall shout. Please don't exceed
The courtesy you owe to my Patricio.
You'll find, in Dos Hermanos, there are Romans,
Aemilias, and Lucreces who avenge.

DON JUAN: Just hear two words: and hide the blushing scarlet
Of your fair cheeks deep down within your heart,
The richer and more precious for your sake.

AMINTA: Go, go! My husband's coming.

DON JUAN: I'm your husband.
So what have you to marvel at?

AMINTA: Since when?

DON JUAN: From now on, and forever, I am he!

AMINTA: But who arranged the marriage?

DON JUAN: My delight.

AMINTA: And who was it that married us?

DON JUAN: Your eyes.

AMINTA: By what authority?

DON JUAN: Why, that of sight!

AMINTA: But does Patricio know?

DON JUAN: Yes! He forgets you.

AMINTA: Has he forgotten me?

DON JUAN: Yes. I adore you.

AMINTA: How?

DON JUAN: Thus, with all my heart I swoon before you.

AMINTA: Get out!

DON JUAN: How can I when you see I'm dying
With love for you alone.

AMINTA: What shameless lying!

DON JUAN: Aminta, listen and you'll know the truth,
Since women are the friends of truth. I am
A noble knight, the heir of the Tenorios,
The conquerors of Seville. And my father,
Next to the King, is honored and esteemed
Beyond all men in court. Upon his lips
Hang life or death according to his word.
Travelling on my road, by merest chance,

I came and saw you. Love ordains these things,
And guides them, so that even he, himself,
Forgets that they were anything but chance.
I saw you, I adored you, I was kindled
So that I am determined now to wed you—
Even though the King forbids it, and my father
In anger, and with threats, tries to prevent it—
I have to be your husband. What's your answer?

AMINTA: I don't know what to say. Your so-called "truths"
Are covered with deceitful rhetoric:
Because if I am married to Patricio
(As is well known) the fact is not annulled
Even if he deserts me.

DON JUAN: Non-consummation,
Either by malice or deceit, is reason
For an annulment.

AMINTA: In Patricio all
Was simple truth.

DON JUAN: Tush! Come, give me your hand,
And let's confirm our vows.

AMINTA: You're not deceiving?

DON JUAN: I'd be the one deceived.

AMINTA: Then swear before me
To carry out your promised word.

DON JUAN: I swear
By this white hand, a winter of pure snow.

AMINTA: Swear, then, to God. Pray that he curse your soul
If you should fail.

DON JUAN: If in my word and faith
I fail, I pray to God that by foul treason
I'm murdered by a man . . .
[Aside]   I mean a dead one.
For living man, may God forbid!

AMINTA: This promise
Has made me your own wife.

DON JUAN: My very soul
I offer you between my outstretched arms.

AMINTA: My life and soul are yours!

DON JUAN: Ah, my Aminta,
            Tomorrow you will walk in silver buskins
            Studded with tacks of gold from heel to toe.
            Your alabaster throat will be imprisoned
            In necklaces of diamonds and rubies,
            And your white fingers, in their flashing rings,
            Will seem transparent pearls.

AMINTA: From now, to yours
            My will bows down, and I am yours alone.

DON JUAN: [*Aside*] Little you know the trickster-man of Se-
                                                        ville.

            [*Exeunt* AMINTA *and* DON JUAN.]

Near Tarragona.

            [*Enter* ISABEL *and* FABIO *in travelling clothes.*]

ISABEL: He robbed me of my master,
            By treason, Fabio, of the man whom I adored!
            O pitiless disaster
            To truth! Oh night abhorred—
            Black mask of day, who aided the deceit,
            Antipod of the sun, and spouse of sleep!

FABIO: What serves it, Isabel,
            Always upon your sorrows so to dwell?—
            If Love is naught but cunning,
            Always through fields of scorn and anger running;
            If he who laughs today,
            Tomorrow has to weep his woes away?
            The sea is swelled with anger
            And from this mighty tempest and its clangor,
            Out of the foamy welter,
            Duchess, the galleys now have sun for shelter
            Beneath the towers that crown
            This rocky strand.

ISABEL: Where are we?

FABIO: At the town

Of Tarragona. Hence,
By land, we'll reach the city of Valénce
In very little time;
The palace of the sun, a most sublime
And stately city. There,
For several days you may divert your care;
And then to Seville sailing,
You'll see the world's eighth wonder. What if fail-
　　　　　　　　　　　　　　　　　　　　　ing

To win Octavio's hand?
Don Juan is more famous in the land!
Then why so sad? They say
He's made a count already. Anyway,
The King himself is giving
Your hand to him. Of all the nobles living,
The nearest to the King
His father is—the first in everything.

ISABEL:　My sadness is not due
To marrying Don Juan, since it's true
He is most nobly born
And the world knows it. What makes me forlorn
Is honor which, though wife,
I must lament the years of all my life.

FABIO:　A fishermaid appears
Sighing most tenderly and bathed in tears;
Surely she's come to you
Some favor or some sympathy to woo.
So while I fetch your train
You two may all the sweetlier complain
Together.

[*Exit* FABIO *and enter* THISBE.]

THISBE:　Sea of Spain,
Rough sea, with waves of fire, and fleeting foam!
Burned Troy of my poor home!
O fire, conceived and hatched deep in the main
Which waves brought forth to turn
Again to running water, though it burn

With flames in these salt tears!
Cursèd be the wood that on the wave careers
To work the woe that was Medea's;
Cursèd be those that had the mad ideas
Of twisting hemp or lint
To crucify the canvas on a splint
And be the engines of deceiving—
Serpents of rope their deep enchantments weaving.

ISABEL: Why, lovely fishermaid,
Do you complain so sadly of the sea?

THISBE: Why, madam, I have made
A thousand such: . . . and happy must you be
To laugh at such a thing!

ISABEL: I also have such sad complaints to sing.
Where are you from?

THISBE: Behind
There, where, sore-wounded by the wind,
You see those huts; the gales
Over them so victoriously rampage
That through their shattered pales
Each bird can find a nesting place, their rage
Forces so many a rift!
Of these great bulls, are you the prize they left,
O beautiful Europa, in this cart.

ISABEL: Though much against my heart,
They're taking me to Seville to be wed.

THISBE: If my sad lot has bred
Some pity in you, and if you as well
Some woes of the injurious sea can tell,
Then take me with you, and I'll be your slave.
I have a private audience with the King to crave
For reparation of an evil hoax
Played by a noble on us humble folks.
Lifeless and stranded by the angry wave,
Was Don Juan de Tenorio, whom to save,
I sheltered until he was out of danger,

When this ungrateful and relentless stranger
Proved to my foot a viper in the grass.
With promises of marriage he confused me
And for his own mere pleasure then abused me.
Woe to the woman who believes men's oaths!
He ran away and left me to my woe.
Say, have I right to vengeance then, or no?

ISABEL: O cursèd woman, hold your tongue,
By which even to death I have been stung!
[*After reflecting*] But, if it's grief that's actuating
you,
It's not your fault. Proceed! But is it true?

THISBE: How happy, were it false . . .

ISABEL: Woe to the woman who believes men's oaths!
Who's coming with you?

THISBE: One old fisherman,
My father, and the witness of my wrongs.

ISABEL: No vengeance can suffice so great an evil.
Come in my company, and welcome, both!

THISBE: Woe to the woman who believes man's oath!

    [*Exeunt* THISBE *and* ISABEL.]

A *church in Seville.*

    [*Enter* DON JUAN *and* CATALINÓN.]

CATALINÓN: That we are in this church I'm glad;
I tell you things are looking bad.

DON JUAN: How so?

CATALINÓN: First, that Octavio has got to know
That hoax in Italy. The Marquis, too,
Knows that the message which he got from you
And which you said his cousin gave, was faked.
Then, Isabela's on the way: she's staked
A marriage claim, and also it is spoken . . .

DON JUAN: [*Hitting him a blow*] Here, hold your tongue!

CATALINÓN: Look, master, you have broken
A molar in my mouth.

DON JUAN: Then hold your jaw.
Who told you all this nonsense?

CATALINÓN: Nonsense?

DON JUAN: Yes.

CATALINÓN: It's gospel truth!

DON JUAN: I don't care if it is.
And what if Duke Octavio tries to kill me—
Have I not hands as well? Where is our lodging?

CATALINÓN: Down in the darkest hidden street.

DON JUAN: That's good.

CATALINÓN: Here in this church it's Holy Ground.

DON JUAN: Just so.
D'you think they'll kill me here in broad daylight?
And have you seen Patricio, the bridegroom from
Hermanos?

CATALINÓN: I saw him, too, looking both grim and sad.

DON JUAN: For two whole weeks, Aminta has not known
How she's been tricked.

CATALINÓN: So thoroughly she's hoaxed,
She goes about calling herself the countess!

DON JUAN: God! What a funny hoax.

CATALINÓN: Funny enough:
And one for which that girl must weep forever.

DON JUAN: [*They both look at the sepulchre*] Whose sepulchre
is this?

CATALINÓN: Here Don Gonzalo
Lies buried.

DON JUAN: What? The same one as I killed?
They've done him very nobly for a tomb.

CATALINÓN: This tomb was ordered by the King. What says
That writing there?

DON JUAN: [*Reads*] "Here, trusting in the Lord
For vengeance on a traitor, the most loyal
Of all true knights lies buried." What a joke!
So you think you'll avenge yourself on me?

[*Pulling the beard of the statue*]
So now you sprout a beard of solid stone,
Good gaffer?

CATALINÓN: There are beards that can't be plucked.
You watch yourself with beards that are too strong!

DON JUAN: O Statue, fine Stone Don, tonight I will await you
at my inn
For supper. There we can arrange a duel,
Although it won't be easy fighting me;
A granite rapier must be stiff to handle.

CATALINÓN: Come, sir, it's getting dark. We'd better go!

DON JUAN: [*To the statue*] How long this vengeance seems
to be in coming,
Especially if you are going to wreak it!
You musn't be so motionless and sleepy!
And if you're willing still to wait till death
Why, what a lot of chances you are wasting
That for so long a time you give me credit!

[*Exeunt* DON JUAN *and* CATALINÓN.]

Room in an inn.

[*Enter* SERVANTS.]

1ST SERVANT:
We must prepare the room, because Don Juan
Dines here tonight.

2ND SERVANT: The tables are prepared.
If he's so late there's nothing one can do
But let the drinks warm, and the food grow cold.
But who could order *order* from Don Juan—
The ace of all disorder?

[*Enter* DON JUAN *and* CATALINÓN.]

DON JUAN: You've locked the doors?

CATALINÓN: I've locked the doors exactly as you ordered.

DON JUAN: Then bring my supper, quick.

1ST SERVANT: It's here already.

DON JUAN: Catalinón, sit down.

CATALINÓN: I sup more slowly.

DON JUAN: Sit down, I tell you.

CATALINÓN: Well; if you insist.

1ST SERVANT:
          [*Aside*] He must be for a journey, now, as well,
          To sup with his own lackey.

DON JUAN: Come, sit down.
     [*A big knock is heard on the outside door.*]

CATALINÓN: Say, that's some knock!

DON JUAN: It must be someone calling.
          See who it is.

1ST SERVANT: I fly, sir, to obey you.
     [*Exit* SERVANT.]

CATALINÓN: What if the police have come?

DON JUAN: What if they have?
          No need for fear!
     [*Enter* SERVANT, *excitedly*.]

1ST SERVANT: Oh, sir, terrible, terrible!

DON JUAN: What's this? You're all atremble.

CATALINÓN: He has seen something evil. One can tell it.

DON JUAN: Don't make me lose my temper. Speak, man,
                                                  speak!
          What have you seen? Some Devil's terrified you?
          Go, you, and see whatever's at the door.
          Go on! Go, quick!

CATALINÓN: Who, I?

DON JUAN: Yes, you, at once.
          Yes, you, get your feet moving. Aren't you going?

CATALINÓN: Who's got the keys?

2ND SERVANT: Only the bolt is slid.

DON JUAN: What's up with you then? Move! Why don't you
                                                  go?

CATALINÓN: What if the raped and ravished have arrived
          To have their final vengeance. [*He leaves*]
          [*Outside*] Oh, Lord . . . Saint Antonio.

DON JUAN: What's all this?

CATALINÓN: God help me! You can kill me if you like.

DON JUAN: Who's killing you? What is it? What have you
seen?

CATALINÓN: Master . . . there . . . I saw . . . well, when I
got there . . .
[Aside] But what has seized me? What has
snatched my mind?
[Aloud] I got there to the door . . . then, after,
I was blind . . .
But there I saw . . . I swear to God . . . I saw it.
I spoke and said, "Who are you?" Then he an-
swered.
I opened and called with a . . . with a . . .

DON JUAN: With what or whom?

CATALINÓN: I don't know! Don't ask *me!*

DON JUAN: How wine confuses people. Here! That candle!
I'll go and see myself who it can be. [*Goes*]

DON GONZALO:
Don Juan Tenorio.

DON JUAN: What's this? Who are you?

DON GONZALO:
It's I.

DON JUAN: But who on earth are you?

DON GONZALO:
Don Gonzalo de Ulloa. Once the Commander of
Calatrava.
The person you invited here to dine.

DON JUAN: Why, there's enough for both of us, and more,
If you've brought any friends along with you;
The table's set already. Sit down here.

CATALINÓN: May God be with me now in my sore need
With Saint Panuncio and San Antón.
What? Do the dead eat too?

DON GONZALO:
Yes, they do.

DON JUAN: Catalinón, sit down with us.

CATALINÓN: Excuse me.

I take it that he's dined.

DON JUAN: You've lost your head.
Are you afraid of a dead man? What then?
If he were living, how much more you'd fear him!
What an illiterate and rustic fear!

CATALINÓN: Dine with your guest, sir. I have supped already.

DON JUAN: You wish to make me angry?

CATALINÓN: Sir, I stink,
And that's the reason I would not offend you,
I smell too bad.

DON JUAN: Sit down! I'm waiting for you.

CATALINÓN: [Aside] I'm almost dead with fear. My bum has
                                                     misbehaved.

DON JUAN: You others there. What about you? You're trem-
                                                     bling?

CATALINÓN: I never liked to eat with foreigners,
Who come from other countries.—Me, my lord?
You'd have me feasting with a *guest of stone?*

DON JUAN: What stupid fear! If he is stone, what matters?

CATALINÓN: It knocks me all to pieces all the same!

DON JUAN: Speak to him courteously.

CATALINÓN: Sir, are you well?

DON GONZALO:
          Yes.

CATALINÓN: That "other life," is it a pleasant country?
What is it like—all plains, or steep sierras?

DON GONZALO:
          Yes.

CATALINÓN: Do they give prizes there for poetry?

DON GONZALO:
          Yes.

CATALINÓN: And are there lots of taverns there? Why, surely,
If Noah lives around there, there must be!

DON JUAN: Fetch wine.

CATALINÓN: Señor Dead-man, tell me, in your country,
Do the drinks there have ice in them?

DON GONZALO:
>   Yes, they do.

CATALINÓN: Ah! With ice!
>   What a good country!

DON JUAN: If you want a song
>   I'll make them sing.

DON GONZALO:
>   Yes, please do!

DON JUAN: Then sing!

CATALINÓN: The Señor Dead-man
>   Has real good taste.

DON JUAN: He's nobly bred, and so
>   He is a friend of pleasure, naturally.
>   Come! Sing!

SINGERS:
>   *If you expect it of us men*
>   *That our deserts shall find adjusting—*
>   *But not till after death, why then,*
>   *A long, long time you are for trusting!*

CATALINÓN: Either he finds the heat is overpowering
>   Or else he is a man who eats but little.
>   I cannot keep from trembling at my dinner.
>   It seems that they don't drink much over there
>   And so I'll drink, for both of us [*Drinks*] a pledge
>   Of stone. I feel less terrified already.

SINGERS:
>   *If that's the date you ladies give*
>   *To enjoy all for whom I'm lusting—*
>   *You grant a long, long time to live*
>   *And burnish up my joys from rusting.*
>   *If you expect it of us men*
>   *That our deserts shall find adjusting,*
>   *But not till after death, why then*
>   *A long, long time you are for trusting!*

CATALINÓN: Which, of all the ladies you have cheated,
>   Do they make mention?

DON JUAN: I laugh at them all,
>   My friend, on this occasion. Why, in Naples

With Isabel . . .

CATALINÓN: She's not so badly cheated
Since you will have to marry her, quite rightly.
But that poor girl who saved you from the sea,
You treated in a pretty sorry fashion.
You cheated Doña Anna.

DON JUAN: Hold your jaw!
For here is someone who has suffered for her,
And waits for his revenge.

CATALINÓN: He is a man
Of mighty valor being made of stone,
And you of flesh. It's not a pleasant problem.

DON GONZALO:
Ask your servants to clear the table and then to
                                        leave us.

KING: Here, clear this table;
The rest should go, and leave us both together.

CATALINÓN: It's bad! For God's sake, master, don't remain!
For here's a dead man that with one sole fisticuff
Could floor a giant.

DON JUAN: All of you, get out!
Were I Catalinón, then I might flinch . . .
But go; for he desires it so.

[Exeunt all but DON JUAN and DON GONZALO. Door shuts.]
                                        The door's shut
And I am at your service. What's your will—
Shade, Vision, or Phantasma? If your soul
Is travailing in pain; if you await
Some satisfaction or relief, then tell me—
And I will give my word to do whatever
You command me. Are you in the Grace
Of God? Or was it that I killed you recklessly
In a state of mortal sin. Speak! I am anxious.

DON GONZALO:
And as a gentleman you'll keep your word?

DON JUAN: I keep my word, with men, being a knight.

DON GONZALO:
> Then give your hand on it. Don't be afraid!

DON JUAN: What! *Me* afraid? Were you both Hell and Death,
> I'd dare to give my hand. [*He gives his hand*]

DON GONZALO:
> Now lower both your hand and voice: tomorrow
> At ten, I'll be awaiting you for supper;
> You'll come!

DON JUAN: Why, I expected something far
> More dangerous than what you ask of me.
> Tomorrow I shall be your guest; but where?

DON GONZALO:
> In my side chapel, by my tomb.

DON JUAN: Alone?

DON GONZALO:
> No, you can bring your servant, and you'll honor
> Your word, as I have done the same to you?

DON JUAN: Of course! I am Tenorio born and bred.

DON GONZALO:
> And I—a born Ulloa.

DON JUAN: I'll be there
> And without fail.

DON GONZALO: I trust your word. Good-by.
> [*He goes toward the door*]

DON JUAN: Wait, let me get a torch to light your way!

DON GONZALO:
> My soul requires no light. *I am in Grace.*
> [*Exit* DON GONZALO, *staring at* DON JUAN.]

DON JUAN: God save me! All my body's bathed in sweat.
> My very heart seems frozen here inside.
> For when he took me by the hand and squeezed it
> It seemed I was in Hell. Such was the heat.
> And yet his breath and voice were like the blizzard
> Of an infernal frost. Yet all these things,
> Begot by fear on the imagination,
> Are quite unreal. To fear the dead is baseness.

If I am not afraid of noble bodies
With all their powers, alive with wits and reason—
To fear dead bodies is a stupid thing.
Tomorrow I will go there to the chapel
Where he invited me, that all of Seville
May make a living legend of my valor.

[*Exit* DON JUAN.]

The palace in Seville.

[*Enter the* KING, DON DIEGO *and retinue.*]

KING: So Isabela has arrived at last, good Don Diego.
DON DIEGO: Against her will, sire.
KING: She does not like this marriage?
DON DIEGO: She feels the worst at losing her good name.
KING: It is some other cause that thus torments her.
Where is she?
DON DIEGO: She has taken up her lodging
With the Discalcèd Nuns.
KING: Then fetch her here:
And at her leisure she may serve the Queen.
DON DIEGO: And if her marriage must be with Don Juan,
Then, please, command it, that he may appear.
KING: Yes, let him come here, full-dressed as a bride-
groom;
I'll have this marriage famed throughout the land.
For from today Don Juan is the Count
Of Lebrija: to rule it and possess it.
If Isabel has lost a Duke, her equal,
At least she's won a most outstanding Count.
DON DIEGO: For this great kindness, I could kiss your feet.
KING: You have deserved my favors worthily.
I still am far behindhand in requiting
Your services. It seems, too, that today
The Lady Anna should be wedded also.

DON DIEGO: What! With Octavio?

KING: Should it not be
That Duke Octavio must save the shame
Of this great scandal? Doña Anna and the Queen
Have begged the Marquis' life: since now the father
Is dead, she wants a husband of her choice;
For now she loses one, she wins the other.
Go to Triana's fort, and there inform him
That for his injured cousin's sake, he's pardoned.

DON DIEGO: Now I have seen what most I have desired!

KING: This evening, then, the weddings will take place.

DON DIEGO: All's well that ends well. It should be quite easy
To show the Marquis he was truly wooed
By his own cousin.

KING: Also, warn Octavio.
That Duke is always luckless with his women;
For him they're all appearances and rumors.
They say he's furious with Don Juan.

DON DIEGO: I shouldn't be surprised, since he found out
The truth about that dirty trick he played,
Which has done so much damage on all sides.
Here comes the Duke.

KING: Don't leave my side at all,
For in this crime you, too, are implicated.

   [*Enter* DUKE OCTAVIO.]

OCTAVIO: Give me your feet, Unconquered Majesty!

KING: Rise, Duke. Put on your hat. What is your trouble?

OCTAVIO: I come to ask a right that should be granted.

KING: Duke, if it's just, I swear to grant it. Name it.

OCTAVIO: Already, Sire, you know by letters from
Your own Ambassador, and the whole world
Knows by the tongue of rumor, how Don Juan,
With Spanish arrogance in Naples lately,
In my own name, defiled the sacred virtue
Of a great lady.

KING: Don't go any further!

| | I know of your misfortune. What's your plea? |

OCTAVIO: To fight it out with him in open country,
Since he's a traitor.

DON DIEGO: No, his blood's too noble . . .

KING: Don Diego!

DON DIEGO: Sire!

OCTAVIO: Why, who are you to speak
Before the King in such a fashion?

DON DIEGO: I
Am one who holds his peace when the King bids
                                                    it.

Otherwise I would answer with this sword.

OCTAVIO: You're far too old!

DON DIEGO: I once was young in Italy;
My sword was known from Naples to Milan.

OCTAVIO: Your blood is frozen. "I was once," is nothing
To "I am now."

DON DIEGO: I am both "was" and "am."
                                        [Clutching his sword]

KING: Come, come, you two, restrain yourselves. Enough:
Be silent, Don Diego; for my person
You have shown disrespect. As for you, Duke,
After the marriages are celebrated
We'll speak of this affair at greater leisure:
Don Juan's my creation and my henchman,
And of this trunk a branch. So keep your distance!

OCTAVIO: Your Majesty, I'll do as you command.

KING: Come, Don Diego.

DON DIEGO: [Aside]   Oh, my son, my son,
How badly you repay the love I bear you!

KING: Duke.

OCTAVIO: Sire.

KING: Tomorrow we shall have you married.

OCTAVIO: So be it, if it is Your Highness' wish.

KING: Come, Don Diego. We will leave you, Duke;
The court is at your disposal.

[*Exeunt* KING, DON DIEGO *and retinue. Enter* GASENO *and* AMINTA.]

GASENO: This gentleman may tell us where to find
             Don Juan Tenorio. Sir, is Don Juan Tenorio round
                                                  about?

OCTAVIO: You really mean Don Juan Tenorio?

AMINTA: Yes, that's the one I mean, and no mistake.

OCTAVIO: Oh, yes. He's here. What do you want with him?

AMINTA: Why, that young man's my bridegroom. So he is.

OCTAVIO: What's that?

AMINTA: You, being of the palace, haven't
             Yet heard of it! That's strange.

OCTAVIO: He didn't tell me.

GASENO: Can that be possible?

OCTAVIO: Well, so it seems.

GASENO: Lady Aminta is most honorable,
             And now they're marrying: she is by lineage
             One of the non-converted ancient Christians
             And is the heir to our own cattle
             Which we rule just like counts or marquises.
             Don Juan took her from Patricio
             And was betrothed to her.

OCTAVIO: [*Aside*] This must be just another
             Of his foul tricks, and for my own revenge
             They're giving it away.
             [*To Gaseno*]   What is your wish?

GASENO: I want to see the marriage celebrated
             Because the time is passing—or, if not,
             I'll take it to the King.

OCTAVIO: And very justly too.

GASENO: All I require is reason and just law.

OCTAVIO: [*Aside*] It just fits in, in keeping with my thoughts.
             [*Aloud*] Today there is a wedding in the palace.

AMINTA: Why then it must be mine!

OCTAVIO: To make quite sure,
             I have a little plan. You come with me,

Lady, where you'll be dressed in courtly fashion.
Then into the King's quarters come with me . . .

AMINTA: Give me your hand and lead me to Don Juan.

OCTAVIO: This is a wise precaution.

GASENO: Reason prompts it.

OCTAVIO: [Aside] So these good people give me my revenge
Against that traitor villain, base Don Juan,
And his foul injuries to Isabel.

[Exeunt all.]

A street

[Enter DON JUAN and CATALINÓN.]

DON JUAN: Stop here awhile; this is the church.

CATALINÓN: How did the King receive you?

DON JUAN: Far more lovingly
Than if he were my father.

CATALINÓN: Did you see
The Duchess Isabel?

DON JUAN: Yes. Her, also.

CATALINÓN: How did she seem?

DON JUAN: An angel.

CATALINÓN: She received you
Kindly?

DON JUAN: Her face seemed bathed in milk
And blushing with her blood, like a white rose
With all its dews lit by the red aurora.

CATALINÓN: And so the wedding is this evening, sir?

DON JUAN: Yes: without fail.

CATALINÓN: If it had been before,
Perhaps you'd not have harmed so many women.
But now, you take a wife, with heavy charges
And grave responsibilities.

DON JUAN: Are you being
Impertinent and stupid once again?

CATALINÓN: You might at least have waited till tomorrow.

Today is most unlucky!

DON JUAN: What day is it?

CATALINÓN: A Tuesday.

DON JUAN: Oh, to Hell with all that nonsense
Which only fools and madmen take to heart.
That day alone's unlucky, cursed, and foul,
When I run out of money. Other days—
All other days—are revelry and laughter.

CATALINÓN: Come, let us go, for you must dress in style.
They're waiting for you now; and it grows late.

DON JUAN: We have another business first in hand.
So they'll just have to wait.

CATALINÓN: What other business?

DON JUAN: To sup with the dead man.

CATALINÓN: What need for that?

DON JUAN: Well, don't you know? I gave my word upon it.

CATALINÓN: And if you broke it, sir; what could it matter?
A jasper figure can't expect so much
From a live man as to insist on vows.

DON JUAN: The Dead Man, then, could say I was a *coward*.

CATALINÓN: But anyway, you see the church is *shut*.

DON JUAN: Knock, then.

CATALINÓN: What does it matter if I knock?
There's nobody to open it inside,
And all the sacristans are sleeping.

DON JUAN: Knock
Here at this postern.

CATALINÓN: [*Knocks*] It is open.

DON JUAN: Enter.

CATALINÓN: Let friars enter with their stoles and hyssops!

DON JUAN: Then follow me, and hold your tongue. Be silent.

CATALINÓN: Silent?

DON JUAN: Yes.

CATALINÓN: I am silent. Oh, may God,
Please, bring me out alive from such a feast.

[*Enter and exit by different doors.*]

It's very dark for such a great big church.
Oh, sir, protect me; someone grabbed my cloak!

[*Enter* DON GONZALO.]

DON JUAN: Who's that?

DON GONZALO: It's I.

CATALINÓN: Oh, I am dead with fright!

DON GONZALO:
        I am the Dead Man: do not be afraid.
        I did not think that you would keep your word,
        Since you delight in breaking it so often—

DON JUAN: I suppose that you imagine me a coward!

DON GONZALO:
        Why, yes! Because, that night, you fled from me
        When you killed me.

DON JUAN: I fled from recognition.
        But here I stand before you. What's your will?

DON GONZALO:
        Why, only to invite you here to supper.

CATALINÓN: Pray let us be excused. Here all the victuals
        They serve are *cold—cold* supper and *cold* lunches.

DON JUAN: We'll sup then.

DON GONZALO: Well, to do so, you must lift
        The lid, here, off this tomb.

DON JUAN: Why, if you wish it,
        I'll lift these pillars too!

DON GONZALO:
        [*The tomb slides back*] You're very willing.

DON JUAN: Yes, I have strength and courage in my body.

CATALINÓN: This table must have come from Guinea's coast,
        It is so black. Are there none here to wash it?

DON GONZALO:
        Be seated.

DON JUAN: Where?

CATALINÓN: See, two black servants come
        With stools.

[*Enter two figures in black with stools.*]

> So here, too, people go in mourning
> With flannel made in Flanders?

DON JUAN: You! Sit down!

CATALINÓN: What, me, sir? I've already fed this evening.

DON JUAN: Don't answer back!

CATALINÓN: All right, I will not answer.
> [Aside] Oh God, in safety get me out of this!
> [Aloud] What dish is this?

DON GONZALO: Tarantulas and vipers.

CATALINÓN: Really? How nice!

DON GONZALO: That is our diet here.
> But *you're* not eating.

DON JUAN: I shall eat it,
> Though all the snakes in hell be on one plate!

DON GONZALO:
> I'd like to have them sing to you a little.

CATALINÓN: What sort of wine do they have here?

DON GONZALO: There, taste it.

CATALINÓN: Vinegar and bile—that's what this wine is!

DON GONZALO:
> Well, that's the sort of wine that we press here.
> Here, sing, my choristers.

SINGERS: [Singing]
> *Let all those know who judge God's ways*
> *And treat His punishments with scorn:*
> *There is no debt, but that one pays;*
> *No date, but it is bound to dawn.*

CATALINÓN: How terrible. I've heard this tune before
> And now it is addressed to me.

DON JUAN: [Aside]   My breast
> Is frozen, and the ice is breaking through it.

SINGERS: [Singing]
> *While in the world one's flesh is lusting*
> *It is most wrong for men to say,*
> *"A long long time in me you're trusting—"*
> *For very shortly dawns the day.*

CATALINÓN: What is this fricassée?

DON GONZALO: Of finger-nails.

CATALINÓN: Then they must be the finger-nails of tailors,
They are so sharp, and clawlike, and rapacious.

DON JUAN: Now I have eaten; let them clear the table.

DON GONZALO:
Give me your hand. Don't be afraid! Your *hand.*

DON JUAN: "Afraid," you say. *Me* frightened? Here's my hand.
[*He gives it*]
I'm roasting, burning! Do not burn me so
With your fierce fire.

DON GONZALO: That's nothing to the fire
Which you have sought yourself! The wondrous
ways
Of God, Don Juan, are not fathomable!
And so He wishes now for you to pay
Your forfeits straight into the hands of Death.
This is God's justice. What you've done, you pay
for.

DON JUAN: I'm roasting. Do not grip my hand so hard.
I'll kill you with this dagger! But the blows
Strike only empty air. Look. With your daughter
I did no harm. She saw the hoax in time.

DON GONZALO:
That does not matter. It was your *intention.*

DON JUAN: Then let me send for a confessor quickly,
So to absolve my soul before I die.

DON GONZALO:
Impossible. You've thought of it too late.

DON JUAN: Oh, I am burning! Oh, I am roasting, burning!
I'm dying! [*He falls dead*]

CATALINÓN: There is no escape. I, too,
Must die for having been your boon companion.

DON GONZALO:
Such is God's justice. What is done is paid for.
[*The tomb sinks noisily with* DON JUAN *and* DON GONZALO.
CATALINÓN *crawls in.*]

CATALINÓN: So help me God! What's this? The chapel's burn-
ing
With wondrous light. And I'm left with the corpse
To watch with it and guard it. To his father
I'll drag his body and proclaim the news.
Saint George, and Holy Lamb of God, protect me
That I may come in safety to the street.
[*Exit* CATALINÓN.]

The palace.

[*Enter* KING, DON DIEGO *and retinue.*]
DON DIEGO: The Marquis of Mota wants to kiss your royal feet.
KING: Then let him enter: call the Count Don Juan
As well, that he be kept no longer waiting.
[*Enter* PATRICIO *and* GASENO.]
DON DIEGO: Who is this rustic rushing in? What do you want;
See you not the King?
PATRICIO: Where are such foul monstrosities permitted
That your own servants should affront, unpun-
ished,
The humble people.
KING: What is that you say?
PATRICIO: Don Juan Tenorio, treacherous, detestable,
Stole my young wife the evening of our marriage.
And here I have the witnesses.
[*Enter* THISBE, ISABEL *and retinue.*]
THISBE: Sire, if Your Highness will not do me justice
On Don Juan Tenorio, both to God and men
I will complain through all my days to come!
When dying he was swept ashore, I gave him
Both life and hospitality. With lust
And promises of marriage he repaid
This kindness: he abused me and then left me.
KING: What do you say?
ISABEL: She's telling you the truth.
[*Enter* AMINTA *and* DUKE OCTAVIO.]

DON DIEGO: And yet another comes
In bridal gown.

AMINTA: Where is my spouse?

KING: Who is he?

AMINTA: What, you don't
Know, even yet? Don Juan Tenorio,
With whom I've come this evening to be wedded,
Because he owes it to my name and honor
And, being noble, will not break his word.

[*Enter* SERVANT.]

SERVANT: The Marquis de la Mota to kiss the King's feet.

[*Enter* MARQUIS DE LA MOTA.]

MARQUIS: It's time to drag some truths into the light,
My lord. Know then that of the selfsame crime
For which you sentenced me, Don Juan is guilty
(A cruel trick to play on a best friend)
And I've the witnesses to prove it here.

KING: Could any shamelessness compare to this?

DON DIEGO: Sire, to reward my services to you,
Let him be made to expiate his crime
So that the heavens themselves don't shoot their
                                        lightning
At me, for having bred so foul a son.

KING: And so it's thus my favorites behave!

DON DIEGO: Sire, here comes his servant,
Green with terror; full with news.

[*Enter* CATALINÓN.]

CATALINÓN: My lords, all listen to the greatest wonder
That ever happened in this world:—and kill me
If listening, you don't believe it's true:
Don Juan, making fun of the Commander—
Having divested him of life and honor,
And all the gems and ornaments of life—
Pulling the beard upon his granite statue,
Insulted him by asking him to dine.
Oh that he'd never done so! Then the statue
Went to his house, inviting him in turn,

And then (to make it short, and not to tire you)
When they had finished supper, took his hand
And squeezed it till he squeezed his life out, saying
"God ordered me to kill you thus, and punish
Your monstrous crimes. For what you've done,
                                        you pay."

KING: What are you saying?
CATALINÓN: It's the gospel truth.
Don Juan pleaded, first, that he had not
Seduced the Lady Anna, who discovered
The fraud in time.

MARQUIS: For this delightful news
A thousand gifts I wish to give you.

KING: Just punishment from heaven has been dealt.
Now let them all be married, since the cause
Of all their harm is dead.

OCTAVIO: Since Isabela's
A widow now, I wish to marry her.

MARQUIS: And I to wed my cousin.

PATRICIO: And us others
With our own girls. For now THE TRICKSTER OF SE-
                    VILLE AND THE GUEST OF STONE
Is ended.

KING: Take the tomb to San Francisco,
The great church in Madrid, and there install it
And so preserve this memory through all time.

THE GREAT THEATER
OF THE WORLD

PEDRO CALDERÓN DE LA BARCA

Translated freely by Mack Hendricks Singleton

[*Enter the* AUTHOR *in a starry mantle with nine rays of light in groups of threes on his hat.*]

AUTHOR: This earth, this gleaming tapestry that lieth before my feet, is heaven's fairest masterpiece—the mirror and reflection of heaven's great embroidery. Subtly contrived—in shades and shadows and retreating visual planes—it would outshine the rich refulgence, even, of heaven's celestial sphere; and, on its emerald-carpeted meadows, upflash in myriad hosts the sweet fresh smiling flowers, impatient ever to shame the teeming stars above—those other flowers of heaven. Observe this transitory paradise—this mortal lavishness. Behold the windy air where little feathered galleons do sail their singing flight. See too the seas adjacent, and the Ocean, and finny fish that there their briny courses fly. Mark how yon bolt of lightning's fiery wrath doth sear and scourge each blinded eye. And there, not least, observed beyond—the solitary hills, of man the lonely lair, and sylvan beast. Behold, in monstrous war internecine, the massy, wild confliction of the elements—tempestuous battleground of fire and air, of air and earth, and fire and earth and water. Oh thou of various aspect, many-hued, where Nature all her treasure doth amass, thou art the first rich miracle of time, fashioned most marvellously, and beyond surpass. This happy concourse of the elements, from ashes risen like Phoenix, the immortal bird, shall be confined and limited within a single word. I, then, thou brave new tapestry before my feet unfurled, decree a name to name thee, and thee I name the World.

WORLD: Who summons me from my concealment in the dark and adamantine center of earth's great globe?

AUTHOR: World, thy Creator summons thee. Only a breath, a slightest turn of hand, suffice me to knead thy formless matter into ordered substance.

WORLD: What is Thy command?

AUTHOR: Thou art my creation, and my most shadowy desire must produce thy acquiescence immediately. Though Nature for my delight outdoeth herself in daily spectacle, still would I see a work cast in a different mold. Know that Man's life is but a play from cradle to the grave. Prepare, therefore, to perform the Play of Life, whose spectator shall be heaven. Thou, World, shall set the stage, I will the play direct, and men and women (whom I most loved of all created things) shall be the actors in it; and in this quadripartite World's Great Playhouse they shall put on their play with seemly skill and due comportment. To each we give the part that he may act most fittingly. Now, therefore, World, order thy stage and the settings place, and gather together appropriate properties. I will then appoint rehearsals, and thou—from first to last— shall be the Great World's Theater, and Man the cast.

WORLD: Oh my Creator, before whose word and majesty all nature suppliant kneels, I bend my will immediately to Thy words. I am rejoiced to be the World's Great Theater. Mine shall be the craftsmanship, though the miracle be thine: I only execute Thy dread command. And that men may play their roles judiciously, I will array a stage and its appurtenances in stateliest propriety. To whet sweet pleasure's expectation, before the act begins, all Nature shall by a thick and sable veil be covered over. There chaos reigns, and dire confusion. Now do the mists primeval flee dispelled, and all enshrouding vapors. Straightway the theater is lighted up (without light there is no play), and two great luminaries gleam forth—the sun's bright gold by day, and the nocturnal orb's pale light; and unnumbered

gems celestial do diadem the night. In the First Act of the
World's Great Play shall be displayed the simple candor of
primitive Natural Law. A garden first appears, with images
bedecked of wondrous beauty—tactful perspectives so dex-
trously contrived that man at nature's artistry might wonder,
thus to paint so artlessly. Scarce burst from roseate bud, the
dewy flowers' bewilderment salutes the world's first dawning.
There do the trees bend low with savory fruits mellifluous
(except that one where envy's asp distils his hellish venom).
Up flash the myriad beads of liquid crystal, shattered from
gentle brooklet's pebbly bed; and shimmering beams of Dawn
weep countless pearls diminutive. And for just proportion's
sake, within this heaven terrestrial, there shall be scattered
about, occasional virgin fields untilled; and mountains and
valleys shall be created and stand in fit decorum; and my wise
discernment shall guide rivers there—the great sea's arms—
through the grooved earth in numberless courses divergent.
The first scene shall show no habitations; but you shall see
directly how I establish nations, and cities shape, and raise up
mighty fortresses. And when importunate mountains fatigue
the down-pressed earth and obstruct the lucid air, all shall—
alas!—be overwhelmed by water in wrathful inundation. Far
off, on yonder vast and liquid plain, see!—a ship, an Arc, now
sails her course uncharted midst the waxings and the wanings
of the waves, and the whirlings of the winds and clouds and
tempests. With steady fluctuance it forward bears, harboring in
its deep recesses man, and all manner of birds and beasts and
other living things. An iris sign-of-peace doth now behue the
heavens—saffron-pale, violet-sapphire, and crimson-velvet sombre. The guild of waves withdraws—obedient to its statutes and
the decrees of first primitive Natural Law. And earth again
reveals her wasted features wan, and shakes off her neck the
dire oppression of the waters. Now doth the Second Act begin,
heralded by Israel's progeny, that dry-shod crossed the Red
obedient Sea. The waves shall heap them high, and summit
toward th'amazed, incredulous sky. Then shall two columns
incandescent in the desert illuminate the wandering host's

bright journey toward their Promised Land. Moses shall later snatch the Written Law from cloud in flight across a mountain-top. Finally, the Second Act shall end when a dying sun fadeth away in dire eclipse; and the sapphire broad-spread firmament shall quake and tremble, and the geometry of heaven shall be confused. The everlasting hills will shake, and the walls of cities shall fall upon the inhabitants thereof. And then the Third Act will begin, heralded by the Law of Grace, whose attributes are known to every man. Thus with three acts, three laws, and one decree the story of the World will have run its course. And at the final end the stage and all its rich embellishments shall be swept by flames—and so bring fire to our fiesta. My voice fails me, and my hand grows palsied, when I pause to think of that dread day. But let us dwell no more upon that burning horror, and let us pray it be postponed till distant ages have passed away.

Now have I briefly outlined the broad action of the World's Great Drama, and we may next proceed directly to the performance we must give. All the basic preparations have been made; but not mine is the task to choose what dress the different actors wear, for in Thy mind, Creator, and in Thy mind alone, a final choice has been prepared, for in the mystery of Thy timeless prescience all men before their entrance on the stage have been assigned the role and station of their lives. The stage is now constructed; and, that men may come from Thy all-knowing Presence into the world and act their parts, and then to Thee return, here have I two doors constructed—the cradle and the grave. The properties are waiting, too. For the actor who plays the King I have set purple and laurel aside; for the brave warrior—courage, weapons and triumphs; and for the scholar—writings and studies and schools. For the churchman, obedience; insults, for the villain; honors for the nobleman; and liberties for the common man. I shall give rough tools to the rude peasant, who, for Adam's folly, must till the earth in the sweat of his brow from morning sun till moon. To the leading-lady I give adornments and perfections—the despair of imitation. The beggar alone shall have no gown, and only nakedness shall be his raiment. When this is fitly done, none may complain he did not receive appropriate properties with which to play his part. If any man plays trivially, this is *his* fault—not mine.

Now all is ordered and expectant. Come then, ye mortals, and apparel yourselves to play your part in the Great Theater of This World.

AUTHOR: Mortals—and I may call you mortal though you have never lived, for mortal have I willed you be—come then, ye mortals, hastening to this shadowy bower, where shaded by palms, laurels and cedars, your Author and Director awaits you to assign today to each of you the role that he must play!

[*Enter* RICH MAN, KING, PEASANT, BEGGAR, WISDOM, BEAUTY, *and a* CHILD.]

KING: Mindful of our obedience, though yet unborn, we come to await Thy pleasure; for in our Sovereign Author's mind we have existed forever, though never given form and breath. We have no soul, no sense, no mind, nor any potency. We are but formless dust beneath Thy feet. Breathe Thou upon this dust, and we shall live and act the parts assigned us in the Great Theater of This World.

BEAUTY: We are but thoughts in Thine imagination—inchoate men and women we and neither animate nor tangible; nor know we aught of good or evil. Choose us our parts to play, for individual choices have we none.

PEASANT: Oh Sovereign Author mine, of whose resplendent Being my shadowy thought is now aware, and aware ever shall be—I am Thy creature, contrived and fashioned by Thy celestial hand—give me, I pray Thee, the part that I shall play; and if I err in it and go astray, the fault shall not with the choice Thou madest be; the blame shall fall alone on me.

AUTHOR: If men might choose to be or not to be, no man would choose to bear life's heavy yoke unless he might be ruler and director of all other men—and all forgetful that what he thinks is life is only drama, the signs and symbols and reflections of some other life to come. I, therefore, since not all men may play the part of kings and governors, shall in my wisdom choose for each man the role he best can act on earth. Here is the assignment of your work. Be thou the King.

[*The* AUTHOR *gives each his part.*]

KING: My lot is honor and power and glory.

AUTHOR: The leading lady, thou.

BEAUTY: Right gladly will I play that part.

AUTHOR: The Rich Man, thou.

RICH MAN: Then I shall bask in all magnificence.

AUTHOR: And thou, the Peasant.

PEASANT: Is that a trade or benefice?

AUTHOR: Hard labor, that.

PEASANT: I'll make a poor peasant, I will. By Thy life, Lord, I am a child of Adam, and all that, but give me not that kind of work. Even though Thou giv'st me properties, I still suspect I'll be a failure as a peasant. I'm too lazy. And being so new to life, I may delve poorly, nor shall I labor well. If "I don't wish to" would aught avail me, I would say, "I don't wish to." But in the presence of so august an Author, "I don't wish to" would do me little good. So, of all the actors in the play I shall do my part the worst. And yet: I should not complain; Thou knowest my frailties and my scarce wit, and Thou'st given me a part that suits my meager talent perfectly. Thou showest me Thy love for my deficient self; and so I'll play the part Thou givest me—although I'll be a little leisurely about it and not wear myself out.

AUTHOR: Thou shalt play the part of Wisdom.

WISDOM: A happy lot.

AUTHOR: The beggar, thou.

BEGGAR: That part Thou gavest me, alas!

AUTHOR: And thou, Child, shalt die unborn.

CHILD: Then little practice for so brief a line.

AUTHOR: Thus hath my foreknowledge marked out the designated path each man must follow. I am Distributive Justice, and I, and I alone, foreknow what every man's appointed lot will be.

BEGGAR: I would most happily escape this Beggar's part assigned to me, though I cannot speak objection very openly.

Heed, therefore, Lord, not what I say but what I leave unsaid. Why befalls it me to act the part of Beggar in this Play? Shall it for me alone be Tragedy? Have not I the same soul, sense, being, as hath the King? Why must our parts, then, different be? Had I been fashioned from some other clay, then I, in sense deficient, should have been an alien to this our human line. Yet such was not Thy will. Oh, it is harsh and bitter—cruel—to play a part so mean, so vile, when yonder sceptered King's no more a man than I.

AUTHOR: It matters not what part a man doth play in Life's great Drama. What he must do is play the best he can the part that's given him. And when the play is over, Beggar and King shall once again be equals, and shall be judged as equals. So, Beggar, soften thy affliction for the while, for I have willed it that if the Beggar play his part effectively and if the King should do less well, then shall the Beggar have the prize, for when the final curtains close, the actors will receive reward as each one merits. We do not care what part a man has played; we only care how well he played it. And when the final words are spoken then shall I summon those who acted best to sit beside me at my Table, and sup with me in Paradise. And the Beggar and the King shall have like welcome there.

BEAUTY: Tell us, Lord, the title of our play.

AUTHOR: *Do Good, for God is God.*

KING: Then must we exercise all care lest our defects should mar a drama with such great mystery laden.

RICH MAN: We shall need rehearsals, then.

BEAUTY: How shall we rehearse the play if we have neither soul nor any being until we say our lines?

BEGGAR: And yet no play should be performed without some practice.

PEASANT: I thoroughly agree with what the Beggar said, for beggar and peasant tread the selfsame earth and speak the selfsame language. Even a play that has previously been done requires a little rehearsal. How, then, shall this our play, untried, be properly performed without some practice?

AUTHOR: Mark this, as heaven is your critic: ye are born but once to live and once to die—and only once.

BEAUTY: But how shall we know when to make appropriate our exits and our entrances?

AUTHOR: That ye all must discover as the play moves on. Be ever zealous to perform your best, for you will be summoned to me, all, when life's great play is over.

BEGGAR: And if we grow confused? Forget our lines?

AUTHOR: I shall set a Prompter here to help you mend your flaws, and guide you when you stumble. My *Law* shall be your Prompter, and ever wakeful, a luminous and everlasting light, it will guide your faltering steps. Free Will I gave you, every one —to know, to choose, and follow right or wrong. Let no complaint be uttered that ye knew not right from wrong, for the Prompter's voice shall soothe each doubt and clarify obscurity. Now is the theater all prepared; now shall ye tread your lives out, from cradle to the grave.

WISDOM: Why tarry we then?

ALL: Let us hasten to Do Good, for God is God.

[*As they start to the stage,* WORLD *halts them.*]

WORLD: Now all is ready to perform the Play of Life. What properties are required?

[KING *shows* WORLD *his part; then takes the purple and laurels.*]

BEAUTY: And I: hues of jasmine and the tinted rose and smiling, chaste carnation. Petal on petal the flowers of May, and ray on ray the light of day, shall shower their loveliness on me. The sun himself shall swoon to see my beauty; and as the sunflower ever turns her head to see the sun's rich ruby red, so will the sun my sunflower be and turn his smiling eyes on me.

WORLD: That was said most vainly.

BEAUTY: That is the part that I am playing, for I am Beauty's very self.

WORLD: Crystal liquid, carmine, snow, and crimson red shall showers of tints upon thee shed. [*Gives* BEAUTY *a bouquet*]

RICH MAN: My part requires wealth and comfort and happiness.

WORLD: The deep abysses of my being shall now be violated to wrest thee gold and silver from my hoarded treasuries.

RICH MAN: I am o'erwhelmed and dazed by such resplendent riches.

WISDOM: For the part that I shall play I need a little earth— and nothing more.

WORLD: What part is thy part?

WISDOM: Wisdom.

WORLD: Then, Wisdom, prayers and fasting shalt thou have. [*Gives her sackcloth and scourges*]

WISDOM: I were not Wisdom did I ask for more.

WORLD: Who art thou that unrequesting stand'st upon my stage, and silently?

CHILD: For my brief appearance nothing shall I need, for I will die before my birth, and I shall be within Thy precinct only the fragment of a little moment in journey swift from that dark prison of the womb to the other silent prison—the prison of the tomb. I only ask a grave to lie in.

WORLD: [*To* PEASANT]: What, lout, requesteth thou? Give me thy part to see.

PEASANT: I will not.

WORLD: From this gross boorishness I clearly see thou'lt earn thy bread in the sweat of thy brow.

PEASANT: Such is my burden.

WORLD: Well, Peasant, here's thy hoe. [*Gives him a hoe*]

PEASANT: This is Adam's legacy. Father Adam, if he'd been wise, should have known how his wife could babble. He should have let her dine alone on apple; but I suppose he'll say he couldn't resist her. Well, that's why his hands, and mine, are all blister.

BEGGAR: Now that they have all received their appointed fortunes, then let me have the woe prescribed for me. Nor purple nor laurels, nor tinted hues, nor gold and silver, shall be my properties—but only rags—rags only.

WORLD: What need'st thou?

BEGGAR: Affliction, woe, anguish, poverty, pain, pity, sighs, moans, contempt, vexations, impatience, insults, disdain, affronts, shame, hunger, thirst, nakedness, weeping, lamentation, filth, vileness, hardships, and desperate indigence—with nothing ever to give but ever pleading to receive. That is what poverty is.

WORLD: I'll give thee nothing, for one who plays the Beggar's part may not receive a thing from World. And so, to perform my task meticulously, I will even take away from thee what rags thou wearest now, and from thy body I will all its raiment tear, and thou shalt go forth naked, naked and cold and bare. [*Takes his clothes*]

BEGGAR: Thus doth the World give to him that hath; and from him that hath not, it taketh away.

WORLD: Now is the stage filled with various estates: a king with wide dominion, beauty that steals the gaze of every eye, the tamed high wielders of power, beggars pressed direly, peasants, and servants of the Church—and all have come to enact their parts in this great play today. I am the theater, and I have given them costumes and properties—outrages, even, and alms. Now, Author Omnipotent, come forth to witness the performance that men will here present before Thee. Let the center of the earth be opened up, for there the scene shall be.

[*While music plays, two globes open up. Within one is the throne of glory, where sits the* AUTHOR. *In the other there is a stage with two doors—and on one is painted a cradle, and on the other is painted a coffin.*]

AUTHOR: This is the play I have devised for my enjoyment. And from this throne eternal will I turn my sight upon my players there below. Oh ye who make your entrance in the cradle and your exit in the coffin, see that you do your parts right well, for your very Author, who sees you moving in your terrestrial vale, marks how ye do succeed, or how ye fail.

[WISDOM *enters with an instrument.*]

WISDOM:
[*Singing*]
Let praise be lifted high to heaven's all-seeing King,
Let every voice be raised, His glorious praise to sing.

> Praise Him above, ye sparkling pilgrims of the night,
> And loud Hosannas sing, Oh sun, moon, fire and light.
> Let all the years and seasons magnify His might—
> Earth's tapestry by day, the frosty stars by night,
> Declare His glory, Oh ye smiling flowers dew-pearled
> And worship Him forever, the Judge of all the world!

AUTHOR: No other song hath to mine ears more sweetly sounded ever than that one bright hymn which Daniel did sing to temper Nebuchadnessar's wrath and lull the fury of the King.

WORLD: Who will recite the Prologue?

[*Enter the* LAW OF GRACE, *with paper in hand. She goes to a high place above where the* WORLD *stands.*]

LAW OF GRACE: I am the Law of Grace, and I shall speak the Prologue to our play. And I shall prompt you with this script, in which Thou'st summarized, oh Lord, the contents of our play: [*Singing*]

> Love thy neighbor as thyself,
> and Do Good, for God is God.

WORLD: The Law of Grace is now become the Prompter. But I must be still: the performance begins.

[*Enter* BEAUTY *and* WISDOM *through the cradle-door.*]

BEAUTY: Come: let us disport amid these sweet and smiling meadows—May's bright domain and Sun's rich golden tapestry.

WISDOM: Remember'st not I take no pleasure to forsake my little habitation? I may not interrupt my quiet routine, nor do I wish to quit me of that meek, mild yoke which I have chosen to bear.

BEAUTY: Must chill austerity forever press thee down? Shall not one single day be given to these little simple pleasures? Why hath God fashioned the nodding flowers if not to please us with their gentle fragrance? Why hath He created birds—those feathered little lutes—if not to lull our ears fatigued, with fluted trills and cadences? And may we not without reproach allow our hands to rest upon His craftsmanship? Why hath He sweetened the heavy-hanging fruit if not to give our palates some delight? Why hath He formed the valleys and the hills and sun and clouds and sky save to instruct man's curious eye?

Oh, it is ingratitude, ingratitude, to disdain enjoyment of this wondrous fabric of our glorious Lord's Creation!

WISDOM: It is not unlawful to revere Creation's beauties if we remember us of their Creator ever; but I have chosen the cloister for my part, and I have put away the blinding vanities of this pale world. Thus have I merited Wisdom's name.

BEAUTY: And I have chosen the ways of Beauty—to see, be seen.

WORLD: Beauty and Wisdom were never loving sisters.

BEAUTY: Snares shall I lay for chillest hearts and downcast eyes most coyly reticent.

WORLD: Only one of these hath read her lines aright.

WISDOM: What shall I do, the better to exercise discretion?

BEAUTY: How shall I display my loveliness more strikingly?

LAW OF GRACE: *Do Good, for God is God.*

WORLD: Beauty heareth not the Prompter.

[*Enter* RICH MAN.]

RICH MAN: Heaven hath beneficently bestowed upon me her countless treasures and powers without earthly bound or bourne. Therefore, I'll spend my lavish gold on mundane pleasures. Whatever I wish—that I shall buy. My table with flesh and fowl shall be oppressed; and when night's gentle slumber steals in to seal my somnolent eyes, it will find me couched beneath the lascivious canopy of Venus' sacred self. And these shall be my guides and my companions: sloth, lust, gluttony, envy, and ambition.

[*Enter* PEASANT.]

PEASANT: Was greater labor ever seen than mine? Dreary was that sentence that made me earn my bread in the sweat of my brow. I daily fight with hoe, ploughshare, and sickle—and stumps and growing grains when May showers and April rains. But I cannot have the spring unless I take the rain that goes with it. When those fellows out there levy taxes they always start first with the peasant. Well, I toil and sweat over my crops, so anyone who wants my grain will have to pay me what I ask him for it. And, believe me, I intend to ask more than the ceiling prices those people have put on things. I won't budge either. Come April, if it doesn't rain (and I pray to God it won't), I am going to make a pile of ducats on the grain I've stored up. And around here I'll be like Nabal in the Old Testament: everybody will have to come to me for food. Why shouldn't I profit from their necessity? What else can I do?

LAW OF GRACE [Singing]: Do Good, for God is God.

WISDOM: Didst not hear the Prompter's voice?

PEASANT: I was temporarily deaf.

WORLD: Stubborn, this fellow.

PEASANT: More than you can imagine, World.

[Enter BEGGAR.]

BEGGAR: Who hath ever seen more misery than is my lot to bear? The earth's my only bed, and heaven itself my only canopy. Frost and the heat descend upon me, and hunger and thirst, they tread me down. Help me, I pray thee, Lord—help me in this dark night of my affliction!

RICH MAN: How shall I show my riches more conspicuously?

LAW OF GRACE [Singing]: Do Good, for God is God.

BEGGAR: I have heard some voice that comforteth my woe.

WISDOM: Now is the King himself come hither to these gardens.

RICH MAN: Why must my arrogance bend low before his eyes —or any man's?

BEAUTY: I shall stand before his presence. Mayhap my beauty will even captive kings.

PEASANT: Me, I'll stand here in the rear. The only thing he'll do if he sees me is raise my taxes. That's the only favor I can expect from him.

[Enter THE KING.]

KING: Far as the farthest horizon that eyes can see and farther still than thought can fly, stretch infinite my teeming realms and territories, prostrate and suppliant before my royal gaze. Is there perchance aught in all the world that is my need?

LAW OF GRACE [Singing]: To Do Good, for God is God.

WORLD: With what skill the Prompter seeketh to correct each player's fault!

BEGGAR: When I in mean and low necessity lift up mine eyes

from this my downcast state, I see that other men are richly endowed with ease and sweet contentment in their appointed stations. The King, our Lord Supreme, savors his regal majesty with never a thought of me. My Lady Beauty, with vanity surfeited, knoweth not what need and sorrow be. Lost in her lonely orisons, the pensive nun doth softly serve our Lord, and hath no fear of winter's wind or summer's parching blasts. The Peasant, homeward from his weary fields returning, hath ever found to welcome him some decent fare of pleasant country messes. The Rich Man hath too much of much. But I, alas! alone of men—I have no ounce of earthly goods and must perforce call out for alms to every man. They all may live and never have a thought of me; but it is not a Beggar's privilege to forget his fellow men. Now, I will see what Beauty hath to give me.—Alms, I pray thee, maiden, in God's dear, blessèd name.

BEAUTY: Ye brooks that are my mirrors, tell me: what garlands shall I don today? How, too, ringlet my sunny tresses, say?

BEGGAR: Seest thou not me?

WORLD: Fool, fruitless will be that plea. Why should she, that hath no proper care for her own well-being, take any heed of thee?

BEGGAR [To RICH MAN]: From thine abundance, sir, give me some little mite, I pray.

RICH MAN: Canst thou not knock at the door as others properly do? Must thou thus intrude upon me? Thou couldst have made thy plea at the threshold of my vestibule, and not come here.

BEGGAR: Treat me not harshly.

RICH MAN: Annoying Beggar, get thee forthwith gone.

BEGGAR: Can one that so much ill-spends on his pleasures deny to me one little farthing?

RICH MAN: Yes.

WORLD: How like unto Lazarus and the rich man in the parable!

BEGGAR: My misery knoweth no bound. I'll even ask the King. Alms, my lord; alms.

KING: We have a royal almoner; ask him for alms, not me.

WORLD: The presence of his ministers doth salve the conscience of the King.

BEGGAR: Peasant, God's blessing on thy grain hath brought to thee its great multiplication. Canst thou not in charity give me to eat?

PEASANT: God may have given me much grain, but I should never have had it without, myself, plowing and sowing and sweating it out. Mark this: hast thou—great stout fellow that thou art—no little shame to go about a-begging? Art thou content to be a knave? If thou hast hunger, take this hoe and with it earn thy daily bread.

BEGGAR: In this play I'm doing the part of a beggar, not a peasant.

PEASANT: Well, friend, the Author hath not commanded thee to beg and nothing more, hath He, perchance? Or sit idly by, perchance? Toil and sweat are also the Beggar's proper part.

BEGGAR: Let it be, then, for dear God's love. Oh, thou hast spoken harshly to me, brother.

PEASANT: Thou'rt insistent, insistent, insistent.

BEGGAR [To BEAUTY]: Give me thou some comfort then.

WISDOM: Take thou this bread—and, brother, forgive me. [Gives him a loaf of bread]

BEGGAR: How reasonable it was that thou shouldst give me bread, for Religion with the Bread of Life sustaineth us every one.

WISDOM: Alas! [She almost falls]

KING: How now!

BEGGAR: It is Religion swooneth!

KING: Let me uphold her! [Gives her his hand]

BEGGAR: That was well done, for none could have better lent her aid than thou.

AUTHOR: I might well correct the flaws my actors make; but I have given them all Free Will—Free Choice—to mend their own deficiencies. Free Will is far superior to all other human attributes, and if it be duly exercised, it may govern man's each move and passion. Men I created free, for if not free, what proof could they have given me of their integrity? I formed them free, and free they must remain. Thus I permit them all to act their parts according to their will; but when they miss their mark, I send them warnings and correction through my obedient handmaiden's voice, the Law of Grace.

LAW OF GRACE: *Do Good, for God is God.* I have counselled you every one; if therefore ye err, ye err. [*Singing*] *Love thy neighbor as thyself, for God is God.*

KING: If life is really just a play, then do we travel all the selfsame way. Shall we not lighten the burden of this common journey, and each one tell a tale?

BEAUTY: Without such commerce World were not World.

KING: Come: let us have a story from everyone.

WISDOM: That were tedious. 'T were better each one here should paint in words the secret thoughts that lie ensconced within the rich festoons of his most secret fantasies.

KING: Well, I'll begin. My mind's eye perceiveth my utter majesty, the grandeur and the glory of my imperial sway. On all that I call my own hath Nature lavished numberless perfections, and, in variety, infinite. Obedient to my governance stand lofty fortresses adamant; and Beauty herself is my bondswoman. So hath it been decreed—that some should follow and some should lead. Heaven itself hath lent its hand to aid me in the governance of my wild, unequal brood. And I, to subjugate so many stubborn necks beneath my royal yoke must ever call on heavenly wisdom to direct my steps and lend my will assistance.

WORLD: That was well said. He calleth on heaven's wisdom as did the mighty Solomon.

VOICE [*Singing backstage near the coffin-door*]: King of this transitory fleeting realm, lull now thy towering ambition, for thou hast nearly played thy total part in this great Theater of the World. Only a little moment is given thee now to utter thy sad last lines—and then forever say farewell—forever.

KING: The doleful voice speaks forth and calleth me: my part is played; reason and discourse flee from me. Whither shall I go? Where turn my steps? To the cradle's no returning: then must I take the other way to death's eternal ocean. I am become as water; and the way of water is to seek the sea. Heavenly Author, forgive my great transgressions; sorely I repent me now, and I shall go hence with obedient will. My time hath run out; my words are still.

[KING *leaves by coffin-door.*]

WORLD: How nobly the King hath sought forgiveness in his closing lines!

BEAUTY: Now do his vassals have no overlord. The King—our King—is dead.

PEASANT: With showers in May and King out of the way, I think my luck will come to stay.

WISDOM: Oh doleful day, Oh day of tribulation!

BEAUTY: All is confounded, forlorn and broken. What shall we do alone? Our lord and King hath gone hence.

RICH MAN: Let us return again and speak our recitations. Beauty, we'll hear thy piece—a pretty thing.

BEAUTY: Well then, I'll speak, and dry the tears I've shed.

WORLD: The dead forget the living, as the living forget the dead!

PEASANT: Particularly if they leave you a bit of property and help you out of the red.

BEAUTY: I see my beauty as in a glass before mine eyes, and it is clear and fair and lovable. It hath no envy of the King's once glittering triumphs or his broad empire—teeming, vast—for vaster empire shall I have, and marshalled all 'neath Beauty's gleaming banner. The King was only master of men's flesh and bones, but I shall steal their hearts away. They shall be Beauty's slaves. Mine is the fairer realm in every part, for Beauty reigns eternal in every human heart. And if Philosophy in man a little world doth see, then a little heaven shall womanly beauty be.

WORLD: She hath forgotten Ezekiel's words: When Beauty's loveliness had been by pride assailed, its luster fled, its color paled.

VOICE [*Singing*]: All human loveliness is like a little flower. It blossoms at morn and blooms its brief hour; and at the close of one swift day, its beauty withers and fades away.

BEAUTY: A doleful voice commandeth death to Beauty. No, no, it shall not be. Beauty may never perish, or from the world depart. And yet 'tis true, alas! The rose that bared her bosom to the sun, the rose bedecked with red and pearly white shall at night's coming be consumèd quite. The emerald bud will open never again, when beauty's rose at night is foully slain. And yet to me what matters it that flowers should fade 'twixt dawn and dewy dusk? Am I a flower ephemeral? Shall I like mortal roses be a brief parenthesis between what-was-not and what-will-never-be? Nay, the sun that saw me blossom first, shall see my loveliness forever bloom. Say, shall the Eternal die?

VOICE [*Singing*]: Eternal is thy spirit; but thy roseate beauty's fair array is but the garland of an autumn day.

BEAUTY: I will protest no more, nor vainly contend against all odds. From the cradle came I hither; to the sepulcher go hence.—Why played I not a better part?

[*Exit* BEAUTY.]

WORLD: That part well ended in repentance.

RICH MAN: Now Beauty's sparkling presence is no more.

PEASANT: If on feast days there's bread, wine, and meat available—sucking-pig, preferably—I can get along quite well without having Beauty around.

WISDOM: She hath left sorrow to us, and we are covered over with lamentation.

BEGGAR: Alas, alas! What shall we do?

RICH MAN: Return to our recitations.

PEASANT: When I go out to till and toil in the fields I fear not cold nor heat. I fear not that; for what I really fear is the lukewarm heart I bear within this chilly breast that gives thanks to the fields that bring me again, but not to God who grew the grain.

WORLD: He hath done well to see that the first step in the mending of the sin of ingratitude was to have acknowledged himself to be a debtor.

BEGGAR: I begin now to have some liking for that Peasant, even though the other day he had harsh words for me.

VOICE [*Singing*]: The end of thy appointed task is come to

thee, Peasant, and thou shalt henceforth labor in other vineyards: but where, God knows, God knows.

PEASANT: Voice, if I may appeal this sentence, then let me do
so in a higher court. I ought not die now, but at some more
appropriate time. I haven't put my affairs in order yet. I am a
wretched sort of peasant, and my vineyards proclaim me so—
thistle after thistle and flower after flower. The weeds are so
high there, a spectator in the distance cannot tell whether
it's a vineyard or growing wheat. And compared to my neighbor's grain, mine is a mere poor dwarf. Some of you might say
that if my farm *is* in bad shape it would be a good idea for me
to move along now. And I reply: "If he does not leave some
of the fruits of his toil to his heir and so carry out the injunc-
tions of his forefathers, what shall he, fruitless, do, Lord? But
now I see I shall not even have one day of grace, for the Voice
there said my time has come. The grave is yawning to swallow
me down. If I have acted my part deficiently, I only regret I
cannot regret having done it better.

WORLD: At first I judged him boorish; but now he shows
me with those last remarks how wrong I was. The Peasant ended
well!

RICH MAN: The Peasant hath left his hoes, his plows, his dust,
and sweat and weariness.

BEGGAR: And us—afflicted.

WISDOM AND BEGGAR: Alas! Alas!

WISDOM: What shall we do?

RICH MAN: Return to our recitations. And to do my share, I
too will now recite my piece.—If the life of man is like a rose
ephemeral and only lasts from dawn to darkling eve, then let
us all rejoice to have at least that brief reprieve. My belly shall
be my deity, till death's slow step draw nigh. Let us eat, drink
and be merry, for tomorrow we shall die.

WORLD: That is false doctrine—Isaiah hath told us so.

WISDOM: Who will speak next?

BEGGAR: I follow next.—Let that day perish, Oh Lord, wherein I was born upon this earth; perish the chill night when I was
conceived to bear such woe. May day never dawn to dispel

those sombre shades; may darkness reign there, and Stygian night forever. Eternal be that fearful night; let the stars of the twilight thereof be dark—neither let it behold the eyelids of the morn; and let that day have no morning, and let the night be moonless and without stars. Yet make I not my dismal moan for this my outcast state. I would not trouble heaven's ears with mournful din. I only grieve that I was born in deepest sin.

WORLD: Thus, cursing day, likewise did Job curse sin.

VOICE: Now shall happiness and sorrow be brought to an accounting, both.

BEGGAR: Oh joyful words!

RICH MAN: Dost thou not tremble to hear that voice?

BEGGAR: I tremble.

RICH MAN: Shalt thou not seek to flee away?

BEGGAR: No. For to tremble when God's voice speaketh is natural in sinful man. Flight were vain; for if Power could not escape this dread command, nor Beauty, then whither shall these rags and tatters fly? I give my thanks instead to lay me down in death and quit me of my burdens.

RICH MAN: Hast no regret to leave the Theater of the World?

BEGGAR: I have no happiness to leave behind me. With right good will go I hence.

RICH MAN: Oh, I am slain, for I loved naught but worldly goods.

BEGGAR: Oh comfort and joy!

RICH MAN: Oh woe, woe; woe, affliction and woe!

[*Exeunt* RICH MAN *and* BEGGAR.]

WORLD: They go hence differently.

WISDOM: I now am the only actor left in World's Great Theater.

WORLD: Religion is the last of all to leave me.

WISDOM: Religion will never, never end; but now my time is come, for I am not Religion's self—only an humble devotee who chose that path to follow. Now, even before the Voice makes ready to call me hence I find myself prepared to go, and waiting for the grave. Have I in life itself not buried been? Now, last of all our cast today, I too go hence from the play our Author will present again and on the morrow. Oh ye that fail today and end in grief and sorrow, profit from Wisdom's words, and mend your faults tomorrow!

[*The earth's globe closes.*]

AUTHOR: I have prepared punishments and recompense for those who've acted in this play. Now shall they see what proper guerdon their work hath merited.

[*The celestial globe closes with the* AUTHOR *in it.*]

WORLD: Brief was the play, as life itself is brief—that little moment 'twixt our entrances and exits. The actors have left the stage and are now returned to their first primeval being. Dust they were; they are now to dust returned. I must collect from all of them the properties I gave them to embellish their performance and the stage, for all they had was theirs for only the brief duration of our little play. Alert, I'll place me at this door, and take their properties away; for dust they were and now to dust return they.

[*Enter the* KING.]

What was thy part that thou shouldst be the first to go hence?

KING: Hath the World so soon forgotten who I was?

WORLD: World little heeds nor long remembers who men were.

KING: I was one who ruled the whole wide world. I judged, and governed many states; inherited and acquired me much renown; wisely executed many an excellent project; had many a favorite; left many histories. I sat upon a burnished throne hedged round with purple, laurels and scepters flashing.

WORLD: Give me the crown, and doff thy clothèd majesty. All pomp and circumstance are stilled when monarchs silenced be. Time casts their withered laurels down—their faded majesty. Naked and bare thou shalt bid thy last farewell to this life's play. The purple robes that were the insignia of thy majesty—that, another shall wrap round him; nor shalt thou steal from these hungry hands thy laurels or thy flashing scepters.

KING: Must thou then seize my loved embellishments? Why takest from me away what once thou gavest me willingly?

WORLD: I never gave thee aught; I only lent thee some little baubles—trinkets—for thy part. All that was thy pageantry and circumstance must now return to me.

KING: World hath the fame of being a golden treasury, but that is because World never gives but only lends a little while. Shall I then carry no reward, no little guerdon, from what once my kingly state was?

WORLD: The Author hath stored up for thee whatever of punishment or reward thy performance merited. It behooves not me to pronounce judgment on thy work. I only take from thee the dress and costume of thy earthly state; for from this World shalt thou most surely go as naked and bare as when thou first didst enter here.

[Enter BEAUTY.]

WORLD: And who wert thou?

BEAUTY: I was the cynosure of every eye.

WORLD: What were thy properties that once I gave to thee?

BEAUTY: The bright perfection of my beauty—nothing more.

WORLD: Where is that beauty now?

BEAUTY: In the grave, in the grave.

WORLD: Thus Nature showeth a World amazed how briefly Beauty reigns and falls to dust. That single property I bestowed upon thee lieth in the earth consumed, and neither thou nor I again shall hold it ever in our keeping. Lost—lost and gone is what to thee I lent: both flame and candle now are wholly spent. Behold thee in this glass.

BEAUTY: I have seen.

WORLD: Where is the loveliness with which I clothed thee? Shall I not have it back again? Where is it now?

BEAUTY: The grave hath all consumed. There low-fallen lie all shades subdued, jasmine and coral and flowers many-hued, and the pristine, virgin rose. Ivory and crystal broken lie, and shattered there; and all my arts and fantasies; all signs and symbols of what my one-time beauty was. There lie eclipsed the splendors and the glancing rays of loveliness. There only shades and shadows lie; their beauty's mask consumed—and I.

[Enter PEASANT.]

WORLD [To PEASANT]: Who wert thou?

PEASANT: I am one that courtly men treated with vile and barbarous contempt—one ever recipient of base and low address.

WORLD: Leave with me what once I gave thee.

PEASANT: What gavest thou me?

WORLD: A hoe.

PEASANT: Verily, a gem, that hoe.

WORLD: With the hoe that once I gave thee hast thou played thy part—for good or ill, as will be seen.

PEASANT: This miser World is even envious of the hoe that brought us in our livelihood. He will not, alas! allow us to take that with us—not even that—when we go hence.

[*Enter the* RICH MAN *and the* BEGGAR.]

WORLD: Who are these?

RICH MAN: One who, if he might choose, from thee, Oh World, would never go away.

BEGGAR: And one who, if he might choose, World, would never wish to stay.

WORLD: Why weep ye then—the one to leave, the other to remain?

RICH MAN: I weep for these bright treasures that I must leave behind.

BEGGAR: I weep, the surcease of my woe, to find.

WORLD: Give me back those properties. [*Snatches them back*]

PEASANT: I who had nothing shall nothing leave.

[*Enter* CHILD.]

WORLD: Child, thou wert of this company; yet hast thou spoken here no line.

CHILD: The only life thou gavest me was death. What didst on me bestow, there in the grave it lieth low.

[*Enter* WISDOM.]

WORLD: When thou didst knock upon the door of life, what adornments didst thou seek?

WISDOM: Faith, haircloth, scourges, and obedience.

WORLD: Leave all those properties with me, for none may take his glories hence.

WISDOM: That cannot be, for all those pristine glories may

now accompany me. Uprightness, sacrifice, and prayer may not be left in this World below.

WORLD: 'Tis true: I never may withhold good works; they, and they alone may all be taken hence.

KING: Oh had I had more kingdoms!

BEAUTY: And had I wished more beauty.

RICH MAN: Oh had I had more riches!

PEASANT: Had I but labored more!

BEGGAR: Oh had I suffered greater misery!

WORLD: It is too late, for when Death's dread summons comes, none shall garner further merits. Now have I heaped together the august trappings of majesty and withered Beauty's fragile bloom. Likewise have I bent the neck of haughty vanity. Now in death's democracy, scepters and plowshares are all one; and the moment is come when ye shall enter the Theater of Truth and leave yon Fiction's Playhouse far behind.

KING: And thou who once did welcome us most winsomely —thou send'st us now downcast and expatriate forth.

WORLD: My reason know: The cradle like the crescent silver moon receives the new-born babe in warm embrace; but when the journey's done, the cradle, overturned, becomes a sheltering tomb. This was the way of life, the course of earthly doom. I once was, to receive you, cradle; I say farewell—a tomb.

BEGGAR: Now hath the wild World cast us forth from his domain. Let us then repair to that great Supper which our Author hath laid for us.

KING: Where is thy respect, thus to precede my way and enter first? Hast so swiftly forgotten whose vassal once thou wert? Remember'st thou not, vile mendicant?

BEGGAR: Thou'st played thy part, Oh King, and I. In this dim dressing-room all are alike in death's equality. What once thou wert, no man remembereth now.

RICH MAN: Thou didst but yesterday seek alms from me. Hast thou no memory?

BEGGAR: Enough to recall the none thou gavest me.

BEAUTY: Hast no recollection how once my beauty charmed thine eyes?

WISDOM: In this great dressing-room, death's dark and silent vestry, are we all equalled each to each and like to like. There's no hierarchy or precedence in death's shrouded kingdom—no rank or file or order. All categories broken lie; wasted, all protocol.

RICH MAN: Wouldst go before me still, Sir Villain Peasant?

PEASANT: In time's bleak gray oblivion all arrogant ambition now lieth cold and withered; dead. Thou once wert midday sun; now but an evening shadow.

RICH MAN: My heart is sore affrighted to know that I must see our Author's face.

BEGGAR: Author of earth and heaven, this company of players that hath performed life's human comedy approacheth now to that Great Supper thou'st prepared before us. Let the curtains forthwith be drawn away, and we shall see Thy throne and canopy, behold Thy Day.

[*The celestial globe is seen again. There is a table within it, on which are chalice and host. The* AUTHOR *is seated there. Exit* WORLD.]

AUTHOR: This table now awaits you, and this Bread—adored by heaven and reverenced even by hell itself. They who shall sup with me will presently be known; known, too, those who through misjudgment or forgetfulness of my many mercies have erred their parts. First, the Beggar and Saintly Wisdom shall sup with me; and now freed from World's requirements and the need of physical food, they shall forever adore this heavenly Bread and glorify it through all eternity.

[BEGGAR *and* WISDOM *go up.*]

BEGGAR: What fortune, mine! Oh, had I but suffered more—more grinding hardships, anguish more dreadful! For that one who suffers in God's holy name shall merit heavenly recompense forever and forever and forever.

WISDOM: I, who performed my many penances have now been blessed beyond all bourne and measure by this great recompense now given to me. Happy is he that weepeth to confess his errors!

KING: Then shall not also I merit divine forgiveness? 'Midst royal pomp, and circumstantia, I ever sought Thy pardon.

AUTHOR: Beauty and Power shall likewise to my table ascend, because they sought forgiveness for their grievous sin of pride; but not ascend at present. So shall the Peasant also tarry awhile away, for though he gave the Beggar nothing 'twas not because he did not wish to give. Pious was his intent. He only wished to help the Beggar help himself.

PEASANT: That was my only wish: I had no use for vagabonds—that's all.

AUTHOR: Therefore shall ye all receive reward; but first must ye plead more mercy, and I consign you all to languish for a period in the precincts of Purgatory's confinement drear.

WISDOM: Author Divine, I was low-pressed, and the King lent me his hand and lifted me up. Now lend I him mine, and do beseech Thee pardon him.

[WISDOM *gives the* KING *her hand and he ascends.*]

AUTHOR: I will remit my verdict, since Religion herself hath been King's advocate. Now since hope is ever present, let future ages run their course, time speed away.

PEASANT: Indulgences rain down upon my miseries now; close they crowd about me. These sacred words from Rome's blest Pontiff will free me from this Stygian night.

CHILD: If no mistake I made, great Lord, why grant'st Thou me no guerdon?

AUTHOR: Nothing didst thou do for either good or ill. Thou therefore neither reward nor punishment shalt receive. Blind, thou shalt nothing have; thou art a child of sin.

CHILD: Then fearful night will blind me in dismal and perpetual darkness lugubrious; and I shall have no hope for glory or grief—for either grief or glory.

RICH MAN: If Power and Beauty have blanched to see our great Creator's face—even though with tears they washed the sin away of partial pride—and if the Peasant whose low wail oft softened very stones now stands a-tremble before our Author's gaze, how shall I, unworthy that I am, lift up mine eyes to see my Lord? Yet I cannot hold me back. Oh where shall my vast sinfulness find shelter against the Lord's most righteous justice? Author!

AUTHOR: With what bold arrogance name'st thou my name? I fashioned thee, and now thou ever shalt shamefast be, and from my company go hence for all eternity. My power casts thee down into a torment that with dreadful fire shall devour thy pride and arrogance forever and forever.

RICH MAN: Oh woe, woe! I fall, in devouring flames enwrapped, dragging my earthly shadow into this fiery pit; and locked and immured forever in adamantine rock, this shape and form I called my own, will through all eternity enterrèd be.

WISDOM: But glory I shall have forever and forever.

BEAUTY: I shall not lose the hope I had for glory.

PEASANT: Nor I, nor I.

RICH MAN: All hope of glory's lost!

CHILD: Lost, lost, indeed.

AUTHOR: Of these remaining, Beauty first shall sit before the Table's mystery ineffable and after that the Peasant shall take his place beside her. For they have labored long; now merit glory.

[BEAUTY *and the* PEASANT *go up.*]

BEAUTY: Eternal joy!

PEASANT: Oh heavenly crown!

RICH MAN: My woe and misfortune drag me down.

KING: Triumph eternal!

RICH MAN: Oh doleful day!

WISDOM: Alleviation for all!

BEGGAR: Peace, peace for all.

RICH MAN: Poison and gall, poison and gall.

CHILD: Punishment for all, and glory; but never punishment or glory for me.

AUTHOR: The angels in heaven, and men on earth, hell's very demons, even, low kneel before this sacred Bread; now let the joyful sounds of earth, hell, heaven this Bread proclaim in sweet harmonious concord resonant. Let joyful pipes sing out their hymns, bright banners be unfurled, to praise God's holy majesty, the Author of the World.

[*Sound of hornpipes is heard. The* TANTUM ERGO *is sung many times.*]

WORLD [*To audience*]:

The World's a stage, and you have seen Life's play;
Now with applauding hands, our fears allay.

Rinehart Editions